Arminius Speaks

Arminius Speaks

Essential Writings on Predestination, Free Will, and the Nature of God

JAMES ARMINIUS

Edited by John D. Wagner

Foreword by Robert E. Picirilli

WIPF & STOCK · Eugene, Oregon

ARMINIUS SPEAKS
Essential Writings on Predestination, Free Will, and the Nature of God

Contents previously published in *The Works of James Arminius*, published in 1825, 1828 (volumes 1 and 2) by Longman, Hurst, Rees, Orme, Brown and Green; and 1875 (volume 3) by Thomas Baker.

Wipf & Stock
An Imprint of Wipf and Stock Publishers
199 W. 8th Ave., Suite 3
Eugene, OR 97401

www.wipfandstock.com

ISBN 13:978-1-61097-030-3

Manufactured in the U.S.A.

Dedicated to the

Society of Evangelical Arminians

Contents

Foreword

JOHN D. WAGNER HAS done us all a service in presenting these selections from Arminius. The three-volume set of Arminius' works, while it can be found in many theological libraries, is not always easily available. And the set is imposing. One encounters difficulty deciding where to turn to find the key discussions. The contents are not arranged in an orderly manner. Most people, on looking at the small-print table of contents, tend to find it mysterious and intimidating. Mr. Wagner has selected from this *corpus* several of the most helpful writings of this sixteenth-century theologian whose name has been given to a theology of salvation that offers saving grace to everyone.

Arminius was born Jacob Harmenszoon in Holland in 1559 or 1560. He took the Latin name Jacobus (= James) Arminius for his theological pursuits. After study at Leiden, Geneva, and Basel, he returned to his homeland to serve first as a pastor and subsequently as a professor of theology at Leiden. His study of the Scriptures led him to resist the unconditional predestination of Calvin and Beza that dominated the Reformed churches, and that resistance led to serious upheaval in the Dutch church. Those who were influenced by him filed a "remonstrance" with the authorities of the Dutch state (which had extensive power over the church) and came to be known as Remonstrants. They, in turn, were condemned by the Synod of Dort in 1618–19.

As a result, the "Arminian" position on the theology of salvation came to be summarized—with oversimplification—as counter to the five points—"TULIP"—of the "Calvinism" that prevailed at Dort-- Total Depravity, Unconditional Election, Limited Atonement, Irresistible Grace, and (Necessary) Perseverance of Saints. Instead, Arminianism champions the Biblical teaching that salvation is by faith, that Jesus died for all, and that God does not arbitrarily elect some to be saved and others to be damned but freely offers salvation to all.

The trouble is that the name Arminianism has come to be used so broadly that it means different things to different people. This is the reason it is important to get back to Arminius himself. More than one Calvinist, on carefully studying Arminius, has found that he was not "Arminian" after all—at least not as that view is often understood. Both while he was alive, and ever since, Arminius has been unfairly accused of sentiments that were not his. Those who read him carefully know well that he did not make saving faith a work, that he affirmed that God's grace is to be credited entirely with anyone's salvation from beginning to end. He was no Pelagian, as he took pains to make clear. Anyone who reads the selections in this volume should come away convinced of this.

I call the soteriology of Arminius (and of the very first generation of his followers) "Reformation Arminianism" in order to distinguish it from other forms. Not that Arminius was one of the Magisterial Reformers. But he lived, ministered, and died a member of the Reformed church. And his theology is firmly rooted in the Reformation. With Luther and Calvin, Arminius believed and taught *sola gratia, sola fide,* and *solo Christo*-- salvation by grace alone, through faith alone, by Christ alone.

I am grateful to Mr. Wagner for making these important writings more easily accessible. The *Public Disputations* (originally twenty-five) were theses discussed during the period 1603–09 before Arminius' theology classes at Leiden.[1] The *Declaration of Sentiments*, arguably his most important writing, resulted from Arminius' appearance before the States General of Holland on October 30, 1608, where he was ordered to put the views he had expressed into written form. The *Examination of Perkins' Pamphlet* was a response to a 1602 treatise of William Perkins, a fellow of Christ's College at Cambridge, a high Calvinist. The *Defense against Several Articles* (originally thirty-one) was probably published in 1609, answering (as Arminius said) articles invented and secretly circulated by his enemies, accusing him and others of novelty, heterodoxy, error, and heresy. The *Letter to Hippolytus* was to an ambassador from Prince Frederick IV, following a personal audience with him. In all of these one detects that Arminius was an embattled but capable and Biblical theologian.

Anyone who desires to know what Arminius really said will do well to read these selections and will share the indebtedness of the church

1. The modern spelling is *Leiden,* but the traditional Dutch spelling used by Arminius is *Leyden.*

to this editor. Indeed, I commend Arminius' sentiments to any reader. They are well worth serious consideration and they require evaluation in the light of careful Biblical exegesis.

Robert E. Picirilli, PhD

Professor Emeritus of Greek and New Testament

Free Will Baptist Bible College

Public Disputations

ON THE FREE WILL OF MAN AND ITS POWERS

THE WORD, *ARBITRIUM*, "CHOICE," or "free will," properly signifies both the faculty of the mind or understanding, by which the mind is enabled to judge anything proposed to it, and the judgment itself the mind forms according to that faculty. But it is transferred from the mind to the will on account of the very close connection subsisting between them. Liberty, when attributed to the will, is properly an affection of the will, though it has its root in the understanding and reason. Generally considered, it is various:

- freedom from the control or jurisdiction of one who commands, and from an obligation to render obedience.

- freedom from the inspection, care, and government of a superior.

- freedom from necessity, whether this proceeds from an external cause compelling, or from a nature inwardly determining absolutely to one thing.

- freedom from sin and its dominion.

- freedom from misery.

Of these five modes of liberty, the first two appertain to God alone; to whom also on this account, *autexousia*, perfect independence, or complete freedom of action, is attributed. But the remaining three modes may belong to man, nay in a certain respect they do pertain to him. And, indeed, the former, namely, freedom from necessity always pertains to him because it exists naturally in the will, as its proper attribute, so that there cannot be any will if it is not free. The freedom from misery, which pertains to man when recently created and not then fallen into sin, will again pertain to him when he shall be translated in body and soul into celestial blessedness. But about these two modes also, of freedom from necessity and from misery, we have here no dispute. It remains, therefore, for us, to discuss that which is a freedom from sin and its dominion, and which is the principal controversy of these times.

It is therefore asked, is there within man a freedom of will from sin and its dominion, and how far does it extend? Or rather, what are the powers of the whole man to understand, to will, and to do that which is good? To return an appropriate answer to this question, the distinction of a good object, and the diversity of men's conditions, must both enter into our consideration. The good things presented to man are three: natural, which he has in common with many other creatures; animal, which belong to him as a man; and spiritual, which are also deservedly called Celestial or Divine, and which are directly related to him as being a partaker of the Divine Nature. The states, or conditions, are likewise three: that of primitive innocence, in which God placed him by creation; that of subsequent corruption, into which he fell through sin when destitute of primitive innocence; and, lastly, that of renewed righteousness, to which state he is restored by the grace of Christ.

But because it is of little importance to our present purpose to investigate what may be the powers of free will to understand, to will, and to do natural and animal good things, we will omit them. We will enter on the consideration of spiritual good, that concerns the spiritual life of man, which he is bound to live according to godliness, inquiring from the Scriptures what powers man possesses, while he is in the way of this animal life, to understand, to will, and to do spiritual good things. Those alone are truly good and pleasing to God. In this inquiry the office of a director will be performed by a consideration of the three states, of which we have already treated, varied as such consideration must be in the relation of these powers to the change of each state.

In the state of Primitive Innocence, man had a mind endued with a clear understanding of heavenly light and truth concerning God, and his works and will, as far as was sufficient for the salvation of man and the glory of God. He had a heart imbued with "righteousness and true holiness," and with a true and saving love of good, and powers abundantly qualified or furnished perfectly to fulfill the law which God had imposed on him. This admits easily of proof, from the description of the image of God, after which man is said to have been created (Gen 1:26,

27), from the law divinely imposed on him, which had a promise and a threat appended to it (2:17), and lastly from the analogous restoration of the same image in Christ Jesus (Eph 4:24, Col 3:10).

But man was not so confirmed in this state of innocence, as to be incapable of being moved, by the representation presented to him of some good (whether it was of an inferior kind and relating to this animal life, or of a superior-kind and relating to spiritual life), inordinately and unlawfully to look upon it and to desire it, and of his own spontaneous as well as free motion, and through a preposterous desire for that good, to decline from the obedience which had been prescribed to him.

Having Turned Away

Nay, having turned away from the light of his own mind and his chief good, which is God, or, at least, having turned towards that chief good not in the manner in which he ought to have done, and besides having turned in mind and heart towards an inferior good, he transgressed the command given to him for life. By this foul deed, he precipitated himself from that noble and elevated condition into a state of the deepest infelicity, which is under the dominion of sin. For "to whom ye yield yourselves servants to obey," (Rom 6:16) and "of whom a man is overcome, of the same is he brought in bondage," and is his regularly assigned slave (2 Pet 2:19).

In this state, the free will of man towards the true good is not only wounded, maimed, infirm, bent, and weakened; but it is also imprisoned, destroyed, and lost. And its powers are not only debilitated and useless unless they are assisted by grace, but it has no powers whatever except such as are excited by Divine grace.[1] For Christ has said, "Without me ye can do nothing." St. Augustine, after having diligently meditated upon each word in this passage, speaks thus: "Christ does not say, without me ye can do but little; neither does He say, without me ye can do any arduous thing, nor without me ye can do it with difficulty. But he says, without me ye can do Nothing! Nor does he say, without me ye cannot

---

1. It is important to note that Arminius believed in a prevenient, non-irresistable grace prior to regeneration. "It is very plain, from the Scriptures, that repentance and faith cannot be exercised except by the gift of God. But the same Scripture and the nature of both gifts very clearly teaches that this bestowment [via grace] is by persuasion." *The Works of James Arminius*, III: 334. Such grace is effective within a person who "does consent and believe and is converted." Ibid., 335.

complete anything; but without me ye can do Nothing." That this may be made more manifestly to appear, we will separately consider the mind, the affections or will, and the capability, as contra-distinguished from them, as well as the life itself of an unregenerate man.

The mind of man, in this state, is dark, destitute of the saving knowledge of God, and, according to the Apostle, incapable of those things which belong to the Spirit of God. For; "the natural man receiveth not the things of the Spirit of God" (1 Cor 2:14), in which passage man is called "natural," not from the animal body, but from anima, the soul itself, which is the most noble part of man, but which is so encompassed about with the clouds of ignorance, as to be distinguished by the epithets of "vain" and "foolish." Men themselves, thus darkened in their minds, are denominated "mad" or foolish, "fools," and even "darkness" itself (Rom 1:21, 22; Eph 4:17, 18; Titus 3:3; Eph 5:8).

This is true, not only when, from the truth of the law which has in some measure been inscribed on the mind, it is preparing to form conclusions by the understanding; but likewise when, by simple apprehension, it would receive the truth of the gospel externally offered to it. For the human mind judges that to be "foolishness" which is the most excellent "wisdom of God" (1 Cor 1:18, 24). On this account, what is here said must be understood not only of practical understanding and the judgment of particular approbation, but also of theoretical understanding and the judgment of general estimation.

To the darkness of the mind succeeds the perverseness of the affections and of the heart, according to which it hates and has an aversion to that which is truly good and pleasing to God; but it loves and pursues what is evil. The Apostle was unable to afford a more luminous description of this perverseness, than he has given in the following words:

"The carnal mind is enmity against God: for it is not subject to the law of God, neither indeed can be. So then, they that are in the flesh cannot please God" (Rom 8:7–8).

For this reason, the human heart itself is very often called deceitful and perverse, uncircumcised, hard and stony" (Jer 17:9; Ezek 36:26). Its imagination is said to be "only evil continually" and "evil from his youth" (Gen 6:5; 8:21). And "out of the heart proceed evil thoughts, murders, adulteries," etc. (Matt 15:19).

Exactly correspondent to this darkness of the mind, and perverseness of the heart, is the utter weakness of all the powers to perform that which is truly good, and to omit the perpetration of that which is evil, in a due mode and from a due end and cause. The subjoined sayings of Christ serve to describe this impotence. "Neither can a corrupt tree bring forth good fruit" (Matt 7:18). "How can ye, being evil, speak good things?" (Matt12:34).

The following relates to the good which is properly prescribed in the gospel: "No man can come to me, except the Father . . . draw him" (John 6:44). As do likewise the following words of the Apostle: "The carnal mind . . . is not subject to the law of God, neither indeed can be" (Rom 8:7), therefore, that man over whom it has dominion, cannot perform what the law commands. The same Apostle says, "For when we were in the flesh, the motions of sins . . . did work in our members," or flourished energetically (Rom 7:5). To the same purpose are all those passages in which the man existing in this state is said to be under the power of sin and Satan, reduced to the condition of a slave, and "taken captive by him [the Devil] at his will" (Rom 6:20; 2 Tim 2:26).

To these let the consideration of the whole of the life of man placed under sin, be added, of which the Scriptures exhibit to us the most luminous descriptions. And it will be evident, that nothing can be spoken more truly concerning man in this state, than that he is altogether dead in sin (Eph 2:1; Rom 3:10–19). To these let the testimonies of Scripture be joined, in which are described the benefits of Christ, which are conferred by his Spirit on the human mind and will, and thus on the whole man (1 Cor 6:9–11; Gal 5:19–25; Eph 2:2–7; 4:17–20; Titus 3:3–7).

Deprived by Sin

For, the blessings of which man has been deprived by sin, cannot be rendered more obviously apparent, than by the immense mass of benefits to believers through the Holy Spirit; when, in truth, nature is understood to be devoid of all that which, as the Scriptures testify, is performed in man and communicated by the operation of the Holy Spirit. Therefore, if "where the Spirit of the Lord is, there is liberty" (2 Cor 3:17); and if "the Son therefore shall make you free, ye shall be free indeed" (John 8:36) it follows, that our will is not free from the first fall. That is, it is not free to good, unless it be made free by the Son through his Spirit.

But far different from this is the consideration of the free will of man, as constituted in the third state of Renewed Righteousness. For when a new light and knowledge of God and Christ, and of the Divine will, have been kindled in his mind; and when new affections, inclinations and motions agreeing with the law of God, have been excited in his heart, and new powers have been produced in him; it comes to pass, that, being liberated from the kingdom of darkness, and being now made "light in the Lord," (Eph 5:8) he understands the true and saving good.

After the hardness of his stony heart has been changed into the softness of flesh, and the law of God according to the covenant of grace has been inscribed on it, (Jer 31:32–35) he loves and embraces that which is good, just, and holy. And that, being made capable in Christ, cooperating now with God, he prosecutes the good which he knows and loves, and he begins himself to perform it in deed.

But this, whatever it may be of knowledge, holiness and power, is all begotten within him by the Holy Spirit; who is, on this account, called "the spirit of wisdom and understanding, the spirit of counsel and might, the spirit of knowledge and the fear of Jehovah" (Isa 11:2), "the Spirit of grace" (Zech 12:10), "of faith" (2 Cor 4:13), "the Spirit of adoption" into sons (Rom 8:15–16), and "the Spirit of holiness" (Rom 1:4), and to whom the acts of illumination, regeneration, renovation, and confirmation, are attributed in the Scriptures.

But two things must be here observed. The first is that these works of illumination and regeneration are not completed in one moment; but that are advanced and promoted, from time to time, by daily increase. For "our old man is crucified with him, that the body of sin might be destroyed" (Rom 6:6), and that "the inward man is renewed day by day" (2 Cor 4:16). For this reason, in regenerate persons, as long as they inhabit these mortal bodies, "the flesh lusteth against the Spirit" (Gal 5:17). Hence it arises, that they can neither perform any good thing without great resistance and violent struggles, nor abstain from the commission of evil.

Nay, it also happens, that, either through ignorance or infirmity, and sometimes through perverseness, they sin, as we may see in the cases of Moses, Aaron, Barnabas, Peter and David. Neither is such an occurrence only accidental. But, even in those who are the most perfect, the following Scriptures have their fulfillment: "In many things we offend all" (Jas 3:2), and "There is no man that sinneth not" (1 Kgs 8:46).

The second thing to be observed is, that as the very first commencement of every good thing, so likewise the progress, continuance and confirmation, nay, even the perseverance in good, are not from ourselves, but from God through the Holy Spirit. For, "he which hath begun a good work in you, will perform it until the day of Jesus Christ" (Phil 1:6); and "we are kept by the power of God through faith" (1 Pet 1:5). "The God of all grace" will "make you perfect, stablish, strengthen, settle you" (1 Pet 5:10).

But if it happens that persons fall into sin who have been born again, they neither repent nor rise again unless they be raised up again by God through the power of his Spirit, and be renewed to repentance. This is proved in the most satisfactory manner, by the example of David and of Peter. "Every good gift and perfect gift is from above, and cometh down from the Father of lights" (Jas 1:17), by whose power the dead are animated that they may live. The fallen are raised up that they may recover themselves, the blind are illuminated that they may see, the unwilling are incited that they may become willing, the weak are confirmed that they may stand, the willing are assisted that they may work and may cooperate with God. "Unto him be glory in the church by Christ Jesus throughout all ages, world without end. Amen" (Eph 3:21).

*   *   *

"Subsequent or following grace does indeed assist the good purpose of man; but this good purpose would have no existence unless through preceding or preventing grace. And though the desire of man, which is called good, be assisted by grace when it begins to be; yet it does not begin without grace, but is inspired by Him, concerning whom the Apostle writes thus, thanks be to God, who put the same earnest care into the heart of Titus for you. If God incites anyone to have 'an earnest care' for others, He will 'put it into the heart' of some other person to have 'an earnest care' for him."[2]

"What then, you ask, does free will do? I reply with brevity, it saves. Take away free will, and nothing will be left to be saved. Take away grace, and nothing will be left as the source of salvation. This work [of salvation] cannot be effected without two parties—one, from whom it may come: the other, to whom or in whom it may be wrought. God is the author of salvation. Free will is only capable of being saved. No one,

2. St. Augustine, *Contra. 2 Epist. Pelag.* l. 2. c. 9. Note: Because many of Arminius' reference sources published during or before his era are extremely rare today, his citations have been left in original form.

except God, is able to bestow salvation; and nothing, except free will, is capable of receiving it."[3]

On Divine Predestination

We call this decree "Predestination," in Greek, *proorismon* from the verb *proorizein* which signifies to determine, appoint, or decree anything before you enter on its execution. According to this general notion, Predestination, when attributed to God, will be his decree for the governance of all things, to which divines usually give the appellation of providence (Acts 2:28; 17:26). It is customary to consider in a less general notion, so far as it has reference to rational creatures who are to be saved or damned, for instance, angels and men.

It is taken in a stricter sense about the Predestination of men, and then is usually employed in two ways. For it is sometimes accommodated to both the elect and the reprobate. At other times, it is restricted to the elect alone, and then it has reprobation as its opposite. According to this last signification, in which it is almost constantly used in Scripture (Rom 8:29), we will address Predestination.

Predestination, therefore, as it regards the thing itself, is the decree of the good pleasure of God in Christ, by which he resolved within himself from all eternity, to justify, adopt and endow with everlasting life, to the praise of his own glorious grace, believers on whom he had decreed to bestow faith (Eph 1; Rom 9).

The genus of Predestination we lay down as a decree which is called in Scripture *prothesis tou theou* "the purpose of God," (Rom 9:11) and *ton Boulen tou theleuatos autou,* "the counsel of his [God's] own will" (Eph 1:11). This decree is not legal, according to what is said, "That the man which doeth those things shall live by them;" (Rom 10:5), but it is evangelical, and this is the language which it holds:

"This is the will of him that sent me, that everyone who seeth the Son, and believeth on him, may have everlasting life" (John 6:40; Rom 10:9). This decree, therefore, is peremptory and irrevocable, because the final manifestation of "the whole counsel of God" concerning our salvation, is contained in the gospel (Acts 20:27; Heb 1:2; 2:2, 3).

The cause of this decree is God, "according to the good pleasure" or the benevolent affection "of his will" (Eph 1:5). And God indeed is

---

3. Bernardus Silvestris, *De Libero Arbit. et Gratia.* The author was a twelfth-century scholastic theologian.

the cause, as possessing the right of determining as he wills both about men as his creatures, and especially as sinners, and about his blessings (Jer 18:6; Matt 20:14, 15), "according to the good pleasure of his will," by which, being moved with and in himself, he made that decree. This "good pleasure" not only excludes every cause it could take from man, or could be imagined to take from him; but it likewise removes whatever was in or from man, that could justly move God not to make that gracious decree (Rom 11:34, 35).

As the foundation of this decree, we place Jesus Christ, the mediator between God and men (Eph 1:4), "in whom I [the Father] am well pleased" (Matt 3:17; Luke 3:22); "in whom God was "reconciling the world unto himself, not imputing their trespasses unto them." God "hath made him to be sin for us, . . . that we might be made the righteousness of God in him" (2 Cor 5:19, 21).

His purpose was "to bring in everlasting righteousness" (Dan 9:24), adoption to be acquired, the spirit of grace and of faith was to be obtained (Gal 4:5, 6, 19), eternal life procured (John 6:51), and all the plenitude of spiritual blessings prepared, the communication of which must be decreed by Predestination. He is also constituted by God the Head of all those persons who will, by divine Predestination, accept of the equal enjoyment of these blessings (Eph 1:22; 5:23; Heb 5:9).

We attribute Eternity to this decree, because God does nothing in time, which He has not decreed to do from all eternity. For "Known unto God are all his works from the beginning of the world" (Acts 15:18), and "He hath chosen us in him [Christ] before the foundation of the world" (Eph 1:4). If it were otherwise, God might be charged with mutability.

We say that the object or matter of Predestination is two-fold—divine things, and persons to whom the communication of those divine things has been predestinated by this decree.

These divine things receive from the Apostle the general appellation of "spiritual blessings" (Eph 1:3). Such are, in the present life, justification, adoption as sons (Rom 8:29, 30), and the spirit of grace and adoption (Eph 1:5; John 1:12; Gal 4:6, 7). Lastly, after this life, eternal life. (John 3:15, 16). The whole of these things are usually comprised and enunciated, in the Divinity schools, by the names of Grace and Glory.

We circumscribe the Persons within the limits of the word "believers," which presupposes sin: for no one believes on Christ except a sinner, and the man who acknowledges himself to be that sinner. (Matt 9:13;

11:28). Therefore, the plenitude of those blessings, and the preparation of them which has been made in Christ, were necessary for none but sinners. But we give the name of "believers," not to those who would be such by their own merits or strength, but to those who by the gratuitous and peculiar kindness of God would believe in Christ (Rom 9:32; Gal 2:20; Matt 11:25; 13:11; John 6:44; Phil 1:29).

The form is the decreed communication of these blessings to believers, and in the mind of God the pre-existent and pre-ordained relation and ordination of believers to Christ their Head. The fruit of this, they receive through a real and actual union with Christ their Head. In the present life, this fruit is gracious, through the commencement and increase of the union. In the life to come, it is glorious, through the complete consummation of this union (2 Tim 1:9, 10; John 1:16, 17; 17:11, 12, 22–24; Eph 4:13, 15).

The end of Predestination is the praise of the glorious grace of God: for since grace, or the gratuitous love of God in Christ, is the cause of Predestination, it is equitable that to the same grace the entire glory of this act should be ceded (Eph 1:6; Rom 11:36).

Decree of Predestination

But this decree of Predestination is "according to election," as the Apostle says (Rom 9:11). This election necessarily implies reprobation. Reprobation therefore is opposed to Predestination, as its contrary and is likewise called "a cast[ing] away" (Rom 11:1), being "ordained to . . . condemnation," (Jude 4) and "appointed . . . to wrath" (1 Thess 5:9).

From the law of contraries, we define reprobation to be a decree of the wrath, or of the severe will, of God. He resolved from all eternity to condemn to eternal death unbelievers, who, by their own fault and the just judgment of God, would not believe, for the declaration of his wrath and power (John 3:18; Luke 7:30; John 12:37, 40; 2 Thess 2:10, 11; Rom 9:22).

Though by faith in Jesus Christ the remission of all sins is obtained, and sins are not imputed to them who believe (Rom 4:2–11); yet the reprobate will be compelled to endure the punishment, not only of their unbelief (by the contrary of which they might avoid the chastisement due to the rest of their sins), but likewise of the sins they have committed against the law, being "everlasting destruction from the presence of the Lord, and from the glory of his power" (2 Thess 1:9).

To each of these decrees, that of Predestination and that of reprobation, is subjoined its execution. The acts are performed in that order in which they have been appointed in and by the decree itself. The objects both of the decree and of its execution are the same, and entirely uniform, or invested with the same formal relation (Ps 115:3; 33:9, 11).

Great is the use of this doctrine, as thus delivered from the Scriptures. For it serves to establish the glory of the grace of God, to console afflicted consciences, to terrify the wicked and to drive away their security.

But it establishes the grace of God when it ascribes the whole praise of our vocation, justification, adoption, and glorification, to the mercy of God alone, and takes it entirely away from our own strength, works and merits (Rom 8:29, 30; Eph 1:14).

It comforts afflicted consciences that are struggling with temptation, when it renders them assured of the gracious good will of God in Christ, which was from all eternity decreed to them, performed in time, and which will endure forever (Isa 54:8). It also shows, that the purpose of God according to election stands firm, not of works, but of Him that calleth (1 Cor 1:9; Rom 9:11).

It is capable of terrifying the ungodly because it teaches that the decree of God concerning unbelievers is irrevocable (Heb 3:11, 17–19); and that "they . . . who believed not the truth but had pleasure in unrighteousness" are to be adjudged to eternal destruction (2 Thess 2:12).

This doctrine therefore ought to resound, not only within private walls and in schools, but also in the assemblies of the saints and in the church of God. Yet one caution ought to be strictly observed, that nothing be taught concerning it beyond what the Scriptures say, that it be propounded in the manner which the Scriptures have adopted, and that it be referred to the same end as that which the Scriptures propose when they deliver it. This, by the gracious assistance of God, we think we have done. "Unto Him be glory in the church by Christ Jesus throughout all ages, world without end. Amen" (Eph 3:21).

"For the power of the Lord is great, and he is honored of the lowly. Seek not out things that are too hard for thee, neither search the things that are above thy strength. But what is commanded thee, think thereupon with reverence, for it is not needful for thee to see with thine eyes the things that are in secret. Be not curious in unnecessary matters: for more things are shewed unto thee than men understand." (Ecclesiasticus 3:23)[4]

ON THE RIGHTEOUSNESS AND EFFICACY OF THE PROVIDENCE OF GOD CONCERNING EVIL

The consideration of evil, called "the evil of culpability" or "of delinquency," has induced many persons to deny the providence of God concerning creatures endowed with understanding and freedom of will, and concerning their actions.

They have thought that because God is good and just, omniscient and omnipotent, he would have entirely prevented sin from being committed, if in reality he cared by his providence for his rational creatures and their actions (Mark 10:18; Ps 147:5; Rev 4:8; Mal 2:17; 3:14).

This is because they can conceive in their minds no other administration of Divine Providence concerning evil, than such as would involve God himself in the culpability, and would exempt from all criminality the creature, as if he had been impelled to sin by an irresistible act of God's efficiency.

For this reason, then, since a belief in the Providence of God is absolutely necessary (Luke 12:28), from whom a considerable part of his government is taken away if it be denied that he exercises any care over rational creatures and their actions; we will endeavor briefly to explain the efficiency of Divine Providence concerning evil. At the same time we will demonstrate from this efficiency, that God cannot possibly be aspersed with the charge of injustice, and that no stain of sin can attach to him. On the contrary, this efficiency is highly conducive to the commendation of God's righteousness.

But in sin are to be considered not only the act (under which we likewise comprise the omission of the act), but also "the transgression of the law." The act has regard to a natural good, and is called the material cause of sin. The transgression is a moral evil, and is called the formal cause of sin. An investigation into both of them is necessary, when we treat upon the efficiency of God concerning sin. For it is occupied about the act as it is an act, and as it is done against the law which prohibits its commission about the omission of the act as such, and as it is against

---

4. This is a book accepted as part of the Biblical canon by Catholics and Eastern Orthodox, but not by Protestants.

the law which commands its performance. But this efficiency is to be considered:

- with regard to the beginning of sin, and its first conception in the heart of a rational creature;

- its attempt, and, through this attempt, its perpetration; and,

- with regard to sin when finished. The efficiency of God concerning the beginning of sin is either its hindrance or permission, as well as the administration both of arguments and occasions inciting to sin, and an immediate concurrence to produce the act. The Divine efficiency concerning the progress of sin comprises its direction and determination and concerning the completion of sin, it is occupied in punishing or pardoning.

The First efficiency of God concerning sin, is hindrance or the placing of a hindrance, which, both with regard of the efficiency and of the object, is three-fold. With respect to efficiency: For

- the impediment is either of sufficient efficacy, but such as does not hinder sin in the act (Matt 11:21, 23; John 18:6);

- or it is of such great efficacy as to render it impossible to be resisted;

- or it is of an efficacy administered in such a way by the wisdom of God, as in reality to hinder sin with regard to the event, and with certainty according to the foreknowledge of God, although not necessarily and inevitably (Gen 20:6). With respect to the object, it is likewise three-fold: for a hindrance is placed either on the power, the capability, or the will of a rational creature.

The impediment placed on the power, is that by which some act is taken away from the power of a rational creature, for the performance of which it has an inclination and sufficient powers. This is done by legislation, through which it comes to pass that the creature cannot perform that act without sin (Gen 2:16, 17).

The impediment placed on the capability, is that by which this effect is produced, that the creature cannot commit the deed, for the performance of which it possesses an inclination, and powers which, without this hindrance, would be sufficient. But this hindrance is placed on the capability in four ways: First, by depriving the creature of the essence and life, which are the foundation of capability (1 Kings 19; 2 Kings 1).

Secondly, by the removal or diminution of capability (1 Kgs 13:4; Rom 6:6). Thirdly, by the opposition of a greater capability, or at least of one that is equal (2 Chr 26:18–21; Gal 5:17). Fourthly, by the withdrawing of the object towards which the act tends (John 8:59).

Impediment is Placed

An impediment is placed on the will when, by some argument, it is persuaded not to will the perpetration of a sin, whether this argument be taken from the impossibility or the difficulty of the thing (Matt 21:46; Hos 2:6, 7) from its unpleasantness or inconvenience, its uselessness or injuriousness (Gen 37:26, 27) and, lastly, from its injustice, dishonor, and indecency (Gen 39:8, 9).

The Permission of sin is contrary to the hindering of it. Yet it is not opposed to hindrance as the latter is an act which is taken away from the power of a creature by legislation. For, in this case, the same act would be a sin, and not a sin—a sin as it was an act forbidden to the power of the creature, and not a sin as being permitted, that is not forbidden. But permission is opposed to this hindrance, by which an impediment is placed on the power and the will of the creature. This permission is a suspension of all impediments, that God knows, if they were employed, would in fact hinder the sin. And it is a necessary result, because sin might be hindered by a single impediment of this description.

Sin, therefore, is permitted to the power of the creature, when God employs none of those impediments which have been mentioned in the third thesis of this disputation, on which account, this permission has the following, either as conjoint or preceding acts of God. The continuance of essence and life to the creature, the preservation of his power, a care that it be not opposed by a greater power, or at least by one equal to it, and, lastly, the exhibition of the object on which sin is committed (Exod 9:16; John 18:6; 1 Sam 20:31, 32; Matt 26:2, 53).

Sin is permitted also to the will, not by the suspension of every impediment suitable to deter the will from sinning, but by not employing those which in reality would hinder, of which kind God must have an immense number in the treasures of his wisdom and power.

The foundation of this permission is:

- The liberty of choice, which God the Creator, has implanted in his rational creature, and the use of which the constancy of the Donor does not suffer to be taken away from this creature.

- The infinite wisdom and power of God, by which He knows and is able to produce good out of evil. (Gen 1:2, 3; 2 Cor 4:6)

Therefore, God permits that which he does permit, not in ignorance of the powers and the inclination of rational creatures, for he knows all things (1 Sam 23:11, 12). Also, not with reluctance, for it was in his power not to have produced a creature who possessed freedom of will, and to have destroyed him after he was produced (Rev 4:11), not as being incapable of hindering, for how can this be attributed to Him who is both omniscient and omnipotent? (Jer 18:6; Ps 94:9, 10) And not as an unconcerned spectator, or negligent of that which is transacted, because even before anything is done he has already gone through the various actions concerning it, and has, besides, an attentive eye upon it to direct and determine to punish or to pardon it (Ps 81:12, 13). But whatever God permits, he permits it designedly and voluntarily, His will being immediately concerned about its permission, which permission itself is immediately occupied about sin, which order cannot be inverted without injury to divine justice and truth (Ps 5:4, 5).

We must now, with more distinctness, explain by some of the differences of sin, those things which we have spoken thus generally about hindering and permitting.

The distinction of sin, from its causes, into those of ignorance, infirmity, malignity, and negligence, will serve our purpose. For an impediment is placed on a sin of ignorance by the revelation of the divine will (Ps 119:105), on a sin of infirmity, by the strengthening of the Holy Spirit (Eph 3:16), on a sin of malignity, because God will "take the stony heart . . . and will give them a heart of flesh" (Ezek 11:19), and inscribing on it the law of God (Jer 31:33) and on a sin of negligence, by a holy solicitude excited in the hearts of believers (Jer 32:40). From these, it will be easily evident, in the suspension of which of these acts consists the permission of sins under each of the preceding classes.

The distinction of sin according to the relation of the law, which commands the performance of good, and of that which prohibits the commission of evil, has also a place in this explanation. For, against the prohibitory part, an offense is committed either by performing an act, or from an undue cause and end, omitting its performance against the perceptive part either by omitting an act or by performing it in an undue manner, and from an undue cause and end. To these distinctions also, God's hindering and permitting may be adapted. For Joseph's brethren were hindered from killing him, but they were induced to omit that act from an undue cause and end (Gen 37:26, 27).

Following the Counsel

Absalom was hindered from following the counsel of Ahithophel, which was useful to himself, and hurtful to David. But he did not abstain from it through a just cause, and from a good end (2 Sam 17). God hindered Balaam from cursing the children of Israel, and caused him to bless them; but it was in such a manner that he abstained from the former act, and performed the latter with an insincere and knavish mind (Num 23).

We shall more correctly understand the reasons and causes both of hindering and permitting, if, while distinctly considering in sin the act, and the transgression of the law, we apply to each of them the divine hindrance and permission. But though, in sin, the act and the transgression of the law are inseparably connected, and therefore neither can be hindered or permitted without the other. Yet they may be distinguished in the mind, and God may hinder and permit sometimes with regard to the act or to the transgression alone; at other times, principally with regard to the one of them or to both, and these his acts may become objects of consideration to us. God hindered Elijah from being forcibly brought to Ahaziah to be killed, not as that was a sin, but as it was an act. This is apparent from the end and the mode of hindering.

From the end, because it was His will that the life of His prophet should be spared, not lest Ahaziah should sin against God. From the mode of hindering, because Ahaziah destroyed two companies of fifty men each who had been sent to seize him, which was a token of divine anger against him and the men, by which sin is not usually hindered as such, but as it is an act which will prove injurious to another. But through Grace, sin is hindered as such (2 Kgs 1).

God permitted Joseph to be sold, when he hindered his murder. He permitted his selling, not more as it was a sin than as it was an act; for by the sale of Joseph, as it was an act, God obtained his end (Gen 37:1, 20; Ps 105:17). But God hindered David from laying violent hands on Saul, not so much as it was an act, as in reference to its being a sin. This appears from the argument by which David was induced to refrain. "The Lord forbid," said he, "that I should do this thing unto my master, the Lord's anointed, to stretch forth mine hand against him . . ." (1 Sam 24:6).

God permitted Ahab to kill Naboth, rather as it was a sin than as it was an act. For thus Ahab filled up the measure of his iniquities, and accelerated the infliction of punishment on himself. For, by some other way than this, God could have taken Naboth to himself (1 Kgs 21). But Abimelech was hindered from violating the chastity of Sarah, both as it was an act by which indelible grief would have been brought down upon Abraham, whom He greatly loved, and as it was a sin; for God was unwilling that Abimelech should defile himself with this crime, because "in the integrity of [his] heart," he would have done it (Gen 20:6). On the contrary, God permitted Judah to know Tamar, his daughter-in-law, both as an act because God willed to have Christ born in direct descent from Judah, and as it was a sin (Gen 38:18). For it was the will of God thus to show: Nothing is so polluted that it cannot be sanctified in Christ Jesus.

For it is not in vain that Matthew has informed us, that Christ was the Son of Judah by Tamar, as he was also the Son of David by the wife of Uriah (Matt 1:6). This matter when diligently considered by us, conduces both to illustrate the wisdom of God, and to promote our own profit, if in our consciences, we solicitously observe from what acts and in what respect we are hindered, and what acts are permitted to us.

Beside this permission, there is another efficiency of the providence of God concerning the Beginning of Sin. That is, the administration or management of arguments and occasions that incite to an act that cannot be committed by the creature without sin, if not through the intention of God, at least according to the inclination of the creature, and not seldom according to the events which thence arise (2 Sam 12:11, 12; 16:21–23).

But these arguments are presented either to the mind (2 Sam 24:1; 1 Chr 21:1; Ps 105:25) or to the senses, both external and internal (Job 1 & 2; Isa 10:5–7); and this indeed, either by means of the service or intervention of creatures, or by the immediate act of God himself. The end of God in this administration is to try whether it be the will of the creature to abstain from sinning, even when it is excited by these incentives (for small praise is due to the act of abstaining, in those cases in which such excitements are absent) and, if it be the will of the creature to yield to these alluring attractions, to effect his own work by the act of the creature. God is not impelled by necessity, as if He was unable to complete his own work without the aid of the creature, but through a desire to demonstrate his manifold wisdom.

Consider the arguments by which the brethren of Joseph, through their own malice, were incited to will his murder: these were Joseph's accusation, by which he disclosed to his father the deeds of his brethren, the peculiar affection which Jacob cherished for Joseph, the sending of a dream, and the relation of it. Consider also the occasions or opportunities, the mission of Joseph to his brethren at his father's request, and the opportune appearance of the Ishmaelites who were traveling into Egypt, (Gen 37:28).

Efficiency of God

The last efficiency of God concerning the beginnings of sin, is the divine concurrence, which is necessary to produce every act, because nothing whatever can have an entity except from the first and chief Being, who immediately produces that entity. The concurrence of God is not his immediate influx into a second or inferior cause, but it is an action of God immediately flowing into the effect of the creature, so that the same effect in one and the same entire action may be produced simultaneously by God and the creature.

Though this concurrence is placed in the mere pleasure or will of God, and in his free dispensation, yet he never denies it to a rational and free creature, when he has permitted an act to his power and will. For these two phrases are contradictory, "to grant permission to the power and the will of a creature to commit an act," and "to deny the divine concurrence without which the act cannot be done."

But this concurrence is to the act as such, not as it is a sin. And therefore God is at once the effecter and the permitter of the same act, and the permitter before he is the effecter. For if it had not been the will of the creature to perform such an act, the influx of God would not have been upon that act by concurrence. And because the creature cannot perform that act without sin, God ought not, on that account, to deny the divine concurrence to the creature who is inclined to its performance. For it is right and proper that the obedience of the creature should be tried, and that he should abstain from an unlawful act and from the desire of obeying his own inclinations, not through a deficiency of the requisite divine concurrence. In this respect, he abstains from an act as it is a natural good, but it is the will of God that he should refrain from it as it is a moral evil.

The preceding considerations relate to the beginnings of sin. In reference to the progress of sin, a two-fold efficiency of divine providence occurs: direction and determination. The direction of sin is an act of divine providence, by which God wisely, justly, and powerfully directs sin wherever he wills, "reaching from one end to another mightily, and sweetly ordering all things" (Wisdom 8:1). In the divine direction is likewise contained a leading away from that point whither it is not the will of God to direct it. This direction is two-fold, unto an object, and unto an end. Direction unto an object is when God allows the sin, which he permits, to be born, not at the option of the creature, towards an object which, in any way whatsoever, is exposed and liable to the injury of sin; but which he directs to a particular object that sometimes has been no part of the sinner's aim or intention, or that he has at least not absolutely intended (Prov 16:9; 21:1).

Of this we have a signal example in Nebuchadnezzar, who, when he had prepared himself to subjugate nations, preferred to march against the Jews rather than the Ammonites, through the divine administration of his divinations (Ezek 21:19–22). Direction unto an end is, when God does not allow the sin, which he permits, to be conducive to any end which the creature intends. But he uses it for that end that he himself wills, whether the creature intends the same end (by which he would not still be excused from sin), or whether he has another purpose which is directly contrary. The sale of Joseph into Egypt, the temptation of Job, and the expedition of the king of Assyria against the Jews, afford illustrations of these remarks (Gen 1:20, 21; Job 1 & 2; Isa 10:5–12).

The determination of sin is an act of divine providence by which God places a measure or check on his permission, and a boundary on sin, that it may not, at the option and will of the creature, wander in infinitum. This mode and boundary are placed by the circumscription of the time, and the determination of the magnitude. The circumscription of the time is, when the space of time in which the permitted sin could continue, is diminished and circumscribed so as to stop itself (Matt 24:22). In this part also, regard must be had to the act as such, and to the sin as such. God places a boundary to the duration of the act, when he takes the rod of iniquity from the righteous, lest they commit any act unworthy of themselves (Ps 125:3) and when "he deliver[s] the godly out of temptation" (2 Pet 2:9).

God places a boundary to the duration of the sin when he hedges up the way of the Israelites with thorns, that they may no longer commit idolatry (Hos 2:6, 7); when "He commandeth all men every where to repent," after He "in times past suffered all nations to walk in their own ways" (Acts 14:16; 17:30).

A boundary is fixed to the magnitude of sin, when God does not permit sin to increase to excess and assume greater strength. This also is done with respect to it as an act, or as a sin.

In the former respect, as an act, God hindered the wrath of the enemies of the children of Israel, who "had swallowed us up quick" though he had permitted the foes to rise up against them (Ps 124:2, 3). He permitted "no temptation taken" the Corinthians "but such as is common to man" (1 Cor 10:13). He hindered the devil from putting forth his hand against the life of Job (1 & 2). He prevented Shishak, the king of Egypt, from "destroy[ing]" the Jews, and permitted him only to subject them to servitude (2 Chr 12:7–9).

God Hindered David

In respect to it as a sin, God hindered David from contaminating himself with the blood of Nabal and his domestics, which he had sworn to shed, and with whom he was then in a state of contention (1 Sam 25:22, 26). He also prevented David from going forth to battle in company with the army of Achish (27:2; 29:6, 7), to whom he had fled, and "before them . . . feigned himself mad" (21:13). Thus, at the same time he hindered him from destroying his own countrymen, the Israelites, and from bringing disasters on the army of Achish. For he could have done neither of these things without the most flagrant wickedness; though the sin, also, as an act, seems thus to have been hindered.

On account of this divine permission, the offering of arguments and opportunities, also on account of this direction, determination, and divine concurrence, God is said himself to do those evils which are perpetrated by men and by Satan: to have sent Joseph down into Egypt (Gen 45:8); to have taken the property of Job (1 & 2); to have done openly "and before the sun" what David had perpetrated "secretly" against Uriah (2 Sam 12:11, 12; 16:11, 21–22). This mode of speech is adopted for the following reasons:

- The principal parts, in the actions employed to produce such effects, belong to God himself.

- The effects and issues, which result from all these, even from actions performed by the creature, are not so much in accordance with the intention of the creatures themselves, as with the purpose of God (Isa 10:5–7).

- The wisdom of God knows, if an administration of this kind be employed by him, that will certainly arise, or ensue, which cannot be perpetuated by the creature without wickedness; and because His will decrees to employ this administration (1 Sam 23:11–13).

- God, who is the universal cause, moves into the effect with a stronger influence than the creature does, whose entire efficacy depends upon God.

Lastly, we address the efficiency of divine providence concerning sin already perpetrated, which consists in its punishment and remission. This efficiency is occupied about sin as it is such: For sin is punished and pardoned as it is an evil, and *because* it is an evil.

The punishment of sin is an act of the providence of God, by which sin is repaid with the punishment that is due to it according to the justice of God. This punishment either belongs to the present life, or to that which is to come.

The latter is the eternal separation of the whole man from God, and his anguish and torture in the lake of fire (Matt 25:41; Rev 20:15).

The punishment inflicted in this life, is either corporal or spiritual. Those chastisements that relate to the body, and to the state of the animal life, are various; but the enumeration of them is not necessary for our purpose. But spiritual punishment must be diligently considered as a punishment of a previous sin, as to be also the cause of other subsequent sins, through the malice of him on whom it is inflicted. It is a privation of grace, and a delivering up to the power of evil. But privation is either that of habitual grace, or that of assisting grace.

The former is through the blinding of the mind, and the hardening of the heart (Isa 6:9, 10). The latter is the withdrawing of the assistance of the Holy Spirit, who is wont, inwardly to "helpeth our infirmities" (Rom 8:26), and outwardly to repress the temptations of Satan and the world both on the right hand and on the left. In this holy service, he also engages the ministry and the care of good angels (Heb 1:14; Psalm 91:11).

A delivering up to the power of evil is, either giving sinners "over to a reprobate mind" and to the efficacy of error (Rom 1:28; 2 Thess

2:9–11), or to the desires of the flesh and to the lusts of sin (Rom 1:24), or lastly to the power of Satan, "the god of this world" (2 Cor 4:4), "that now worketh in the children of disobedience" (Eph 2:2). But because from this punishment arise many other sins, and this not only according to the certain knowledge of God, by which He knows that if He thus punishes, they will thence arise, but likewise according to his purpose by which He resolves thus to punish—hence occur the following expressions: "I will harden Pharaoh's, heart" etc. (Exod 4:21; 7:3).

"Notwithstanding, they [sons of Eli] harkened not unto the voice of their father, because the Lord would slay them" (1 Sam 2:25). "But Amaziah would not hear [Joash, king of Israel]; for it came of God, that he might deliver them into the hand of their enemies, because they sought after the gods of Edom" (2 Chr 25:20). This consideration distinguishes the governance of God concerning sins, so far as it is occupied concerning either those sinners who are hardened, or those who are not hardened.

Act of Providence

The pardon or remission of sin is an act of the Providence of God, by which the guilt of sin is forgiven, and the punishment due to sin on account of its guilt is taken away. As this remission restores, to the favor of God, the man who had previously been an enemy; so it also causes the Divine administration respecting him to be afterwards entirely gracious, so far as equity and justice require. That is, through this pardon, he is free from those spiritual punishments which have been enumerated in the preceding thesis (Ps 2:10–12). And though not exempt from corporal chastisements, he is not visited with them through the anger of God as the punisher of sin, but only through the desire of God thus to declare that He hates sin, and besides so to chastise as to deter the sinner from again falling into it (2 Sam 12:11–13).

For which reason, the government of Providence with regard to this man is entirely different from that under which he remained before he obtained remission (Ps 119:67; 1 Cor 11:32; Ps 32:1, 6). This consideration is exceedingly useful for producing in man a solicitous care and a diligent endeavor to obtain grace from God, which may not only be sufficient to preserve him in future from sinning but which may likewise be so administered by the gracious Providence of God, as God knows to be best fitted to keep him in the very act from sin.

This is the efficiency of Divine Providence concerning sin, which cannot be accused of the least injustice.

For with respect to the hindering of Sin, that which is employed by God is sufficient in its own nature to hinder, and by which it is the duty of the creature to be hindered from sin, by which also he might actually be hindered unless he offered resistance and failed of the proffered grace. But God is not bound to employ all the methods possible to Him for the hindrance of sin (Rom 1 and 2; Isa 5:4; Matt 11:21–23).

But the cause of sin cannot be ascribed to the Divine Permission. Not the efficient cause, for it is a suspension of the Divine efficiency. Not the deficient cause, for it pre-supposed that man had a capability not to commit sin, by the aid of Divine grace, which is either near and ready. Or if it be wanting, it is removed to a distance by the fault of the man himself.

The presenting of arguments and occasions does not cause sin, unless, *per accidens*, accidentally. For it is administered in such a manner, as to allow the creature not only the spontaneous but also the free use of his own motions and actions. But God is perfectly at liberty in this manner to try the obedience of his creature.

Neither can injustice be ascribed with any propriety to the Divine concurrence. For there is no reason in existence why God ought to deny his concurrence to that act which, on account of the precept imposed, cannot be committed by the creature without sin (Gen 2:16, 17), which concurrence God would grant to the same act of the creature, if a law had not been made.

Direction and determination have no difficulty. Punishment and pardon have in them manifest equity, even that punishment which contains blinding and hardening, since God is not wont to inflict it except for the deep demerit and the almost desperate contumacy of his intelligent creature (Isa 6:7; Rom 1; 2 Thess 2:9–12).

ON THE VOCATION OF MEN TO SALVATION

The title contains three terms—vocation, men, salvation,

- The word Vocation denotes a total and entire act, consisting of all its parts, whether essential or integral, what parts soever are necessary for the purpose of men being enabled to answer the Divine Vocation (Prov 1:24; Matt11:20, 21; 23:37).

- Men may be considered in a two-fold respect, either as placed in the state of animal life without sin, or as obnoxious to sin. We consider them here in this last respect (Gen 2:16, 17; Matt 9:13).

- Salvation, by a Synecdoche, in addition to vocation itself by which we are called to salvation, contains also whatsoever is necessary, through the appointment of God, for obtaining salvation or life eternal (Luke 19:9; 2 Cor 6:2).

We define Vocation, a gracious act of God in Christ, by which, through his word and Spirit, He calls forth sinful men, who are liable to condemnation and placed under the dominion of sin, from the condition of the animal life, and from the pollutions and corruptions of this world (2 Tim 1:9; Matt 11:28; 1 Pet 2:9, 10; Gal 1:4; 2 Pet 2:20; Rom 10:13–15; 1 Pet 3:19; Gen 6:3) unto "the fellowship of Jesus Christ" and of his kingdom and its benefits. And that, being united unto Him as their Head, they may derive from him life, sensation, motion, and a plenitude of every spiritual blessing, to the glory of God and their own salvation (1 Cor 1:9; Gal 2:20; Eph 1:3, 6; 2 Thess 3:14).

The efficient cause of this vocation is God the Father in the Son. The Son himself, as appointed by the Father to be the Mediator and the king of his church, calls men by the Holy Spirit; as He is the Spirit of God given to the Mediator; and as He is the Spirit of Christ the king and the head of his church, by whom both "the Father and the Son hitherto work" (1 Thess 2:12; Eph 2:17; 4:11, 12; Rev 3:20; John 5:17). But this vocation is so administered by the Spirit, that the Holy Spirit is himself its effecter: for He appoints bishops, sends forth teachers, endues them with gifts, grants them his assistance, and obtains authority for the word and bestows efficacy upon it (Heb 3:7; Acts 13:2; 20:28; 1 Cor 12:4, 7, 9, 11; Heb 2:4).

The Inwardly-moving cause is the grace, mercy and (philanthropy) "love of God our Savior toward man" (Titus 3:4, 5), by which He is inclined to relieve the misery of sinful man, and to impart unto him eternal felicity (2 Tim 1:9, 10). But the disposing cause is the wisdom and justice of God; by which he knows how it is proper for this vocation to be administered, and wills it to be dispensed as it is lawful and befitting; and from which is formed the decree of his will concerning the administration and its mode (1 Cor 1:17, 18).

The external cause, which outwardly moves God, is Jesus Christ by his obedience and intercession (2 Tim 1:9). But the instrumental cause is the word of God, administered by means of men, either through preaching or writing, which is the ordinary method (1 Cor 12:28–30; 2 Thess 2:14); or without human assistance, when the word is immediately proposed by God inwardly to the mind and the will, which is extraordinary. And this is in fact both the word of the law and that of the Gospel, which are subordinate in the operations apportioned to each other.

The matter or subject of vocation is mankind constituted in the animal life; men worldly, natural, animal, carnal, sinful, alienated from the life of God, and dead in sins. They are therefore unworthy to be called, and unfit to answer to the call, unless by the gracious estimation of God they are accounted worthy, and by his powerful operation they are rendered fit to comply with the vocation (Matt 9:13; Titus 2:12; Eph 2:11, 12; 4:17, 18; 5:14; John 5:25; 6:44; Matt 10:11–13; Acts 16:14).

Very Administration

The form of vocation is placed in the very administration of the word and of the Holy Spirit. God hath instituted this administration so, as He knows to be suitable and becoming to himself, and to his justice tempered with mercy in Christ; always reserving to himself the full and free power of not employing, for the conversion of men, all the methods possible to himself according to the treasures of his wisdom and power, and of bestowing unequal grace on those who are [in every respect] equals, and equal grace on those who are unequal, nay, of employing greater grace on those who are more wicked (Rom 9:21–26; 10:17–21; 11:25, 29–33; Ezek 3:6; Matt 11:21, 23).

But in every vocation the point of commencement, and that of termination, come to be considered. The point of commencement, whence men are called by divine vocation, is not only the state of this animal life, but likewise that of sin and of misery on account of sin, that is, out of guilt and condemnation (1 Pet 2:9; 2 Pet 1:4; Eph 2:1–6; Rom 6:17, 18). The point of termination is, first, the state of grace, or a participation of supernatural good and of every spiritual blessing, during the present life, in Christ, in whom resides a plenitude of grace and truth; and, afterwards, the state of glory, and the perfect fruition of God himself (Eph 1:3, 4; John 1:14, 16; Rom 8:28–30).

The proximate end of vocation is, that they who have been called answer by faith to God and to Christ who give the call, and that they thus become the covenanted people of God through Christ the Mediator of the New Covenant; and, after having become believers and parties to the covenant, that they love, fear, honor, and worship God and Christ, render in all things obedience to the divine precepts "in righteousness and true holiness," and that by this means they "make their calling and election sure" (Prov 1:24; Heb 3:7; Rev 3:20; Eph 2:11–16; Titus. 3:8; Deut 6:4, 5; Jer 32:38, 39; Luke 1:74, 75; 2 Pet 1:1, 10).

The remote end is the salvation of the elect and the glory of God, in regard to which the very vocation to grace is a means ordained by God, yet through the appointment of God it is necessary to the communication of salvation (Phil 1:6; Eph 1:14). But the answer by which obedience is yielded to this call, is the condition which, through the appointment of God, is also requisite and necessary for obtaining this end (Prov 1:24–26; Acts 13:46; Luke 7:30). The glory of God, who is supremely wise, good, merciful, just and powerful, is so luminously displayed in this communication both of his grace and glory, as deservedly to raise into rapturous admiration the minds of angels and men, and to employ their loosened tongues in celebrating the praises of Jehovah (Rev 4:8–11; 5:8–10).

Vocation is partly external, partly internal. External vocation is by the ministry of men, who propound the word of the law and of the gospel, and who are on this account called "workers together with God, planters, waterers, builders, and ministers by whom the [members of the] church believe" (1 Cor 1:5–9; 3:3–6). Internal vocation is by the operation of the Holy Spirit illuminating the mind and affecting the heart, that serious attention may be given to those things which are spoken, and that faith or credence may be given to the word. The efficacy consists in the concurrence of both the internal and external vocation (Acts 16:14; 2 Cor 3:3; 1 Pet 1:22).

But that distribution is not of a genus into its species, but of a whole into its parts, or of the entire vocation into partial acts which concur to produce one conclusion—which is, obedience yielded to the call. Hence an assemblage, or congregation of those who are called, and of those who answer to the call, is denominated "the Church" (1 Cor 3:5, 6; Rom 1:5), which is itself, in the same manner, distinguished into the visible and the invisible—the visible, that "maketh confession with the mouth," and the invisible, "that believeth with the heart" (Rom 10:10). Similarly, man himself is likewise distinguished into "the outward" and "the inward" (2 Cor 4:16).

Lest With the Mystics

But we must be cautious, lest with the mystics and the enthusiasts, we consider the Word which is propounded by the ministry of men as only preparatory; and believe that another word is inwardly employed, which is perfective, or, (which is the same thing,) lest we suppose, that the Spirit by his internal act illuminates the mind into another knowledge of God and Christ, than that which is contained in the word outwardly propounded, or that he affects the heart and the soul with other meanings, than those which are proposed from the very same word (1 Pet 1:23, 25; Rom 10:14–17; 2 Cor 3:3–6; 1 Cor 15:1–4).

The accidental result of vocation, and that which is not of itself intended by God, is the rejection of the word of grace, the condemning of the divine counsel, the resistance offered to the Holy Spirit. The proper and per se cause of this result is, the malice and hardness of the human heart. But this result is, not seldom succeeded by another, the just judgment of God, avenging the contempt shown to his word and call, and the injury done to his Holy Spirit; and from this judgment arise the blinding of the mind, the hardening of the heart, "the giving over to a reprobate mind," and "the delivering unto the power of Satan" (Acts 13:46; Luke 7:30; Acts 7:51; 2 Thess 3:2; 2 Cor 4:4; Ps 81:11–14; Isa 63:10; Isa 6:9–10; John 12:37–40).

But, because "known unto our God are all his works from the beginning of the world" (Acts 15:18), and as God does nothing in time which He has not decreed from all eternity to do, this vocation is likewise instituted and administered according to God's eternal decree. So that what man soever is called in time, was from all eternity predestinated to be called, and to be called in that state, time, place, mode, and with that efficacy, in and with which he was predestinated. Otherwise, the execution will vary from the decree; which charge of mutability and change cannot be preferred against God without producing mischievous effects (Eph 3:5, 6, 9–11; Jas 1:17, 18; 2 Tim 1:9).

2

A Declaration of the Sentiments of James Arminius

Part 1

*On Predestination, Divine Providence, the freedom of the will,
the grace of God, the Divinity of the Son of God,
and the justification of man before God.*

BEFORE MY DEPARTURE FROM Leyden for the convention at the
Hague, five articles were put into my hands. They were said to have
been transmitted to some of the provinces, to have been perused by certain ministers and ecclesiastical assemblies, and considered by them as
documents which embraced my sentiments on several points of religion.

Those points of which they pretended to exhibit a correct delineation, were Predestination, the Fall of Adam, Free Will, Original Sin, and
the Eternal Salvation of Infants. When I had read the whole of them, I
thought that I plainly perceived, from the style in which they were written, who was the author of them. As he was then present, (being one of
the number summoned on that occasion) I accosted him on this subject,
and embraced that opportunity freely to intimate to him that I had good
reasons for believing those articles to have been of his composition. He
did not make any attempt to deny the correctness of this supposition,
and replied, "that they had not been distributed precisely as my articles,
but as those on which the students at Leyden had held disputations."

In answer to this remark, I told him, "Of one thing he must be very
conscious, that, by the mere act of giving circulation to such a document,

he could not avoid creating a grievous and immediate prejudice against my innocence, and that the same articles would soon be ascribed to me, as if they had been my composition: when, in reality," as I then openly affirmed, "they had neither proceeded from me, nor accorded with my sentiments, and, as well as I could form a judgment they appeared to me to be at variance with the word of God."

After he and I had thus discoursed together in the presence of only two other persons, I deemed it advisable to make some mention of this affair in the convention itself, at which certain persons attended who had read those very articles, and who had, according to their own confession, accounted them as mine. This plan I accordingly pursued; and just as the convention was on the point of being dissolved, and after the account of our proceedings had been signed, and some individuals had received instructions to give their high mightinesses the States General a statement of our transactions, I requested the brethren "not to consider it an inconvenience to remain a short time together, for I had something which I was desirous to communicate."

This Proposal

They assented to this proposal, and I told them "that I had received the five articles which I held in my hand and the tenor of which I briefly read to them; that I discovered they had been transmitted by a member of that convention, into different provinces; that I was positive concerning their distribution in Zealand and the diocese of Utrecht; and that they had been read by some ministers in their public meetings, and were considered to be documents which comprehended my sentiments." Yet, notwithstanding, I protested to the whole of that assembly, with a good conscience, and as in the presence of God, "that those articles were not mine, and did not contain my sentiments."

Twice I repeated this solemn asseveration, and besought the brethren "not so readily to attach credit to reports that were circulated concerning me, nor so easily to listen to any thing that was represented as proceeding from me or that had been rumored abroad to my manifest injury." To these observations, a member of that convention answered, "that it would be well for me, on this account, to signify to the brethren what portion of those articles obtained my approbation, and what portion I disavowed, that they might thus have an opportunity of becoming acquainted in some degree with my sentiments."

Another member urged the same reasons; to which I replied, "that the convention had not been appointed to meet for such a purpose, that we had already been long enough detained together, and that their high mightinesses, the States General were now waiting for our determination," in that manner, we separated from each other, no one attempting any longer to continue the conversation, neither did all the members of the convention express a joint concurrence in that request, nor employ any kind of persuasion with me to prove that such an explanation was in their judgment quite equitable. Besides, according to the most correct intelligence which I have since gained, some of those who were then present, declared afterwards, "that it was a part of the instructions which had been previously given to them, not to enter into any conference concerning doctrine; and that, if a discussion of that kind had arisen, they must have instantly retired from the convention."

These several circumstances therefore prove that I was very far from being "solicited by the whole assembly" to engage in the desired explanation. Since none of these objections have any existence in this august assembly, I proceed to the declaration of my sentiments.

Having in this manner refuted all those objections which have been made against me, I will now endeavor to fulfill my promise, and to execute those commands which your Lordships have been pleased to lay upon me. I entertain a confident persuasion, that no prejudice will be created against me or my sentiments from this act, however imperfectly I may perform it, because it has its origin in that obedience which is due from me to this noble assembly, next to God, and according to the Divine pleasure.

I. ON PREDESTINATION

The first and most important article in religion on which I have to offer my views, and which for many years past has engaged my attention, is the Predestination of God, that is, the Election of men to salvation, and the Reprobation of them to destruction. Commencing with this article, I will first explain what is taught concerning it, both in discourses and writings, by certain persons in our Churches, and in the University of Leyden. I will afterwards declare my own views and thoughts on the same subject, while I shew my opinion on what they advance.[1]

---

1. Although Arminius uses the term "Predestination," he is critiquing the Calvinistic

On this article there is no uniform and simple opinion among the teachers of our Churches; but there is some variation in certain parts of it in which they differ from each other.

1. *The first opinion, which I reject, but which is espoused by those [Supralapsarians] who assume the very highest ground of this Predestination.*

This opinion, as it is generally contained in their writings, is to this effect:

"(a.) God by an eternal and immutable decree has predestinated from among men (whom he did not consider as being then created, much less as being fallen) certain individuals to everlasting life, and others to eternal destruction, without any regard whatever to righteousness or sin, to obedience or disobedience, but purely of his own good pleasure, to demonstrate the glory of his justice and mercy; or (as others assert) to demonstrate his saving grace, wisdom, and free uncontrollable power.

"(b.) In addition to this decree, God has preordained certain determinate means which pertain to its execution, and this by an eternal and immutable decree. These means necessarily follow by virtue of the preceding decree, and necessarily bring him who has been predestinated, to the end which has been foreordained for him. Some of these means belong in common both to the decree of election and that of rejection, and others of them are specially restricted to the one decree or to the other.

"(c.) The means common to both the decrees, are three: the first is, the creation of man in the upright [or erect] state of original righteousness, or after the image and likeness of God in righteousness and true holiness. The second is, the permission of the fall of Adam, or the ordination of God that man should sin, and become corrupt or vitiated. The third is, the loss or the removal of original righteousness and of the image of God, with the result of a being concluded under sin and condemnation.

"(d.) For unless God had created some men, he would not have had any upon whom he might either bestow eternal life, or superinduce everlasting death. Unless he had created them in righteousness and true holiness, he would himself have been the author of sin, and would by this means have possessed no right either to punish them to the praise of his justice, or to save them to the praise of his mercy. Unless they had

version of that concept, meaning supralapsarian double predestination.

themselves sinned, and by the demerit of sin had rendered themselves guilty of death, there would have been no room for the demonstration either of justice or of mercy.

"(e.) The means preordained for the execution of the decree of election, are also these three. The first is, the preordination, or the giving of Jesus Christ as a Mediator and a Savior, who might by his merit deserve, [or purchase] for all the elect and for them only, the lost righteousness and life, and might communicate them by his own power [or virtue]. The second is, the call [or vocation] to faith outwardly by the word, but inwardly by his Spirit, in the mind, affections and will; by an operation of such efficacy that the elect person of necessity yields assent and obedience to the vocation, in so much that it is not possible for him to do otherwise than believe and be obedient to this vocation. From hence arise justification and sanctification through the blood of Christ and his Spirit, and from them the existence of all good works.

Force and Necessity

"And all that, manifestly by means of the same force and necessity. The third is, that which keeps and preserves the elect in faith, holiness, and a zeal for good works; or, it is the gift of perseverance; the virtue of which is such, that believing and elect persons not only do not sin with a full and entire will, or do not fall away totally from faith and grace, but it likewise is neither possible for them to sin with a full and perfect will, nor to fall away totally or finally from faith and grace.

"(f.) The two last of these means [vocation and perseverance,] belong only to the elect who are of adult age. But God employs a shorter way to salvation, by which he conducts those children of believers and saints who depart out of this life before they arrive at years of maturity; that is, provided they belong to the number of the elect (known to God alone), for God bestows on them Christ as their Savior, and gives them to Christ, to save them by his blood and Holy Spirit, without actual faith and perseverance in it [faith]. This he does according to the promise of the covenant of grace: *I will be a God unto you, and unto your seed after you.*

"(g.) The means pertaining to the execution of the decree of reprobation to eternal death, are partly such as peculiarly belong to all those who are rejected and reprobate, whether they ever arrive at years of maturity or die before that period; and they are partly such as are proper only to some of them. The means that is common to all the reprobate, is desertion in sin, by denying to them that saving grace which is sufficient and necessary to the salvation of any one. This negation [or denial] consists of two parts. For, in the first place, God did not will that Christ should die for them [the reprobate] or become their Savior, and this neither in reference to the antecedent will of God (as some persons call it), nor in reference to his sufficient will, or the value of the price of reconciliation. This price was not offered for reprobates, either with respect to the decree of God, or its virtue and efficacy. But the other part of this negation [or denial] is, that God is unwilling to communicate the Spirit of Christ to reprobates, yet without such communication they can neither be made partakers of Christ nor of his benefits.

"(h.) The means that belongs properly only to some of the reprobates, is obduration [the act of hardening], which befalls those of them who have attained to years of maturity, either because they have very frequently and enormously sinned against the law of God, or because they have rejected the grace of the gospel."

"To the execution of the first species of induration, or hardening, belong the illumination of their conscience by means of knowledge, and its conviction of the righteousness of the law. For it is impossible that this law should not necessarily detain them in unrighteousness, to render them inexcusable.

"For the execution of the *second species* of induration, God employs a call by the preaching of his gospel, which call is inefficacious and insufficient both in respect to the decree of God, and to its issue or event. This calling is either only an external one, which it is neither in their desire nor in their power to obey. Or it is likewise an internal one, by which some of them may be excited in their understandings to accept and believe the things which they hear, Yet it is only with such a faith as that with which the devils are endowed when they believe and tremble. Others of them are excited and conducted still further, so as to desire in a certain measure to taste the heavenly gift. But the latter are, of all others, the most unhappy, because they are raised up on high, that they may be brought down with a heavier fall. And this fate it is impossible for them to escape, for they must of necessity return to their vomit, and depart or fall away from the faith.

"(i.) From this decree of Divine election and reprobation, and from this administration of the means which pertain to the execution of both of them, it follows, that the elect are necessarily saved, it being impossible for them to perish—and that the reprobate are necessarily damned, it being impossible for them to be saved. All this is from the absolute purpose [or determination] of God, which is altogether antecedent to all things, and to all those causes which are either in things themselves or can possibly result from them."

These opinions concerning predestination are considered, by some of those who advocate them, to be the foundation of Christianity, salvation and of its certainty. On these sentiments they suppose, "is founded the sure and undoubted consolation of all believers, which is capable of rendering their consciences tranquil; and on them also depends the praise of the grace of God, so that if any contradiction be offered to this doctrine, God is necessarily deprived of the glory of his grace, and then the merit of salvation is attributed to the free will of man and to his own powers and strength, which ascription savors of Pelagianism."

These then are the causes offered why the advocates of these sentiments labor with a common anxiety to retain the purity of such a doctrine in their churches and why they oppose all those innovations which are at variance with them.

2. MY SENTIMENTS ON THE PRECEDING SCHEME OF PREDESTINATION

But, for my own part, to speak my sentiments with freedom, and yet with a salvo in favor of a better judgment, I am of opinion, that this doctrine of theirs contains many things that are both false and impertinent, and at an utter disagreement with each other; all the instances of which, the present time will not permit me to recount. But I will subject it to an examination only in those parts which are most prominent and extensive. I shall, therefore, propose to myself four principal heads, which are of the greatest importance in this doctrine. When I have in the first place explained of what kind they are, I will afterwards declare more fully the judgment and sentiments which I have formed concerning them. They are the following:

"(a.) That God has absolutely and precisely decreed to save certain particular men by his mercy or grace, but to condemn others by his justice: and to do all this without having any regard in such decree to righteousness or sin, obedience or disobedience, which could possibly exist on the part of one class of men or of the other.

"(b.) That, for the execution of the preceding decree, God determined to create Adam, and all men in him, in an upright state of original righteousness; besides which he also ordained them to commit sin, that they might thus become guilty of eternal condemnation and be deprived of original righteousness.

"(c.) That those persons whom God has thus positively willed to save, he has decreed not only to salvation but also to the means which pertain to it (that is, to conduct and bring them to faith in Christ Jesus, and to perseverance in that faith).. He leads them to these results by a grace and power that are irresistible, so that it is not possible for them to do otherwise than believe, persevere in faith, and be saved.

"(d.) That to those whom, by his absolute will, God has foreordained to perdition, he has also decreed to deny that grace which is necessary and sufficient for salvation, and does not in reality confer it upon them; so that they are neither placed in a possible condition nor in any capacity of believing or of being saved."

After a diligent contemplation and examination of these four heads, in the fear of the Lord, I make the following declaration respecting this doctrine of predestination.

3. I REJECT THIS PREDESTINATION FOR THE FOLLOWING REASONS:

(1.) Because it is not the foundation of Christianity, of Salvation, or of its certainty.

(a.) It is not the foundation of Christianity. For this Predestination is not that decree of God by which Christ is appointed by God to be the Savior, the Head, and the Foundation of those who will be made heirs of salvation. Yet that decree is the only foundation of Christianity.

For the doctrine of this Predestination is not that doctrine by which, through faith, we as lively stones are built up into Christ, the only corner stone, and are inserted into him as the members of the body are joined to their head.

(b.) It is not the foundation of Salvation:

(i) For this Predestination is not that decree of the good pleasure of God in Christ Jesus on which alone our salvation rests and depends.

(ii) The doctrine of this Predestination is not the foundation of Salvation: for it is not "the power of God to salvation to every one that believeth :" because through it "the righteousness of God" is not "revealed from faith to faith."

(c.) Nor is it the foundation of the certainty of salvation: For that is dependent upon this decree, "they who believe, shall be saved." I believe, therefore, I shall be saved. But the doctrine of this Predestination embraces within itself neither the first nor the second member of the syllogism.

This is likewise confessed by some persons in these words: "we do not wish to state that the knowledge of this [predestination] is the foundation of Christianity or of salvation, or that it is necessary to salvation in the same manner as the doctrine of the Gospel," etc.

This doctrine of Predestination comprises within it neither the whole nor any part of the Gospel. For, according to the tenor of the discourses delivered by John and Christ, as they are described to us by the Evangelist, and according to the doctrine of the Apostles and Christ after his ascension, the Gospel consists partly of an injunction to repent and believe, and partly of a promise to bestow forgiveness of sins, the grace of the Spirit, and life eternal. But this Predestination belongs neither to the injunction to repent and believe, nor to the annexed promise. Nay, this doctrine does not even teach what kind of men in general God has predestinated, which is properly the doctrine of the Gospel; but it embraces within itself a certain mystery, which is known only to God, who is the Predestinator, and in which mystery is comprehended what particular persons and how many he has decreed to save and to condemn.

Further Conclusion

From these premises I draw a further conclusion, that this doctrine of Predestination is not necessary to salvation, either as an object of knowledge, belief, hope, or performance. A confession to this effect has been made by a certain learned man, in the theses which he has proposed for discussion on this subject, in the following words: "Wherefore the gospel cannot be simply termed the book or the revelation of Predestination, but only in a relative sense. Because it does not absolutely denote either the matter of the number or the form; that is, it neither declares how many persons in particular, nor (with a few exceptions) who they are, but only the description of them in general, whom God has predestinated."[2]

2. Excerpted from Franciscus Gomarus (1563–1641), a fellow professor of theology at University of Leyden who strongly opposed Arminius's doctrines. Arminius

(2.) *This doctrine was never admitted, decreed, or approved in any Council, either general or particular, for the first six hundred years after Christ.*

(a.) Not in the General Council of Nice, in which sentence was given against Arius and in favor of the Deity and Consubstantiality of the Son of God. Not in the first Council of Constantinople, in which a decree was passed against Macedonius, respecting the Deity of the Holy Spirit. Not in the Council of Ephesus, which determined against Nestorius, and in favor of the Unity of the Person of the Son of God. Not in that of Chalcedon, which condemned Eutyches, and determined, "that in one and the same person of our Lord Jesus Christ, there were two distinct natures, which differ from each other in their essence." Not in the second Council of Constantinople, in which Peter, Bishop of Antioch, and Anthymus, Bishop of Constantinople, with certain other persons, were condemned for having asserted "that the Father had likewise suffered," as well as the Son. Nor in the third Council of Constantinople, in which the Monothelites were condemned for having asserted "that there was only one will and operation in Jesus Christ."

(b.) But this doctrine was not discussed or confirmed in particular Councils, such as that of Jerusalem, Orange, or even that of Mela in Africa, which was held against Pelagius and his errors, as is apparent from the articles of doctrine which were then decreed both against his person and his false opinions.

But so far was Augustine's doctrine of Predestination from being received in those councils, that when Celestinus, the Bishop of Rome, who was his contemporary, wrote to the Bishops of France, and condemned the doctrines of the Pelagians, he concluded his epistle in these words: "but as we dare not despise, so neither do we deem it necessary to defend the more profound and difficult parts of the questions which occur in this controversy, and which have been treated to a very great extent by those who opposed the heretics.

"Because we believe, that whatever the writings according to the forementioned rules of the Apostolic See[3] have taught us, is amply sufficient for confessing the grace of God, from whose work, credit and authority not a little must be subtracted or withdrawn," etc.

---

responded to Gomarus's writings in 1604.

3. Churches thought to have been founded by apostles.

In reference to the rules which were laid down by Celestinus in that epistle, and which had been decreed in the three preceding particular Councils, we shall experience no difficulty in agreeing together about them, especially in regard to those matters which are necessary to the establishment of grace in opposition to Pelagius and his errors.

(c.) *None of those Doctors or Divines of the Church who held correct and orthodox sentiments for the first six hundred years after the birth of Christ, ever brought this doctrine forward or gave it their approval.* Neither was it professed and approved by a single individual of those who showed themselves the principal and keenest defenders of grace against Pelagius. Of this description, it is evident, were St. Jerome, Augustine, the author of the treatise entitled, *De Vocatione Gentium,* ["The calling of the Gentiles,"] Prosper of Aquitaine, Hilary, Fulgentius, and Orosius. This is very apparent from their writings.

(d.) *It neither agrees nor corresponds with the harmony of those Confessions printed and published together in one volume at Geneva, in the name of the Reformed and Protestant Churches.* If that harmony of Confessions be faithfully consulted, it will appear that many of them do not speak in the same manner concerning Predestination; that some of them only incidentally mention it; and that they evidently never once touch upon those heads of the doctrine, which are now in great repute and particularly urged in the preceding scheme of Predestination, and which I have already adduced. Nor does any single Confession deliver this doctrine in the same manner as it has just now been propounded by me.

Confessions of Bohemia

The Confessions of Bohemia, England and Wirtemburgh, and the first Helvetian [Swiss] Confession, and that of the four cities of Strasburgh, Constance, Memmingen, and Lindau, make no mention of this Predestination. Those of Basle and Saxony, only take a very cursory notice of it in three words. The Augustinian Confession speaks of it in such a manner as to induce the Genevan editors to think, that some annotation was necessary on their part, to give us a previous warning. The last of the Helvetian [Swiss] Confessions, to which a great portion of the Reformed churches have expressed their assent and which they have subscribed, likewise speak of it in such a strain as makes me very desirous to see what method can possibly be adopted to give it any accordance with that doctrine of Predestination which I have just now advanced. Yet this [Swiss] Confession is that which has obtained the approbation of the Churches of Geneva and Savoy.

(e.) Without the least contention or caviling, it may very properly be made a question of doubt, whether this doctrine agrees with the Belgic Confession and the Heidelberg Catechism; as I shall briefly demonstrate.

(f.) In the 14th Article of the Dutch Confession, these expressions occur: "Man knowingly and willingly subjected himself to sin, and, consequently, to death and cursing, while he lent an ear to the deceiving words and impostures of the devil," etc. From this sentence I conclude, that man did not sin on account of any necessity through a preceding decree of Predestination: which inference is diametrically opposed to that doctrine of Predestination against which I now contend. Then, in the 16th Article, which addresses the eternal election of God, these words are contained: "God shewed himself Merciful, by delivering from damnation, and by saving, those persons whom, in his eternal and immutable counsel and according to his gratuitous goodness, he chose in Christ Jesus our Lord, without any regard to their works. And he shewed himself just, in leaving others in that their fall and perdition into which they had precipitated themselves." It is not obvious to me, how these words are consistent with this doctrine of Predestination.

(3.) In the 20th question of the Heidelberg Catechism, we read: "Salvation through Christ is not given [restored] to all them who had perished in Adam, but to those only who are ingrafted into Christ by the faith, and who embrace his benefits." From this sentence I infer, that God has not absolutely predestinated any men to salvation; but that he has in his decree considered [or looked upon] them as believers. This deduction is at open conflict with the first and third points of this Predestination. In the 54th question of the same Catechism, it is said: "I believe that, from the beginning to the end of the world, the Son of God out of the entire race of mankind doth by his word and Spirit gather or collect unto himself a company chosen unto eternal life and agreeing together in the true faith."

In this sentence "election to eternal life," and "agreement in the faith," stand in mutual juxtaposition; and in such a manner, that the latter is not rendered subordinate to the former, which, according to these [Supralapsarian} sentiments on Predestination ought to have been done. In that case the words should have been placed in the following order:

"The son of God calls and gathers to himself, by his word and Spirit, a company chosen to eternal life, *that they may believe and agree together in the true faith.*"

Confessions and Catechism

Since such are the statements of our Confession and Catechism, no reason whatever exists, why those who embrace and defend these [Supralapsarian] sentiments on Predestination, should either violently endeavor to obtrude them on their colleagues and on the Church of Christ; or why they should take it amiss, and put the worst construction upon it, when anything is taught in the Church or University that is not exactly accordant with their doctrine, or that is opposed to it.

(4.) *I affirm, that this doctrine is repugnant to the Nature of God, but particularly to those Attributes of his nature by which he performs and manages all things, his wisdom, justice, and goodness.*

It is repugnant to his wisdom in three ways.

(1.) Because it represents God as decreeing something for a particular end [or purpose] which neither is nor can be good: which is, that God created something for eternal perdition to the praise of his justice.

(a.) Because it states, that the object which God proposed to himself by this Predestination, was, to demonstrate the glory of his mercy and justice: But this glory he cannot demonstrate, except by an act that is contrary at once to his mercy and his justice, of which description is that decree of God in which he determined that man should sin and be rendered miserable.

(b.) Because it changes and inverts the order of the two-fold wisdom of God, as it is displayed to us in the Scriptures. For it asserts, that God has absolutely predetermined to save men by the mercy and wisdom comprehended in the doctrine of the cross of Christ, without having foreseen this circumstance, that it was impossible for man (and that, truly, through his own fault) to be saved by the wisdom revealed in the law and which was infused into him at the period of his creation. The Scripture asserts, on the contrary, that "it pleased God by the foolishness of preaching to save them that believe;" that is, "by the doctrine of the cross, after that in the wisdom of God the world by wisdom knew not God" (1 Cor 1:21).

(2.) It is repugnant to the justice of God, not only in reference to that attribute denoting in God a love of righteousness and a hatred of iniquity, but also in reference to its being a perpetual and constant desire in him to render to everyone that which is his due.

(a.) It is at variance with the first of these ideas of justice in the following manner: Because it affirms, that God has absolutely willed to save certain individual men, and has decreed their salvation without having the least regard to righteousness or obedience. The proper inference from that, is, that God loves such men far more than his own justice [or righteousness].

(b.) It is opposed to the second idea of his justice: Because it affirms, that God wishes to subject his creature to misery (which cannot possibly have any existence except as the punishment of sin), although, at the same time he does not look upon [or consider] the creature as a sinner, and therefore as not obnoxious either to wrath or to punishment. This is the manner in which it lays down the position that God has willed to give to the creature not only something which does not belong to it, but is connected with its greatest injury. That is another act directly opposed to his justice. In accordance, therefore, with this doctrine, God, in the first place, detracts from himself that which is his own [or his right], and then imparts to the creature what does not belong to it, to its great misery and unhappiness.

(3.) It is also repugnant to the Goodness of God. Goodness is an affection [or disposition] in God to communicate his own good so far as his justice considers and admits to be fitting and proper. But in this doctrine the following act is attributed to God, that, of himself, and induced to it by nothing external, he wills the greatest evil to his creatures; and that from all eternity he has preordained that evil for them, or predetermined to impart it to them, even before he resolved to bestow upon them any portion of good. For this doctrine states, that God willed to damn; and, that he might be able to do this, he willed to create; although creation is the first egress [or going forth] of God's goodness towards his creatures. How vastly different are such statements as these from that expansive goodness of God by which he confers benefits not only on the unworthy, but also on the evil, the unjust and on those who are deserving of punishment, which trait of Divine beneficence in our Father who is in heaven, we are commanded to imitate (Matt 5:45).

Such a doctrine of Predestination is contrary to the nature of man, in regard to his having been created after the Divine image in the knowledge of God and in righteousness, in regard to his having been created with freedom of will, and in regard to his having been created with a disposition and aptitude for the enjoyment of life eternal. These three circumstance, respecting him, may be deduced from the following brief expressions: "Do this, and live" (Rom 10:5). "In the day that thou eatest thereof, thou shalt surely die" (Gen 2:17). If man is deprived of any of these qualifications, such admonitions as these cannot possibly be effective in exciting him to obedience.

This doctrine is inconsistent with the Divine image, which consists of the knowledge of God and holiness. For according to this knowledge and righteousness man was qualified and empowered, he was also laid under an obligation to know God, to love, worship, and serve him. But by the intervention, or rather by the prevention, of this Predestination, it was preordained that man should be formed vicious and should commit sin, that is, that he should neither know God, love, worship, nor serve him; and that he should not perform that which by the image of God, he was well qualified and empowered to do, and which he was bound to perform.

Declaration as Following

This is tantamount to such a declaration as the following, which anyone might make: "God did undoubtedly create man after his own image, in righteousness and true holiness; but, notwithstanding this, he foreordained and decreed, that man should become impure and unrighteous, that is, should be made conformable to the image of Satan."

This doctrine is inconsistent with the freedom of the will, in which and with which man was created by God. For it prevents the exercise of this liberty, by binding or determining the will absolutely to one object, that is, to do this thing precisely, or to do that. God, therefore, according to this statement, may be blamed for the one or the other of these two things (with which let no man charge his Maker!), either for creating man with freedom of will, or for hindering him in the use of his own liberty after he had formed him a free agent. In the former of these two cases, God is chargeable with a want of consideration, in the latter with mutability. And in both, with being injurious to man as well as to himself.

This Predestination is prejudicial to man in regard to the inclination and capacity for the eternal fruition of salvation, with which he was endowed at the period of his creation. For, since by this Predestination it has been predetermined, that the greater part of mankind shall not be made partakers of salvation, but shall fall into everlasting condemnation. And since this predetermination took place even before the decree had passed for creating man, such persons are deprived of something, for the desire of which they have been endowed by God with a natural inclination. This great privation they suffer, not in consequence of any preceding sin or demerit of their own, but simply and solely through this sort of Predestination.

This Predestination is diametrically opposed to the Act of Creation.

For creation is a communication of good according to the intrinsic property of its nature. But creation of this description, whose intent or design is to make a way through itself by which the reprobation that had been previously determined may obtain its object, is not a communication of good. For we ought to form our estimate and judgment of every good, from the mind and intention of Him who is the donor, and from the end to which or on account of which it is bestowed. In the present instance, the intention of the donor would have been, to condemn, which is an act that could not possibly affect anyone except a creature; and the end or event of creation would have been the eternal perdition of the creature. In that case creation would not have been a communication of any good, but a preparation for the greatest evil both according to the very intention of the Creator and the actual issue of the matter; and according to the words of Christ, "It had been good for that man, if he had never been born!" (Matt 26:24).

Reprobation is an act of hatred, and from hatred derives its origin. But creation does not proceed from hatred. It is not therefore a way or means, which belongs to the execution of the decree of reprobation.

Creation is a perfect act of God, by which he has manifested his wisdom, goodness and omnipotence. It is not therefore subordinate to the end of any other preceding work or action of God. But it is rather to be viewed as that act of God, which necessarily precedes and is antecedent to all other acts that he can possibly either decree or undertake. Unless God had formed a previous conception of the work of creation, he could not have decreed actually to undertake any other act; and until he had executed the work of creation, he could by no means have completed any other operation.

All the actions of God which tend to the condemnation of his creatures, are strange works or foreign to him; because God consents to them, for some other cause that is quite extraneous. But creation is not an action that is foreign to God, but it is proper to him. It is eminently an action most appropriate to Him, and to which he could be moved by no other external cause, because it is the very first of the Divine acts, and, till it was done, nothing could have any actual existence, except God himself; for everything else that has a being, came into existence through this action.

If creation be the way and means through which God willed the execution of the decree of his reprobation, he was more inclined to will the act of reprobation than that of creation. And he consequently derived greater satisfaction from the act of condemning certain of his innocent creatures, than in the act of their creation.

Lastly, creation cannot be a way or means of reprobation according to the absolute purpose of God: because, after the creation was completed, it was in the power of man still to have remained obedient to the divine commands, and not to commit sin. To render this possible, while God had on one part bestowed on him sufficient strength and power, he had also on the other placed sufficient impediments: a circumstance most diametrically opposed to a Predestination of this description.

This doctrine is at open hostility with the nature of Eternal Life, and the titles by which it is signally distinguished in the Scriptures. For Eternal Life is called "the inheritance of the sons of God" (Titus 3:7). But those alone are the sons of God, according to the doctrine of the Gospel, "who believe in the name of Jesus Christ." (John 1:12). It is also called, "the reward of obedience," (Matt 5:12). and of "the labor of love" (Heb 6:10), "the recompense of those who fight the good fight and who run well, a crown of righteousness," etc. (Rev 2:10; 2 Tim 4:7, 8). God therefore has not, from his own absolute decree, without any consideration or regard whatever to faith and obedience, appointed to any man, or determined to appoint to him, life eternal.

This Predestination is also opposed to the nature of Eternal Death, and to those appellations by which it is described in Scripture. For Eternal Death is called "the wages of sin" (Rom 6:23), "flaming fire taking vengeance on them that know not God and obey not the Gospel of our Lord Jesus Christ; who shall be punished with everlasting destruction . . ." (2 Thess 1:8, 9), "everlasting fire prepared for the devil and his angels" (Matt 25:41), "judgment and fiery indignation, which shall devour the adversaries" of God (Heb 10:27). God, therefore, has not, by any absolute decree without respect to sin and disobedience, prepared Eternal Death for any person.

This Predestination is inconsistent with the nature and properties of Sin, because Sin is called "disobedience" and "rebellion," neither of which terms can possibly apply to any person who by a preceding divine decree is placed under an unavoidable necessity of sinning.

Sin is the meritorious cause of damnation. But the meritorious cause that moves the Divine will to reprobate, is according to justice; and it induces God, who holds sin in abhorrence, to will reprobation. Sin, therefore, which is a cause, cannot be placed among the means, by which God executes the decree or will of reprobation.

This doctrine is likewise repugnant to the nature of Divine Grace, and as far as its powers permit, it effects its destruction. Under whatever specious pretenses it may be asserted, that "this kind of Predestination is most admirably adapted and quite necessary for the establishment of grace," yet it destroys it in multiple ways:

Grace is so adaptive and commingled with the nature of man, as not to destroy within him the liberty of his will, but to give it a right direction, to correct its depravity, and to allow man to possess his own proper notions. While, on the contrary, this Predestination introduces such a species of grace, as takes away free will and hinders its exercise.

The representations of grace that the scriptures contain, are such as describe it capable of "being resisted," (Acts 7:51) and "received in vain" (2 Cor 6:1). and that it is possible for man to avoid yielding his assent to it and refuse all cooperation with it (Heb 12:15, Matt 23:37, Luke 7:30). While, on the contrary, this Predestination affirms that grace is a certain irresistible force and operation.

According to the primary intention and chief design of God, grace conduces to the good of those persons to whom it is offered and by whom it is received. While, on the contrary, this doctrine drags along with it the assertion, that grace is offered even to certain reprobates, and is so far communicated to them as to illuminate their understandings and to excite within them a taste for the heavenly gifts, only for this end and purpose, that, in proportion to the height to which they are elevated, the abyss into which they are precipitated may be the deeper, and their fall the heavier; and that they may both merit and receive the greater perdition.

The doctrine of this Predestination is injurious to the Glory of God, which does not consist of a declaration of liberty or authority, nor of a demonstration of anger and power, except to such an extent as that declaration and demonstration may be consistent with justice, and with a perpetual reservation in behalf of the honor of God's goodness. But, according to this doctrine, it follows that God is the author of sin, which may be proved by four arguments:

One of its positions is that God has absolutely decreed to demonstrate his glory by punitive justice and mercy, in the salvation of some men, and in the damnation of others, which neither was done, nor could have possibly been done, unless sin had entered into the world.

This doctrine affirms, that, in order to obtain his object, God ordained that man should commit sin, and be rendered vitiated; and, from this Divine ordination or appointment, the fall of man necessarily followed.

It asserts that God has denied to man, or has withdrawn from him, such a portion of grace as is sufficient and necessary to enable him to avoid sin, and that this was done before man had sinned. This is an act that amounts to the same as if God had prescribed a law to man that would be utterly impossible for him to fulfill, when the nature in which he had been created was taken into consideration.

It ascribes to God certain operations with regard to man, both external and internal, both mediate (by means of the intervention of other creatures). and immediate. These Divine operations being once admitted, man must necessarily commit sin, by that necessity which the schoolmen call "a consequential necessity antecedent to the thing itself," and which destroys the freedom of the will. Such an act does this doctrine attribute to God, and represents it to proceed from his primary and chief intention, without any foreknowledge of an inclination, will, or action on the part of man.

Further Conclusion

From these premises, we deduce, as a further conclusion, that God really sins. Because, according to this doctrine, he moves to sin by an act that is unavoidable, and according to his own purpose and primary intention, without having received any previous inducement to such an act from any preceding sin or demerit in man.

From the same position we might also infer, that God is the only sinner. For man, who is impelled by an irresistible force to commit sin (that is, to perpetrate some deed that has been prohibited), cannot be said to sin, himself.

As a legitimate consequence it also follows, that sin is not sin, since whatever that be which God does, it neither can be sin, nor ought any of his acts to receive that appellation.

Besides the instances I have already recounted, there is another method by which this doctrine inflicts a deep wound on the honor of God. But these, it is probable, will be considered at present to be amply sufficient.

This doctrine is highly dishonorable to Jesus Christ our Savior. It entirely excludes him from that decree of which predestinates the end. And it affirms, that men were predestinated to be saved, before Christ was predestinated to save them; and thus it argues, that he is not the foundation of election.

It denies that Christ is the meritorious cause who again obtained for us the salvation we had lost, by placing him as only a subordinate cause of that salvation which had been already foreordained, and thus only a minister and instrument to apply that salvation unto us. This indeed is in evident congruity with the opinion which states "that God has absolutely willed the salvation of certain men, by the first and supreme decree which he passed, and on which all his other decrees depend and are consequent." If this be true, it was therefore impossible for the salvation of such men to have been lost, and therefore unnecessary for it to be repaired and in some sort regained afresh, and discovered, by the merit of Christ, who was foreordained a Savior for them alone.

This doctrine is also hurtful to the salvation of men. It prevents that saving and godly sorrow for sins that have been committed, which cannot exist in those who have no consciousness of sin. But it is obvious, that the man who has committed sin through the unavoidable necessity of the decree of God, cannot possibly have this kind of consciousness of sin (2 Cor 7:10).

It also removes all pious solicitude about being converted from sin unto God. For he can feel no such concern who is entirely passive and conducts himself like a dead man, with respect not only to his discernment and perception of the grace of God that is exciting and assisting, but also to his assent and obedience to it; and who is converted by such an irresistible impulse, that he not only cannot avoid being sensible of the grace of God which knocks within him.

Likewise of Necessity

But he must likewise of necessity yield his assent to it, and thus convert himself, or rather be converted. Such a person it is evident, cannot produce within his heart or conceive in his mind this solicitude, except he had previously felt the same irresistible motion. And if he should produce within his heart any such concern, it would be in vain and without the least advantage. For that cannot be a true solicitude, which is not produced in the heart by any other means except by an irresistible force according to the absolute purpose and intention of God to effect his salvation (Rev 2:3; 3:2).

It restrains, in persons that are converted, all zeal and studious regard for good works, since it declares "that the regenerate cannot perform either more or less good than they do." For he that is actuated or impelled by saving grace, must work, and cannot discontinue his labor; but he that is not actuated by the same grace, can do nothing, and finds it necessary to cease from all attempts (Titus 3:14).

It extinguishes the zeal for prayer, which yet is an efficacious means instituted by God for asking and obtaining all kinds of blessings from him, but principally the great one of salvation (Luke 11:1–13). But from the circumstance of it having been before determined by an immutable and inevitable decree, that this description of men [the elect] should obtain salvation, prayer cannot on any account be a means for asking and obtaining that salvation. It can only be a mode of worshipping God, because according to the absolute decree of his Predestination he has determined that such men shall be saved.

It takes away all that most salutary fear and trembling with which we are commanded to work out our own salvation (Phil 2:12). for it states "that he who is elected and believes, cannot sin with that full and entire willingness with which sin is committed by the ungodly; and that they cannot either totally or finally fall away from faith or grace."

Because it produces within men a despair both of performing that which their duty requires and of obtaining that towards which their desires are directed. For when they are taught that the grace of God (which is really necessary to the performance of the least portion of good) is denied to the majority of mankind, according to an absolute and peremptory decree of God—and that such grace is denied because, by a preceding decree equally absolute, God has determined not to confer salvation on them but damnation. When they are thus taught, it is scarcely possible for any other result to ensue, than that the individual who cannot even with great difficulty work a persuasion within himself of his being elected, should soon consider himself included in the number of the reprobate. From such an apprehension as this, must arise a certain despair of performing righteousness and obtaining salvation.

This doctrine inverts the order of the Gospel of Jesus Christ. For in the Gospel, God requires repentance and faith on the part of man, by promising to him life everlasting, if he consents to become a convert and a believer (Mark 1:15; 16:16). But it is stated in this [Supralapsarian] decree of Predestination, that it is God's absolute will, to bestow salvation on certain particular men, and that he willed at the same time absolutely to give those very individuals repentance and faith, by means of an irresistible force, because it was his will and pleasure to save them. In the Gospel, God announces eternal death on the impenitent and unbelieving (John 3:36). And those threats contribute to the purpose which he has in view, that he may by such means deter them from unbelief and thus may save them. But by this decree of Predestination it is taught, that God wills not to confer on certain individual men that grace that is necessary for conversion and faith because he has absolutely decreed their condemnation.

God So Loved the World

The Gospel says, "God so loved the world that he gave his only begotten son, that whosoever believeth in him should not perish, but have everlasting life" (John 3:16). But this doctrine declares; "that God so loved those whom he had absolutely elected to eternal life, as to give his son to them alone, and by an irresistible force to produce within them faith on him." To embrace the whole in few words, the Gospel says, "fulfill the command, and thou shalt obtain the promise; believe, and thou shalt live." But this [supralapsarian] doctrine says, "since it is my will to give thee life, it is therefore my will to give thee faith," which is a real and most manifest inversion of the Gospel.

This Predestination is in open hostility to the ministry of the Gospel. For if God by an irresistible power quicken him who is dead in trespasses and sins, no man can be a minister and one of the "laborers together with God" (1 Cor 3:9). Nor can the word preached by man be the instrument of grace and of the Spirit, any more than a creature could have been an instrument of grace in the first creation, or a dispenser of that grace in the resurrection of the body from the dead.

By this Predestination the ministry of the gospel is made "the savor of death unto death" in the case of the majority of those who hear it, (2 Cor 2:16) as well as an instrument of condemnation, according to the primary design and absolute intention of God, without any consideration of previous rebellion.

According to this doctrine, baptism, when administered to many reprobate children (who yet are the offspring of parents who believe and are God's covenant people), is evidently a seal [or ratification] of nothing, and thus becomes entirely useless, in accordance with the primary and absolute intention of God, without any fault [or culpability] on the part of the infants themselves, to whom it is administered in obedience to the Divine command.

It also hinders public prayers from being offered to God in a becoming and suitable manner, that is, with faith, and in confidence that they will be profitable to all the hearers of the word; when there are many among them, whom God is not only unwilling to save, but whom by his absolute, eternal, and immutable will (antecedent to all things and causes whatever), it is his will and pleasure to damn. In the meantime, when the apostle commands prayers and supplications to be made for all men, he adds this reason, "for this is good and acceptable in the sight of God our Saviour; who will have all men to be saved, and to come unto the knowledge of the truth" (1 Tim 2:4).

The constitution of this doctrine is such, as very easily to render pastors and teachers slothful and negligent in the exercise of their ministry: Because, from this doctrine it appears to them as though it were impossible for all their diligence to be useful to any persons, except to those only whom God absolutely and precisely wills to save, and who cannot possibly perish. It is as though all their negligence could be hurtful to none, except to those alone whom God absolutely wills to destroy, who must of necessity perish, and to whom a contrary fate is impossible.

This doctrine completely subverts the foundation of religion in general, and of the Christian Religion in particular.

The foundation of religion considered in general, is a two-fold love of God; without which there neither is nor can be any religion: The first of them is a love for righteousness [or justice] which gives existence to his hatred of sin. The second is a love for the creature who is endowed with reason, and (in the matter now before us), it is a love for man, according to the expression in Hebrews, "for he that cometh to God must believe that he is, and that he is a rewarder of them that diligently seek Him" (11:6). God's love of righteousness is manifested by this circumstance, that it is not his will and pleasure to bestow eternal life on any except on "those who seek him." God's love of man consists in his being willing to give him eternal life, if he seek Him.

A mutual relation subsists between these two kinds of love, which is this. The latter species of love, which extends itself to the creatures, cannot come into exercise, except so far as it is permitted by the former [the love of righteousness]. The former love, therefore, is by far the most excellent species. But in every direction there is abundant scope for the emanations of the latter [the love of the creature] except where the former [the love of righteousness] has placed some impediment in the range of its exercise.

First of These Consequences

The first of these consequences is most evidently proved from the circumstance of God's condemning man on account of sin, although he loves him in the relation in which he stands as his creature; which would by no means have been done, had he loved man more than righteousness, [or justice] and had he evinced a stronger aversion to the eternal misery of man than to his disobedience. But the second consequence is proved by this argument, that God condemns no person, except on account of sin; and that he saves such a multitude of men who turn themselves away [or are converted] from sin; which he could not do, unless it was his will to allow as abundant scope to his love for the creatures, as is permitted by righteousness [or justice] under the regulation of the Divine judgment.

But this [Supralapsarian] doctrine inverts this order and mutual relation in two ways:

(a.) The one is when it states, that God wills absolutely to save certain particular men, without having had in that his intention the least reference or regard to their obedience. This is the manner in which it places the love of God to man before his love of righteousness, and lays down the position—that God loves men (as such) more than righteousness, and evinces a stronger aversion to their misery than to their sin and disobedience.

(b.) The other is when it asserts, on the contrary, that God wills absolutely to damn certain particular men without manifesting in his decree any consideration of their disobedience. In this manner it detracts from his love to the creature that which belongs to it, while it teaches, that God hates the creature, without any cause or necessity derived from his love of righteousness and his hatred of iniquity. In which case, it is not true, "that sin is the primary object of God's hatred, and its only meritorious cause." The great influence and potency this consideration possesses in subverting the foundation of religion, may be appropriately described by the following analogy: Suppose a son to say, "My father is such a great lover of righteousness and equity, that, notwithstanding I am his beloved son, he would disinherit me if I were found disobedient to him. Obedience, therefore, is a duty which I must sedulously cultivate, and which is highly incumbent upon me, if I wish to be his heir."

Suppose another son to say: "My father's love for me is so great, that he is absolutely resolved to make me his heir. There is, therefore, no necessity for my earnestly striving to yield him obedience; for, according to his unchangeable will, I shall become his heir. Nay, he will by an irresistible force draw me to obey him, rather than not suffer me to be made his heir." But such reasoning as the latter is diametrically opposed to the doctrine contained in the following words of John the Baptist: "And think not to say within yourselves, We have Abraham to our father: for I say unto you, that God is able of these stones to raise up children unto Abraham" (Matt 3:9).

But the Christian religion also has its superstructure built upon this two-fold love as a foundation. This love, however, is to be considered in a manner somewhat different, in consequence of the change in the condition of man, who, when he had been created after the image of God and in his favor, became by his own fault a sinner and an enemy to God.

God's love of righteousness [or justice] on which the Christian religion rests, is, first, that righteousness he declared only once, which was in Christ; because it was his will that sin should not be expiated in any other way than by the blood and death of his Son, and that Christ should not be admitted before him as an advocate, deprecator and intercessor, except when sprinkled by his own blood. But this love of righteousness is, secondly, that which he daily manifests in the preaching of the gospel, in which he declares it to be his will to grant a communication of Christ and his benefits to no man, except to him who becomes converted and believes in Christ.

God's love of miserable sinners, on which likewise the Christian religion is founded, is, first, that love by which he gave his Son for them, and constituted him a Savior of those who obey him. But this love of sinners is, secondly, that by which he hath required obedience, not according to the rigor and severity to which he was entitled by his own supreme right, but according to his grace and clemency, and with the addition of a promise of the remission of sins, provided fallen man repent. The [supralapsarian] doctrine of Predestination is, in two ways, opposed to this two-fold foundation: first, by stating, "that God has such a great love for certain sinners, that it was his will absolutely to save them before he had given satisfaction, through Christ Jesus, to his love of righteousness [or justice], and that he thus willed their salvation even in his own fore-knowledge and according to his determinate purpose."

Completely Overturns

Besides, it totally and most completely overturns this foundation, by teaching it to be "God's pleasure, that satisfaction should be paid to his justice [or righteousness] because he willed absolutely to save such persons:" which is nothing less, than to make his love for justice, manifested in Christ, subordinate to his love for sinful man whom it is his will absolutely to save. Secondly, it opposes itself to this foundation, by teaching, "that it is the will of God absolutely to damn certain sinners without any consideration of their impenitency;" when at the same time a most plenary and complete satisfaction had been rendered, in Christ Jesus, to God's love of righteousness [or justice] and to his hatred of sin. So that nothing now can hinder the possibility of his extending mercy to the sinner, whosoever he may be, except the condition of repentance.

Unless some person should choose to assert, what is stated in this doctrine, "that it has been God's will to act towards the greater part of mankind with the same severity as he exercised towards the devil and his angels, or even with greater, since it was his pleasure that neither Christ nor his gospel should be productive of greater blessings to them than to the devils, and since, according to the first offense, the door of grace is as much closed against them as it is against the evil angels." Yet each of those angels sinned, by himself in his own proper person, through his individual maliciousness, and by his voluntary act; while men sinned, only in Adam their parent, before they had been brought into existence.

But, that we may more clearly understand the fact of this two-fold love being the foundation of all religion and the manner in which it is so, with the mutual correspondence that subsists between each other, as we have already described them, it will be profitable for us to contemplate with greater attention the following words in Hebrews: "He that cometh to God, must believe that He is, and that He is a rewarder of them that diligently seek Him" (11:6).

In these words two things are laid down as foundations to religion, in opposition to two fiery darts of Satan, which are the most pernicious pests to it, and each of which is able by itself to overturn and extirpate all religion. One of them is security, the other despair. Security operates, when a man permits himself, that, how inattentive soever he may be to the worship of God, he will not be damned, but will obtain salvation. Despair is in operation, when a person entertains a persuasion, that, whatever degree of reverence he may evince towards God, he will not receive any remuneration.

In what human mind soever either of these pests is fostered, it is impossible that any true and proper worship of God can there reside. Now both of them are overturned by the words in Hebrews. For if a man firmly believes, "that God will bestow eternal life on those alone who seek Him, but that He will inflict on the rest death eternal," he can on no account indulge himself in security. And if he likewise believes, that "God is truly a rewarder of those who diligently seek Him," by applying himself to the search he will not be in danger of falling into despair. The foundation of the former kind of faith by which a man firmly believes, "that God will bestow eternal life on none except on those who seek Him," is that love which God bears to his own righteousness [or justice] and which is greater than that which he entertains for man. And, by this alone, all cause of security is removed. But the foundation of the latter kind of faith, "that God will undoubtedly be a rewarder of those who diligently seek Him," is that great love for man which neither will nor can prevent God from effecting salvation for him, except he be hindered by his still greater love for righteousness or justice.

Yet the latter kind of love is so far from operating as a hindrance to God from becoming a rewarder of those who diligently seek Him, that on the contrary, it promotes in every possible way the bestowment of that reward. Those persons, therefore, who seek God, can by no means indulge in a single doubt concerning his readiness to remunerate.

Acts as a Preservative

And it is this which acts as a preservative against despair or distrust. Since this is the actual state of the case, this two-fold love, and the mutual relation each part of it bears to the other and which we have just unfolded, are the foundations of religion, without which no religion can possibly exist. That doctrine, therefore, which is in open hostility to this mutual love and to the relation that mutually subsists between them, is, at the same time, subversive of the foundation of all religion.

Lastly, this doctrine of Predestination has been rejected both in former times and in our own days, by the greater part of the professors of Christianity. But, omitting all mention of the periods that occurred in former ages, facts themselves declare, that the Lutheran and Anabaptist Churches, as well as that of Rome, account this to be an erroneous doctrine.

However highly Martin Luther and Philip Melancthon might at the very commencement of the reformation, have approved of this doctrine, they afterwards deserted it. This change in Melancthon is quite apparent from his latter writings: And those who style themselves "Luther's disciples," make the same statement respecting their master, while they contend that on this subject he made a more distinct and copious declaration of his sentiments, instead of entirely abandoning those which he formerly entertained. But Melancthon believed this doctrine did not differ greatly from the fate of the Stoics: This appears from many of his writings, but more particularly in a certain letter he addressed to Gasper Peucer, and in which, among other things, he states: "Laelius writes to me and says, that the controversy respecting the Stoical Fate is agitated with such uncommon fervor at Geneva, that one individual is cast into prison because he happened to differ from Zeno. O unhappy times! When the doctrine of salvation is thus obscured by certain strange disputes!"

All the Danish Churches embrace a doctrine quite opposed to this, as is obvious from the writings of Hemmingius in his treatise on Universal Grace[4], in which he declares that the contest between him and his adversaries consisted in the determination of these two points: "Do

---

4. Nicolaus Hemmingius, *Tractatus de Gratia Universali seu Salutari Omnibus Hominbus.* Hemmingius (1513–1600) was a prominent Danish Lutheran theologian.

the Elect believe?" or "Are believers the true elect?" He considers "those persons who maintain the former position, to hold sentiments agreeable to the doctrine of the Manichees and Stoics; and those who maintain the latter point, are in obvious agreement with Moses and the Prophets, with Christ and his Apostles."

Besides, by many of the inhabitants of these our own provinces, this doctrine is accounted a grievance of such a nature, as to cause several of them to affirm, that on account of it, they neither can nor will have any communion with our Church. Others of them have united themselves with our Churches, but not without entering a protest, "that they cannot possibly give their consent to this doctrine." But, on account of this kind of Predestination, our Churches have been deserted by not a few individuals, who formerly held the same opinions as ourselves. Others, also, have threatened to depart from us, unless they be fully assured that the Church holds no opinion of this description.

There is likewise no point of doctrine which the Papists, Anabaptists, and Lutherans oppose with greater vehemence than this, and through whose sides they create a worse opinion of our Churches or procure for them a greater portion of hatred, and thus bring into disrepute all the doctrines which we profess. They likewise affirm "that of all the blasphemies against God which the mind of man can conceive or his tongue can express, there is none so foul as not to be deduced by fair consequence from this opinion of our doctors."

Lastly, of all the difficulties and controversies that have arisen in these our churches since the time of the Reformation, there is none that has not had its origin in this doctrine, or that has not, at least, been mixed with it. What I have said here will be found true, if we bring to our recollection the controversies at Leyden in the affair of Koolhaes, at Gouda in that of Herman Herberts, at Horn with respect to Cornelius Wiggerston, and at Mendenblich in the affair of Tako Sybrants. This consideration was not among the last of those motives that induced me to give my most diligent attention to this head of doctrine, and endeavor to prevent our Churches from suffering any detriment from it. Because, from it the Papists have derived much of their increase. While all pious teachers ought most heartily to desire the destruction of Popery, as they would that of the kingdom of Antichrist, they ought with the greatest zeal, to engage in the attempt, and as far as it is within their power, to make the most efficient preparations for its overthrow.

The preceding views are, in brief, those I hold respecting this novel doctrine of Predestination. I have propounded it with all good faith from the very expressions of the authors themselves, that I might not seem to invent and attribute to them anything I was not able clearly to prove from their writings.

3

A Declaration of the Sentiments of James Arminius

Part 2

II. A SECOND KIND OF PREDESTINATION.

BUT SOME OTHER OF our doctors state the subject of God's Predestination in a manner somewhat different. We will cursorily touch upon the two modes which they employ.

Among some of them the following opinion is prevalent:

1. God determined within himself, by an eternal and immutable decree, to make (according to his own good pleasure) the smaller portion out of the general mass of mankind partakers of his grace and glory, to the praise of his own glorious grace. But according to his pleasure he also passed by the greater portion of men, and left them in their own nature, which is incapable of everything supernatural [or beyond itself] and did not communicate to them that saving and supernatural grace by which their nature (if it still retained its integrity) might be strengthened, or by which, if it were corrupted, it might be restored—for a demonstration of his own liberty. Yet after God had made these men sinners and guilty of death, he punished them with death eternal for a demonstration of his own justice.

2. Predestination is to be considered in respect to its end and to the means which tend to it. But these persons employ the word "Predestination" in its special acceptation for election and oppose it to reprobation.

(a.) In respect to its end (which is salvation, and an illustration of the glorious grace of God), man is considered in common and absolutely, such as he is in his own nature.

(b.) But in respect to the means, man is considered as perishing from himself and in himself, and as guilty in Adam.

3. In the decree concerning the end, the following gradations are to be regarded.

(a.) The prescience of God, by which he foreknew those whom he had predestinated.

Then (b.) The Divine prefinition [predetermination] by which he foreordained the salvation of those persons by whom he had foreknown.

First, by electing them from all eternity: and secondly, by preparing for them grace in this life, and glory in the world to come.

4. The means which belong to the execution of this Predestination, are

(a.) Christ himself; (b.) An efficacious call to faith in Christ, from which justification takes its origin; and (c.) The gift of perseverance unto the end.

5. As far as we are capable of comprehending their scheme of reprobation it consists of two acts, that of preterition and that of predamnatian. It is antecedent to all things, and to all causes that are either in the things themselves or which arise out of them. That is, it has no regard whatever to any sin, and only views man in an absolute and general aspect.

6. Two means are foreordained for the execution of the act of preterition:

(a.) Dereliction [or abandoning] in a state of nature, which by itself is incapable of everything supernatural: and

(b.) Non-communication [or a negation] of supernatural grace, by which their nature (if in a state of integrity) might be strengthened, and (if in a state of corruption) might be restored.

7. Predamnation is antecedent to all things, yet it does by no means exist without a foreknowledge of the causes of damnation. It views man as a sinner, obnoxious to damnation in Adam, and as on this account perishing through the necessity of Divine justice.

8. The means ordained for the execution of this predamnation, are

(a.) just desertion, which is either that of exploration [or examination] in which God does not confer his grace, or that of punishment when God takes away from a man all his saving gifts, and delivers him over to the power of Satan.

(b.) induration or hardening, and those consequences which usually follow even to the real damnation of the person reprobated.

III. A THIRD KIND OF PREDESTINATION

But others among our doctors state their sentiments on this subject in the following manner:

1. Because God willed within himself from all eternity to make a decree by which he might elect certain men and reprobate the rest, he viewed and considered the human race not only as created but likewise as fallen or corrupt, and on that account obnoxious to cursing and malediction. Out of this lapsed and accursed state God determined to liberate certain individuals and freely to save them by his grace, for a declaration of his mercy; but he resolved in his own just judgment to leave the rest under the curse [or malediction] for a declaration of his justice. In both these cases God acts without the least consideration of repentance and faith in those whom he elects, or of impenitence and unbelief in those whom he reprobates.

2. The special means that relate particularly to the execution both of election and reprobation, are the very same as those which we have already expounded in the first of these kinds of Predestination, with the exception of those means common both to election and reprobation. This [third] opinion places the fall of man, not as a means fore-ordained for the execution of the preceding decree of Predestination, but as something that might furnish a fixed purpose or occasion for making this decree of Predestination.

IV. MY JUDGMENT RESPECTING THE TWO LAST SCHEMES OF PREDESTINATION

Both these opinions, as they outwardly pretend, differ from the first in this point that neither of them lays down the creation or the fall as a mediate cause foreordained by God for the execution of the preceding decree of Predestination. Yet, with regard to the fall, some diversity may be perceived in the two latter opinions. For the second kind of Predestination places election, with regard to the end, before the fall; it also places before that event preterition [or passing by] which is the first part of reprobation. The third kind does not allow any part of election and reprobation to commence till after the fall of man.

But, among the causes that seem to have induced the inventors of the two latter schemes to deliver the doctrine of Predestination in this manner, and not to ascend to such a great height as the inventors of the first scheme have done, this is not the least. They have been desirous of using the greatest precaution, lest it might be concluded from their doctrine that God is the author of sin, with as much show of probability as (according to the intimation of some of those who yield their assent to both the latter kinds) it is deducible from the first description of Predestination.

Yet if we be willing to inspect these two latter opinions a little more closely, and in particular if we accurately examine the second and third kind and compare them with other sentiments of the same author concerning some subjects of our religion, we shall discover, that the fall of Adam cannot possibly, according to their views, be considered in any other manner than as a necessary means for the execution of the preceding decree of Predestination.

1. In reference to the second of the three, this is apparent from two reasons comprised in it: The first is that which states God to have determined by the decree of reprobation to deny to man that grace necessary for the confirmation and strengthening of his nature, that it might not be corrupted by sin; which amounts to this, that God decreed not to bestow that grace necessary to avoid sin, and from this must necessarily follow the transgression of man, as proceeding from a law imposed on him. The fall of man is therefore a means ordained for the execution of the decree of reprobation.

The second of these reasons is that which states the two parts of reprobation to be preterition and predamnation. These two parts, according to that decree, are connected together by a necessary and mutual bond, and are equally extensive. For, all those whom God passed by in conferring Divine grace, are likewise damned. Indeed no others are damned, except those who are the subjects of this act of preterition. From this therefore it may be concluded, that "sin must necessarily follow from the decree of reprobation or preterition." If it were otherwise, it might possibly happen, that a person who had been passed by, might not commit sin, and from that circumstance might not become liable to damnation; since sin is the sole meritorious cause of damnation: and thus certain of those individuals who had been passed by, might neither be saved nor damned, which is great absurdity.

This second opinion on Predestination, therefore, falls into the same inconvenience as the first. For it not only does not avoid that [conclusion of making God the author of sin] but while those who profess it make the attempt, they fall into a palpable and absurd self-contradiction while, in reference to this point, the first of these opinions is alike throughout and consistent with itself.

2. The third of these schemes of Predestination would escape this rock to much better effect, had not its patrons, while declaring their sentiments on Predestination and providence, employ certain expressions, from which the necessity of the fall might be deduced. Yet this necessity cannot possibly have any other origin than some degree of Predestination.

(a.) One of these explanatory expressions is their description of the Divine permission, by which God permits sin. Some of them describe it thus: "Permission is the withdrawing of that Divine grace, by which, when God executes the decrees of his will through rational creatures, he either does not reveal to the creature that divine will of his own by which he wills that action to be performed, or does not bend the will of the creature to yield obedience in that act to the Divine will." To these expressions, the following are immediately subjoined: "If this be a correct statement, the creature commits sin through necessity, yet voluntarily and without restraint." If it be objected that "this description does not comport with that permission by which God permitted the sin of Adam," we also entertain the same opinion about it. Yet it follows, as a consequence, from this very description, that "other sins are committed through necessity."

(b.) Of a similar tendency are the expressions which some of them use, when they contend, that the declaration of the glory of God, which must necessarily be illustrated, is placed in "the demonstration of mercy and of punitive justice." But such a demonstration could not have been made, unless sin, and misery through sin, had entered into the world, to form at least some degree of misery for the least sin. And in this manner is sin also necessarily introduced, through the necessity of such a demonstration of the Divine glory. Since the fall of Adam is already laid down to be necessary, and, on that account, to be a means for executing the preceding decree of Predestination; creation itself is likewise at the same time laid down as a means subservient to the execution of the same decree.

For the Fall cannot be necessarily consequent upon the creation, except through the decree of Predestination, which cannot be placed between the creation and the Fall, but is prefixed to both of them, as having the precedence, and ordaining creation for the fall, both of them for executing one and the same decree to demonstrate the justice of God in the punishment of sin, and his mercy in its remission.

Because, if this were not the case, that which must necessarily ensue from the act of creation had not seen intended by God when he created, which is to suppose an impossibility. But let it be granted, that the necessity of the Fall of Adam cannot be deduced from either of the two latter opinions, yet all the preceding arguments produced against the first opinion, are, after a trifling modification to suit the varied purpose, equally valid against the two latter. This would be very apparent, if, to demonstrate it, a conference were to be instituted.

V. MY OWN SENTIMENTS ON PREDESTINATION

I have hitherto been stating those opinions concerning the article of Predestination inculcated in our churches and in the University of Leyden, and of which I disapprove. I have at the same time produced my own reasons, why I form such an unfavorable judgment concerning them. I will now declare my own opinions on this subject, which are of such a description as, according to my views, appear most conformable to the word of God.

- The first absolute decree of God concerning the salvation of sinful man, is that by which he decreed to appoint his Son, Jesus Christ, as Mediator, Redeemer, Savior, Priest and King, who might destroy sin by his own death, might by his obedience obtain the salvation which had been lost, and might communicate it by his own virtue.

- The second precise and absolute decree of God, is that in which he decreed to receive into favor those who repent and believe, and, in Christ, for his sake and through Him, to effect the salvation of such penitents and believers as persevered to the end; but to leave in sin, and under wrath, all impenitent persons and unbelievers, and to damn them as aliens from Christ.

- The third Divine decree is that by which God decreed to administer in a sufficient and efficacious manner the means which were necessary for repentance and faith; and to have such administration instituted according to the Divine Wisdom, by which God knows what is proper and becoming both to his mercy and his severity, and according to Divine Justice, by which He is prepared to adopt whatever his wisdom may prescribe and put it in execution.

- To these succeeds the fourth decree, by which God decreed to save and damn certain particular persons. This decree has its foundation in the foreknowledge of God, by which he knew from all eternity those individuals who would, through his preventing grace, believe, and, through his subsequent grace would persevere, according to the before-described administration of those means which are suitable and proper for conversion and faith; and, by which foreknowledge, he likewise knew those who would not believe and persevere.

Predestination, when thus explained, is:

(1.) The foundation of Christianity, and of salvation and its certainty.

(2.) It is the sum and the matter of the gospel; nay, it is the gospel itself, and on that account necessary to be believed in order to salvation, as far as the two first articles are concerned.

(3.) It has had no need of being examined or determined by any council, either general or particular, since it is contained in the scriptures clearly and expressly in so many words; and no contradiction has ever yet been offered to it by any orthodox Divine.

(4.) It has constantly been acknowledged and taught by all Christian teachers who held correct and orthodox sentiments.

(5.) It agrees with that harmony of all confessions, which has been published by the protestant Churches.

(6.) It likewise agrees most excellently with the Dutch Confession and Catechism. This concord is such, that if in the Sixteenth article these two expressions "those persons whom" and "others," be explained by the words "believers" and "unbelievers" these opinions of mine on Predestination will be comprehended in that article with the greatest clearness. This is the reason why I directed the thesis to be composed in the very words of the Confession, when, on one occasion, I had to hold a public disputation before my private class in the University. This kind of Predestination also agrees with the reasoning contained in the twentieth and the fifty-fourth question of the Catechism.

(7.) It is also in excellent accordance with the nature of God: with his wisdom, goodness, and righteousness; because it contains the principal matter of all of them, and is the clearest demonstration of the Divine wisdom, goodness, and righteousness [or justice].

(8.) It is agreeable in every point with the nature of man in what form soever that nature may be contemplated, whether in the primitive state of creation, in that of the Fall, or in that of restoration.

(9.) It is in complete concert with the act of creation, by affirming that the creation itself is a real communication of good, both from the intention of God, and with regard to the very end or event; that it had its origin in the goodness of God; that whatever has a reference to its continuance and preservation, proceeds from Divine love; and that this act of creation is a perfect and appropriate work of God, in which he is at complaisance with himself, and by which he obtained all things necessary for an unsinning state.

(10.) It agrees with the nature of life eternal, and with the honorable titles by which that life is designated in the scriptures.

(11.) It also agrees with the nature of death eternal, and with the names by which that death is distinguished in scripture.

(12.) It states sin to be a real disobedience, and the meritorious cause of condemnation; and on this account, it is in the most perfect agreement with the Fall and with sin.

(13.) In every particular, it harmonizes with the nature of grace, by ascribing to it all those things which agree with it [or adapted to it], and by reconciling it most completely to the righteousness of God and to the nature and liberty of the human will.

(14.) It conduces most conspicuously to declare the glory of God, his justice and his mercy. It also represents God as the cause of all good and of our salvation, and man as the cause of sin and of his own damnation.

(15.) It contributes to the honor of Jesus Christ, by placing him for the foundation of Predestination and the meritorious as well as communicative cause of salvation.

(16.) It greatly promotes the salvation of men. It is also the power, and the very means that lead to salvation by exciting and creating within the mind of man sorrow on account of sin, a solicitude about his conversion, faith in Jesus Christ, a studious desire to perform good works, and zeal in prayer and by causing men to work out their salvation with fear and trembling. It likewise prevents despair, as far as such prevention is necessary.

(17.) It confirms and establishes that order according to which the gospel ought to be preached, by requiring repentance and faith and then by promising remission of sins, the grace of the spirit, and life eternal.

(18.) It strengthens the ministry of the gospel, and renders it profitable with respect to preaching, the administration of the sacraments and public prayers.

(19.) It is the foundation of the Christian religion; because in it, the two-fold love of God may be united together God's love of righteousness [or justice], and his love of men, may, with the greatest consistency, be reconciled to each other.

(20.) Lastly: This doctrine of Predestination has always been approved by the great majority of professing Christians, and even now, in these days, it enjoys the same extensive patronage. It cannot afford any person just cause for expressing his aversion to it; nor can it give any pretext for contention in the Christian Church.

It is therefore much to be desired, that men would proceed no further in this matter, and would not attempt to investigate the unsearchable judgments of God at least that they would not proceed beyond the point at which those judgments have been clearly revealed in the scriptures.

Most Potent Lords

This, my most potent Lords, is all that I intend now to declare to your mightinesses, respecting the doctrine of Predestination, about which there exists such a great controversy in the Church of Christ. If it would not prove too tedious to your Lordships, I have some other propositions which I wish to state, because they contribute to a full declaration of my sentiments, and tend to the same purpose as that for which I have been ordered to attend in this place.

There are certain other articles of the Christian religion, which possess a close affinity to the doctrine of Predestination, and that are in a great measure dependent on it. Of this description are the providence of God, the free-will of man, the perseverance of saints, and the certainty of salvation. On these topics, if not disagreeable to your mightinesses, I will in a brief manner relate my opinion.

VI. THE PROVIDENCE OF GOD

I consider Divine Providence to be that solicitous, continued, and universally present inspection and oversight of God, according to which he exercises a general care over the whole world, but evinces a particular concern for all his [intelligent] creatures without any exception, with the design of preserving and governing them in their own essence, qualities, actions, and passions. This is all done in a manner that is at once worthy of himself and suitable to them, to the praise of his name and the salvation of believers. In this definition of Divine Providence, I by no means deprive it of any particle of those properties which agree with it or belong to it. But I declare that it preserves, regulates, governs and directs all things and that nothing in the world happens fortuitously or by chance.

Beside this, I place in subjection to Divine Providence both the free-will and even the actions of a rational creature, so that nothing can be done without the will of God, not even any of those things done in opposition to it. Only we must observe a distinction between good actions and evil ones, by saying, "God both wills and performs good acts," but that "He only freely permits those which are evil." Still farther than this, I very readily grant, that even all actions whatever, concerning evil, that can possibly be devised or invented, may be attributed to Divine Providence employing solely one caution, not to conclude from this concession that God is the cause of sin.

This I have testified with sufficient clearness, in a certain disputation concerning the Righteousness and Efficacy of Divine Providence concerning things that are evil, discussed at Leyden on two different occasions, as a divinity act, at which I presided. In that disputation, I endeavored to ascribe to God whatever actions concerning sin I could possibly conclude from the scriptures to belong to him. And I proceeded to such a length in my attempt, that some persons thought proper on that account to charge me with having made God the author of sin.

The same serious allegation has likewise been often produced against me, from the pulpit in Amsterdam on account of those very theses; but with what show of justice such a charge was made, may be evident to anyone, from the contents of my written answer to those

Thirty-one Articles formerly mentioned, which have been falsely imputed to me, and of which this was one.

VII. THE FREE WILL OF MAN

This is my opinion concerning the free will of man: In his primitive condition as he came out of the hands of his creator, man was endowed with such a portion of knowledge, holiness and power, as enabled him to understand, esteem, consider, will, and to perform the true good, according to the commandment delivered to him. Yet none of these acts could he do, except through the assistance of Divine Grace. But in his lapsed and sinful state, man is not capable, of and by himself, either to think, to will, or to do that which is really good; but it is necessary for him to be regenerated and renewed in his intellect, affections or will, and in all his powers, by God in Christ through the Holy Spirit, that he may be qualified rightly to understand, esteem, consider, will, and perform whatever is truly good.

When he is made a partaker of this regeneration or renovation, I consider that, since he is delivered from sin, he is capable of thinking, willing and doing that which is good, but yet not without the continued aids of Divine Grace.

VIII. THE GRACE OF GOD

In reference to Divine Grace, I believe:

1. It is a gratuitous affection by which God is kindly affected towards a miserable sinner, and according to which he, in the first place, gives his Son, "that whosoever believes in him might have eternal life," and, afterwards, he justifies him in Christ Jesus and for his sake, and adopts him into the right of sons, unto salvation.

2. It is an infusion (both into the human understanding and into the will and affections) of all those gifts of the Holy Spirit that appertain to the regeneration and renewing of man such as faith, hope, charity, etc. For, without these gracious gifts, man is not sufficient to think, will, or do anything that is good.

3. It is that perpetual assistance and continued aid of the Holy Spirit, according to which He acts upon and excites to good the man who has been already renewed, by infusing into him salutary cogitations. It is also by inspiring him with good desires, that he may thus actually will

whatever is good; and according to which God may then will and work together with man, that man may perform whatever he wills.

In this manner, I ascribe to grace the commencement, the continuance and the consummation of all good. To such an extent do I carry its influence, that a man, though already regenerate, can neither conceive, will, nor do any good at all, nor resist any evil temptation, without this preventing and exciting, this following and co-operating grace.

From this statement it will clearly appear, that I by no means do injustice to grace, by attributing, as it is reported of me, too much to man's free-will. For the whole controversy reduces itself to the solution of this question, "Is the grace of God a certain irresistible force?" That is, the controversy does not relate to those actions or operations which may be ascribed to grace (for I acknowledge and inculcate as many of these actions or operations as any man ever did), but it relates solely to the mode of operation, whether it be irresistible or not. With respect to which, I believe, according to the scriptures, that many persons resist the Holy Spirit and reject the grace that is offered.

IX. THE PERSEVERANCE OF THE SAINTS

My sentiments respecting the perseverance of the saints are, that those persons who have been grafted into Christ by true faith, and have thus been made partakers of his life-giving Spirit, possess sufficient powers [or strength] to fight against Satan, sin, the world and their own flesh, and to gain the victory over these enemies yet not without the assistance of the grace of the same Holy Spirit. Jesus Christ also by his Spirit assists them in all their temptations, and affords them the ready aid of his hand; and, provided they stand prepared for the battle, implore his help, and be not wanting to themselves, Christ preserves them from falling.

So that it is not possible for them, by any of the cunning craftiness or power of Satan, to be either seduced or dragged out of the hands of Christ. But I think it is useful and will be quite necessary in our first convention, [or Synod] to institute a diligent inquiry from the Scriptures, whether it is not possible for some individuals through negligence to desert the commencement of their existence in Christ, to cleave again to the present evil world, to decline from the sound doctrine which was once delivered to them, to lose a good conscience, and to cause Divine grace to be ineffectual.

Though I here openly and ingenuously affirm, I never taught that a true believer can, either totally or finally fall away from the faith, and perish. Yet I will not conceal, that there are passages of scripture which seem to me to wear this aspect; and those answers to them which I have been permitted to see, are not of such a kind as to approve themselves on all points to my understanding. On the other hand, certain passages are produced for the contrary doctrine [of unconditional perseverance] which are worthy of much consideration.

X. THE ASSURANCE OF SALVATION

With regard to the certainty [or assurance] of salvation, my opinion is, that it is possible for him who believes in Jesus Christ to be certain and persuaded, and, if his heart condemn him not, he is now in reality assured, that he is a son of God, and stands in the grace of Jesus Christ. Such a certainty is wrought in the mind, as well by the action of the Holy Spirit inwardly actuating the believer and by the fruits of faith, as from his own conscience, and the testimony of God's Spirit witnessing together with his conscience. I also believe, that it is possible for such a person, with an assured confidence in the grace of God and his mercy in Christ, to depart out of this life, and to appear before the throne of grace, without any anxious fear or terrific dread: and yet this person should constantly pray, "O Lord, enter not into judgment with thy servant!"

But, since "God is greater than our hearts, and knoweth all things," and since a man judges not his own self, yea, though a man know nothing by himself, yet is he not thereby justified, but he who judgeth him is the Lord (1 John 3:19; 1 Cor 4:3). I dare not [on this account] place this assurance [or certainty] on an equality with that by which we know there is a God, and that Christ is the Savior of the world. Yet it will be proper to make the extent of the boundaries of this assurance, a subject of inquiry in our convention.

XI. THE PERFECTION OF BELIEVERS IN THIS LIFE

Beside those doctrines on which I have treated, there is now much discussion among us respecting the perfection of believers, or regenerated persons, in this life, It is reported, that I entertain sentiments on this subject, which are very improper, and nearly allied to those of the Pelagians, viz: "that it is possible for the regenerate in this life perfectly to keep God's precepts." To this I reply, though these might have been my sentiments yet I ought not on this account to be considered a Pelagian, either partly or entirely, provided I had only added that "they could do this by the grace of Christ, and by no means without it."

But while I never asserted that a believer could perfectly keep the precepts of Christ in this life, I never denied it, but always left it as a matter which has still to be decided. For I have contented myself with those sentiments which St. Augustine has expressed on this subject, whose words have frequently quoted in the University, and have usually subjoined, that I had no addition to make to them.

St. Augustine says, "Four questions may claim our attention on this topic. The first is, was there ever yet a man without sin, one who from the beginning of life to its termination never committed sin? The second, has there ever been, is there now, or can there possibly be, an individual who does not sin, that is, who has attained to such a state of perfection in this life as not to commit sin, but perfectly to fulfill the law of God?

"The third, is it possible for a man in this life to exist without sin? The fourth, if it be possible for a man to be without sin, why has such an individual never yet been found?" St. Augustine says, that such a person as is described in the first question never yet lived, or will hereafter be brought into existence, with the exception of Jesus Christ. He does not think that any man has attained to such perfection in this life as is portrayed in the second question. With regard to the third, he thinks it possible for a man to be without sin, by means of the grace of Christ and free will. In answer to the fourth, man does not do what it is possible for him by the grace of Christ to perform, either because that which is good escapes his observation, or because in it he places no part of his delight. From this quotation it is apparent that St. Augustine, one of the most strenuous adversaries of the Pelagian doctrine, retained this sentiment, that "it is possible for a man to live in this world without sin."

Beside this, the same Christian father says, "Let Pelagius confess that it is possible for man to be without sin, in no other way than by the grace of Christ, and we will be at peace with each other." The opinion of Pelagius appeared to St. Augustine to be this, "that man could fulfill the law of God by his own proffer strength and ability; but with still greater facility by means of the grace of Christ." I have already most abundantly stated the great distance at which I stand from such a sentiment; in addition to which I now declare, that I account this sentiment of Pelagius to be heretical, and diametrically opposed to these words of Christ, "Without me ye can do nothing" (John 15:5). It is likewise very destructive, and inflicts a most grievous wound on the glory of Christ.

I cannot see that anything is contained in all I have hitherto produced respecting my sentiments, on account of which any person ought to be "afraid of appearing in the presence of God," and from which it might be feared that any mischievous consequences can possibly arise. Yet because every day brings me fresh information about reports concerning me, "that I carry in my breast destructive sentiments and heresies," I cannot possibly conceive to what points those charges can relate, except perhaps they draw some such pretext from my opinion concerning the Divinity of the Son of God, and the justification of man before God.

Indeed, I have lately learned that there has been much public conversation, and many rumors have been circulated, respecting my opinion on both these points of doctrine, particularly since the last conference [between Gomarus and myself] before the Counselors of the Supreme Court. This is one reason why I think, that I shall not be acting unadvisedly if I disclose to your mightinesses the real state of the whole matter.

XII. THE DIVINITY OF THE SON OF GOD

With regard to the Divinity of the Son of God and the Greek word *autotheos* [God in his own right] both of which have been discussed in our University in the regular form of scholastic disputations, I cannot sufficiently wonder what the motive can be, which has created a wish in some persons to render me suspected to other men, or to make me an object of suspicion to themselves. This is still more wonderful, since this suspicion has not the least ground of probability on which to rest, and is at such an immense distance from all reason and truth, that, whatever reports have been spread abroad respecting this affair to the prejudice of my character, they can be called nothing better than "notorious calumnies."

At a disputation held one afternoon in the University, when the thesis that had been proposed for disputation was the Divinity of the Son of God, one of the students happened to object, "that the Son of God was *autotheos*, and that he therefore had his essence from himself and not from the Father." In reply to this I observed, "that the word *autotheos* was capable of two different acceptations, since it might signify either 'one who is truly God,' or 'one who is God of himself 'and that it was with great propriety and correctness attributed to the Son of God according to the former signification, but not according to the latter."

The student, in prosecution of his argument, violently contended, "that the word was justly applicable to the Son of God, principally according to the second of these significations: and that the essence of the Father could not be said to be communicated to the Son and to the Holy Spirit, in any other than in an improper sense; but that it was in perfect correctness and strict propriety common alike to the Father, the Son, and the Holy Ghost."

He added "this with the greater confidence because he had the younger Trelcatius of pious memory [but who was then living], as an authority in his favor on this point; for that learned Professor had written to the same purport in his *Common Places*." To these observations I answered, "that this opinion was at variance with the word of God, and with the whole of the ancient Church, both Greek and Latin, which had always taught, that the Son had His Deity from the Father by eternal generation." To these remarks I subjoined, "that from such an opinion as this, necessarily followed the two mutually conflicting errors, Tritheism and Sabellianism; that is:

"1. It would ensue as a necessary consequence, from these premises, that there are three Gods, who have together and collaterally the Divine essence, independently of this circumstance that one of them (being only personally distinguished from the rest) has that essence from another of the persons. Yet the proceeding of the origin of one person from another (that is, of the Son from the Father), is the only foundation that has ever been used for defending the unity of the Divine Essence in the Trinity of Persons.

"2. It would likewise follow as another consequence, that the Son would himself be the Father, because he would differ from the Father in nothing but in regard to name, which was the opinion of Sabellius. For, since it is peculiar to the Father to derive his Deity from himself, or (to speak more correctly) to derive it from no one, if, in the sense of being 'God of himself,' the Son be called *autotheos*, it follows that he is the Father."

Some account of this disputation was dispersed abroad in all directions, and it reached Amsterdam. A minister of that city, who now rests in the Lord, having interrogated, me respecting the real state of this affair, I related the whole of it to him plainly, as I have now done. I requested him to make Trelcatius of blessed memory acquainted with it as it had actually occurred, and to advise him in a friendly manner to amend his opinion, and to correct those inappropriate words in his *Common Places*.[1] This request the minister from Amsterdam engaged to fulfill in his own way.

In all this proceeding I am far from being liable to any blame, for I have defended the truth and the sentiments of the Catholic and Orthodox Church. Trelcatius undoubtedly was the person most open to animadversion; for he adopted a mode of speaking which detracted somewhat from the truth of the matter. But such has always been either my own infelicity or the zeal of certain individuals that, as soon as any disagreement arises, all the blame is instantly cast upon me, as if it was impossible for me to display as much veracity [or orthodoxy] as any other person. Yet on this subject I have Gomarus himself consenting with me. For, soon after Trelcatius had published his book, a disputation on the Trinity having been proposed in the University, Gomarus did in three several parts of his theses express himself in such terms as were diametrically opposed to those of Trelcatius.

The very obvious difference in opinion between those two professors I pointed out to the Amsterdam minister, who acknowledged its existence. Yet, notwithstanding all these things, no one endeavored to vindicate me from this calumny; while great exertion was employed to frame excuses for Trelcatius, by means of a qualified interpretation of his words, though it was utterly impossible to reconcile their palliative explanations with the plain signification of his unperverted expressions. Such are the effects the partiality of favor and the fervor of zeal can produce!

The milder and qualified interpretation put upon the words of Trelcatius, was the following: "the Son of God may be styled *autotheos*, or may be said to have his Deity from himself, in reference to his being God, although he has his Deity from the Father, in reference to his being the Son." For the sake of a larger explanation, it is said, "God, or the Divine Essence, may be considered both absolutely and relatively. When regarded absolutely, the Son has his Divine essence from himself; but, when viewed relatively, he derives it from the Father." But these are new

---

1. Lucas Trelcatius, *A Briefe (sic) Institution of the Common Places of Sacred Divinitie.*

modes of speaking and novel opinions, and such as can by no means consist together.

His Being the Son

For the Son, both in regard to his being the Son, and to his being God, derives his Deity from the Father. When he is called God, it is then only not expressed that he is from the Father, which derivation is particularly noted when the word Son is employed. Indeed, the essence of God can in no manner come under our consideration, except it be said, "that the Divine Essence is communicated to the Son by the Father." Nor can it possibly in any different respect whatever be said, that this essence is both "communicated to him" and "not communicated;" because these expressions are contradictory, and can in no diverse respect be reconciled to each other. If the Son has the Divine Essence from himself in reference to its being absolutely considered, it cannot be communicated to him.

If it be communicated to him in reference to its being relatively considered, he cannot have it from himself in reference to its being absolutely considered.

I shall probably be asked, "Do you not acknowledge, that, to be the Son of God, and to be God, are two things entirely distinct from each other?" I reply, undoubtedly I subscribe to such distinction. But when those who make it proceed still further, and say, "Since to be the Son of God signifies that he derives his essence from the Father, to be God in like manner signifies nothing less than that he has his essence from himself or from no one." I deny this assertion, and declare, at the same time, that it is a great and manifest error, not only in sacred theology, but likewise in natural philosophy. For, these two things, to be the Son and to be God, are at perfect agreement with each other. But to derive his essence from the Father, and, at the same time, to derive it from no one, are evidently contradictory, and mutually destructive the one of the other.

But, to make this fallacy still more apparent, it must be observed, how equal in force and import are certain double ternary and parallel propositions, when standing in the following juxtaposition:

God is from *eternity*, possessing the Divine Essence from eternity.

The Father is from *no one*, having the Divine Essence from no one.

The Son is from *the* Father, having the Divine Essence from the Father.

The word "God" therefore signifies, that He has the true Divine Essence; but the word "Son" signifies, that he has the Divine Essence from the Father. On this account, he is correctly denominated both God and the Son of God. But since he cannot be styled the Father, he cannot possibly be said to have the Divine Essence from himself or from no one. Yet much labor is devoted to the purpose of excusing these expressions, by saying, "when the son of God in reference to his being God is said to have his essence from himself, that form of speech signifies nothing more, than that the Divine essence is not derived from anyone."

But if this be thought to be the most proper mode of action that should be adopted, there will be no depraved or erroneous sentiment that can be uttered that may not thus find a ready excuse. For though God and the divine Essence do not differ substantially, yet whatever may be predicated of the Divine Essence can by no means be equally predicated of God. That is because they are distinguished from each other in our mode of framing conceptions, according to which mode all forms of speech ought to be examined, since they are employed only with a design that through them we should receive correct impressions. This is very obvious from the following examples, in which we speak with perfect correctness when we say, "*Deum mortuum esse*," and "the Essence of God is communicated;" but very incorrectly when we say, "God is communicated."

That man who understands the difference existing between concrete and abstract, about which there were such frequent disputes between us and the Lutherans will easily perceive what a number of absurdities will ensue, if explanations of this description be once tolerated in the Church of God. Therefore, in no way whatever can this phrase, "the Son of God is *autotheon*," ['God of himself,' or 'in his own right,'] be excused as a correct one, or as having been happily expressed. Nor can that be called a proper form of speech that says, "the Essence of God is common to three persons;" but it is improper, since the Divine Essence is declared to be communicated by one of them to another.

The observations which I now make, I wish to be particularly regarded, because it may appear from them how much we are capable of tolerating in a man whom we do not suspect of heresy; and, on the contrary, with what avidity we seize upon any trivial circumstance by which we may inculpate another man whom we hold under the ban of suspicion. Of such partiality, this incident affords two manifest examples.

XIII. THE JUSTIFICATION OF MAN BEFORE GOD

I am not conscious to myself, of having taught or entertained any other sentiments concerning the justification of man before God, than those which are held unanimously by the Reformed and Protestant Churches, and which are in complete agreement with their expressed opinions.

There was lately a short controversy in relation to this subject, between John Piscator, Professor of Divinity in the University of Herborn in Nassau, and the French churches. It consisted in the determination of these two questions:

1. "Is the obedience or righteousness of Christ, which is imputed to believers and in which consists their righteousness before God, only the passive obedience of Christ?" which was Piscator's opinion. Or

2. "Is it not, in addition to this, that active righteousness of Christ that he exhibited to the law of God in the whole course of his life, and that holiness in which he was conceived?" which was the opinion of the French churches. But I never mingled myself with the dispute, or undertook to decide it. For I thought it possible for professors of the same religion to hold different opinions on this point from others of their brethren, without any breach of Christian peace or the unity of faith. Similar peaceful thoughts appear to have been indulged by both the adverse parties in this dispute. For they exercised a friendly toleration towards each other, and did not make that a reason for mutually renouncing their fraternal concord. But concerning such an amicable plan of adjusting differences, certain individuals in our own country are of a different judgment.

A question has been raised from these words of the Apostle Paul: "And therefore it (faith) was imputed to him for righteousness" (Rom 4:22). The inquiry was:

(a.) Whether those expressions ought to be properly understood, "so that faith itself, as an act performed according to the command of the gospel, is imputed before God for or unto righteousness—and that of grace; since it is not the righteousness of the law."

(b.) Whether they ought to be figuratively and improperly understood, "that the righteousness of Christ, being apprehended by faith, is imputed to us for righteousness." Or, (c.) Whether it is to be understood "that the righteousness, for which, or unto which, faith is imputed, is the instrumental operation of faith;" which is asserted by some persons. In the theses on justification, which were disputed under me when I was moderator, I have adopted the former of these opinions not in a rigid manner, but simply, as I have likewise done in another passage which I wrote in a particular letter. It is on this ground that I am accounted to hold and to teach unsound opinions concerning the justification of man before God.

But how unfounded such a supposition is, will be very evident at a proper season, and in a mutual conference. For the present, I will only briefly say, "I believe that sinners are accounted righteous solely by the obedience of Christ; and that the righteousness of Christ is the only meritorious cause on account of which God pardons the sins of believers and reckons them as righteous as if they had perfectly fulfilled the law. But since God imputes the righteousness of Christ to none except believers, I conclude that, in this sense, it may be well and properly said, to a man who believes, faith is imputed for righteousness through grace, because God hath set forth his Son, Jesus Christ, to be a propitiation, a throne of grace [or mercy seat], through faith in his blood."

Whatever interpretation may be put upon these expressions, none of our Divines blame Calvin or considers him to be heterodox on this point; yet my opinion is not so widely different from his as to prevent me from employing the signature of my own hand in subscribing to those things which he has delivered on this subject, in the third book of his Institutes. This I am prepared to do at any time, and to give them my full approval. Most noble and potent Lords, these are the principal articles, respecting which I have judged it necessary to declare my opinion before this august meeting, in obedience to your commands.

XIV. THE REVISION OF THE DUTCH CONFESSION AND THE HEIDELBERG CATECHISM

But, besides these things, I had some annotations to make on the Confession of the Dutch Churches and on the Heidelberg Catechism; but they will be discussed most appropriately in our Synod, which at the first opportunity we hope to obtain through your consent, or rather by means of your summons. This is the sole request which I prefer to your mightinesses, that I may be permitted to offer a few brief remarks on a certain clause, subject to which their high mightinesses, the States

General, gave their consent to the convening of a National Synod in this province (Holland), and the substance of which was, that in such Synod the Confession and Catechism of the Dutch Churches should be subjected to examination.

This clause has given great umbrage to many persons, not only because they account it unnecessary, but likewise unjust, to subject the Confession and Catechism to examination. They also suppose that I and a certain individual of great reputation, are the persons who prevailed with the States General to have such a clause inserted. But it is by no means true that the revision of the Confession and Catechism is unnecessary and unjust, or that we were the instigators of their high mightinesses in this affair. With regard to the last of these two suppositions, so far were we from having any concern with the origin of that clause, that, eleven or twelve years ago, at the pressing importunity of the Churches that prayed for a National Synod, the States of South Holland and West Friezland at last judged it proper to consent to it by their decree, on no other condition than that in such Synod the Confession of the Dutch Churches should be subjected to examination.

Yet we, at that time, neither endeavored by our advice, nor by our influence, to promote any such measure. But if we had with all our might made the attempt, we should have been doing nothing but what was compatible with our official duties; because it is obviously agreeable to reason as well as to equity, and quite necessary in the present posture of affairs, that such a measure should be adopted.

First: That it may openly appear to all the world that we render to the word of God alone such due and suitable honor, as to determine it to be beyond (or rather above) all disputes, too great to be the subject of any exception, and worthy of all acceptation.

Secondly: Because these pamphlets are writings that proceed from men, and may, on that account, contain within them some portion of error, it is therefore, proper to institute a lawful inquiry, that is, in a National Synod, whether or not there be anything in those productions which requires amendment.

1. The first inquiry may be, whether these human writings are accordant, in every part, with the word of God, with regard to the words themselves, the construction of the sentences and the correct meaning.

2. Whether they contain whatever is necessary to be believed unto salvation, so that salvation is, according to this rule, not denied to those things to which it appertains.

3. Whether it [the rule of these formularies] does not contain far too many particulars, and embrace several that are not necessary to be believed unto salvation, so that salvation is consequently attributed to those things to which it does not belong.

4. Whether certain words and forms of speech are not employed in them, that are capable of being understood in different ways and furnishing occasion for disputes. Thus, for example, in the Fourteenth article of the Confession, we read the following words, "Nothing is done without God's ordination" [or appointment]. If by the word "ordination" is signified, "that God appoints things of any kind to be done," this mode of enunciation is erroneous, and it follows as a consequence from it, that God is the author of sin. But if it signifies, that "whatever it be that is done, God ordains it to a good end," the terms in which it is conceived are in that case correct.

5. Whether things utterly repugnant to each other may not be discovered in them. For instance, a certain individual who is highly honored in the church, addressed a letter to Professor Piscator. In it, he exhorted Piscator to confine himself to the Heidelberg Catechism on the doctrine of Justification. For this purpose he cited three passages, which he considered to be at variance with Piscator's sentiments. But the learned Professor replied, that he confined himself completely within the doctrinal boundaries of the Catechism; and then quoted out of that formulary ten or eleven passages as proofs of his sentiments. But I solemnly declare, I do not perceive by what method these several passages can possibly be reconciled with each other.

6. Whether everything in these writings is digested in that due order in which the Scripture requires them to be placed.

7. Whether all things are disposed in a manner the most suitable and convenient for preserving peace and unity with the rest of the reformed Churches.

Thirdly: A National Synod is held for the purpose of discovering whether all things in the Church are in a proper state or right condition. One of the chief duties which appertains to such an assembly, is, the examination of doctrine, whether it be that which is admitted by unanimous consent, or that for which particular Divines contend.

Fourthly: An examination of this description will obtain for these writings a greater degree of authority, when after a mature and rigid examination they shall be found to agree with the word of God, or shall be made conformable to it in a still greater measure. Such an examination will also excite within the minds of men a greater value for Christian ministers, when they perceive that these sacred functionaries hold in the highest estimation that truth revealed in Scripture, and that their attachment to it is so great as to induce them to spare no labor in order to render their own doctrine more and more conformable to that revealed truth.

Fifthly: There are several individuals in the ministry who have certain views and considerations respecting some points contained in these writings, which they reserve in secret and reveal to no one, because they hope such points will become subjects of discussion in a National Synod. Because such a convention has been promised, some of them have suffered themselves to be persuaded not to give the least publicity to any of the views or considerations which they have formed on these subjects.

National Synod

Besides, this will be the design of a National Synod: That their high mightinesses the States General may be pleased to establish and arm with public authority certain ecclesiastical sanctions, according to which everyone may be bound to conduct himself in the Church of God. That this favor may be obtained from their high mightinesses and that they may execute such a measure with a good conscience, it is necessary that they be convinced in their own understandings, that the doctrine contained in the formulary of union is agreeable to the word of God. This is a reason that ought to induce us spontaneously to propose an examination of our Confession before their high mightinesses, and to offer either to show that it is in accordance with the word of God, or to render it conformable to that Divine standard.

Sixthly: A further reason is drawn from the example of those who are associated together under the Augustinian Confession, and from the conduct of the Swiss and the French Churches, that have within two or three years enriched their Confessions with one entirely new article. And the Dutch Confession has itself been subjected to examination since it was first published: some things having been taken away from it and others added, while some of the rest have undergone various alterations.

Numerous other reasons might be produced, but I omit them because I consider those already mentioned to be quite sufficient for proving, that the clause concerning examination and revision, as it is termed, was with the greatest justice and propriety inserted in the instrument of consent of which we have made previous mention.

I am not ignorant, that other reasons are adduced, in opposition to these. One in particular, is made a principal subject of public conversation, and is accounted among all others the most solid. To it, therefore I consider it necessary to offer a brief reply. It is thus stated: "By such an examination as this, the doctrine of the Church will be called in question; which is neither an act of propriety nor of duty.

"1. Because this doctrine has obtained the approbation and suffrages of many respectable and learned men; and has been strenuously defended against all those who have offered it any opposition.

"2. Because it has been sealed with the blood of many thousand martyrs.

"3. Because from such an examination will arise, within the Church, confusion, scandal, offenses, and the destruction of consciences; and, out of the Church, ridicule, calumnies and accusations."

To all these I answer:

1. It would be much better, not to employ such odious forms of speech, as to call in question, and others of that class, when the conversation is only respecting some human composition, which is liable to have error intermixed with its contents. For with what right can any writing he said to be called in question or in doubt, which was never of itself unquestionable, or ought to be considered as indubitable?

2. The approbation of Divines, the defense of a composition against its adversaries, and the sealing of it with the blood of martyrs, do not render any doctrine authentic or place it beyond the limits of doubt; because it is possible both for Divines and martyrs to err, a circumstance which can admit of no denial in this argument.

3. A distinction ought to be made between the different matters contained in the Confession. For while some of them make a near approach to the foundation of salvation and are fundamental articles of the Christian religion, others of them are built up as a superstructure on the foundation, and of themselves are not absolutely necessary to

salvation. The doctrines of this former class are approved by the unanimous consent of all the Reformed, and are effectually defended against all gainsaying adversaries. But those of the latter class become subjects of controversy between different parties: and some of these are attacked by enemies not without some semblance of truth and justice.

The blood of martyrs has sealed those of the former class but by no means those of the latter. In reference to this affair, it ought to be diligently observed, what was proposed by the martyrs of our days, and on what account they shed their blood. If this be done, it will be found, that no man among them was even interrogated on that subject I consider it equitable to make a prominent part in the deliberations of a Synod, and, therefore, that no martyr ever sealed it with his blood.

I will produce an example: When a question was raised about the meaning of Romans 7, one individual said, "The passage was quoted in the margin of the Confession exactly in the same sense as he had embraced it, and that the martyrs had with their own blood sealed this Confession." But, in reply to this, it was stated, "If the strictest search be instituted throughout the entire large *History of the Martyrs*, as it is published by the French, it will be discovered that no martyr has at any period been examined on that passage, or has shed his blood on that account."

Blood of the Martyrs

To sum up the whole: The blood of the martyrs tends to confirm this truth, that they have made profession of their faith "in simplicity and sincerity of conscience." But it is by no means conclusive, that the Confession they produced is free from every degree of reprehension or superior to all exception, unless they had been led by Christ into all truth and therefore rendered incapable of erring.

4. If the Church be properly instructed in that difference which really does and always ought to exist between the word of God and all human writings, and if the Church is also rightly informed concerning that liberty she and all Christians possess, and which they will always enjoy, to measure all human compositions by the standard rule of God's word, she will neither distress herself on that account, nor will she be offended on perceiving all human writings brought to be proved at the touchstone of God's word. On the contrary, she will rather feel far more abundant delight, when she sees that God has bestowed on her in this

country such pastors and teachers, as try at the chief touchstone their own doctrine, in a manner at once suitable, proper, just, and worthy of perpetual observance. That they do this, is to be able exactly and by every possible means to express their agreement with the word of God, and their consent to it even in the most minute particulars.

5. But it is no less proper, that the doctrine once received in the Church should be subjected to examination, however great the fear may be "lest disturbances should ensue, and lest evil disposed persons should make such revision an object of ridicule, calumny or accusation," or should even turn it to their own great advantage [by representing the matter so as to induce a persuasion], "that those who propose this examination are not sufficiently confirmed in their own religion ;" when, on the contrary, this is one of God's commands: "search and try the spirits whether they be of God" (1 John 4:1). If cogitations of that description had operated as hindrances in the minds of Luther, Zwingli, and others, they would never have pried into the doctrine of the Papists, or have subjected it to a scrutinizing examination.

Nor would those who adhere to the Augustinian Confession have considered it proper to submit that formulary again to a new and complete revision, and to alter it in some particulars. This deed of theirs is an object of our praise and approval. And we conclude, that when Luther towards the close of his life was advised by Philip Melancthon to bring the eucharistic controversy on the sacrament of the Lord's Supper to some better state of concord (as it is related in the writings of our own countrymen), he acted very improperly in rejecting that counsel, and in casting it back as a reproach on Philip, for this reason, as they state his declaration, "lest by such an attempt to effect an amicable conclusion, the whole doctrine should be called in question."

Besides, if reasons of this kind ought to be admitted, the Papists with the best right and the greatest propriety formerly endeavored to prevent the doctrine, which had for many preceding centuries been received in the Church, from being called in question or subjected again to examination.

But it has been suggested, in opposition to these reasons, "that if the doctrine of the Churches be submitted to an entirely new revision as often as a National Synod shall be held, the Church would never have anything to which it might adhere or on which it might fully depend, and it will be possible to declare with great justice, concerning Churches thus circumstanced, that, 'they have an anniversary faith,' are tossed to and fro, and carried about with every wind of doctrine (Eph 4:14)."

1. My first answer to these remarks, is, the Church always has Moses and the Prophets, the Evangelists and the Apostles, that is, the Scriptures of the Old and of the New Testament; and these Scriptures fully and clearly comprehend whatever is necessary to salvation. Upon them the Church will lay the foundation of her faith, and will rest upon them as on an immovable basis, principally because, how highly soever we may esteem Confessions and Catechisms every decision on matters of faith and religion must obtain its final resolution in the Scriptures.

2. Some points in the Confession are certain and do not admit of a doubt: these will never be called in question by anyone, except by heretics. Yet there are other parts of its contents that are of such a kind, as may with the most obvious utility become frequent subjects of conference and discussion between men of learning who fear God, for the purpose of reconciling them with those indubitable articles as nearly as is practicable.

3. Let it be attempted to make the Confession contain as few articles as possible; and let it propose them in a very brief form, conceived entirely in the expressions of Scripture. Let all the more ample explanations, proofs, digressions, redundancies, amplifications and exclamations, be omitted; and let nothing be delivered in it, except those truths which are necessary to salvation. The consequences of this brevity will be, that the Confession will be less liable to be filled with errors, not so obnoxious to obloquy, and less subject to examination.

Practice of Ancient Church

Let the practice of the ancient Church be produced as an example, that comprehended, in as brief a form of words as was practicable, those articles which she judged necessary to be believed. Some individuals form a distinction between the Confession and the Catechism with respect to revision; and, since the Confession is the peculiar property of the Dutch Churches, and is on that account found in the hands of comparatively few people, they conclude, "that it is possible without any difficulty to revise it in a Synod and subject it to examination." But since the Catechism belongs not only to us, but likewise and principally to the Churches of the Palatinate, and is therefore to be found in the hands of all men, the same persons consider the examination of it "to be connected with great peril."

But to this I reply, if we are desirous of constituting the Heidelberg Catechism a formulary of concord among the teachers of the Churches, and if they are obliged to subscribe it, it is still necessary to subject it to examination. For no Churches whatever ought to hold such a high station in our esteem, as to induce us to receive any writing of their composition without, at the same time, reserving to ourselves the liberty of submitting it to a nice scrutiny.

And I account this to be the principal cause, why the Churches of different provinces, although at perfect agreement with each other on the fundamental points of Christian doctrine, have each composed for themselves their own Confessions. But if the Heidelberg Catechism is not allowed to become a formulary of this kind, and if a suitable liberty is conceded in the explanation of it, it will then be unnecessary either to revise it or subject it to examination. That is provided, I repeat, that the obligatory burden of subscription be removed, and a moderate liberty be conceded in its explanation.

This is all that I had to propose to your mightinesses, as to my most noble, potent, wise and prudent masters. While I own myself bound to render an account of all my actions, to the members of this most noble and potent assembly (next after God), I at the same time present to them my humble and grateful acknowledgments, because they have not disdained to grant me a courteous and patient audience.

I embrace this opportunity solemnly to declare, that I am sincerely prepared to institute an amicable and fraternal conference with my reverend brethren (at whatever time or place and on whatever occasion this honorable assembly may judge proper to appoint), on all the topics which I have now mentioned, and on any other concerning which it will be possible for a controversy to exist, or at some future period to arise. I also make this additional promise, that I will in every conference conduct myself with equanimity, moderation and docility, and will show myself not less actuated by the desire of being taught, than by that of communicating to others some portion of instruction. And, since in the discussion of every topic on which it will be possible to institute a conference, two points will become objects of attention.

First: "Whether that be true which is the subject of the controversy," and, secondly, "Whether it be necessary to be believed unto salvation," and since both these points ought to be discussed and proved out of the Scriptures, I here tender my sacred affirmation, and solemnly bind myself hereafter to observe it, that, however cogently I may have proved by the most solid [human] arguments any article to be agreeable to the word of God, I will not obtrude it for an article of belief on those of my brethren who may entertain a different opinion respecting it, unless I have plainly proved it from the word of God and have with equal clearness established its truth, and the necessity unto salvation that every Christian should entertain the same belief.

If my brethren will be prepared to act in this manner, as far as I know the complexion of my own opinions, there will not easily arise among us any schism or controversy. But, that I may on my part remove every cause of fear that can possibly invade this most noble assembly, occupied and engaged as its honorable members now are with important concerns on which in a great measure depends the safety of our native country and of the Reformed Churches, I subjoin this remark, "that to hinder my toleration of any matters in my brethren, they must be very numerous and very important. For I am not of the congregation of those who wish to have dominion over the faith of another man, but am only a minister to believers, with the design of promoting in them an increase of knowledge, truth, piety, peace and joy in Jesus Christ our Lord."

Brethren Cannot Perceive

But if my brethren cannot perceive how they can possibly tolerate me, or allow me a place among them, in reference to myself I indulge in no hope that a schism will on this account be formed. May God avert any such catastrophe, since far too many schisms have already arisen and spread themselves abroad among Christians. It ought rather to be the earnest endeavor of everyone, to diminish their number and destroy their influence.

Yet, even under such circumstances [when I shall be rejected from the communion of my brethren], in patience will l possess my soul; and though in that case I shall resign my office, yet I will continue to live for the benefit of our common Christianity as long as it may please God to lengthen out my days and prolong my existence. Never forgetting this sentiment, *Sat Ecclesae, sat Patriae daturm*: Enough has been done to satisfy the Church of Christ and my country!

4

An Examination of Predestination and Grace in Perkins' Pamphlet

Part 1

WILLIAM PERKINS, WAS A prominent Cambridge theologian and leader of the Puritan movement in the sixteenth century. The following was written by Arminius in 1602 in response to Perkins' *A Christian and plain Treatise on the Mode and Order of Predestination, and on the Amplitude of Divine Grace*, originally published in Latin in 1598.

Reverend Sir, and Beloved Brother in Christ,

While I was lately, and with eagerness, examining a certain library abundantly supplied with recently published books, a pamphlet presented itself to me.

When I observed that it bore your name, which was already well known to me by previously published works of a high character, I thought that I must diligently read and consider it, and see whether you, who are devoted to the most accurate learning, could remove, in that work, the difficulties which have long disquieted my mind. I, therefore, read it once and again, with impartiality, as far as I could, and with candor, as you desire. But, in reading, I perceived that all my difficulties were not removed by your work, while I thought that some things, written by you, deserved to be examined in the light of truth. Accordingly, I judged it not improper to commence a friendly discussion with you concerning your treatise.

This I do, with the greater freedom and confidence, because, in the second page of your pamphlet, you say, to the encouragement of my mind, that you "have written these things, that, by those devoted to theological investigation"—among whom I willingly reckon myself—"they may be read without prejudice or acerbity of mind, duly weighed, and judged by the pure word of God." This I undertake, and pledge myself to do according to my ability; asking of you that in return, you will, with the same disposition, read my remarks, weigh them, and examine and judge them by the rule of the same Scriptures.

May God grant that we all may fully agree, in those things necessary to His glory, and to the salvation of the church. And that, in other things, if there cannot be harmony of opinions, there may at least be harmony of feelings, and that we may "keep the unity of the Spirit in the bond of peace."

With this desire, then, expressed at the beginning of our discussion, I enter on the subject itself, following in the track, which, in your writing, you have pursued before me. I will commence with your "Epistle to the Reader," and then proceed, with the divine help, to the treatise itself.

Examination of the Epistle

In your Epistle to the Reader, you lay down two fundamental principles, on which this doctrine of Predestination and Divine Grace, can and must be built. The first is "the written word of God;" the second is "the common ideas, and the principles which God has infused into the minds of men." I have no opposition to make at this point, only let this be added, that, when, on account of the darkness of our minds, and the weakness and diversity of the human judgment (which you regret), it is not possible for us to agree concerning these matters, we must recur, for definite and final decision, to that which is first and equivalent to all other things: the word of God.

Of the first principle, laid down by you, I remark that it is true; but care must be used, lest anything not in accordance with human judgment, should be attributed to God, and defended as just, on the consideration that it is declared to be unjust by corrupt human judgment; unless it can be made clear, by a conclusive argument, that it is suitably ascribed to the Deity. For, it is sufficient, for the sake of referring any action or work to God to say that He has justly performed it; though, from the antecedent, God has done this, will follow, of necessity, the consequent; therefore, it is just.

Of the second: I concede that it is true. For He is the first cause, and the cause of causes, who, from the foreseen free act of rational creatures, takes occasion to make any decree, and to establish a certain order in events; which decree He would not have made, and which order He would not have established, if the free second causes had acted otherwise. The Apostle says, "the creature was made subject to vanity, not willingly, but by reason of Him who hath subjected the same" (Rom 8:20).

To this vanity the creature would not have been subjected, if he, for whose sake it was created by God, had remained in his original integrity. The decree, in reference to sending Christ into the world, depends on the foresight of the Fall; for he is "the Lamb of God, which taketh away the sin of the world" (John 1:29). He "was made a little lower than the angels, for the suffering of death" (Heb 2:9); "as the children are partakers of flesh and blood, he also himself likewise took part of the same; that through death he might destroy him that had the power of death, that is, the devil" (Heb 2:14). He was constituted a "high priest, ordained for men, that he might offer both gifts and sacrifices for sins" (Heb 5:1).

The decrees of God, by which He ordains to punish His creatures, are universally on this principle, according to the Scriptures: "That be far from thee to do after this manner, to slay the righteous with the wicked: shall not the Judge of all the earth do right?" (Gen 18:25) "Whosoever hath sinned against me, him will I blot out of my book" (Exod 32:33).

"I said, indeed, that thy house, and the house of thy father, should walk before me forever, but now the Lord saith, be it far from me; for them that honor me I will honor, and they that despise me shall be lightly esteemed" (1 Sam 2:30). But it is not therefore to be supposed that the imposing of penalties depends on second causes. So far from it, they would put forth every effort to escape punishment, if they could do so either by reason or force.

I could wish also that the word "ordaining" were used in its proper sense: from which they seem to me to depart, who interpret it—to decree that something shall be done. For its true meaning is to establish the order of things done, not to appoint things to be done that they may be done; though it is used sometimes by the fathers in the latter sense. But then God is denied by the fathers to be the ordainer of evils. Thus says

Augustine: "God knows how to ordain, not crime, but the punishment of crimes."

Of the third: It is characteristic of a wise being to do nothing in vain. But he does something in vain, who does it not to attain some end. But God is infinitely wise. Let me caution you, then, not to extend the phrase, "to regard with indifference," farther, or to interpret it otherwise than is suitable. There is a real distinction between doing and permitting.

He who permits anything, that he may attain some end, does not regard it with indifference. From this it is clear that not to regard with indifference is not the same as to do or to make. Of this also I remind you for a certain reason. Then consider whether the phrase you use is correct. The word "prudently" seems to be too feeble to be applied to so great wisdom.

And it is not a usual form of expression to say that an action is performed "in view of a certain end," but for the sake of that end. The statement, He does not will or decree that which He cannot, is ambiguous, and not sufficiently full. It is ambiguous, because it may be understood to mean that He cannot will or decree, or that He cannot do. It is not sufficiently full, because there should be an addition, so that the statement would be this: "He does not will or decree to do or permit that which He cannot do or permit." For which reason also your conclusion is likewise imperfect, and, to the expression, "He has decreed thus to do," add, "or permit."

Decree of God

Of the fourth: The decree of God is two-fold; that of efficacious action and that of permission. Both are immutable. The creature, however free, cannot change himself by his own act, or receive any change from another, contrary to either of these decrees, and without the certain and fixed determination of the former or the latter. But it is not merely necessary that God should fix these, and not other, limits of the change, as if the creature if this was possible without the divine superintendence of the change might be able either to change himself, or to receive change from another, to such an extent that God could not bring it into order, and have occasion for the illustration of his glory. For to Him even *nothing* ought to be material for the declaration of His glory: and any change from nothing to something, produced by Him, ought to serve the same purpose.

Of the fifth: All "the judgments of God," whatever they may be, whether hidden or partly known to us, "are to be honored," and to be adorned with the praise of justice, provided, however, that it be manifest that they are the judgments of God. But under this pretense, no judgments are to be attributed to God which the Scripture does not assign to Him; much less those which are contrary to the righteousness of God revealed in the Scriptures.

Thus Augustine says: "As man becomes more like God, so the more does the damnation of perishing men move him: it moves also our Savior himself, and caused his tears, not once only, to flow. It moves also God Himself; who says:

"What, says He, shall I do to my vineyard?" (Isa 5:4) "O that my people had harkened unto me" (Ps 81:13). "I have no pleasure in the death of a sinner" (Ezek 18:23).

"But it so moves God, that He is yet delighted in the destruction of His enemies, who are refractory and refuse to repent: (Isa 1:24) For His righteousness demands that. It moves Him, I say, because they are unwilling to be saved, not because, when they are unwilling to be saved, He devotes them to just destruction. It so moves Christ, the Savior, that he shall yet, willingly, banish, from his presence, unbelievers and evil doers, and adjudge them to eternal fire. For this is demanded by the office of Judge. It so moves a pious man, that he may not utter any objection against God in reference to His various decrees, and the execrations of His righteous judgments on the obstinate. This is required by the obedience the creature owes to his Creator and Redeemer."

Concerning that objection, I may be allowed, with the leave of Augustine, to say that it is not the offspring of infirm and weak human nature, but of the refractory disposition of the Jews and of those like them, of whom the apostle speaks (Rom 9:20). It is indeed true that we, when compared with God, "are as grasshoppers," yea, and "are counted to Him as less than nothing'" (Isa 40:17, 22). But, in such exaggerations of human insignificance, we are to be careful not to do injustice to the creation of God. For man was made in the image of God, and therefore, even to God Himself, man, not any beast, is the noblest creature, with whom, as the wisdom of God declares, are His delights (Prov 8:31).

Of the sixth: The concurrence of God with second causes to perform any act, or produce any work, is two-fold, of the general, and the special aid of His grace. It is most certain that nothing good can be performed by any rational creature without this special aid of His grace. But whether it is the province of the divine will, absolutely willing it, to communicate this gracious aid, and by this communication, to absolutely work good in us, is in controversy among theologians. This is not improperly so, since the word absolutely cannot be found in the Scriptures, and it has not yet been proved that its equivalent is found in the Scriptures.

Of the seventh: So also it is certain that "no evil can be avoided if God does not prevent it." But there is dispute concerning the mode of prevention; whether it is by the omnipotent action of the Deity operating on the human will according to the mode of nature, from which there exists a necessity of prevention, or by such an action as operates on the will, according to the mode of the will as respects its freedom, from which the certainty of prevention exists.

Of the eighth: It cannot be concluded from an event that God has willed something, but we may know either this fact, that He was unwilling to hinder an event which He foresaw would occur. Otherwise the distinction, which exists between the action and the permission of God, is destroyed. For some things occur because God produces them but others, because He permits them to occur, according to Augustine and to truth itself. But to will that anything should occur, and to be unwilling to prevent its occurrence, are not the same things. For, in the former case, the event is resolved into the will of God as its first and special cause. In the latter, it is resolved affirmatively into a second cause, and negatively into the divine will, which has not prevented it, which prevention also is produced either by power according to the mode of nature, or by persuasion according to the mode of free will. But concerning permission and prevention we shall treat more fully hereafter in their own place.

Divine Gifts and Effects

Of the ninth: But let us examine this idea; "to be able to perform," "to will to do," and "actually to do," are divine gifts and effects on men. But there should be this additional remark, that God gives to no one the power of doing right, unless He is ready also to give the will and the act itself, that is, by the further aid of grace, to concur with man in willing and in actually doing that good, for which He has received sufficient strength, unless the man on his part may interpose, or, as the schoolmen say, may have interposed some obstacle.

"For unto everyone that hath shall be given; but from him that hath not shall be taken away even that which he hath" (Matt 25:29). Were this not so, the power would have been given in vain. But the all-wise God doth nothing in vain. Thus He gave to Adam the faculty of observing the law which He had enacted, and He was prepared to give him whatever else was needed, in addition to that faculty, for actual obedience, namely, both to will and to do, unless Adam willingly and by voluntary motion turned himself away from God, and from His grace. I see here a labyrinth which I will not now enter, because I should not be permitted to make my egress from it, except by the thread and guidance of an accurate explication of the mode of the concurrence of God with man in the performance of any good thing; which explication does not belong to this place, or, as I indeed, acknowledge, to my abilities.

Of the tenth: That "God presides over the whole world, and all things created by Himself, and administers and governs all and each of them" is certain. But this is not only in justice, but also in mercy, even so far as He, in His infinite wisdom, knows what place ought to be assigned to each.

But, indeed, do all those axioms seem to you to be natural and common notions. They, indeed, belong to nature, as it was when it comes from the hand of its Creator, surely not to it, as it has been darkened by sin. For to few among men is it given to know and understand those things. The whole troop of Pelagians and Semi-Pelagians in the church itself, do not know them. What the opinion of many of the Greek and Latin philosophers was concerning most of them, is apparent from an expression used by not one of them only: "What we are, is given to us by the Gods; what of good we are, we have from ourselves." To this notorious falsity, Augustine in more than one passage, sharply opposes himself.

On these principles in part, as a foundation, you build up a doctrine of Predestination, which is, indeed, beset with difficulties. This is caused by the fact, that men do not fear to add to the Scriptures, whatever they think proper, and are accustomed to attribute as much as possible to their own conceptions, which they style natural ideas. I cannot but praise your effort. For light ought, by all means, to be thrown upon truth by all, to the utmost of their ability. Calumnies and accusations, by which the truth is assailed and beset, are to be refuted. Minds, embittered against it, are not only to be softened and soothed, but also, to be induced to embrace it.

It cannot be made an objection against you, that you adduce the opinions of the ancient theologians, especially those whom you quote, some caution being observed, lest we go too far in that direction. For the Fathers are themselves also liable to diverse interpretations, and, indeed, more than the divine and inspired writers, as they were endued with knowledge of the truth, which was less in degree and in clearness, and they could express the thoughts of their minds only with less accuracy and fitness. When I consider this, I doubt whether they have consulted the best interests of the church, who have thought that, in this age, the opinions of the Fathers are to be considered by them as authority in matters of religion. But the die is cast, and we must advance, whithersoever the fates of the Church bear us.

In reference to your declaration, that you present the testimony of the ancient doctors and schoolmen, for the sake of exhibiting an agreement in that part of doctrine, I do not see how that is so. For I am quite persuaded that nothing can be thought of, more adapted to bring that whole doctrine of Predestination and the grace of God into confusion, and to overwhelm it with darkness, than the effort on the part of anyone to bring forward and unite together all the opinions of the Fathers and the schoolmen, in reference to it. But I desire that you may not at once pronounce him an unjust estimator or judge, who dares to assert that the dogmas, which you present in this treatise, are found neither in the Scriptures nor in the Fathers. For if you shall, after reasons have been adduced by that estimator, arbiter or judge, be able to sustain your statement, you will find him not struggling against it, with an unfair and obstinate mind, but ready to yield to what is proved to be the truth with becoming equanimity. Nor will it be an easier matter to persuade me that the dogmas of which you here treat, are, in that same mode and sense, proposed and set forth in all the Reformed Churches. I say this, lest you should think that you can bear down one thinking differently by the prejudgment of those churches.

Examination of the Treatise

I come now to the treatise itself, which I will examine with somewhat more care and diligence. You will not complain if, in some places, I may with the closest criticism also subject some of the nicer points to the most rigid scrutiny. For who would not consent that a serious and solid discussion should be, as it were, spiced by a friendly diversity and a pleasant contest concerning the more accurate handling of a subject.

You begin, and rightly so, with a definition of Predestination.[1] But that definition does not seem to be adapted to the Predestination set forth in the Scriptures. For the Predestination of which the Scriptures treat, is of men in their relation as sinners. It is made in Christ; it is to blessings which concern, not this animal life, but the spiritual life, of which a part also are communicated in this animal life, as is clearly evident from Eph 1, where, among the spiritual blessings to which we have been predestinated in Christ are enumerated "adoption of children," (verse 5), "redemption through his blood, the forgiveness of sins," (verse 7), "having made known unto us the mystery of his will," (verse 9), which blessings are given to the predestinated in this life. The apostle well say "the life, which I now live in the flesh, I live by the faith of the Son of God," (Gal 2:20); signifying that he, in this animal life, was a partaker of spiritual gifts, and from them lived a spiritual life. But perhaps you did not wish to give an accurate definition, but only by some description to give us an idea of Predestination. I may concede this, yet in that description there seem to be many things which ought to be noticed.

For the word "counsel," by which you have desired to explain one kind of Predestination is not a kind of Predestination, but pertains to its efficient cause; for a decree is made by "counsel," which decree can be fitly considered a kind of Predestination—if indeed counsel can be attributed to God, by which He may decree anything, as in the Scripture—e.g. Acts 4:28, and Eph. 1:11. This I say, is apparent from the passages quoted. For in the former (Acts 4:28), "counsel" is said to determine before or predestinate things to be done; in the latter (Eph 1:11), it is said that God "worketh all things," even institutes Predestination after the counsel of His own will.

There is in this life an equality of the pious and the wicked as to external blessings, but they are to be considered generally. For in individual cases there is a great difference both among the pious and the wicked, and so great indeed is it that, to those, who are dissatisfied with that inequality, it may need a defense by an argument for reducing it,

---

1. "Predestination is the counsel of God touching the last end or estate of man out of this temporal or natural life." William Perkins, *The Works of That Famous and Worthy Minister of Christ in the Universitie (sic) of Cambridge, Mr. William Perkins*: II: 606.

hereafter, to an equality. Indeed it is said of the pious and the faithful, "if in this life, only, we have hope in Christ, we are, of all men, most miserable" (1 Cor 15:19).

I approve what you say concerning "the final cause of Predestination," when rightly understood. That is, if a declaration of the glory of God through mercy and justice is attributed to Predestination, so long as it is the foreordination of sinners who shall believe in Christ to eternal life, and on the contrary, the predamnation of sinners who shall persevere in sins to eternal death; who shall believe, through the gracious gift of God, and who shall persevere in sins through their own wickedness and the just desertion of God. But if you think that God, from eternity, without any pre-existence of sin, in His prescience, determined to illustrate His own glory by mercy and punitive justice, and, that He might be able to secure this object, decreed to create man good but mutable, and ordained farther that he should Fall, that in this way there might be a place for that decree, I say that such an opinion cannot, in my judgment, be established by any passage of the word of God.

That this may be made plainer, a few things must be said concerning the glory of God and the modes of its manifestation. No one can doubt that God, since He is the first and Supreme Efficient Cause of all His own acts and works, and the single and sole cause of many of them, has always the manifestation of His own perfection, that is, His own glory, proposed to Himself, as His chief and highest object. For the first and supreme cause is moved to produce any effect, by nothing, out of itself otherwise it would not be the first and supreme cause. Therefore, not only the act of Predestination, but also every other divine act has "the illustration of the glory of God" as its final cause. Now it is equally certain and known to all, who have even approached the threshold of sacred letters, that the manifestation of the divine perfection and the illustration of his glory consists in the unfolding of His essential attributes by acts and works comparable to them. But an inquiry is necessary concerning those attributes, by the unfolding of which He determined to illustrate His own glory, first, by which, in the second place, and so on, by successive steps.

It is certain that He could not, first of all, have done this by means of mercy and punitive justice. For the former could be exercised only towards the miserable, the latter only towards sinners. But since, first of all, the external action of God both was and must be taken up, so to speak, with nothing, it is therefore evident that goodness, wisdom, and omnipotence were, first of all, to be unfolded, and that by them the glory of God was to be illustrated. These, therefore, were unfolded in the creation, by which God appeared to be supremely good and wise, and omnipotent.

But, as God made all His creatures with this difference, that some were capable of nothing more than they were at their creation, and others were capable of greater perfection, He was concerned, as to the former, only with their preservation and government, accomplished by goodness, wisdom and power of the same kind and measure, since preservation is only a continuance of creation, as the latter is the beginning of the former.

Beyond Natural Condition

And government may not go beyond the natural condition of the creatures, unless when it seems good to God to use them, for the sake of men for supernatural purposes, as in the bread and wine used, in the Lord's Supper, to signify and seal unto us the communion of the body and the blood of Christ. As to the latter, which He made capable of greater perfection, as angels and men, the same attributes were to be unfolded, but in a far greater measure. In the former case, the good communicated is limited, as each creature receives that which is appropriate to itself, according to the diversity of their natures, but, in the latter, there is a communication of supreme and infinite good, which is God, in the union with whom consists the happiness of rational creatures.

Reason demanded that this communication should be made contrary to justice, wherefore He gave a law to His creatures, obedience to which was made the condition on which that communication should be made. Therefore, this was the first decree concerning the final cause of rational creatures, and the glory of God to be illustrated by justice and the highest goodness—highest as to the good to be communicated, not absolutely; by goodness joined to justice, in the case of those who should be made partakers of the highest good, through steadfastness in the truth; by punitive justice, in the case of those who should make themselves unworthy of it by their disobedience.

Then we see that justice, rewarding obedience, which was its office, according to the gracious promise of God, and punishing disobedience as it deserves, according to the just threatenings of God, holds the first place. In the former case, justice joined to goodness, in the latter, puni-tive justice opposed to the gracious communication of the highest good, without any mention of mercy, unless it may be considered as preserving the creature from possible misery, which could, by its own fault, Fall into misery; as mercy is not considered when it is predetermined by the decree of Predestination.

That decree was peremptory in respect to the Fallen angels, as in accordance with it, they are condemned: wherefore the Predestination and reprobation of angels was comprehended in this. But what grace was prepared for the former in Predestination and was denied to the latter in Reprobation, and in what respects, I do not now argue. But it was not peremptory in reference to men, whom God did not decree to treat according to that highest rigor of the law, but in the salvation of whom He decreed to exhibit all His goodness, which Jehovah showed to Moses in these, His attributes, "The Lord, Lord God, merciful and gracious, long-suffering, and abundant in goodness and truth." (Exod 26:6) Therefore, the Predestination and Reprobation of men were not considered in that decree.

For since Adam sinned, and in him all who were to be his descen-dants by natural propagation, all would have been devoted to eternal condemnation without hope of pardon. For the decree of Predestination and Reprobation is peremptory. So far, then, no Predestination of men unto life, and no reprobation unto death had any place. And since there could be no Predestination and Reprobation, except in accordance with those attributes by which men are at once saved or damned but the pre-destinated may be saved at once by mercy, and the reprobate may be damned at once by justice opposed to that mercy it follows that there was no fixed Predestination and reprobation of men, in reference to whom there could be no place for mercy and justice opposed to it.

But there could be no place for them in reference to men who were not miserable, and not sinners. Predestination includes the means by which the predestinated will certainly and infallibly come to salvation, and Reprobation includes the denial of those same means, but those means are the remission of sins and the renewing of the Holy Ghost, and its perpetual assistance even to the end, which are necessary and communicable to none, except sinners. I conclude that there was no Predestination and Reprobation in reference to men, in whose case these means were neither necessary nor communicable.

Finally, since God can love no sinner unto salvation, unless he is reconciled to Himself in Christ, hence it is, that there could be no place for Predestination, except in Christ. And since Christ was ordained and given for sinners, it is certain that Predestination and its opposite, Reprobation, could have no place before human sin—its existence as foreseen by God—and the appointment of Christ as Mediator, and indeed his performance, in the prescience of God, of the functions of the office of Mediator, which pertains to reconciliation. Nor does it follow from this that God either made man with an uncertain design, or failed of the end at which He aimed. For He prescribed to Himself, both in the act of creation, and in that of glorification, and its opposite, condemnation, the illustration of His own glory as an end. And He obtained it by goodness, wisdom and power in creation. He obtained it in a greater measure, and joined with justice in glorification and condemnation.

Mode of Illustrating

But, though the mode of illustrating His glory by mercy, which is a certain method of communicating goodness and the approach of the same to a miserable creature, and by justice, opposed to that mercy, could have no place except from the occasion of human sin, yet the decree of God is not, therefore, dependent on the man. For He foresaw from eternity what would be in the future, and in ordaining, concerning the future, to that end. He freely arranged it according to His own choice, not compelled by any necessity as if He could not, in some other way, have secured glory to Himself from the sin of man. But that the glory of God does not consist merely in the illustration of mercy and, its opposite justice, is evident from the fact that, then, He would not have obtained glory from the act of creation, nor from the Predestination and reprobation of angels. It is to be understood, that mercy is not an essential attribute of the Deity distinct from goodness itself, as in the womb and the offspring of goodness; indeed, it is goodness itself extending to the sinful creature and to misery.

It can for this reason be said in simple terms that in all His eternal acts, God determined to declare His own glory by goodness, wisdom, and omnipotence, with the addition of justice when equity demanded it at the prescription of wisdom. But also that He adapted the mode to the state, or rather to the change of the object, in reference to which He had determined to unfold those attributes. In reference to this thing

Tertullian says, in a beautiful and erudite manner, "God must, of necessity use all things in reference to all being, He must have as many feelings, as there are causes of them; anger for the wicked. and wrath for the ungrateful, and jealousy for the proud, and whatever else would not be for the advantage of the evil; so also, mercy for the erring, and patience for those not yet repentant, and honor for the deserving, and whatever is necessary for the good. All these feelings He has in His own mode, in which it is fit that He should feel them, just as man has the same, equally after his own manner."[2]

Predestination does not arise merely from goodness simply considered, the province of which is, indeed, to communicate itself to the creature. It is also from that mode of mercy, which goes out from that goodness to the miserable to remove their misery, of grace in Christ, which goes out from it to sinners to pardon their sins, of patience and long-suffering, going forth from the same goodness towards those who, for a long time, struggle against it, and do not at once obey the call, thus prolonging the delay of conversion. So also reprobation is not merely fixed by justice, the opposite of that goodness, simply considered, but by justice tempered by some mercy and patience. For God "endured with much long-suffering the vessels of wrath fitted for destruction" (Rom 9:22).

From these things, thus considered, I may be allowed, with your kind permission, to conclude that Predestination has not been sufficiently well defined or described by you. If anyone is inclined to consider the series and order of the objects of the knowledge and the will of God, he will be more and more confirmed in the truth of the things briefly set forth by me.

The passage from Augustine, is in agreement with these views, if one wishes to gather his complete opinion from other passages. Fulgentius and Gregory most clearly support me in the passages quoted by you. For, if the act of Predestination is the preparation for the remission of sins or the punishment of the same, then it is certain that there is place for Predestination only in reference to sinners. If also the act of Predestination is the pre-election of some who are to be redeemed from their depravity, and the leaving of others in their depravity, from this also it is evident that Predestination has to do with men considered as sinners. That sentiment of the schoolmen agrees most fully with the

2. Tertullian, *Adversus Marcion*, Lib. 2, Cap 16.

same views. For it openly declares that Predestination depends on the foresight of the Fall, when they say that the perfection and goodness of God, who predestinates, is represented by the mode of mercy and punitive justice, which mode, as I have now frequently said, can have place only in reference to sinners.

If anyone acknowledges that this is indeed true, but says that God has arranged this, as an occasion for Himself, by decreeing that man should Fall, and by carrying forward that decree to its end or limit, we ask the proof of that assertion, which, in my judgment, he will be unable to give. For that sentiment is at variance with the justice of God, as it makes God the author of sin, and introduces an inevitable necessity for sin. This I will prove. For if that decree existed, man could not abstain from sin, otherwise the decree would have been made in vain, which is an impious supposition.

For "the counsel of the Lord standeth forever" (Ps 33:11). We remark also that the human will would have been circumscribed and determined by that decree, so that it could not turn itself except in one direction, in which there would be sin. By that act its freedom would be lost, because it would move the will, not according to the mode of free will, but according to the mode of nature. Such an act it could not resist, nor would there be any volition in that direction, indeed, there would not be the power to put forth that volition on account of the determination of the decree.

Consider also, that, by that sentiment, mercy and justice are considered as means resulting from Predestination, while they are the primary causes of Predestination, as is evident from the fact that the final cause of Predestination may be resolved into the manifestation of mercy and justice.

Creation and Fall of Man

Here, observe, also, in what way you make the creation and the Fall of man the means in common lying at the foundation of the counsel, or rather the decree of Predestination, I think, indeed, that both the creation, and the Fall preceded every external act of Predestination, as also the decree concerning the creation of man, and the permission of his Fall preceded, in the Divine mind, the decree of Predestination. I think, also, that I have partly proved this, in my preceding remarks. But it will be well to look at this with a little more diligence.

Every act, which has reference to an object, is posterior in nature, to its object. It is called an object relatively. Therefore, it has an absolute existence prior to the existence of its relation to the act. The object, then, exists in itself, before it can be under the influence of the act which tends towards it. But man is the object of Predestination. Therefore, man is prior to the act of Predestination. But man is what he is by creation. Therefore, creation is prior to Predestination, that is, in the divine mind, or the decree concerning the creation of man is prior to the decree of Predestination, and the act of creation is prior to the execution of the decree of Predestination. If anyone should reply that God, in the internal act of Predestination, is employed with man considered as not created, but as to be made, I answer that this could neither take place, nor be so understood by a mind judging rightly.

For Predestination is a decree, not only to illustrate the divine glory, but to illustrate it in man, by the mode of mercy and justice. From this, it follows that man must also exist in the divine mind before the act of Predestination, and the Fall of man must itself, also, be previously foreseen. The attributes of God, by which creation is affected, are, therefore, considered as prior, in the divine nature, to those in which Predestination originates. Goodness, simply considered, wisdom, and power, operating upon nothing, are, therefore, prior to mercy and punitive justice. Add, also, that since Predestination originates, on the one hand, in mercy, and on the other, in justice, in the former case having reference to salvation, in the latter to damnation, it cannot be that any means exist pertaining, in common, to the execution of election and of reprobation. For they are provided neither in mercy nor in justice.

There exists, then, no means of Predestination, common to both parts of the decree. If you wished to define the creation of man that should have been done with greater accuracy. But if you wished only to describe it, there is yet, in that description, something which I may note. "Man was made mutable," as was demanded by the very condition of that nothing from which he was made, and of the creature itself, which neither could nor ought to be raised, by creation, to the state of the Creator, which is immutability. But he was made mutable in such a sense that actual change from good to evil would follow that possible mutability, only by the voluntary and free act of man.

But the act of the creature does not remain free when it is so determined in one direction, that, if that determination continues, there cannot but be a change.

But of the "permission of the Fall," we must treat at somewhat greater length: for very much depends on this for the expediting of this whole matter. It is certain that God can by the act of His own absolute power prevent all things whatever, which can be done by the creature, and it is equally certain that He is not absolutely under obligation to any one to hinder him from evil. But He cannot, in His justice, do all that He can in His absolute power. He cannot, in His justice (or righteousness), forget the "work and labor of love" of the pious (Heb 6:10). The absolute power of God is limited by the decree of God, by which He determined to do anything in a particular direction. And though God is not absolutely under obligation to anyone, He can yet obligate Himself by His own act, as, for instance, by a promise, or by requiring some act from man. He is obligated to perform what He promises, for He owes to Himself the immutability of His own truth, whether He has promised it absolutely or conditionally.

By requiring an act, He places Himself under obligation to give ability and the strength without which that act cannot be performed; otherwise, He would reap where He had not sown. It is plain, from these positions, that God, since He conceded the freedom of the will, and the use of that freedom, ought not, and indeed could not, prevent the Fall in any mode which would infringe on the use of that freedom; and farther, that He was not obligated to prevent it in any other way than by the bestowment of the ability which should be necessary and sufficient to the avoidance of the Fall. Permission is not, therefore, a "cessation from the act of illuminating and that of inclining" to such an extent that, without those acts, a man could not avoid sin.

Justly and Deservedly Charged

For, in that case, the fault could be justly and deservedly charged upon God, who would be the cause of sin, by way of removing or not bestowing that which is necessary for the performance of an act which Himself has prescribed by His own law. From which it also follows that the law is unjust, as it is not in proportion to the strength of the creature on which it is imposed, whether that deficiency of strength arises from the nonbestowal or the removal of it before any fault has been committed by the creature.

Permission is, indeed, a cessation of the act of hindrance, but that cessation is to be so explained that it may not be reduced to an efficient cause of sin, either directly, or by way of the denial or removal of that, without which sin cannot be avoided. In reference to this permission, if it is fitly explained, it can be doubtless said that "God not only foreknows it, but He even wills it by an act of volition" affirmatively and immediately directed to the permission itself, not to that which is permitted. As it cannot be said concerning this, that God wills that it should not be done, for He permits it, and not unwillingly, so, also, it cannot be truly said that God wills it. For permission is an act intermediate between volition and nolition, the will being inactive.

But the cause, in view of which He permits sin, is to be found not only in the consequent, but in the antecedent. In the antecedent, because God constituted man so that he might have a free will, and might, according to the freedom of his will, either accord obedience or refuse it. He could not rescind this constitution, which Himself had established, in view of His own immutability, as Tertullian clearly shows, in his argument against Marcion[3]. In the consequent, because He saw that He could use sin as an occasion for demonstrating the glory of His own grace and justice. But this consequent does not naturally result from that sin. From this, it follows that even from the highest evil (if there be any highest), evil only, could result per se, or there would be an injury to the divine majesty, opposed to the divine good; but that consequent is an incidental result of sin, because God knows and wills to elicit, by His wisdom, goodness and power, His own glory from it, as light from darkness.

As, then, evil is not good, per se, so it is not absolutely good that evil should occur. For if this is true, then God not only permits it, but is its author and effector. But it is incidentally good that evil should occur, in view of that wisdom, goodness, and power of God, of which I have spoken, by which God takes from sin the material for illustrating his own glory. Therefore, sin is not, in this respect, the means per se, for illustrating the glory of God, but only the occasion not made for this purpose, nor adapted to it by its own nature, but seized by God and used in this direction with wonderful skill, and praiseworthy perversion.

---

3 Tertullian, *Against Marcion*, Lib. 2, Cap. 5, 6, and 7.

No absolute good in the universe would be prevented, even if God should prevent evil, provided that prevention should not be affected in a manner not adapted to the primitive constitution of man. And God is free to prevent sin, but in a way not at variance with the freedom of the will. Any other method of prevention would be absolutely contrary to the good of the universe, inasmuch as one good of the universe consists even in this, that there should be a creature endued with free will, and that the use of his own free will should be conceded to the creature without any divine interference. But if the existence of evil or sin should absolutely contribute to the good and the perfection of the universe, then God ought not only not to hinder sin, but even to promote it, else He would fail in His duty to His own work, and do injury to His own perfection. I admit that, without the existence of sin, there would not be that place for the patience of the martyrs, or for the sacrifice of Christ; but the patience of the martyrs and the sacrifice of Christ are not necessary results of the existence of sin.

Indeed we shall see, by considering the natural effect of sin, that from it would result impatience in those who are afflicted, and by it the wrath of God would be kindled. That not only could, but in fact, would, prevent the bestowment of any good, even the least, and much more that of his Son, unless God should be, at the same time, merciful, and could, in His wisdom, find a way by which He might prevent the natural effect of sin, and using sin as the occasion, might promote other effects, contrary to the very nature of sin.

The passages cited from Augustine and Gregory, are not only not opposed to, but actually in favor of this opinion. For they do not say that it would have been good absolutely that evils should occur, but that God judged it better to bring good out of evils than to prevent them; thus comparing two acts of the Deity, and esteeming the one better than the other. I may be allowed to observe, in reference to the remark of Gregory, that he is not sufficiently accurate, when he compares the evils we suffer on account of sins with the blessing of redemption as something greater. For he ought to compare our sins and faults, not the evils we suffer on their account, with the blessing of redemption. If he had done this, and had carefully considered the words of the apostle, "We are not to do evil that good may come," (Rom 3:8), he would have judged otherwise, or, at least, would have expressed his views more fitly, without making such a transition, and without substituting the punishment of sin for sin itself. It is indeed right, for men and for any believer, to say with entire confidence that there can be no redemption so excellent and no method of redemption so glorious that, for the sake of obtaining either, any sin, however small, is to be committed.

For the Redeemer "was manifested that he might destroy the works of the devil," (1 John 3:8) i.e., sins; they are not, therefore, to be committed in order that the Son of God, the Redeemer, might come. For that circular form of reasoning, the Son of God came that he might destroy the works of the devil, and sin was committed that it might be destroyed by the Son, is not only contrary to the Scriptures, but also hostile to all truth, as it leads infinitely astray.

Proved That the Fall

From this it is also easily proved that the Fall cannot be called a happy transgression, except by a catachrestic hyperbole, which, while it may be adapted to declamations, panegyric orations, and rhetorical embellishments, should be far removed from the solid investigation of truth. To these is always to be added the remark, which I have made, frequently and with reiteration, that redemption could not have resulted from transgression, except as the latter might afford an occasion for it, by the arrangement of God, in accordance with His will, that the transgression should be expiated, and washed away by a Redeemer of such character and dignity.

But the distinction which you make between "the permission of the Fall" and "the permitted Fall" seems to me to be of no force. For the permission of the Fall is not less by the Divine arrangement than the permitted Fall. For God ordained His own permission for a certain end. But consider whether it is not absurd to distinguish between "the permission of the Fall" and "the permitted Fall." In the latter case, I speak of the Fall, not considered in that it is a Fall, but in that it is a permitted Fall: as you must, of necessity, consider, when you style it "the means of the decree," which appellation is not appropriate to the Fall except on account of the adjunct "permitted."

For not the Fall but the permission of the Fall, tended to the glory of God; not the act of many which is the Fall, but the act of God, which is permission, having immediate reference to that act of man according to the prescript of the Divine arrangement, tended to His glory. But I acknowledge that permission is the means of the decree, not of

Predestination, but of providence, as the latter is distinguished from the former. I speak now of providence, as governing and administrative, which is not only not prior, in nature and order, to Predestination, but is also the cause of the mission of the Son as the Redeemer, who is our head, in whom Predestination is made, as the apostle teaches (Eph 1:3–6).

But how can it be true that the Fall is permitted by God, and yet that "it would not have occurred unless God had willed it"? I wish that it might be explained how God could, at once, will that the Fall should occur, and permit the same; how God could be concerned, by His volition, with the Fall both mediately and immediately: mediately by willing the permission, and immediately by willing the Fall itself. I wish also that these things may be harmonized, how the Fall could occur by the will of God, and yet the will of God not be the cause of the Fall, which is contrary to the express declaration of God's word, "Our God is in the heavens; He hath done whatever He pleased" (Ps 115:3).

Also, in what way could God will the Fall, and yet be "a God that hath no pleasure in wickedness" (Ps 5:4), since the Fall was wickedness. The distinctions which are presented are not sufficient to untie the knot, as I shall show in the case of each of them separately. For they distinguish between the Fall and the event of the Fall; between the will of open intimation and that of His good-pleasure, revealed or hidden; between the Fall as it was sin, and as it was the means of illustrating the divine glory.

They say that God willed that the Fall should occur, but did not will the Fall; that He willed the Fall according to His good pleasure and His hidden will, not according to His will, of open intimation, revealed and approving that He willed the Fall, not as it was sin, but as it was the means of illustrating His own glory.

The first distinction is verbal, and not real. He, who willed that the Fall should occur, willed also the Fall. He who willed that the Fall should occur, willed the event of the Fall, and He, who willed the event of the Fall, willed the Fall. For the event of the Fall is the Fall, as the event of an action is the action itself. But if He willed the Fall, He was the cause of the Fall. For "He hath done whatsoever He pleased" (Ps 115:3). If anyone replies, that He willed that the Fall should occur by the act of another, not by His own act, I answer it could not be that God should will that the Fall should occur by the act of another, and not by His own act. For it would not happen by the act of another, unless he should interpose with His own act, and, indeed, with an act, such that, from it, the act of another should necessarily exist. Otherwise that which He wished should occur by the act of another, would not be effected or occur by that act of another. The force of the argument is not increased: whether God willed that the Fall should occur, mediately, by the act of another, or, immediately, by His own act.

These are mediately connected, the act of God and the act of another, that is of man, or the Fall. The Fall proceeded from the act of man, but that depends of necessity on the act of God; otherwise it could happen that the act of another should not be performed, and thus it could happen that the Fall should not occur, which, nevertheless, God willed should occur. It is not, therefore, denied that God is the cause of the Fall, except immediately; it is conceded that He is so, mediately.

Declaration of Anyone

No one, indeed, ever wished to deduce from the declaration of anyone, that God is the immediate cause of the sin perpetrated by man, for he would deduce a contradiction in terms, as they say in the schools, unless, indeed, the subject might be the general concurrence of God with man, in producing an act which cannot be produced by man without sin. The distinction of the will into that of hidden and revealed, while it may have place elsewhere, cannot avail here. For the hidden will of God is said to be efficacious; but if, in its exercise, God willed that the Fall should occur, it is certainly a necessary conclusion, also, that He effected the Fall, that is, He must be the cause of the Fall; for whatever God wills, even by His hidden will, the same, also, He does both in heaven and on the earth; and no one can resist His will, namely, that which is hidden.

But I may remark concerning that distinction in the will, that I think that it may be said, that neither of these can be so contrary, or opposed to the other, that God, by one, wills that to be done, which, by the other, He wills not to be done, and vice versa. God wills by His revealed and approving will, that man should not Fall, it cannot, therefore, be true that God, by any will, considered in any way whatever, can will that man should Fall. For though there may be distinction in the will of God, yet no contradiction can exist in it. But it is a contradiction, if God, by any act of His own will, should tend towards an object, and at the same time towards its contrary.

The third distinction, in which it is said that God wills sin, not as such, but as the means of illustrating His own glory, defends God from the charge of efficiency in sin no more than the two preceding. For that assertion remains true: God doeth whatsoever He wills, but He wills sin, therefore, He effects sin, not indeed as it is such, but as it is the means of illustrating His own glory. But if God effects sin, as it is the means to such an end, it cannot be effected, unless man commits sin as such. For sin cannot be made a means, unless it is committed.

There exists, indeed, that distinction of sin into separate and diverse respects, not really, and in fact, but in the mode of considering it. But that we may make that distinction correctly, as it is indeed of some use, it must be said that God permits sin as such, but for this reason, because He had the knowledge and the power to make it the means, yea, rather, to use it as the means of illustrating His own glory. So that the consideration of sin as such was presented to the Divine permission, the permission itself being, in the mean time, caused both by the consideration that the sin could be the means of illustrating the Divine glory, and by the arrangement that the sin, permitted, should be, in fact, the means for illustrating that same glory.

The simile you present of the mutable decaying house is not applicable for many reasons. For in the first place, in its fall, the house is passive; but in the Fall of man he is active, for he sins. Secondly, that house is, not only mutable, that is, capable of decay, but subject to decay; but man, though capable of sinning, was still not subject to sin. Thirdly, that house could not stand if attacked by the winds; but man could preserve his position, even though tempted by Satan. Fourthly, the necessary props were not placed under that house; but man received strength from God, sufficient for steadfastness against the onset of Satan, and was supported by the assistance of divinity itself. Fifthly, the builder anticipated the ruin of the house, and in part willed it, because he was unwilling to prevent the Fall when he could have done it; God, indeed, foresaw sin, but He did not will it. Indeed, He endeavored to prevent it by precept and the bestowment of grace, necessary and sufficient for the avoidance of sin.

Farther than this, He must not prevent, lest He should destroy the constitution which He had established. The ideas, I will the ruin, and I will it, so far as I will not to prevent it, do not agree. For the ruin and the permission of the ruin cannot be at the same time the immediate object of the will. For God cannot be concerned in the Fall, at the same time, both by an affirmative and by a negative act of the will. The act of willing the Fall was affirmative, the act of not willing to prevent is negative, intermediate between two opposite affirmative acts, namely, between the act of volition and that of nolition concerning the Fall. It is altogether true, that so much causality or efficiency is to be attributed to the builder as there is of will, directed to the ruin of the house, attributed to him.

Let us now consider the application of the similitude. God left Adam to himself, but yet Adam was not deserted by God; for He placed under him as it were a triple prop, lest he might sin or Fall. He gave him a precept, that he might, in obedience, not choose to sin. He added a threat that he might fear to sin on account of the annexed and following punishment; He bestowed grace that he might be able in fact to fulfill the precept, and avoid the threatened punishment. It may be lawful, also, to call the promise, which was placed in opposition to the threatening, and which was sealed by the symbol of the tree of life, a fourth prop. The reason, in view of which, God left man to himself, was not that his ability might be tested by temptation, for from the actual occurrence of the Fall, his inability to stand could be neither proved nor disproved. But because it was suitable that there should be such a trial of the obedience of him whom God had made the ruler of his own will, the lord and the head of his own voluntary sets.

Permission Instituted

Nor was permission instituted to this end, that it might be seen what the creature could do, if the Divine aid and government over him should cease for a time, both because the Divine aid and government was not deficient, and because it was already certain that man could do nothing without the government and general aid of God, and nothing good without the special aid of His grace.

That "God was not the cause of that defection" is a theological axiom. But you, by removing those acts, do not remove the cause of the defection from the Deity. For God can be regarded as the cause of sin, either by affirmative or negative acts. You, indeed, take from Him the affirmative acts, namely, the inclining of the mind to sin, the infusion of wickedness, and the deprivation of the gift, already bestowed, but you attributed to Him a negative act, the denial or non-bestowal of strengthening grace. If this strengthening grace was necessary to the avoidance of sin, then, by that act of denial, God became the Author of sin and of Adam's Fall. But if you attribute the denial or the non-bestowal of strengthening grace to God, not absolutely, but on account of the transgression of Adam, because he did not seek the Divine aid, I approve what you say, if you concede that it was in the power of Adam to seek that aid. Otherwise it was denied to him to seek that also, and so we go on without end.

You say: "There are two parts or species of Predestination, the decree of Election and that of Reprobation," concerning which it must be stated that one cannot exist without the other, and that, one being supposed, the other must be also. This is signified by the word election, otherwise, Predestination may be considered per se and without an opposite, and so all men universally would be predestinated unto life. In that case, there would be no election, which includes the idea of reprobation, as united to it by a necessary consequence and copula. Election and Reprobation are opposed to each other both affirmatively and negatively. Negatively, because election refers to the act of the will by which grace and glory are conferred, reprobation, that by which they are not conferred.

Affirmatively, since reprobation refers to the act of the will, which inflicts punishment on account of sin.

It is worthy of consideration that God, both in the decree of Election and in that of Reprobation, was concerned with men considered as sinners. For the grace provided by election or Predestination, is the grace of the remission of sins, and the renewal of the Holy Ghost; and the glory He has prepared by the same decree, is out of the ignominy to which man was liable on account of sin. Reprobation, also, is a denial of that grace and a preparation of the punishment due to sin, not in that it was due, but that it was, through mercy, not taken away.

Isidorus and Angelomus, quoted by you, express this condition of the object both of Election and Reprobation. The former, when he says— "the reprobate are left, and predestinated to death," the latter, when he says—of "the unbelieving people some are predestinated to everlasting freedom, but others are left in their own impiety, and condemned to perpetual death by occult dispensation, and occult judgment."

Your definition of Election is obscure from the want of some word. It seems that the phrase to be illustrated ought to have been added, thus: "The decree of Election is that by which God destines certain men to

His glorious grace to be illustrated in their salvation and heavenly life, obtained through Christ," otherwise the phraseology is not sufficiently complete.

But the definition, even when completed, in that way, seems to me to have been, ineptly arranged, as the parts are not arranged according to their mutual relations. For "salvation" and "heavenly life" hold the relation of the material prepared for the decree of election; "certain men" hold the place of the object or subject for which that salvation is prepared; the "illustration of His glorious grace" is the end of election; "Christ" is here made the means of obtaining that salvation and life. The order of all these in the definition according to their mutual relations, ought to be: "The decree of election is that, by which God destined certain men to salvation and heavenly life, to be obtained through Christ, to the praise of His glorious grace."

In this definition, however, Christ does not seem to me to obtain that place he deserves, and which the Apostle assigns to him. For Christ according to the Apostle is not only the means by which the salvation, already prepared by election, but, so to speak, is the meritorious cause, in respect to which the election was made, and on whose account that grace was prepared. For the apostle says that we are chosen in Christ (Eph 1:4), as in a mediator, in whose blood salvation and life is obtained for us, and as in our "head," (Eph. 1:22) from whom those blessings flow to us.

God Chooses in Christ

For God chooses no one unto eternal life except in Christ, who prepared it by his own blood for them who should believe on his name. From this it seems to follow that, since God regards no one in Christ unless they are engrafted in him by faith, election is peculiar to believers, and the phrase "certain men," in the definition, refers to believers. For Christ is a means of salvation to no one unless he is apprehended by faith.

Therefore, that phrase "in Christ" marks the meritorious cause by which grace and glory are prepared, and the existence of the elect in him, without which they could not be elected in him. The definition, then, is susceptible of this form. "Election is the decree of God, by which, of Himself, from eternity, He decreed to justify in (or through) Christ, believers, and to accept them unto eternal life, to the praise of His glorious grace." But you will say, "Then faith is made dependent on the human will, and is not a gift of divine grace." I deny that sequence, for there was no such statement in the definition. I acknowledge that the cause of faith was not expressed, but that was unnecessary. If any one denies it, there may be added after "believers" the phrase "to whom He determined to give faith."

But we should observe whether, in our method of consideration, the decree, by which God determined to justify believers and adopt them as sons, is the same with that by which He determined to bestow faith on some, but to deny the same to others. This seems to me not very probable. For there are, here, two purposes, each determined by the certain decree of God; their subjects are also diverse, and different attributes are assigned to them. I think that this ought to have been noticed in treating correctly of the order and mode of Predestination.

I do not much object to your statement that "the act of the divine mind is two-fold, regarding the end, and the means to the end, or to salvation," but that remark does not seem correct to me, in which you say that "the former is commonly called the decree, and the latter the execution of the decree," for such is your marginal annotation, each of these is an act of the decree, as you acknowledge; but an act of the decree is internal, and precedes its execution whether it is in reference to the end or the means.

The passage in Rom 9, does not favor your idea as you claim. For it does not distinguish the purpose from election, nor does it make the election prior to the purpose of damning or conferring salvation, but it says that the purpose is "according to election," not without election or apart from election, as is clearly evident from the words of the apostle. For they are as follows: *ina he kat eklogen tou theou prothesis mene*, that is "that the purpose of God according to election might stand" (verse 11), from which it is apparent that, by these words, is described the purpose of God, which is "according to election."

But that this may be more plainly understood, we may examine briefly the design and the scope of the apostle. The Jews objected that they, by virtue of the covenant and the divine word, committed to them, were the peculiar people of God, and, therefore, that honor could not be taken away from them, without the disgrace and the violation of the divine decree. They asserted, however, that the honor referred to, and the title of the people of God was taken from them by the Apostle Paul, when he made those only, who should believe in the Christ whom he preached, partakers of the righteousness of God, and of eternal salvation. Since they had not believed in that Christ, it followed, according to the doctrine of the apostle, that they were strangers to the righteousness of God and eternal salvation, and unworthy to be longer considered the people of God. But since they considered this to be contrary to the decree and the covenant of God, they concluded that it was, at the same time, absurd and foreign to the truth.

The apostle answers that the covenant, decree, or word of God hath not "taken none effect," (verse 6) but remains firm, even if many of the Jews should not be reckoned among the people of God, because that decree or covenant did not comprehend all Israelites, universally without election and distinction; for that decree was "according to election," as set forth in those words of God announcing his purpose. For God said "In Isaac," not in Ishmael, "shall thy seed be called." Also "The elder," Esau, "shall serve the younger," Jacob.

The apostle asserts that God declared most clearly in these words, that He did not regard the whole progeny of Abraham, or that of Isaac, or of Jacob, or all of their individual descendants, as His people, but only those who were "the children of the promise" to the exclusion of "the children of the flesh." The Apostle reasons, most conclusively from those words of God, that the purpose of God is according to election, and that it, therefore, embraces, in itself, not all the Israelites, but, while it claims some, it rejects others.

Not Wonderful or Contrary

From which it follows that it is not wonderful or contrary to the purpose or covenant of God, that some of the Jews are rejected by God, and those indeed, who are specially excluded by that decree according to those words of God, as "the children of the flesh," i.e. those who were seeking to be justified "by the works of the law" and according to the flesh. Compare Rom 9:7–11 and 30–32, also 10:3–5 with 4:1–3.

In Rom 8:29, those acts, I refer now to the decree and the execution of the decree, are clearly distinguished. In the decree two things are mentioned, foreknowledge and Predestination, "for whom He did foreknow, He also did predestinate to be conformed to the image of His Son." It is inquired: what is the import of this foreknowledge or prescience? Some explain it thus: "whom He foreknew," i.e. whom He previously loved, and affectionately regarded as His own, as indeed the simple word "to know" is sometimes used, as "I know you not" (Matt 25:12). "The Lord knoweth the way of the righteous" (Ps 1:6). Others say that foreknowledge, or prescience of faith in Christ, is here signified.

You assent to the former, and reject the latter, and with good reason, if it has the meaning, which you ascribe to it. But it is worthy of consideration whether the latter meaning of the work "foreknow" may not be so explained, as not only not to impinge upon the former, but also to harmonize with it most completely so that the former cannot be true without the latter. This will be evident, if it shall be demonstrated that God can "previously love and affectionately regard as His own" no sinner unless He has foreknown him in Christ, and looked upon him as a believer in Christ.

To prove this I proceed thus: God acknowledges, as His own, no sinner, and He chooses no one to eternal life except in Christ, and for the sake of Christ. "He hath chosen us in Him," (Eph 1:4); "wherein He hath made us accepted in the Beloved," (verse 6). "Nor any other creature shall be able to separate us from the love of God which is in Christ Jesus our Lord" (Rom 8:39). "God was in Christ reconciling the world unto Himself" (2 Cor 5:19).

For, if God could will to anyone eternal life, without respect to the Mediator, He could also give eternal life, without the satisfaction made by the Mediator. The actual bestowment of eternal life is not more limited, than the purpose to bestow it. God truly loved the world, and, on account of that love, gave His own Son as its Redeemer (John 3:16). But the love, here spoken of, is not that by which He wills eternal life, as appears from the very expression of John, for he interposes faith in Christ between that love and eternal life. Hence God acknowledges no one, in Christ and for Christ's sake, as His own, unless that person is in Christ. He who is not in Christ, cannot be loved in Christ. But no one is in Christ, except by faith; for Christ dwells in our hearts by faith, and we are engrafted and incorporated in him by faith. It follows then that God acknowledges His own, and chooses to eternal life no sinner, unless He considers him as a believer in Christ, and as made one with him by faith. This is proved by the following testimonies:

"As many as received him, to them gave He power to become the sons of God, even to them that believe on his name" (John 1:12).

But to those, to whom He gave this power, and to them, considered in one and the same manner, He also decreed to give this power, since the decree of Predestination effects nothing in him who is predestinated, and there is, therefore, no internal change in him, intervening between the decree and the actual bestowment of the thing, destined and prepared by the decree.

"God so loved the world that He gave His only begotten Son that whosoever believeth in him shall not perish, but have everlasting life" (John 3:16). "They which be of faith are blessed with faithful Abraham" (Gal 3:9). "Without faith it is impossible to please him" (Heb 11:6).

Hence he is not in error who says that foreknowledge or prescience of faith in Christ is signified in Rom 8:29, unless he adds the assertion that the faith, referred to, results from our own strength and is not produced in us by the free gift of God.

The same explanation is proved true from the following member: "whom He did foreknow, He also did predestinate to be conformed to the image of He Son." No one is conformed to the image of the Son of God if he does not believe on him. Therefore, no one is predestinated by God to that conformity, unless he is considered as a believer, unless one may claim that faith itself is included in that conformity believers have with Christ—which would be absurd, because that faith can by no means be attributed to Christ, for it is faith in him, and in God through him. It is faith in reference to reconciliation, redemption, and the remission of sins. It is true, also, since it is the means of attaining that conformity.

But you say: "They, who are predestinated to be justified and to become the sons of God, are also predestinated to believe, since adoption and justification are received by faith." I deny that consequence; indeed I assert that just the contrary can be concluded from that argument, if the act of Predestination is one and the same. This I will prove: If adoption and justification is received by faith, then they, who are predestinated to be justified and to become the sons of God, are, of necessity, considered as believers.

Destined to Anyone

For that, which is destined to anyone by Predestination, will certainly be received by him. And as he is when he receives it, such he was considered to be, when he was predestinated to receive it. Therefore, the believer alone was predestinated to receive it. From which I again conclude, that no one is chosen by God to adoption and the communication of the gift of righteousness, unless he is considered by Him as a believer. You add:

"It cannot be said correctly, that God foreknew that men would believe, and then predestinated them to faith, since those, whom He foreknew to believe, He thus foreknew because He decreed that they should believe."

But what relation has this to the matter? Such an affirmation is not made by the defenders of the sentiment to which I have referred. You confound two kinds of Predestination, and unite together acts of a different character. The Predestination in which God decreed to justify and adopt as sons believers in Christ, is not the same with that, in which He decreed, by certain means, to give faith to these and not to those. For the decree, is in this case, concerning the bestowment of faith in that, concerning the justification and adoption of believers; which, cannot, indeed, be the same decree, on account of the diversity of the subject and the attribute.

Otherwise it is true, that "God first foreknew that men would believe, and then predestinated them to faith." For He foreknew that they would believe by His own gift, which decree was prepared by Predestination.

These things, having been thus plainly set forth, may throw some light on this whole discussion, in reference to Predestination. This we will do, at greater extent, hereafter, when we shall subjoin our own view of the mode and order of Predestination.

Those testimonies, which you cite from the Fathers and schoolmen, can be very easily harmonized with what has been said by us, yet to avoid prolixity, I will dispense with that labor. One thing, however, I will observe; namely, that the explanation of Peter Lombard, however true it may be elsewhere, it is not adapted to the passage in Rom 8:29.

For the Apostle has there presented the object of Predestination (conformity to the image of Christ), in a different light from that in which it is set forth or presented by Lombard, namely, "that they should believe the word preached unto them." I will add, also, that you do not rightly conclude, because the word foreknowledge is used elsewhere by the Holy Spirit for the purpose of God, that, in the passage under discussion, it cannot signify prescience of faith.

Further, in the decree of election, you refer to two acts, one "the purpose of choosing certain men to His love and grace, by which choice, men are made vessels of mercy and honor;" the other, "the purpose of saving, or of the bestowment of glory." This is not an unimportant distinction, if all things are correctly understood. For those things, that

God prepares in election, are contained in grace and glory. But your statement, "Some, by the divine purpose, were chosen to the eternal love of God," must be explained to refer to that communication of love, by which God determined to communicate Himself to some.

If you regard, in a different light, that love of God which embraces us, it must be considered as preceding, in the order of nature, that decree or the Divine purpose by which grace and glory are prepared for us, grace, I say, which is the means of attaining to glory. Otherwise if you understand, by that word, the gracious disposition of God towards us, it coincides with the love of God, and is to be placed above the purpose or decree of God as its cause. This also is indicated by the order of the predicaments (in the logical sense of that word). For the purpose or decree is placed in the predicament of action, the gracious affection and love, in the preceding predicament of quality. This is evident from Eph 1:5–6, where God is said to have predestinated and adopted us "to the praise of the glory of His grace." If grace, then, is to receive praise from those acts, it must be placed before them as their cause.

Your position that "men to be created," as the object of the former purpose is not correct. For we are now treating of the subject, not as it is, in itself—for we know that the eternal purpose of God is antecedent to the actual existence of man—but as it is presented to the divine mind, in the act of decree, and in that of Predestination. If the object of that purpose is considered with that limitation, it is certain that men, not "to be created," but "already created, and sinners," that is, in the divine mind, are the object of the divine purpose and Predestination.

This is evident, from the love and gracious affection from which, and the grace to which he chose them. For that love is in Christ; in him is that gracious affection of God towards us; the grace prepared for us as a saving means, has placed in Christ, and not elsewhere. This you have, with sufficient clearness, signified, when you said that men, in that grace to which He chose them, were made "vessels of mercy;" which word is misplaced, except when wretchedness and sin have preceded it.

Love and Gracious Affection

But if you think of the love and gracious affection of God, as in God apart from any consideration of Christ, I shall deny that the purpose and decree of Predestination was instituted and established by God, according to those things, so considered, and I shall claim from you the proof, which, in my judgment, you will not be able to give. That is both because the love of God towards those "to be created" is uniform towards all, for in Adam all were created without any difference, and because that love and gracious affection, by which the purpose of Predestination was executed, saves with certainty, the predestinated. But the predestinated are not saved by that love and affection, considered out of Christ.

If you say that the love and gracious affection in God is the same, whether considered in Christ or out of Christ, I admit it. But man, "to be created," and man "having been created, and a sinner," are the same man. Created, and continuing in the condition of creation, he could be saved, by obedience, of the love and gracious affection of God, considered out of Christ. As a sinner, he could not be saved, except by the same feelings, considered in Christ. If you make the sinner the object of Predestination, you ought to add to predestinating grace, a mode adapted to the sinner who is to be saved. If you do not add this, will grace, considered without that mode, be sufficient?

I do not think that you will urge that the grace and love, by which a man, who is not a sinner, can be saved, and which is separate from mercy, is to be considered in Christ, and affects us on account of, and in respect to, him. If, however, you do this, I shall ask the proof. And, after all the proof you may be able to present, it will be proper to say that Christ himself is to be here considered in different relations. In the former case, it is as Mediator preserving and confirming the predestinated in the integrity of their state. In the latter, as Mediator redeeming and renewing the same persons from the state of sin and corruption. I will add that grace and salvation come to us, not by the former, but by the latter mediation.

For he is "Jesus, for he shall save his people from their sins" (Matt 1:21). He is "the Lamb of God, which taketh away the sin of the world" (John 1:29). He is the Redeemer of the world by his flesh given "for the life of the world" (John 6:51); by the destruction of "the works of the devil" (1 John 3:8; Heb 2:14); and by that reconciliation, which consists of in not "imputing their trespasses unto them, and hath committed unto us the word of reconciliation" (2 Cor 5:19).

That act, indeed, is "of the mere will of God," but not "without respect to sin in the creatures;" of sin, which is considered, not as the cause moving God to election, but as a condition, which must exist in the object of that act. And, in this sense, He does injury to no one if He does not elect all, since He is not under obligation to bestow mercy on anyone. But He can ordain no one to punishment, without the prevision of sin, in view of any right He possesses over His creatures. For that right is not unlimited, as many think of unlimited, I say, in such a sense that God can rightly inflict any act, possible to His omniscience, upon any creature considered in any respect, and without injustice bring upon the creature all things which the creature can suffer from his omnipotent Creator.

This can be made plain by the following demonstration: Every right of God over His creatures, depends either on the goodness of God towards His creatures, or on their wickedness towards Him, or on some contract entered into between God and His creatures. Without considering the right, which depends on contract, let us discuss the others. The right, which depends on the goodness of God, or on the wickedness of men, cannot exceed the magnitude of those things severally.

Man received from God, by His goodness in creation, his existence, both that of nature and of supernatural grace. The latter also includes the power of attaining to the highest felicity, and that of a supernatural nature, which God promised to man on the condition of obedience. The opposite of this highest felicity is the deepest misery into which the same man would Fall, justly and according to divine right, if he should transgress that law. Hence, exists the right of God over man, in that he is a creature, according to which He can take from him that very being which He has given, and reduce it to its pristine nothing.

Hence, also, He cannot have the right to condemn to eternal punishment a man unless he has become a sinner. For these four thing: existence, non-existence, happiness, misery, are so mutually connected that, as happiness is better than existence, so misery is worse than non-existence. This, Christ signified when he said "It would have been better for that man if he had not been born" (Matt 26:24). Therefore, the divine right does not permit that He should inflict misery on man, to whom He has given existence, except on the commission of that, by the opposite of which he could obtain felicity, the opposite of that wretchedness. Hence, if He should not elect all, He would do injustice to no one, if the non-elect should be only deprived of the good to which they had no claim. But injustice would be done to them, if, by non-election or reprobation, they must suffer evil which they had not deserved. The right of God does not so far extend itself over them.

There seems to have been need of this explanation, otherwise, we must, of necessity, far into many absurdities, and impinge on the righteousness of God. This, Augustine also, admits, in many passages. I will quote one or two: "God is good, God is just; He can deliver some without merit, because He is good; He cannot damn anyone without demerit, because He is just."[4]

Also: "If it is believed that God damns anyone, who does not deserve it, and is chargeable with no sin, it is not believed that He is far from iniquity."[5]

May be Permitted

I may be permitted, with your leave, to note some things in the explanation of the second act, which seem to have been propounded by you with too little accuracy. For, when you, here, change the formal relation of the object, and consider men, under this act, as "about to Fall," whom, under the first act, you presented as "about to be created," you seem to do it with no good reason. For, in your mode of considering the subject, men "to be created" are the object of both acts. But if all things are duly weighed, the object in both is, in fact, men as sinners, neither more in the former than in the latter, nor more in the latter than in the former act.

Nor was it necessary to use the future participle, since the discussion is, here, concerning the act of the divine mind to which all things are present. I pass over the fact that the ordination to salvation depends on the Fall, as the occasion of making that decree, wherefore, you should have said "Fallen," not "about to Fall." I could wish, also, that there might be an explanation how that act, the purpose of saving and of bestowing of glory, is the same with the act under which they are ordained, on whom that glory is bestowed, and to whom it is manifested; also, how the second act, namely, the purpose of saving, pertains to the execution and completion of the former purpose, namely, that by which He chooses some to His own love and grace.

That "the act referred to has no preparative cause, out of the good-pleasure of God," is true, only let Christ be duly included in that divine good-pleasure. To this, you seem, indeed, to assent, when you say "that

4. St. Augustine, *Against Julian the Pelagian*, Lib. 3, Cap. 18.
5. St. Augustine, *Epistle 106 to Paulinus*.

act is in respect to Christ, the Mediator, in whom we are all elected to grace and salvation."

But when you so explain your meaning that we are said to be elected, in Christ, to grace and salvation, "because he is the foundation of the execution of election," you again destroy what you have said. For, if Christ is only the foundation of the execution of election, the election itself is made without respect to Christ in the decree of God, preceding, in fact, the execution of it. It cannot be said, then, that we are elected in him to grace and salvation, but only that we, having, out of Christ, been previously elected to grace and salvation, are by Christ made partakers of them.

But the Scriptures make Christ the foundation not only of the execution, but of the act of election. For He is, according to the Scriptures, Mediator, not only in the efficacy of the application, but in the merit of obtainment; wherefore, also, when they speak of Christ, the Scriptures affirm that grace and eternal life are bestowed upon us, not only through him, but on account of him, and in him. The direct relation is first presented, because God cannot love the sinner unto eternal life, except in Christ, and on account of Christ, since the justice of God requires that reconciliation should be made by the blood of Christ.

The sum of the whole is, that both acts, that of choosing to grace and the love of God, as well as that of the bestowment of glory and the preparation of the means necessary to salvation, depends upon Christ as their only foundation—upon Christ. He was ordained by God to be High Priest and Mediator by the blood of his cross, the Savior from sins, the Redeemer from the bondage of sin and Satan, the Author and Giver of eternal salvation. Therefore, neither of those acts is in reference to men as "to be created," but both of them in reference to them, as "Fallen sinners, and needing the grace of the remission of sins and the renewing of the Holy Spirit."

Those "five decrees" are well considered as mutually dependent, but they cannot all be attributed, nor are they all subordinate to the "second act;" nor yet, indeed, to the first act. For the first three, namely, the "appointment of the Mediator, the promise of him, as appointed, and the presentation of him, as promised" are in the order of nature and of causes antecedent to all Predestination of men to grace and glory. For Christ, appointed, promised, presented, yet more, having accomplished the work of reconciliation, having obtained eternal redemption, and having procured the Holy Spirit, is the head of all those who are predestinated in him unto salvation, not yet, in the order of nature, predestinated, but to be predestinated. For Christ is the head; we are the members. He was, first, in the order of nature, predestinated to be the head, then we to be the members.

He was first, ordained to be the Savior, then we were ordained, in him, to be saved for his sake and in him. He inverts the order laid down in the Scripture, who says "God first predestinated men, and then ordained Christ to be the head of those predestinated." It need not be inquired, with much prolixity, why many have conceived that the order should be inverted. Yet I think that some passages of the Scripture, in which the love of God towards men is said to be the cause of the mission of his Son, on the one hand, and on the other, that, other passages, in which Christ is said to gather together and to bring to salvation the children of God, and the elect, have given occasion for a conception of this kind—an occasion, not a just cause.

Love Not the Cause

For that love is not the cause of Predestination, and it has no necessary connection with Predestination. And Christ is not only the Savior of those who have been elected and adopted as Sons by God, but he is also the Mediator and head in whom the election and adoption were made. This I have already often said.

Your definition of the "appointment of the Mediator" was not sufficiently complete, for the condition of men was omitted, in reference to which the whole matter of Mediation was arranged. The passage you have cited from 1 Pet 1:18–20, might admonish you of this. For Christ is there said to be the foreordained Mediator who redeemed us by his own "precious blood, as of a lamb without blemish, from vain conversation."

The word "sinners" ought to have been added. For Christ was ordained to be Mediator, not between God and men absolutely considered, but between God and men considered as sinners. From this, I may also deduce a proof of what I have already argued in reference to the object of Predestination. For if Christ is Mediator for sinners, then it follows that no one is loved, in Christ the Mediator, unless he is a sinner. Therefore, no one is predestinated in Christ, unless he is a sinner.

It seems to me that there is, also, some confusion in your discussion of "the promise of the Mediator." For the promise is considered either as the pure revelation of the decree to give and send the Mediator, or as having, united with it, the offering of the Mediator, who was to be given, with all his benefits. The former is a mere prediction of the advent of the Messiah himself, antecedent to his mission. The latter is the offering of the Messiah, in reality to come at a future time, but, in the decree of God, having already discharged the office of Mediator, pertaining, with the gifts obtained by the discharge of the office, to the application of its benefits.

In this latter respect, it is made subordinate to Predestination. Considered in the former respect, it precedes, not Predestination, it is true, for that is from eternity, but the execution of Predestination. The revelation, without the offering, consists in these words, "I will give a Mediator to the world;" but the offering in these words "Believe in the Mediator, whom I will give unto the world, and you shall obtain salvation in him." By that revelation and prediction, God binds Himself to offer the Mediator to the world, whether it should believe or not; but by that offering He demands faith, and by the internal persuasion of the Holy Spirit, added thereto, He effects faith and binds Himself to give salvation to the believer.

It appears from this, that the promise is to be considered with this distinction, that in the former part, only, it is antecedent to the mission of the Messiah, but in the latter part it pertains to the execution of Predestination.

Let us now, passing over that distinction of the promise and the offering, consider the universality of the promise, and the offering, taken jointly and in connection. That universality is not to be measured by the degree of faith.

For faith is posterior to the promise and the offering, as it marks the apprehension and embraces the application of the promise. But a distinction must be made between the promise and offering made by God, with the act of man that apprehends the promise, which is faith, and that act of God that applies to the believer, that which is promised and offered. The promise and the offering extends itself to all who are called: called by the external preaching of the gospel, whether they obey its call or not.

For even they received an invitation, who "would not come" to the marriage, and were, therefore, judged unworthy by God (Matt 22:2–8), since they "rejected the counsel of God against themselves," (Luke 7:30), and by the rejection of the promise, made themselves unworthy (Acts 13:46). It is not that unworthiness, in accordance with which all sinners are alike unworthy, as the Centurion, and the publican, who are, nevertheless, said to have had faith, and to have obtained the remission of their sins from Christ; from which they are, in the Scripture, called "worthy" (Rev 3:4).

But the passages of Scripture cited by you, do not limit the promise made, but the application by faith of the promised thing, with the exception of the second, Matt 11:28, which contains only an invitation to Christ, with the added promise of rest, as an inducement to come, but in reality not to be given, unless they should come to Christ.

You say also, that "an exhortation or command to believe is joined with the promise, and that this is more general than the promise." In this last assertion you are, in my judgment, in an error. For the promise as made, and the command to believe are equally extensive in their relation. If the promise does not refer to all, to whom the command to believe is given, the command is unjust, vain, and useless. It is unjust, since it demands that a man should have faith in the promise, not generally, that it pertains to some persons, but specially, that it was made for himself. But the promise was not made for him, if the command is more extensive than the promise.

Command is in Vain

This command is in vain, since it is in reference to nothing. It commands one to believe, but presents no object of faith, that promise which is the only object of faith, having been taken away. For which reason, also, the command is useless. It can in no way be performed by him, to whom the promise, as made, does not pertain. Indeed, should he attempt to obey the command to believe, he would effect nothing else than the conception in his mind of a false opinion of a falsity. For since the promise was not made to him, he cannot believe that it was made for him, but can only think so, and that falsely. The Scripture, however, everywhere represents the promise and the command to believe as of equal extent.

"Repent and be baptized every one of you in the name of Jesus Christ, for the remission of sins; and ye shall receive the gift of the Holy Ghost. For the promise is unto you and to your children, etc." (Acts 2:38, 39).

"Come unto me all ye that labor" the command; "and I will give you rest," the promise, made to all who are commanded to come (Matt 11:28).

"If any man thirst, let him come unto me and drink," the command; "He that believeth on me, as the Scripture hath said, out of his belly shall flow rivers of living water," the promise, made to all who are commanded to come to Christ and drink (John 7:37, 38). Perhaps some may prefer to join the phrase "drink" to the promise, in this way, "if any one thirst, let him come unto me; if he shall do this, he shall drink so abundantly that out of his belly shall flow rivers of living water." But explained in this way, it equally answers my present purpose.

You may say that you make the promise, in respect, not to its presentation, but to its application, of narrower extent than the command to believe. This, indeed, is correct. But the comparison is then incongruous. As, in the promise, three things are to be considered, the command itself, the obedience yielded to the command, and the reward bestowed on obedience. Of these three items, each answers to each of the things placed in the opposite parallel with it: the promise as made, to the command; faith exercised in the promise made, and the gift or application of the promised good conferred on obedience.

But who does not know that the promise is made to many, by whom it is not apprehended by faith, and that the command is addressed to many, by whom it is not obeyed? Hence you can perceive that it was not fitly said: "the promise relates to believers (that is, the promise, not as merely made, but as applied, for the promise in the latter sense is antecedent to faith); and "the command relates to believers and to non-believers." It belongs to neither. The command is prior to faith, demands faith, and prohibits unbelief.

But what are those things which follow? You seem, most learned Perkins, to be forgetful of yourself, and to be entirely a different person from him whom you have displayed in other of your published works. Again and again I entreat you to be patient with me, as I shall discuss these points with candor and mildness.

First, observe the coherence of that, which follows, with that, which precedes. "For the elect are mingled with the wicked in the same assemblies." What then? Is the promise, as made, therefore, less extensive than the command to believe? You answer affirmatively, for the reason that the promise relates to the elect only, the command pertains to the elect and to the wicked. I reply, that the promise, as made and proposed by God, relates not to the elect only, but to the wicked, whom you place in opposition to the elect: and that the command, is not imposed either on the elect or on those opposed to them, except with the promise joined.

I think that I see what you mean, namely, that, as the promise is not applied except to the elect, so also the same is not proposed except to the elect, that is: according to the divine mind and purpose. How this may be, we shall see hereafter. Meanwhile, I make the same remark in reference to the command. As the command, by which faith is not obeyed except by the elect, so, also, it is not proposed except to the elect, that is, according to the divine mind and purpose. For as, in the former case, the promise is proposed to the non-elect, without the divine purpose of applying the promise; so in the latter case, the command is proposed to the non-elect, without the divine purpose that they should fulfill or obey the command.

If, on account of the absence of the divine efficacy, you think that the promise is not made to the non-elect, on account of the absence of the divine efficacy, I affirm, also, that the command is not imposed on the non-elect. The fact is the same in reference to both. We will, hereafter, more fully discuss that matter.

Secondly, the phrases "elect" and "wicked" are unsuitably placed in opposition to each other, since with the former, "reprobate," and with the latter, "pious," should have been contrasted, according to the rule of opposition. But here the opposition of the two things is unsuitable, since, in one of the opposites, the other is also comprehended. For the wicked, in this case, may comprehend also the elect. For it refers to those who are commanded, in the exhortation of the ministers of the word, to repent. But repentance is prescribed only to the wicked and to sinners, whether they are elect or reprobate, though with a contrary result in each case. I now speak of the call to repentance.

Office of Ministers

Thirdly, you seem to me to limit the office of ministers to the mere calling of sinners to repentance, excluding the presentation of the promise, which is another part of the message entrusted to them. For they say: "Repent and believe the gospel, for the kingdom of heaven is at hand."

Finally, of what importance is it, whether they know, or do not know, "who, and how many are elect and to be converted"? "Then," you will say, "they might arrange their sermons, and present them to each person with an adaptation to his state." This I deny. For Christ knew and understood that Judas was a reprobate, and yet he did not arrange his sermons differently on his account. The preachers of the word must not desist from the functions of their office in any assembly, as long as they may be permitted to discharge them, and there are those who are willing to hear. But when they are cast out, and none whatever listen to their word, they are commanded by Christ to depart, and to shake off the very dust from their feet as a testimony against them. From this it appears, that their rule of teaching and exhorting is not an internal knowledge, which they can have, of the election of some and the reprobation of others, but the external obedience or contumacy of those whom they teach, whether they be elect or reprobate.

You add, moreover, the cause, in view of which, "God wills that they should be admonished to repent, who, as He sees, never will repent, namely, that they may be left without excuse." But this, I say, is neither the only object, nor the chief object, nor the object per se, but incidentally, and the event rather than the object, except in a certain respect, as we shall see. It is not the only object, since there is another, that they should be admonished of their duty, and invited and incited to faith and conversion, "not knowing that the goodness of God leadeth them to repentance" (Rom 2:4); also that God may satisfy Himself, and His own love towards His own creatures also, by that exercise of long suffering and patience.

"What more could have been done to my vineyard, that I have not done in it?" (Isa 5:4) "God endured with much long-suffering the vessels of wrath fitted to destruction (Rom 9:22).

These two objects are, also, of far greater importance than that of rendering the impenitent inexcusable; therefore that is not the chief object. It is not the object per se, because the admonition does not render them inexcusable, unless it is despised and rejected, but this result of the admonition depends on the wickedness of those called. God does not will this result, unless He also foreknows that future admonition will be useless through the wickedness, not through the infirmity, of those who are admonished, and unless He has already frequently invited them in vain to repentance, as in Isa 6:10, "Make the heart of this people fat, and make their ears heavy," etc.

For a distinction should be made between the admonition, as first addressed to a person, and as repeated the second or third time, and the final presentation of the same, after long contumacy.

For the former is done through grace and mercy to miserable sinners, the latter through wrath against the obstinate, who, having hardened themselves by their own sin, have made themselves worthy of divine hardening. Therefore the rendering them inexcusable is rather the event of the admonition than an object proposed to the Deity, except against the obstinate, and those who are incorrigible through their own voluntary wickedness. This event deservedly, indeed, results from that rejected admonition, as the admonition becomes a savor of death unto death to those who were unwilling that it should be to themselves a savor of life unto life, that it might become against them a testimony of contumacy, as they refused to have the remedy of repentance, that they might endure the just and punitive will of God, who refused to obey His merciful and benevolent will.

But someone may reply that no other end was proposed to the Deity, in the exhortation, than that they should be indeed inexcusable, both because God, in the decree of reprobation, determined not to give the repentance and faith, which they could not have, except by His gift, and because God obtained no other end than that of rendering them inexcusable, and yet He is never frustrated in His design. These arguments seem, indeed, to be of some value, and to present no little difficulty, and if they can be fitly answered, by the use of necessary analysis and explanation, there is no doubt but that much light and clearness may in this way be thrown upon the whole subject of which we treat. I will endeavor to do what I may be able, trusting in divine grace, and depending on the aid of the Holy Spirit.

Do you, my friend Perkins, assist me, and if you shall desire anything, which may not be presented by me in the discussion, kindly mention it. I pledge myself that you will find me susceptible of admonition and correction, and ready to give my hand to the truth, when proved to be so.

Facilitate the Discussion

It will facilitate the discussion, if I arrange both the arguments with the parts of the subject under discussion in the form of a syllogism, and then examine the parts of the syllogism by the rule of the truth. That which belongs to the former argument may, in my judgment, be arranged thus: Those to whom God by a fixed decree has determined not to give repentance and faith, He does not admonish to repent and believe with any other object, than that they should be rendered inexcusable. But God has determined, in the decree of reprobation, not to give repentance and faith to the reprobate. Therefore, when God admonishes the reprobate to repent and believe, He does it with no other object than that they should be rendered inexcusable.

I reply to the Major: It seems to depend on a false hypothesis. For it presupposes that "God, by the external preaching of the gospel, admonishes some to repent and believe, to whom He has determined by a fixed decree not to give repentance and faith." This proposition seems to me to disagree with the truth.

In the first place, because it inverts the order of the divine decrees and acts. For the decree, by which God determined to exhort some to repentance and faith, by the external preaching of the gospel, precedes the decree of the non-bestowment of repentance and faith. For the former pertains to the will of God, in the relation of antecedent, the latter, in that of consequent. This can be proved from many very clear passages of the Scripture. In Isa 6, hardening and blinding is denounced against those who refuse to obey "the calling of God," as appears from the fifth chapter. The Apostle Paul manifestly agrees with this in Acts 28:26, 27, citing the declaration of Isaiah against those Jews who did not believe.

Again, it is said, "My people would not hearken to my voice; and Israel would none of me. So I gave them up unto their own heart's lust; and they walked in their own counsels" (Ps 81:11–12). In Hos 1:6, the Israelites are called "not beloved," or "not having obtained mercy," "and not the people of God," only, after they had merited that rejection by the foul crime of unbelief and idolatry.

"The Pharisees and lawyers rejected the counsel of God against themselves, being not baptized of him" (Luke 7:30).

"Paul and Barnabas waxed bold, and said, It was necessary that the word of God should first have been spoken to you; but seeing ye put it from you, and judge yourselves unworthy of everlasting life, lo, we turn to the Gentiles" (Acts 13:46).

The Jews are said in Rom 9:22, to have "stumbled at that stumbling stone," because they had not sought to be justified by faith in Christ, but by the works of the law. In 1 Pet 2:7, 8, Christ is said to be "a rock of

offense, even them which stumble at the word, being disobedient." From
this it appears that the decree of blinding and hardening, of the non-
bestowment of the grace of repentance and faith, pertain to the decree of
God, in the relation of consequent, depending on the foresight of incre-
dulity, disobedience and contumacy. This proposition, then, ought to be
enunciated thus, the subject being changed into the attribute, and vice
versa: "God determined, by a fixed decree, not to give repentance and
faith to those who, as He foresaw, would reject, in their wickedness and
contumacy, the preaching of the gospel, by which they should be called
to repentance and faith." It does not, indeed, follow from this, that God
decreed to give faith to those whom He foresaw to be obedient. For there
is a wide difference between the acts of divine mercy and divine justice.

For the latter have their cause in men, the former have their occasion, indeed, from men, but their cause from God alone. This is the
purport of that passage from Augustine[6], "Esau did not will or run; but
if he had willed or run, he would have found God to be his helper, who
would even have effected that he should will and run by calling him,
unless he had become reprobate by the rejection of the call."

In the second place, because it charges God with hypocrisy, as if He
would demand by an admonition to faith made to such persons, from
them, that they should believe in Christ, whom He had, nevertheless,
made to them, not a Savior, not a savor of life unto life unto the resurrection, but a savor of death unto death, a rock of offense, which charge
must be contradicted both in its statement and proof.

If any assert that God demands faith not of them, but of the elect,
who are mingled with the reprobates, but that this admonition, being
presented by the ministers of the world, ignorant who are elect, and who
are reprobate, is to be presented also, to them, I shall reply that such cannot be called "disobedient," because they do not obey an admonition not
made to themselves. If, however, that hypothesis is false, then the argument that follows is of no weight, since it is presupposed on both sides
that God does exhort to repentance and faith, those to whom He has
determined not to give repentance and faith. For if He does not exhort
such to repentance, He does not exhort them to any end, either that they
may be rendered inexcusable, or any other.

It is in no way unfavorable to my reply that the decree of reprobation was made from eternity. For we must consider what is the first

6. St. Augustine, *Ad Simplicianum*, Lib. 1, Quaes. 2.

external act, either negative or affirmative, towards or in reference to a man, reprobate from eternity by the internal act of God. For the first external act, towards or in reference to a man, when really existing, makes him reprobate in fact, as the internal act of God makes him reprobate in the mind and counsel of God, that is, as is commonly said, a distinction is to be made between the decree and its execution. It is certain that a man cannot be called a reprobate in fact, in reference to whom God has not yet, by an external act, begun to execute the decree of reprobation.

I also remark, that the proposition seems to me to be at variance with the truth, because it regards those who are reprobate, as being rendered inexcusable, while the order should be inverted, and those who are inexcusable should be made reprobates. For reprobation is just, and therefore, the reprobate must have been inexcusable before the act of reprobation; inexcusable in fact, before the external act of reprobation, and, foreseen or foreknown as inexcusable before the decree of reprobation. If they were reprobate on account of original sin, they were inexcusable on this account; if reprobate on account of their unbelief and rejection of Christ, they were inexcusable on account of that unbelief, etc.

Same Proposition

I reply to the same proposition that it is not possible that the exhortation is made, only to this end, that it might render one who should hear it, inexcusable, and should, in fact and of right, render him inexcusable. For the exhortation renders its hearer inexcusable, not as it is heard, but as it is rejected. Moreover a rejection, which must render the person, who rejects, inexcusable, ought not to be inevitable. But the rejection of the exhortation, which is here discussed, is inevitable. First, because the exhortation is addressed to one in reference to whom God has already been employed in the external act of reprobation. But such a man cannot avoid disobedience, according to the sayings of Christ. "Therefore, they could not believe, because that Isaiah said again, He hath blinded their eyes, and hardened their heart" (John 12:39–40). Secondly, since it is only presented to the end that it may be rejected. But this presentation is of the will of God, in the relation of consequent, which is always fulfilled, and attains its end.

Therefore, that rejection is inevitable.

As then the Major is false in these three respects, it follows that the conclusion from the syllogism is not legitimate. But let us look at the Minor. For in reference to this also, and by occasion of it, there will be some things to be said which will be, in no small degree, adapted to our purposes.

The assumption (or minor) was this, "But God has determined, in the decree of reprobation, not to give repentance and faith to the reprobate." I willingly agree to that statement, but let it be correctly understood. It is necessary to explain the non-bestowment or denial of repentance and faith, which is established by the decree of reprobation. For there is another denial of repentance and faith, which is administered by the decree of providence, inasmuch as this is distinguished from the decree of reprobation. If there is not an accurate distinction between these, error cannot be avoided. I say, then, that it is very plain from the Scriptures, that repentance and faith cannot be exercised except by the gift of God.

But the same Scripture and the nature of both gifts very clearly teach that this bestowment is by the mode of persuasion. This is effected by the word of God. But persuasion is effected, externally by the preaching of the word, internally by the operation, or rather the cooperation, of the Holy Spirit, tending to this result, that the word may be understood and apprehended by true faith. These two are almost always joined. For God has determined to save them, who believe by the preaching of the word, and the preaching of the word, without the cooperation of the Holy Spirit, is useless, and can effect nothing. As it is said, "So then neither is he that planteth anything; neither he that watereth; but God that giveth the increase" (1 Cor 3:7).

But God does not will that His word should be preached in vain, as it is said,

"So shall my word be that goeth forth out of my mouth: it shall not return unto me void, but it shall accomplish that which I please, and it shall prosper in the thing whereto I sent it" (Isa 55:11).

It is in vain without the cooperation of the Holy Spirit; and it has, always joined with it, the cooperation of the Holy Spirit. For which reason, the gospel is called "the ministration of the Spirit" (2 Cor 3:8), and they who resist it are said "to resist the Holy Spirit," (Acts 7 & 13, and Matt 12), not only because they oppose the external preaching administered by the command and the guidance of the Holy Spirit, but also because they strive against the cooperation of the Holy Spirit. Whence, also, some are said to sin against the Spirit, in that they wickedly deny, and, through their hate, persecute and blaspheme the truth of which they are persuaded in their own minds, by the persuasion of the Holy Spirit. This internal persuasion of the Holy Spirit is two-fold. It is sufficient and efficacious. In the former sense, since he, with whom it is employed, is able to consent, believe, and be converted.

Decree of Providence

In the latter, because he to whom it is applied, does consent and believe, and is converted. The former is employed, by the decree of providence, with a sure prescience that it will be rejected by the free will of man. The latter is administered by the decree of Predestination, with a sure prescience that he, to whom it is applied and addressed, will in fact consent, believe, and be converted, because it is applied in a way such as God knows to be adapted to the persuasion and conversion of him to whom it is applied. These remarks are made in accordance with the sentiments of Augustine.

Hence also there is a twofold denial of grace, namely, of that which is sufficient, without which he cannot believe and repent, and of that which is efficacious, without which he will not repent or be converted. In the decree of reprobation, sufficient grace is not with propriety, said to be denied, since it is bestowed on many who are reprobate, namely, on those, who by the external preaching of the gospel, are called to faith and repentance. But efficacious grace is denied to them, namely, that grace by which they not only can believe and be converted, if they consent, but by which they also will consent, believe, and be converted, and certainly and infallibly do so.

The assumption (or minor) has this meaning: God has determined by a sure decree of reprobation not to give to some persons repentance and faith, that is, by affording to them efficacious grace, by which they will surely believe and be converted. But God has not by that decree denied the grace, by which they may be able, if they will to believe and to be converted. Indeed by another decree, namely, that of Providence, in distinction from Predestination, He has determined to give to them faith and repentance by sufficient grace, that is, to bestow upon them those gifts in a manner in which they may be able to receive them, by the strength given to them by God, which is necessary and sufficient for their reception. God has, therefore, ordained by the decree of Providence, by which external preaching is addressed to those whom God foreknew as persons who would not repent or believe, to give to them, having this character, sufficient grace and the strength necessary to their faith and conversion to God.

Upon this determination, also, depends the fact that they are without excuse, who are all called by sufficient grace to repentance and faith. But He further decreed not to give efficacious grace to the same persons, and this by the decree of reprobation. But their inexcusableness does not depend upon this denial of efficacious grace. If, indeed, sufficient grace should be withheld, they, who do not believe and are not converted, are deservedly excused, for the reason that, without it, they could neither believe nor be converted. But if these things are explained in this way, according to the view of Augustine, and, perhaps also, in accordance with the sense of the Scriptures, it follows that it cannot be concluded that God admonishes the reprobate to repentance and faith with no other design than that they may be left without excuse.

For according to the decree of providence, by which He gives to them grace sufficient to faith, and exhortation to repentance and faith is addressed and it is to this end, that they may be led to repentance and faith, and that God may satisfy His own goodness and grace, and be clear from the responsibility of their perdition. The exhortation, then, is not made according to the decree of reprobation, Therefore, its design is not to be measured by the decree of reprobation.

The second can also be arranged and disposed in the form of a syllogism; God proposes to Himself in His acts, no end, without attaining it, for He never fails of His purpose. But God, in the admonition which He addresses to the reprobate, attains no other end than that they should be left without excuse. Therefore God, in that admonition, proposes no other end to Himself.

To the Major, I reply that it seems to me to be simply untrue. For God has not determined all His own deeds in accordance with His own will, in the relation of consequent, which is always fulfilled, but He administers many things according to His will, in the relation of antecedent, which is not always fulfilled. Legislation, the promulgation of the Gospel, promising, threatening, admonishing, rebuking are all instituted, according to the will of God, as antecedents By these acts He requires obedience, faith, repentance, conversion, and those acts were instituted to this end; yet God does not always attain those ends. The falsity of this proposition can be proved by the clearest passages of Scripture;

"Wherefore, when I looked that it should bring forth grapes, brought it forth wild grapes" (Isa 5:4);

"How often would I have gathered thy children together, and ye would not" (Matt 23:37); "The Lord is long suffering to us-ward, not willing that any should perish, but that all should come to repentance" (2 Pet 3:9).

The Pharisees are said to have "rejected the counsel of God against themselves" (Luke 7:30), when they might have been brought, by the preaching of John and baptism to a participation in his kingdom. But though God might fail of any particular end, yet He cannot fail in His universal purpose. For, if any person should not consent to be converted and saved, God has still added, and proposed to Himself, another design, according to His will as consequent, that He should be glorified in their just condemnation.

Freed From Falsity

Therefore, that this proposition may be freed from its falsity, it must be amended thus: God proposes to His will, as consequent, no end which He does not attain. If anyone should say that it follows from this that God is either unwise and not prescient of future events, or impotent, I reply that it does not follow. For God does not always propose an end to Himself from His prescience, and further, God does not always please to use His own omnipotence, to accomplish any purpose which He has proposed to Himself.

As to the minor, it also seems to me to be chargeable with falsity. For God, by that admonition, attains another end than that they should be rendered inexcusable, namely, He satisfies His own goodness and love towards us. Add to this that, as the fact of their being without excuse arises, not from the presentment, but from the rejection of the admonition, God has not proposed to Himself their inexcusableness as an end, except after the foresight that the admonition would come to them in vain. In this view, then, their inexcusableness does not arise from the antecedent will of God, administering the admonition, but from the consequent will, furnishing the rejection of the admonition.

It follows, therefore, that a true conclusion cannot be deduced from these false propositions. The words of the Abbot Joachim must be understood according to this explanation, or they will labor under the error, which we have now noticed in your words.

The command of God by which He exacts repentance and faith from those, to whom the gospel is preached, can, in no way, be at variance from the decree of God. For no will or volition of God, whatever may be its character, can be contrary to any other volition. But it may be possible that a decree may be ignorantly assigned to God, which is at variance with His command. Also, a decree of God, which is assigned to Him in the Scriptures, may be so explained, as to be necessarily at variance with the command of God.

The command by which God exacts faith of anyone, declares that God wills that he, on whom the command is imposed, should believe. If, now, anyone ascribes any decree to God, by which He wills that the same person should not believe, then the decree is contrary to the command. For it cannot be that God should, at the same time, will things contradictory, in whatever way or with whatever distinction the will may be considered. But to believe, and not to believe are contradictory, and to will that one should believe, and to will that he, the same person, and considered in the same light, should not believe, are contradictory. The decree is of such a character, that God is said to have determined, according to it, to deny the concurrence of His general government or of His special grace, without which, as He knew, the act of faith could not be performed by him, whom, by His command, He admonishes to believe. For He, who wills to deny to any person the aid necessary to the performance of an act of faith, wills that the same person should not believe.

For he who wills in the cause, is rightly said to will, also, in the effect, resulting, of necessity, from that cause. For, as it cannot be said that God wills that a person should exist longer, to whom He denies the act of preservation, so, also, it cannot be said that He wills that an act should be performed by anyone, to whom He denies His own concurrence and the aid, which are necessary for the performance of the act. For the act of the divine preservation is not more necessary to a man, that he may continue to exist, than the concurrence of the divine aid, in order that he may be able to exercise faith in the gospel.

If, then, that purpose not to do a thing, of which you speak, marks a denial of the concurrence of God, which is necessary to the exercise of faith in the promise, it certainly impinges upon the command, and can, in no way, be harmonized with it. For that denial, being of this character, holds the relation of most general and most efficacious hindrance, as that, which is not, is hindered, that it may not become something, most efficaciously by the purpose of creation (i.e. by a denial of its exercise), and that which is, that it may not longer exist, by the will of preservation (not being exercised). If you understand the "purpose not to do a thing," in such a sense, then, truly, you do not free the will of God from contradiction by either of your answers. You say that "God, in His commands and promises, does not speak of all which He has decreed, but only in part manifests His own will." I grant it.

But I say that whatever God says in His commands and promises, is such in its nature that He cannot, without contradiction, be said to will or determine anything, contrary to it, by any decree; for it is one thing to be silent concerning certain things He wills, and another thing to will that which is contrary to those things He has previously willed. It is certain, from the most general idea of command that the whole will of God is not set forth in a command, but only that which He approves and wills to be done by us. There is no decree of God by which He wills anything.

What Are Expectations?

I wish also that you would consider how ineptly you express what follows. What are these expressions? "God does not will the same thing alike in all. He wills conversion in some, only in respect to their trial and exhortation, and the means of conversion; in others, also: in respect to the purpose of effecting it." If you say those things in reference to the will of God as it requires conversion, they ought to have been differently expressed. If in reference to His will as it effects conversion, they ought, in that case, also, to have been differently expressed. Understood in either sense, the phraseology is not correct. But I think that you are here speaking of the will in the latter sense, according to which God does not will to effect conversion equally in all, for whom He does equally, and of the same right, require it.

For, in some, He wills to effect it only by external preaching, admonition, and sufficient means, for so I explain your meaning. If this is in accordance with your views, it is well, but if not, I would wish that you would inform us what you have understood by the word "means." In others, He wills to effect it, by efficacious means, administered according to the decree of Predestination. There is here, indeed, no conflict of wills, but only different degrees of will, as far as we are concerned, or rather different volitions of God in reference to different objects, according to which God cannot be said to will and not to will the same object, that is, to will the conversion, and not to will the conversion of the same man—the laws of just opposition being here observed. I could wish that it might be explained how "God sincerely wills that the man should believe in Christ, whom He wills to be alien from Christ, and to whom He has decreed to deny the aid necessary to faith," for this is equivalent to not willing the conversion of any one.

To your second answer, I say, that it is not sufficient that you should say that "the revealed will of God is not adverse to the will of good pleasure (*eudokias*);" but the matter of Predestination is to be so treated that the will of good pleasure is not to be opposed to the revealed will; for I think that the limits of that opposition ought to have been thus expressed. For the will which you call that of "good pleasure," ought to be investigated by means of the revealed will. Hence the latter is to be brought into agreement with the former, not the former to be reconciled with the latter. I desire, also, that it should be considered by what right the revealed will is usually considered as distinguished from the will of good pleasure, since the good pleasure of God is frequently revealed. It is the good-pleasure of God that he who beholds the Son and believes on him, should have eternal life.

The Greek word *eudokia* is often used in Scripture, for that will of God, that is inclined towards anyone, which is called "good pleasure" in distinction from the pleasure of God, considered in a general sense.

Reprobation cannot be referred to good pleasure; for every exercise of good pleasure towards men is in Jesus Christ, as the angels sung *Hen hanthropois eudokai* "good will toward men" (Luke 2:14). In Matt 11:25, 26, in which *eudokia* is used in reference to the pleasure of God by which He has hidden the mysteries of the kingdom of heaven from the wise, and revealed them unto babes, I remark that the word is properly to be referred to that concerning which Christ gives thanks to his Father, that is, the revelation of the heavenly mysteries to babes.

Christ does not give thanks to the Father that He has hidden the mysteries from the wise, for he prayed for the wise men of this world who crucified him. For the "princes of this world" are said to have crucified the Lord of glory (1 Cor 2:8), and he is said to have prayed for his persecutors, and particularly for those who crucified him.

In what respect is it true that the revealed will "always agrees, in its beginning, end and scope," with the good pleasure, in the ordinary acceptation of that phrase, since the revealed will has often a different object from that of the will of good pleasure? Also, if both are in reference to the same object, there cannot be the same beginning, and the same end and scope to both except it be also true that God wills by His good pleasure, that which, in His revealed will, He declares that He wills, unless, indeed, that same beginning is considered universally to be God, and the same end to be the glory of God. But that "the revealed will of God seems often to be diverse, and, indeed, in appearance, to be contrary to the decree of God, and also in reference to the mode of proposing it," is true, if you mean that this "seems" so to ignorant men, and to those who do not rightly distinguish between the different modes and the various objects of volition. These two wills of God, however diverse, never seem contrary to those, who rightly look into these things, and so judge of them.

God's Justice

As to the death of Hezekiah, and the destruction of Nineveh, God knew that it belonged to His justice, unless it should be tempered with mercy, to take away the life of Hezekiah, and to send destruction on the Ninevites. For the law of His justice claimed that these things should be denounced against them by Isaiah and Jonah. But God was not willing to satisfy the demands of justice, unless with the intervention of the decree of mercy, by which He determined that neither death should come on Hezekiah, nor destruction upon the Ninevites, unless they should be forewarned to seek the face of God by prayers, and, in this manner, to turn away the evil from themselves; and, if they should do this, they should be spared. But He knew that they would do this, being, indeed, assisted by grace and the divine aid, by which He had determined to cooperate with the external preaching. So He determined to prolong the life of Hezekiah and to preserve the city of the Ninevites from destruction. Here, then, there seems to be not even apparent contrariety.

What you observe concerning "the human and the divine will of Christ," does not affect our present subject of discussion. It is true that there was such a difference; but this is not strange, since those wills belonged not to one origin, though they did belong to one person, embracing in himself two natures and two wills. I may add, also, that Christ willed both to be freed and not to be freed from death. For as a man, he said, "O, my Father, let this cup pass from me," and as a man, also, he corrected himself, "nevertheless, not as I will, but as thou wilt" (Matt 26:39). That this is to be understood of the human will, is apparent, because there is one and the same will, as there is one nature to the Father and to the Son, as divine.

I may say, in a word, that Christ, as to the outward man, willed to be freed from immediate death, but according to the inward man, he subjected himself to the divine will. And, if you will permit, I will say, that there was in him a feeling and a desire to be freed, not a volition. For volition results from the final decision of the reason and of wisdom, but desire follows the antecedent decision of the senses or the feelings.

That "Abraham was favorably inclined towards the Sodomites, who were devoted, by the decree of God, to destruction," the Scripture does not assert. It also does not seem to me to be very probable that "he could pray in faith" for those whom he knew to be devoted, by the decree of God, to irrevocable destruction. For prayer was not to be offered in behalf of such persons. God commands Jeremiah (7:16, 11:14; 14:11) not to pray for the people, which He had, by an irrevocable decree, and by His will as its consequent, destined and devoted to captivity and destruction.

For although it may not be requisite in prayers, offered for anything whatever, that one should certainly believe that the thing, which he seeks, shall be granted, it is necessary that the mind of him who prays should certainly believe that God, in His omnipotence and mercy, is both able and willing to do that which is asked, if He knows that it will be in accordance with His own grace. But that which God has decreed not to do, and what He has signified absolutely that He will not do, He neither can do, nor will He ever will to do, so long as the decree stands. And it is not right for a believer to intercede with God in his prayers for that thing, if the decree of God has been known to him.

Your third answer is, that "God, as a creditor, can require what He Himself may not will to effect." But there is an equivocation or ambiguity in those words. They may be understood, either in reference to that concurrence of God, which is necessary to the doing of that which He commands, or in reference to that efficacious concurrence by which what He commands, is certainly done. If in reference to the latter, it is true. There is no kind of conflict or contrariety between these two: "demand or command that any thing should be done," and "yet not to do it efficaciously." If in reference to the former, it is not true. For God does not command that, in reference to which He denies the aid necessary to effect it, unless anyone, of his own fault, deprives himself of that grace and makes himself unworthy of that aid.

The right of creditor remains, if he who is in debt, is not able to pay by his own fault. But it is not so with the command, in which faith is prescribed. For faith in Christ is not included in the debt which a man was bound to pay according to his primitive creation in the image of God, and the primitive economy under which he lived. For it began to be necessary, after God changed the condition of salvation from legal obedience to faith in Christ.

We come now to "the presentation of the Mediator" consisting both in the fact that the Mediator presented himself to God, the Father, as a victim for the sin of the world, and that the Father, by the word and His spirit, presents the Mediator, having performed the functions of that office, and having obtained remission of sins and eternal redemption to the world, reconciled through him. The former pertains to the provision of salvation, the latter to its application by faith in the same Mediator. The former is the execution of the act of appointment and promise, the latter coincides with the actual offering, which we have previously considered in discussing the promise. But the presentation, as it is defined by you, not immediately antecedent to the application, for between that presentation and the application there intervenes the offering of the Mediator by the word and the Holy Spirit.

Virtue and Efficacy

What you say concerning the virtue and efficacy of the price paid by Christ needs a more careful consideration. You say, that "the efficacy of that price, as far as merit is concerned, is infinite"; but you make a distinction between "actual and potential efficacy." You also define "potential efficacy" as synonymous with a sufficiency of price for the whole world. This, however is a phrase hitherto unknown among theologians, who have merely made a distinction between the efficacy and the sufficiency of the merit of Christ. I am not sure, also, but that there is an absurdity in styling efficacy "potential," since there is a contradiction in terms.

For all efficacy is actual, as that word has been, hitherto, used by theologians. But, laying aside phrases, let us consider the thing itself.

The *lutron* or price of the death of Christ, is said to be universal in its sufficiency, but particular in its efficacy, i.e. sufficient for the redemption of the whole world, and for the expiation of all sins, but its efficacy pertains not to all universally, which efficacy consists in actual application by faith and the sacrament of regeneration, as Augustine and Prosper, the Aquitanian, said. If you think so, it is well, and I shall not very much oppose it. But if I rightly understand you, it seems to me that you do not acknowledge the absolute sufficiency of that price, but with the added condition, if God had willed that it should be offered for the sins of the whole world. So then, that, which the Schoolmen declare categorically, namely, that Christ's death was sufficient for all and for each, is, according to your view, to be expressed hypothetically, that is, in this sense— the death of Christ would be a sufficient price for the sins of the whole world, if God had willed that it should be offered for all men. In this sense, indeed, its sufficiency is absolutely taken away. For if the *lutron* is not a ransom offered and paid for all, it is, indeed, not a *lutron* much less sufficient for all. For the *lutron* is that, which is offered and paid.

Therefore the death of Christ can be said to be sufficient for the redemption of the sins of all men, if God had wished that he should die for all. But it cannot be said to be a sufficient ransom, unless it has, in fact, been paid for all. Hence, also, Beza notes an incorrect phraseology, in that distinction, because the sin offering is said to be absolutely sufficient, which is not such, except on the supposition already set forth. But, indeed, my friend Perkins, the Scripture says most clearly in many places that Christ died for all, for the life of the world, and that by the command and grace of God.

The decree of Predestination prescribes nothing to the universality of the price paid for all by the death of Christ. It is posterior, in the order of nature, to the death of Christ and to its peculiar efficacy. For that decree pertains to the application of the benefits obtained for us by the death of Christ: but his death is the price by which those benefits were prepared.

Therefore the assertion is incorrect, and the order is inverted, when it is said that "Christ died only for the elect, and the predestinate." For Predestination depends, not only on the death of Christ, but also on the merit of Christ's death. Hence Christ did not die for those who were predestinated, but they, for whom Christ died were predestinated, though not all of them. For the universality of the death of Christ extends itself more widely than the object of Predestination. From which it is also concluded that the death of Christ and its merit is antecedent, in nature and order, to Predestination. What else, indeed, is Predestination than the preparation of the grace, obtained and provided for us by the death of Christ, and a preparation pertaining to the application, not to the acquisition or provision of grace, not yet existing? For the decree of God, by which He determined to give Christ as a Redeemer to the world, and to appoint him the head only of believers, is prior to the decree, by which He determined to really apply to some, by faith, the grace obtained by the death of Christ.

You allege these reasons in favor of your views, concerning the death of Christ. "Christ did not sacrifice for those for whom also he does not pray, because intercession and sacrifice are conjoined;" But he prays, not for all, but only for elect and for believers (John 17:9). In his prayer, he offers himself to the Father. Therefore he sacrifices not for all, and, consequently, his death is not a ransom for all men.

I reply that the Major does not seem to me to be, in all respects, true. The sacrifice is prior to the intercession. For he could not enter into the heavens that he might intercede for us in the presence of God, except by the blood of his own flesh. It is also prior, as sacrifice has reference to merit, intercession to the application of merit. For he is called the Mediator by merit and the efficacy of its application. He acquired merit by sacrifice; he intercedes for its application. He does both, as Priest; but he makes that application as King and Head of His church. It is indeed true that Christ, in the days of his flesh, offered up prayers with tears to God, the Father. But those prayers were not offered to obtain the application of merited blessing, but for the assistance of the Spirit, that he might stand firm in the conflict. If, indeed, he then offered up prayers to obtain the application referred to, they depended on the sacrifice, which was to be offered as though it were already offered. In this order, sacrifice and intercession are related to each other.

In reference to the minor, I assert, that Christ prayed also for the non-elect.

He prayed for those who crucified him, for his enemies, among whom also were non-elect persons. For "the princes of this world" crucified him, and to most of them the wisdom and power of God, which is Christ, was not revealed (1 Cor 2). Secondly, the prayer of Christ, contained in John 17, was offered, particularly for those who had believed, and those who should afterwards believe, and, indeed, to obtain and apply to them the blessings merited by the sacrifice of his death. He asks that they may be one with the Father and the Son, as the Father and the Son are one; which He could not ask unless reconciliation had actually been made, or was considered, by God, as having been made. But such is not the character of all the prayers of Christ.

Thirdly, I remark that the word "world," in John 17:9, properly signifies those who rejected Christ, as preached to them in the word of the gospel, and those who should afterwards reject him. This is apparent from the contrast: "I pray not for the world, but for them which thou hast given me," whom he describes as having believed (verse 8) and as believing at a future time (verse 20). The word is used similarly in many other passages: "The world knew him not." (John 1:10); "Light has come into the world, and men loved darkness rather than light" (3:19); "The Spirit of truth, whom the world cannot receive" (14:17); "He will reprove the world of sin, because they believe not on me" (16:8, 9); "How is it that thou wilt manifest thyself unto us, and not unto the world?" (14:22). Therefore the extent of the sacrifice is not to be limited by the narrow bounds of that intercession.

Wish to Learn

I could wish to learn from Illyricus how it can be in accordance with the justice of God, and the infinite value of Christ's sacrifice, that "prayer is expiatory and the rule of the Sacrifice [Canon Sacrificii]." I think, not only that Christ did not ask of the Father to regard favorably his sacrifice, but that it was not possible that He should present such a petition: if that is indeed true, which our churches teach and profess with one voice, then the most complete satisfaction was made to the justice of God by the sacrifice of Christ. But that idea originated in the Polish mass, in which, also, are those words—"Canon Sacrificii."

But the words, which contain your conclusion are remarkable, and have no right meaning. What is meant by this? "Christ was appointed to be the *lutron*, or price by the intercession and oblation of the Son." Intercession is subsequent to *lutron*. Therefore the latter was not appointed by the former. Oblation belongs to the ransom itself, and is therefore prior to the intercession, and could, in no way, be concerned in the appointment of the ransom. But the action itself has the character of an oblation. Hence, also, the ransom itself, as I have already often said, is prior to election. For election is unto life, which has no existence except by the oblation of the ransom; unless we may say that election is unto life, not now existing, nor as yet merited, not even in the decree of God. For he is the "lamb slain from the foundation of the world" (Rev 13:8).

You proceed further, and endeavor, but in vain, to confirm the same sentiment by other arguments. They seem to have some plausibility, but no truth. You say, that "Christ is only the Mediator of those, whose character he sustained on the cross; but he sustained the character of the elect only on the cross. Therefore he is only the Mediator of the elect."

I reply to the major, that it belongs not to the essence or the nature of Mediator to sustain the character of anyone. For he is constituted a Mediator between two dissident parties. Therefore, as Mediator he sustains the character of neither; unless, indeed, the nature of the mediation be, of necessity, such as to demand that the mediator should sustain the character of one of the parties. But this mediation has such a nature as the justice of God required. For it could enter upon no way of reconciliation with a world, guilty of sin, unless the Mediator should pledge satisfaction, and, in fact, should make it in accordance with the right of surety. This is what is said in 2 Cor 5:19, 21: "God was in Christ, reconciling the world unto Himself, for He hath made him to be sin" for the world, that is, a sin offering.

In this sense, also, it is truly said that Christ is not a Mediator, except for those, whose character he sustained. I speak here in respect to the Sacrifice: "For every high priest taken from among men, is ordained for men," etc. (Heb 5:1). Here, also, a distinction may be made between the act, by which reconciliation is obtained, and the completion of that act, which is reconciliation. The act, obtaining reconciliation, is the oblation of Christ on the cross. Its completion is the reconciliation. In respect to the act, he sustained our character, for we deserved death, not in respect to the completion. For the effect, resulting from the oblation, depends on the dignity and excellence of the character of Christ, not of us, whose character he sustained. Indeed, if it be proper to use distinctions of greater nicety, in this place, I may say, that Christ sustained our character, not in respect to action, namely, that of oblation, but of passion. For He was made a curse for us, and an offering for sin. From which it is evident, that, as all men are sinners and obnoxious to the curse, and Christ assumed human nature common to all, it is probable that he sustained the character of all men.

Minor of Syllogism

We see this also in the minor of your syllogism, which is: "Christ sustained the character of the elect only on the cross," in which I notice a two-fold fault, that of falsity and that of incorrect phraseology. Its falsity consists in this, that Christ is said to have sustained on the cross the character of the elect only. I prove it, from the fact that the Scripture no where says this; indeed it asserts the contrary in numerous passages.

Christ is called "the Lamb of God which taketh away the sin of the world" (John 1:29).

God is declared to have "so loved the world that He gave His only begotten Son" (3:16). Christ declares that he will give "his flesh for the life of the world" (6:51). "God was in Christ reconciling the world unto Himself" (2 Cor 5:19). "He is the propitiation for our sins; and not for ours only, but also for the sins of the whole world" (1 John 2:2).

The Samaritans said "We know that this is indeed the Christ, the Savior of the world" (John 4:42).

Also 1 John 4:14, "We have seen and do testify, that the Father sent the Son to be the Savior of the world." That, in the word "world," in these passages, all men, in general, are to be understood, is manifest from these passages and from Scriptural usages. For there is, in my judgment, no passage in the whole Bible, in which it can be proved beyond controversy that the word "world" signifies the elect. Again, Christ is said to have died for all, in Heb 2:9, and elsewhere. He is said to be "the Savior of all men, especially of those that believe" (1 Tim 4:10), which declaration cannot be explained to refer to preservation in this life without perversion and injury. Christ is also styled the "Mediator between God and men" (1 Tim 2:5). He is said to have died for those "without strength, ungodly, and yet sinners" (Rom 5:6–8).

What I said a little while since, is important also on this point. That the case of the whole human race is the same, all being alike conceived and born in sin, and the children of wrath; and that Christ assumed human nature common to all men, not from Abraham only and David, as Matthew traces his genealogy, but also from Adam, to whom Luke goes back in his third chapter. He offered, therefore, the flesh which he had in common with all. "For as much then as the children are partakers of flesh and blood, He also himself likewise took part of the same, etc." (Heb 2:14).

He offered that flesh for the common cause and the common sin, namely, for the sin of the world, in respect to which there is no difference among men, and the Apostle adds this cause in the passage just cited, "that through death he might destroy him that had the power of death."

Let the dignity and excellence of the person, which could offer an equivalent ransom for the sin of all men be added to this. Let the gracious and tender affection of God towards the human race come into consideration, which, in the Scriptures, is usually spoke of by the Greek term *philanthtropia* as in Titus 3:4. That term signifies, in general terms, the love of God towards men; which affection cannot be attributed to God, if He pursues with hatred any man, without reference to his deserts and his sin.

I know that some will reply that God indeed hates no one except on account of sin, but that He destined some to His own just hatred, that is, reprobating some without reference to sin. But in that way the order of things is inverted; for God does not hate because He reprobates, but reprobates because He hates. He reprobates a sinner, because the sinner and sin are justly hateful and odious to Him. Hatred is an affection in the Deity by which He hates unrighteousness and the unrighteous, as there is in Him also love for righteousness and the righteous. Reprobation is an act of God, internal in purpose, external in execution, and the act is, in the order of nature, subsequent to the affection. The destination of anyone to hatred, however it may be considered, has necessarily these two things preceding it, hatred against unrighteousness and the foresight that the individual, by his own fault, will be guilty of unrighteousness, by omission or commission.

I know, indeed, that the *philanthropia* of God, referred to, is not in all respects equal towards all men and towards each individual. But I also deny that there is so much difference, in that divine love, towards men that He has determined to act towards some, only according to the rigor of His own law, but towards others according to His own mercy and grace in Christ, as set forth in his gospel. He willed to treat the Fallen angels according to that rigor, but all men, Fallen in Adam, according to this grace. For every blessing, in which also mercy and long suffering (Exod 33:19 & 34:6–7), are comprehended, He determined to exhibit, in the deliverance and salvation of men.

Some, however, may wish to do away with the distinction, which many theologians make between the Fall of angels and that of man. For they say that the angels fell beyond all hope of restoration, but that men could have a complete restoration, and they assign, as a reason, the fact that angels sinned, by their own motion and impulse, and man, by the instigation and persuasion of an evil angel.

By Way of Definition

To all these things, we may add by way of conclusion, the proper and immediate effect of the death and suffering of Christ, and we shall see that no one of the human race is excluded from it. It is not an actual removal of sins from these or those, not an actual remission of sins, not justification, not an actual redemption of these or these, which can be bestowed upon no one without faith and the Spirit of Christ. But it is reconciliation with God, obtainment from God of remission, justification, and redemption; by which it is effected that God may now be able, as justice, to which satisfaction has been made, interposes no obstacle, to remit sins and to bestow the spirit of grace upon sinful men.

To the communication of these effects to sinners He was already inclined, of His own mercy, on account of which He gave Christ as the Savior of the world. But, by His justice, He was hindered from the actual communication of them. Meanwhile God maintained His own right to bestow on whom He pleased, and with such conditions as He chose to prescribe, those blessings (which are His by nature) the participation in which He, through His mercy, desired to bestow on sinners. But He could not actually do it on account of the obstacle of His justice, but which He can now actually bestow, as His justice has been satisfied by the blood and death of Christ. He, as the injured party, could prescribe the mode of reconciliation, which also He did prescribe, consisting in the death and obedience of His Son and because He has given him to us, to perform in our behalf the functions of the Mediatorial office.

If we decide that any person is excluded from that effect, we decide at the same time, that God does not remit his sins unto him, not because He is unwilling to do so, having the ability, but because He has not the ability, as justice presents an obstacle, and because He willed not to be able. He willed that His justice should be satisfied, before He should remit his sins unto any one, and because He did not will that His justice should be satisfied in reference to that person.

On the other hand, also, if we decide that the nature of the Mediation is such, as you seem to conceive, that the sins of all the Elect are taken from them and transferred to Christ, who suffered punishment for them, and, in fact, freed them from punishment, then obedience was required of him, who rendered it, and, by rendering it, merited eternal life, not for himself, but for them, not otherwise than if we had constituted him Mediator in our place, and through him had paid unto God our debt. We must also consider that, according to the rigor of God's justice and law, immunity from punishment and eternal life are due to the elect. And they can claim those blessings from God, by the right of payment and purchase, and without any rightful claim on the part of God, to demand faith in Christ and conversion to him. It is not easy to tell under how great absurdities, both the latter and the former opinion labor. I will refute each of them by a single argument.

In reference to the former, I argue that if God was unwilling that satisfaction for the sins of any should be rendered to Himself by the death of His Son, then faith in Christ cannot, justly, be demanded of them. They cannot justly be condemned for unbelief, and Christ cannot justly be constituted their judge. The latter, I compute by an argument of very great strength taken from the writings of the Apostle. The righteousness rendered by Christ is not ours in that it is rendered, but in that it is imputed unto us by faith, so that faith itself may be said to be "counted for righteousness" (Rom 4:5). This phrase, if rightly understood, may shed the clearest light on this whole discussion. I conclude, therefore, that Christ bore the character of all men in general, as it is said, and not that of the elect only.

I notice incorrect phraseology in the statement that He bore, on the cross, the character of the Elect, when no one is elect, except in Christ, as dead and risen again, and now constituted by God the Head of the church, and the Savior of them who should believe in him, and obey him unto salvation. Therefore, there were no elect, when he was yet hanging on the cross, that is, both of these events being considered as existing in the foreknowledge of God. Hence He could not have borne, on the cross, the character of the Elect. On this account, likewise, it would be absurdity to say that Christ bore the character of the reprobate, because reprobation had there no place. But he bore the character of men as sinners, unrighteous, enemies to God, apart from any consideration or distinction between Election and Reprobation. It is evident, then, from this reply, that it cannot be concluded from that argument that Christ is the Mediator for the Elect only, the work of the Mediator being now restricted to the oblation made on the cross.

You advance, also, another argument to prove the truth of your sentiment, and say: "Whatever Christ suffered and did as Redeemer, the same things all the redeemed do and suffer in him, and with him. But Christ, as Redeemer, died, rose again, ascended, sat down on the right hand of the Father; Therefore, in him and with him, all the redeemed died, rose again, ascended, sat down at the right hand of the Father." You then assume, as a position by consequence, that "The Elect only die, rise again, ascend, sit at the right hand of the Father, in and with Christ. Therefore, they alone are redeemed." We will inspect and examine both parts of this argument in order.

Notorious Falsity

The proposition, or Major, of this prosyllogism seems to me to be chargeable with notorious falsity, as can, also, be easily demonstrated. For it confounds the sufferings and the actions, by which redemption is effected and obtained, with the completion of redemption itself, and the application of redemption. For redemption does not refer to suffering, or to any action of Christ, but to the completion, the event, and the fruit of that suffering and action. Therefore, the sufferings and the actions of Christ are prior to redemption, but redemption is prior to its application. They, however, are called redeemed from the application. Therefore, that which Christ suffered and did to obtain redemption, the redeemed did not suffer or do.

For they were not at that time redeemed, but by those actions, redemption was obtained and applied to them by faith, and so they as the result, were redeemed. The very nature of things clearly proves that redeemer and redeemed are things so related, that the former is the foundation, the latter, the terminus, not vice versa. Therefore, in the former is comprehended the cause of the other, and indeed the cause, produced by its own efficiency. Whence it follows that the redeemed did not that, which was done by the redeemed, since, in that case, they were redeemed before the act of redemption was performed by the redeemer, and the redemption itself was obtained. If you say that you consider the redeemed not as redeemed, but as men to be redeemed, I reply that in whatever way they are considered it can never be truly said that they did, in and with Christ, what Christ did for the sake of redeeming them. For those to be redeemed were not in Christ or with Christ, therefore, they could neither in him nor with him, suffer or do anything.

You will say that "they suffered and acted in him as a surety and pledge;" but I say in him as constituted a surety not by them, but by God for them, and on him the work of redemption was imposed by God. It is true, indeed, that he assumed from men the nature in which redemption was performed. Yet He, not men in him, offered it. But, if they may be said to have suffered, because their nature suffered in the form of Christ, you see that in this way also the redemption is general for all those to whom the same nature belongs. Perhaps you refer to those passages of Scripture, in which we are said to be "dead with Christ, buried with him and raised with him" (Rom 6:3, 4, 5).

Your explanation is unsatisfactory if it regards them as having reference to our present subject. For those passages treat of the crucifixion, death, burial, and resurrection, which we each, in our own person, endure and experience. But they do not pertain to the meritorious redemption, as the crucifixion, death, etc., of Christ. Again, in those passages, the subject of discussion is that of our engrafting into Christ by faith, and our communion with him, which pertain to the application of redemption. But here, the subject of discussion is the obtaining of redemption, and the acts that pertain to it. Those passages teach that we, being grafted into Christ by faith, received from him the power of the Spirit, by which our old man is crucified, dead and buried, and we are resuscitated and raised again into a new life. From this it is apparent that they have no connection with our present subject.

The right meaning of the assumption, or minor, is that Christ, performing the work of redemption, died, rose again, and ascended into the heavens. For he was not the redeemer before he offered himself to death and rose again from the dead. I remark, more briefly, that Christ died and rose again in that he was Redeemer by the imposition and acceptance of the office, not by the fulfillment of the same. For the death and resurrection of Christ pertain to the function of the office of Redeemer. It now appears, from this, in what sense the conclusion is true, not in that in which you intend it, that they, whom you call "the redeemed," died and rose again in the person of Christ, but as I, a short time since, explained it, in a sense, pertaining, not to the obtainment of redemption, but to the application of the obtained redemption. For Christ is said to have "entered in once into the holy place, having obtained eternal redemption," (Heb 9:12) which redemption he communicates to believers, by the Holy Spirit sent from heaven.

These things being thus considered, your position by consequence does not weigh against the opinion, which I here defend. For it certainly happens to the Elect, only in the sense which we have set forth, with Christ to die, rise again, ascend, and sit at the right hand of the Father. They also, by reason of their being engrafted in Christ, and the application of the benefits of Christ, and of communion with Christ, are said to be "redeemed."

"Thou art worthy to take the book, and to open the seals thereof: for thou wast (sic) slain, and hast redeemed us to God by thy blood out of every kindred, and tongue, and people, and nation; and hast made us unto our God kings and priests; and we shall reign on the earth" (Rev 5:9, 10).

So, also, in Rev 14:3–4, the same are said to have been "redeemed from the earth, and from among men." It is, however, to be observed that this position is not a consequence of the antecedents, unless there be added, to the major, a restrictive phrase, in this way: "Whatever Christ suffered and did this all the redeemed, and they only, suffered and did in Him, and with Him."

Prove This Position

The arguments you adduce to prove this position, are readily conceded by me, in the sense which I have explained. But that, which you afterwards present to illustrate your meaning, deserves notice. For the sins of those, for whom Christ died, are condemned in the flesh of Christ, in such a manner that they may not, by that fact, be freed from condemnation, unless they believe in Christ. For "there is therefore, now, no condemnation to them which are in Christ Jesus, who walk not after the flesh, but after the Spirit" (Rom 8:1).

The error of confounding things, which should be distinct, and uniting those which should be divided, is constantly committed. For obtaining, and the act itself, which obtains, are confounded with the application and the former are substituted for the latter.

You say, also, "the expiatory victim sanctifies those for whom he is a victim For victim and sanctification pertain to the same persons;—But Christ sanctifies only the Elect and believers;—Therefore, Christ is victim for the Elect only and believers."

I answer to your Major, that the expiatory victim sanctifies, not in that it is offered, but in that it is applied. This may be plainly seen in the passage cited by yourself : "For if . . . the ashes of a heifer, sprinkling the unclean, sanctifieth to the purifying of the flesh: How much more shall the blood of Christ, etc." (Heb 9:13, 14). For which reason, it is called in Heb 12:24, "the blood of sprinkling."

In the same manner, those, who not only slew the paschal lamb, but also sprinkled the door posts with its blood, were passed over by the destroying angel. If, then, the phrase "for whom" implies, not the oblation only, but also the fruit and advantage of the oblation, I admit the truth of the major. But we are, here, discussing not the application of the victim Christ, but the oblation only, which, in the Scriptures, is simply said to be "for men" (Heb 5:1). But faith must necessarily intervene between the oblation, and its application which is sanctification. The oblation of the victim then, was made not for believers, but for men as sinners, yet on this condition, that He should sanctify only believers in Christ. Hence, it cannot be considered, even though the minor should be conceded, that Christ offered himself for the Elect only, since Election, as it is made in Christ, offered, dead, risen again, and having obtained eternal redemption by his blood, must be subsequent to the oblation.

You add: "Christ is the complete Savior of those, whom he saves, not only by his merits, but by efficaciously working their salvation." Who denies this? But the distinction is to be observed between these two functions and operations of Christ, the recovery, by his blood, of the salvation, which was lost by sin, and the actual communication or application, by the Holy Spirit, of the salvation obtained by his blood.

The former precedes, the latter requires, in accordance with the divine decree, that faith should precede it. Therefore, though Christ may not be said to completely save those who are not actually saved, yet he is said to be the Savior of others than believers (1 Tim 4:10). I do not see how that passage can be suitably explained, unless by the distinction between sufficient and efficacious salvation, or salvation as recovered and as applied. The passages you cite from the Fathers partly have no relation to the matter now discussed, and partly are related to it, but they teach nothing else than that the death and passion of Christ, which are a sufficient price for the redemption of the sins of all men, in fact, profit the Elect only, and those who believe unto salvation. What you say in reference to the application is correct; but I wish that you would distinguish between it, and those things which precede it.

From what has already been said, the decree, in reference to the bestowment of the Mediator and to the salvation of believers through the Mediator, is prior to the decree of Predestination, in which some are destined to salvation in Christ, and others are left to condemnation out of Christ. But you say that "the decree of election is the cause and the beginning of all the saving gifts and works in men." I grant it, but not in view of the fact that it is the decree of election, but in that it is the desire of the bestowing of grace. In that it is the decree of election, it is the cause that grace is bestowed only on those: for it is the opposite of reprobation, and necessarily supposes it. For there is no election without reprobation, and the term elect itself signifies loved, with the contrast of not loved at least in the same mode and decree, and restricts love to those who are styled elect with the exclusion of those who are styled the non-elect or reprobate. So far then, as saving gifts are bestowed upon anyone in that act which is called election, it is properly love; in that the bestowing is restricted to some, to the exclusion of others, it is called election.

From this, it is apparent, in the first place, that the love that is according to election, would not be less towards the elect than it now is, even if God should declare the same favor, and His own love towards all men in general. Secondly, they who make the love of God, in Christ, the cause of the salvation of men, and that alone, do no injury to grace, even if they deny that such love is according to election, that is, restricted to a few by the decree of God. They may indeed, deny that which is true, but without injury to grace or mercy. For I presupposed that they make the same love to be the cause of salvation, as they do, who contend for election. I know, indeed, that Augustine often said against the Pelagians, that "they who make the grace of God common to all, in effect, deny grace altogether." But this assertion is not, in all respects, true; but it was valid against the Pelagians, and all those who, at that time, made the grace of God universal.

For they explained the grace of God, to be the gift bestowed equally on all by creation, in our original nature. I acknowledge, indeed, that, from the universality of grace, some consequences can be deduced, which will prove that the universality of grace may be indirectly opposed to that grace by which the elect are saved. But it should be known that those consequences are not, all of them, tenable, we examine them accurately, and I wish that you should demonstrate this.

You will thus effect much, not indeed in sustaining the view that you here specially advocate, but in sustaining the doctrine of election and reprobation in general. But it will be said that, by the reprobation of some, that is, by election joined with love, the elect are more fully convinced that the love of God towards themselves is not of debt, than they would be if that same love were bestowed by God upon all without any distinction. I, indeed grant it, and the Scripture often uses that argument. Yet that love toward us, can be proved to be gratuitous, and not of debt, and can be sealed upon our hearts, without that argument.

It appears then, that there is no absolute necessity of presenting that argument. I do not say these things because I wish that the doctrine of election should not be taught in our churches; far be it from me. I do so to show that this subject is to be treated with moderation, and without offense to weak believers, who, for the very reason that they hear that they cannot be certain of salvation, unless they believe that which is taught concerning Election with the rejection of some, begin to doubt whether the sense of certainty of salvation they have at times enjoyed, is to be attributed to the testimony of the Holy Spirit, or to a certain persuasion and presumption in their own minds. I write this from experience. So much in reference to Election. Let us now consider its opposite: Reprobation.

Decree of Reprobation

But you define the decree of reprobation in a two-fold manner. First you say: "It is the work of divine providence, by which God decreed to pass by certain men, as to supernatural grace, that He might declare His justice and wrath in their due destruction." In my opinion, there are in this definition, four faults, which, with your consent, I will exhibit. The first fault is, you have made the decree of Reprobation, "the work, etc.," when, as it exists in God, it can in no way be called a work, which is something apart from that which produces it, existing after an act, and from an act produced by the efficaciousness or efficiency of an agent.

I should prefer then to use the word "act" in this case. The second fault is: you do not well describe the object of that act, when you say "certain men are passed by," without any mention of any condition required in the object, or any reference to the fact that the men spoken of are sinners. For sin is a condition, requisite in a man, to be passed by in reprobation, or, so to speak, in one capable of being passed by. This I shall briefly prove in a few arguments.

First, the Scripture acknowledges no reprobation of men, as having been made by God, unless its meritorious cause is sin. Secondly, since reprobation is the opposite of election, it follows, if divine election has reference to sinners, that reprobation has reference to persons of the same character. But Election, as I have previously shown, has reference to sinners. Thirdly, because that supernatural grace, denied by reprobation, is grace necessary to sinners only: namely that of remission of sins and the renewal of the Holy Spirit. Fourthly, because justice and wrath cannot be declared, except against a sinner, for where there is no sin there can be no place either for wrath or punitive justice (of which you here necessarily speak). Fifthly, because punishment is due to no one, unless he is a sinner, and you say that "the wrath of God and His justice are declared in the due destruction of the Reprobate."

When I make sin the meritorious cause of reprobation, do not consider me as, on the other hand, making righteousness the meritorious cause of Election. For sin is the meritorious cause of the reprobation of all sinners in general. But election is, not only of that grace which is not of debt, and which man has not merited, but also of that grace that takes away demerit. Even if the meritorious cause is supposed, the effect is not at once produced unless by the intervention of His will, to whom it belongs to inflict due punishment, according to the merit of sin. But He has power to punish sin according to its deserts, or to pardon it, of His grace in Christ.

Therefore, in both cases, in election and in reprobation, the free will of God is considered the proximate and immediate cause. If you oppose to me the common distinction, by which sin is said to be required in the object of the execution, but not in the object of the decree itself, I reply that it is not right that God should will to condemn anyone, or will to pass by him without consideration of sin, as it is not right for Him, in fact, to pass by or condemn anyone without the demerit of sin. It is, then, truly said, the cause of the decree and of its execution is one and the same.

Ill-Adjusted Phraseology

Your third fault is that of obscurity and ill-adjusted phraseology. For what is implied in the phrase "to pass by as to supernatural grace," instead of to pass by in the dispensation and bestowment of supernatural grace? There is ambiguity, also, in the word "supernatural." Grace is supernatural, both as it is superadded to unfallen nature, bearing nature beyond itself, and as it is bestowed on fallen nature, changing it, and raising it to things heavenly and supernatural.

The fourth fault is, that you present a result of the preterition which coheres by no necessary copula, with the antecedent cause of the preterition. For sin is not presupposed to that act. Sin does not of necessity exist from that act; one of which facts is necessarily required from the necessity of coherence between the act and its result. If, indeed, you say that sin necessarily results from that preterition, then you make God the Author of sin by a denial of the grace, without which, sin cannot be avoided. But if that grace, which is denied to anyone by preterition, is not necessary for the avoidance of sin, then a man could without it abstain from sin and so not deserve destruction. If he could do this, that declaration of justice and wrath does not result from the act of decreed preterition. But you know that the parts of a definition should mutually cohere by a necessary copula, and that a result should not be proposed, which, even on the supposition of any act, does not result from that same act. For such a result would be incidental, and therefore, ought not to be found in a definition which is independent, and designed to convey absolute knowledge.

Let us now examine the other definition, which you have adduced, perhaps for the very reason, that you thought your former one somewhat unsound. It is this: "The decree of reprobation is the purpose to permit anyone to fall into sin, and to inflict the punishment of damnation on account of sin." I know that this definition is used by the Schoolmen, and, among others, by Thomas Aquinas, for whose genius and erudition I have as high an esteem as anyone; but he, here, seems to me to be under a kind of hallucination. First, because he makes the decree of reprobation to be antecedent to sin, which opinion I have already refuted. Secondly, because he attributes that permission to the decree of reprobation, which ought to be attributed to a certain other, more general decree, that of providence, as I will show. An act that has reference to all men, in general, apart from the distinction between the elect and the reprobate, is not an act of reprobation, for in that act, God had reference to the reprobate only. But it is that act of permission, by which God permitted man to fall into sin, is general, and extending to all men; for in Adam, all sinned (Rom 5:12).

And all are "by nature the children of wrath" (Eph 2:3). That act, then, is not one of reprobation, but of mere general providence, regarding all men entirely without difference, and governing and administering their primitive state in the person of Adam. If you say that both are to be conjoined, the permission of the Fall and the infliction of punishment, and that the whole subject, taken in a complex manner, is the proper act of reprobation, I answer that on that principle, permission, according to which Adam, and in him, all his posterity fell, which is one and univocal, is resolved into two diverse matters. The matter thus becomes two-fold and equivocal; that is, into the decree of reprobation, by which the reprobate are permitted to fall, and the decree of providence, by which even the elect themselves are permitted to fall.

I add another argument, which, in my judgment indeed, is irrefutable.

Reprobation and Election are spoken of as things separate and opposite; one is not without the other. Hence, no act can be attributed to one of them, the opposite of which, either affirmative or negative, may not be attributed to the other. But no act, opposite to that of permission to fall, can be attributed to Election. There is but one act that is opposite to the act of permission, namely, hindrance from falling into sin. But no man, not even one of the elect, is hindered from falling into sin. For the elect themselves sinned in Adam. Therefore, the act of permission is not to be assigned to the decree of Reprobation. If you diligently consider this argument, you will see that it is clearly evident from it that permission to fall was prior both to Reprobation and to Election, and therefore the decree of Permission was prior to the decree of Election and Reprobation: prior, in order and nature. Then, also, that other peculiarity of Reprobation remains, and as it presupposes sin, I conclude that men, as sinners, are the object of Reprobation.

You limit, moreover, the decree of Reprobation to two acts. "The former is the purpose to pass by certain men, and to illustrate justice in them." But what justice, unless it is punitive? If it is punitive, then it coincides with the second act: "the ordination to punishment." Others distinguish that same decree into the negative act of preterition, and the affirmative act of ordination to punishment. If you meant the same thing, you have not expressed it well, for punitive justice superintends the ordination of punishment, but the freedom of the divine will superintends preterition.

Not Caused by Men

Your assertion that "this preterition has not its cause in men" will not be proved by any passage of Scripture, which everywhere teaches that all abandonment is on account of sin. Though this is so, yet it does not follow that "the mere good pleasure of God" is not the cause of abandonment. For God is free to leave or not to leave the sinner, who deserves abandonment; and thus, the will of God is the proximate and immediate cause of abandonment, and indeed the only cause in this respect, that when it is possible for Him not to forsake the sinner, He may yet sometimes do so.

For God dispenses absolutely according to His own will, in reference to the merit of sin, whether in His Son, to take it away, or out of His Son, to punish it. And how, I pray, does it "interfere with the liberty of the good pleasure," I would prefer the word *pleasure*, "of God," if He is said not to be able to forsake one who is not a sinner? For it is only in view of His justice that He is able to forsake one unless he is a sinner. And liberty does not describe the objects with which God is concerned, in the operations of His will, but the mode in which He pleases to operate in reference to any object.

I could wish that you would not attribute any freedom to the will of God that may impinge upon His justice. For justice is prior to the will, and is its rule, and freedom is attributed to the will as its mode. That mode, then, is limited by justice. Yet it will not, therefore, be denied that God is completely free in the acts of His will. Since then He is completely free in the acts of His will, not because He wills all things, but because He wills freely whatever He wills, in what respect is it contrary to the freedom of God, if He is said not to will certain things?

For He cannot, in His justice, will them, and His freedom is not limited by a superior being out of Himself, but by His own justice. In this sense, also, the will of God is said to be "the cause of causes, and out of which, or beyond which no reason is to be sought," which is true also according to my explanation. For if anyone asks, "Why does God leave one, and choose another?" the answer is: "Because He wills it." If it is asked: "But why does He will it?" The cause is found not out of Himself. But there is a cause why He could justly will to leave anyone, and that cause is sin, not effecting actual desertion, but deserving it, and making the sinner worthy of abandonment, and certainly to be abandoned, if God should choose to punish him according to his demerit, which choice is allowed to His free will.

Man is indeed as "clay in the hands of the potter," but it does not follow from this that God can justly make of that clay whatever it might be possible for Him to make by an act of His omnipotence. He can reduce to nothing the clay formed by Himself and made man, for this belongs to Him by supreme right. But He cannot hate the same clay, or be angry with it, or condemn it forever, unless that lump has become sinful by its own fault, and been made a lump of corruption. Thus also Augustine explains the passage in Rom 9, as having reference to the lump of corruption.

But you say, "if God had willed by His eternal decree to pass over men as sinners only, not as men, then He did not make them vessels of wrath, but He found them vessels of wrath, made such by themselves." I reply that ignorance of the phrase, which the apostle uses in Rom 9:22, is shown here. For "to make a vessel unto wrath," does not signify to sin or to make one worthy of wrath through sin. But it signifies to destine to just wrath him who has sinned and so made himself worthy of wrath, which is an act of the divine judgment, peremptory indeed, because it is an act of reprobation, but it has reference to man as a sinner, for sin alone is the meritorious cause of wrath.

If you urge further that in the word "lump," men, not as made but as to be made, are signified, and that this is proved by the force of the word, shall deny that the force and radical meaning of the word is to be, here, precisely insisted upon. This asserts that, in Scriptural use, the word is applied to men, not only as made but as sinners, and as those received into the grace of reconciliation, and transgressing of the covenant of grace; as in the prophet Jeremiah, "Behold as the clay is in the potter's hand, so are ye in mine hand, O house of Israel" (18:6).

In your third argument you turn aside from the controversy, and from the real state of the case, contrary to the law of correct disputation. Therefore, you do not come to the conclusion that is sought, unless you may say that to reject grace is the same as to sin, which two things are indeed often distinguished in the Scriptures. For the Pharisees were already in Adam and indeed, in themselves, sinners before they "rejected the counsel of God against themselves, being not baptized" of John (Luke 7:30). The Jews, mentioned in Acts 13:46, were already sinners, in Adam and in themselves, before they made themselves unworthy of the grace of God, rejecting the word of life. But the question here is whether God passes by sinners, not whether he sees that they will reject grace.

Again, it does not follow that "reprobation, therefore, depends on men," if God reprobates no one unless reprobation and rejection is desired. For an effect cannot be said to depend on that cause which, being in operation, does not certainly produce the effect. But all men as sinners, but some of them, namely, the Elect, are not left. Hence sin is not the cause of rejection, unless by the intervention of the damnatory sentence of the judge, in which it is decreed that sin shall be punished according to its demerit. Who does not know that the sentence depends on the judge, not on the criminal, even if the criminal has deserved that sentence by his own act, without which the judge could neither conceive, nor pronounce, nor execute the sentence. Nor does it follow "that God chooses some, and so they are chosen by Him, and that He rejects others, and, therefore, they are rejected." For sin, as to demerit, is common to the elect and the reprobate, according to the theory, which simply requires that men as sinners should be made the object of Predestination, without any special distinction in the sin itself.

Neglect of Grace

But you present, as a proof, that the foreseen neglect of grace is not the cause of rejection, the statement that "infants," dying out of the covenant of the gospel, have not neglected this grace, and yet are reprobate and "rejected by God." I affirm that they rejected the grace of the gospel in their parents, grandparents, great-grandparents, etc., by which act they deserved to be abandoned by God. I should desire that some solid reason might be presented to me why, since all his posterity have sinned, in Adam, against the law, and on that account, have merited punishment and rejection, infants also, to whom, in their parents, the grace of the gospel is offered, and by whom, in their parents, it is rejected, have not sinned against the grace of the gospel. For the rule of the divine covenant is perpetual, that children are comprehended and judged in their parents.

The fourth argument, which you draw from Rom 9, does not relate to the present subject. For the apostle there treats of the decree, by which God determined to justify and to save those who should be heirs of righteousness and salvation, not by works, but by faith in Christ; not of the decree by which He determined to save these or those, and to condemn others, or of that by which He determined to give faith to some, and to withhold it from others. This might be most easily demonstrated from the passage itself, and from the whole context, and I should do it, if time would permit. But this being granted, yet not acknowledged, namely, that the Apostle excludes works as the basis of the decree, of which he here treats, yet that, which you intend to prove, will not follow.

For Augustine interprets it of works, which were peculiar to each of them (Esau and Jacob), not common to both, such as original sin, in which they were both conceived, when God spoke to Rebecca (verse 12). This interpretation of Augustine is proved to be true from the fact that the apostle regards Jacob, as having done no good, and Esau, no evil, when it was said to their mother Rebecca, "the elder shall serve the younger," as if it might be thought that Esau, by evil deeds, had merited that he should be the servant of his younger brother, who, by his good deeds, had acquired for himself that prerogative.

Therefore, it does not exclude all respect of sin: sins, to which they were both equally subject. That "will" of God, in which "Paul acquiesces," is not that, by which He has purposed to adjudge anyone, not a sinner, to eternal death, but by which of those who are equally sinners, to one He shows mercy, but another He hardens; which words indeed mark the pre-existence of sin. For mercy can be shown to no one, who is not miserable; and no one is miserable, who is not a sinner.

Hardening also has sin as its cause, that is, contumacious perseverance in sin.

But from your last argument, you deduce nothing against those, who make sin a requisite condition in the object of Predestination. For they acknowledge that "it is of the mere will of God that this one is elected, and that one rejected." The passage you also cite from a German author[7] , also places sin as a condition, prerequisite to Predestination. For he is not "delivered" who has not been, first, made miserable and the captive of sin.

---

7. Henricus Steinwerterus, *De Vocatione Gentium.*

The second act of reprobation, you make to be "ordination to punishment," which you distinguish into "absolute and relative." There might be also a place for the same distinction, in the contrary act of election. For absolute election is a reception into favor; relative election is that, by which one person, and not another, is received into favor. You do rightly in making the will of God the cause of absolute ordination, yet not to the exclusion of sin. For it is very true that, in the Deity, there is the same cause of willing and doing that which He has decreed. Sin also has the same relation to ordination as to damnation.

It has the relation of meritorious cause to damnation, hence it has also the relation of meritorious cause to, ordination. There is likewise no probable relation, to which a contrary cannot be conceived. Therefore, it cannot be absolutely denied that "sin is the cause of the decree of damnation." For though it may not be the immediate, proximate or principal cause, yet it is the meritorious cause, without which God cannot justly ordain anyone to punishment. But I should desire the proof that "sin does not precede, in the relation of order, in the divine prescience, that former act" of preterition and rejection. There is indeed, in my judgment, no passage of Scripture that contains that idea; I wish that one may be adduced.

"Relative ordination is that by which this person, and not that, is ordained to punishment, and on the same condition." God has indeed the power of punishing and of remitting sin, according to His will, nor is He responsible to anyone, unless so far as He has bound Himself by His own promises.

Divine Goodness

In this, also, "the liberty of the divine goodness is exhibited," but not in this only. For the same thing is declared in creation itself, and in the dispensation of natural blessings, in this, that He determined that one part of nothing should be heaven, another the earth, a third the air, etc. Indeed He has in creation demonstrated "the same liberty in the bestowment of supernatural blessings." For He has honored some of His creatures with supernatural gifts, as angels and men, and others, indeed all others, He has made without supernatural gifts. He has likewise demonstrated the same freedom, not only in the creation, but in the government and care of His rational creatures, since He has made a communication of supernatural felicity, according to the fixed law and pleasure of His own will.

From which angels and men could understand that God was free to communicate it to them according to His own will. This is declared by the arbitrary prescription of its condition. I make this remark that no one may think, that the act, which we now discuss, was the first act by which God evinced the freedom of His will.

Your words, "and indeed if God should destroy and damn all those who are rejected by Him, yet He would not be unjust," I cannot approve, and you will not, if you compare your previous statements with them. For you said that ordination to punishment is subsequent to sin in the order of nature. And, here, you do not place sin between rejection, which is the first act of reprobation, and damnation, which is the second; while damnation does not follow rejection immediately, but it follows sin. Those words so to speak, also contain a manifest falsity. First, because "the judge of all the earth cannot do right, if He should slay the righteous with the wicked" (Gen 18:25); and sin is the single and only meritorious cause of damnation.

"Whosoever hath sinned against me, him will I blot out of my book" (Exod. 32:33). "The soul that sinneth it shall die" (Ezek 18:4). Secondly, because that rejection is the cause into which sin can be resolved, and, therefore, the cause of sin, by the mode of removal, or non-bestowment of that aid, without which sin cannot be avoided. No small error is committed here, in the fact that, when you do not suppose sin to be previous to rejection and divine preterition, you yet make ordination to punishment subsequent to rejection, without any explanation of the coherence of both those acts.

If you attempt this, you will fall into no less a fault; for you will make God, on account of that rejection, the author of sin, as can be shown by irrefutable arguments. The illustrations you propose, are not adapted to your design, and fail through want of analogy. For it is one thing to kill a beast, by which deed it ceases to exist and is not rendered miserable, or to exclude from your house one whom you do not please to admit, and a very different thing to condemn a man to eternal punishment, which is far more severe than to annihilate the same person.

"The cause of this relative reprobation is the mere will of God without any consideration of sin," namely, that which may have any effect in making a distinction between different persons, but not in giving the power to ordain certain persons to punishment, which power indeed exists in God as Lord and Judge, but cannot really be exercised except towards a sinner who deserves punishment from the equity of divine justice. That which you quote from Augustine and Gregory agrees with this distinction. For both make sin the meritorious cause of reprobation, and consider sin and sinners as altogether prerequisite to Predestination, but attribute the act of separation to the mere will of God.

In this "second act of reprobation," you make two "steps, just rejection, and, damnation on account of sin." It is apparent, from this, that you distinguish between that rejection which you made the first step of reprobation, and this latter rejection. Yet you do not state the distinction between those two rejections, which, however, ought to have been done, to avoid confusion. Yet it may be right to conjecture, since you make the former prior to sin, that you would make the latter consequent upon sin, and existing on account of the desert of sin.

You make the divine rejection two-fold, but do not explain whether you mean, here, the latter, which you consider the first step in the second act of reprobation, or divine rejection in general. It is not the former, in my judgment, for that, as it pertains to the second act of reprobation, is on account of sin. And this is considered by you to be prior to sin. Perhaps it is the same with the rejection, which is the first act of reprobation. If so, you cannot in the passages now referred to, escape the charge of confused discussion.

Let us see how you explain that twofold rejection. You say that the former is "the denial of aid, confirmation, and assisting grace, by which the first is rendered efficacious for the resistance of temptations, and for perseverance in goodness," and you style it "rejection of trial or test" and affirm that it occurs in the case of those "who have not yet forsaken God," illustrating it from the example of the first man, Adam. But I inquire of you, whether you consider that aid, confirmation, and assisting grace so necessary for perseverance in goodness, that, without it, a man could not resist temptation? If you reply affirmatively, consider how you can excuse, from the responsibility of sin, the Deity, who has denied to man, apart from any fault in him, the gifts and aids necessary to perseverance in goodness. If negatively, then indeed, tell me by what right you call this a rejection by God.

Can he be said to be rejected by God, who is adorned and endued with grace, rendering him acceptable, provided with all gifts and aids necessary to perseverance in goodness, and even fortified by the help of the Holy Spirit to resist temptation? If you speak in accordance with Scriptural usage you cannot call it rejection. You will say that it is not called, in an absolute sense, rejection, but *kata ti*, relatively, and in a certain respect, that is, so far that God affords to him, on whom He has bestowed all those things: not efficacious aid, not actual confirmation in goodness, not that assisting grace, without which the former graces are inefficacious. This is apparent, you say, from the event, since, if he had obtained also those helps, he would have been steadfast in goodness, he would not have Fallen.

This you express in quoting from Augustine: "God rejected man, not as to ability, but as to will." If he had possessed the latter, he would have maintained his integrity.

Here we enter, most learned Perkins, on a discussion of the utmost difficulty, and scarcely explicable, at least by myself, as yet but a beginner, and not sufficiently acquainted with those heights of sacred theology. Yet I will venture to present some thoughts, trusting to the grace of Him, who gives wisdom to babes, and sight to the blind. You will assist me in part, that, by our mutual conference, the light may shine with greater brightness. For I have undertaken to write not against you, but to you, for the sake both of learning and of teaching.

Need Explanation

I see here two things which will need explanation from me. First, in reference to sufficient and efficacious grace. Secondly, in reference to the administration and dispensation of both, and the causes of that dispensation.

We have, thus far, examined your doctrine of Predestination. If now it may seem proper to you to correct it according to our observations, it will, without doubt, be free from the liability to be called "Manichean," "Stoic," "Epicurean," or even "Pelagian"; though, as set forth by you, it is free from the imputation of the last error. It cannot be with equal ease acquitted of the former, to him, who shall accurately compare not only your opinion, but the logical consequences of your opinion, with the dogmas of the Manichees, and the Stoics.

Some would deduce Epicurism also from the same opinion, but only by means of a series of conclusions. I wish that you had with sufficient perspicuity vindicated your doctrine from those objections. You, indeed, attempt to do this in answering the various allegations, usually made against the doctrine, set forth by you. We will consider these, with your answers in order.

ALLEGATION 1:

"It is Taught by Us That Certain Men, and Few in Number, Are Elected"

It is true that your theory, manifestly includes the very doctrine which is stated in that allegation. Therefore, in that accusation, no sentiment contrary to your opinion and doctrine is attributed to you. It is also true, that the allegation contains no offense. For the Scripture in plain terms declares that "Many are called, but few are chosen" (Matt 22:14).

"Fear not, little flock" (Luke 12:32). In your reply, you show most clearly that nothing false is charged upon your theory, in that allegation. I do not, indeed, think that there is anyone who can object, on this account, to that theory. For even all heretics, with whom we have become acquainted, think that the elect are few; many of them, and, I would dare to say, all of them, believe that "the few are known to God, and so definitely, that the number can be neither increased nor diminished, and they, who are numbered, cannot be varied." But they offer another explanation of the term election, contrary to, or at least different from your idea.

You ought, then, to have presented this allegation, not in such terms, that it could be made against you only by a foolish opponent—but as it would be stated by those who are opposed to your view. For they do not object to your theory because you say "certain persons, and few in number, are elected by God." You do so because you consider that "God, by a naked and absolute decree, without any reference to sin or unbelief, elected certain men, and that they were few; and that, by the same decree, He rejected the residue of the multitude of men, to whom He did not give Christ, and to whom He did not design that the death of Christ should be of advantage."

But something shall be said of the allegation in that form, under the other allegations referred to by you.

ALLEGATION 2:

"We Teach That God Ordained Men to Hell Fire, and that He
Created Them, That He Might Destroy Them"

In that allegation, the word "men" should have been limited and restricted to certain men, namely, to those about to perish. For no one will
impute to you such an opinion in reference to all men, since all know
that you except and exclude the elect from that number. You ought then,
to have set forth that allegation as thus: "We teach that God ordained
some men, as men, without any consideration of sin, to hell fire, and
created them, that He might destroy them."

This is indeed, a serious allegation, and contains a great slander, if it
is falsely charged upon you. If it is a true charge, you ought, by all means,
to endeavor to free and relieve yourself of it, by a change of sentiment. I
admit that you, and they, who agree with you in opinion, are not accustomed to speak in this way. But it is to be considered whether or not you
assert what is equivalent to this, and if that shall be proved, you are held
convicted of the charge. I will now, for the time, take the place of those
who accuse you, yet being by no means myself an accuser; and do you
must see whether I plead their cause well, and convict you of that charge.

He, who makes hellfire the punishment of sin, who ordains that
the first man, and in him all men, shall sin, who so, by his providence,
governs that first man that he shall of necessity, sin, and shall not be able
in fact to avoid sin, in consequence of which he and all in him, commit
sin, who, finally, certainly and irrevocably decrees in Himself to leave in
Adam (i.e. in depravity) most of these, who shall sin in Adam, and to
punish sin in them by hellfire, is said, most deservedly, to have ordained
to hellfire. This was by an absolute decree for, some and indeed most
men, as men, apart from any consideration of sin, or any demerit on
their part.

There is a connection between their sin and hellfire, from the position of that law that is sanctioned by penalty, and by the decree of God in
reference to withholding the pardon of their sin. Sin is also, of necessity,
connected with the decree of God, and, in truth, it depends on it, so that
man could not but sin, otherwise there would be no place for the decree.
From which it follows, that God has absolutely ordained very many to
hellfire since He ordained men to the commission of sins and absolutely
decreed to punish sin in many.

But I will prove that you and those who agree with you hold each of these opinions. First, you say, and truly, that hellfire is the punishment ordained for sin and the transgression of the law. Secondly, you say that God ordained the first man, and in him, all men should sin. You not only say this, but also adduce the reason of that decree and divine ordination, that God, in that way, might declare His righteousness and mercy, in which His glory chiefly consists, for which there could be no place except through sin and by occasion at it.

Thirdly, you add that God, by His providence, so arranged the primeval state of man that, though, as far as his own liberty was concerned, he might be able to stand and not Fall, yet he should in fact, Fall and commit sin. These two things are mutually connected; for that God might attain the object of His own act of ordination, it was necessary that He should so arrange the whole matter that the object should be attained. But you do not make foreknowledge of sin the foundation of that administration; wherefore it is necessary that you should consider, as presiding over it, the omnipotence of God, to resist which, the man would have neither the power nor the will.

This being so considered, you make a necessity of committing sin. To all these things you add, moreover, the irrevocable decree of God, by which he determined to punish, without mercy and of mere justice, sin committed according to that decree. From this, I think that it is most clearly evident, that when that allegation is made against you, nothing is charged upon you that is foreign to your sentiment.

I now consider the other part of the allegation, in which it is asserted that, according to your doctrine, "God created men that He might destroy them." The truth of this allegation is evident from this, that you say God created men for this purpose, that He might declare, in these, His mercy, and in those, His justice, and indeed His punitive justice, which is the opposite of mercy, and apart from foresight. From this, it follows, as punitive justice destroys men, that God created some men that He might destroy them. For punitive justice and the destruction of man are connected, and the former cannot be declared except by the latter. It is evident then that nothing, foreign to your theory is charged against you in the whole of that allegation.

Indeed I think that you wished to show favor to your own sentiment, when you made the charge less than it deserved. For it is much worse that God should have ordained men to sin, and should have created them that they might sin, than to have ordained them to hellfire, and to have created them that He might destroy them. For if sin is a worse evil than damnation, as it is, evidently, since the former is opposed to divine good, and the latter to human good, then truly is it greater to ordain one to sin than to ordain to hell, to create a man that he might sin, than that he might perish.

Accuracy of Statement

If, however, accuracy of statement is to be sought, it should be affirmed that, if a man is ordained to commit sin, then he otherwise could not have sinned. For sin is a voluntary act, and the decree of God in reference to sin introduces a necessity of sinning. Further, if a man is created that he may be condemned, then he cannot be condemned by God. For condemnation is the act of a just judge. But a just judge does not condemn one unless he is wicked by his own fault, apart from necessity; and he is not wicked, apart from necessity, and of his own fault, who is created that he may sin, and thus perish.

Let us now examine your answer to this second allegation. You think that you blunt and confute it by a distinction in the second act of reprobation, but it is not so. For you freely admit that God, by His absolute purpose, deserted the creature from which desertion, sin, according to your opinion, necessarily exists. Otherwise you cannot connect punitive justice with desertion, except in view of a condition, namely, the contingency that man should sin after that desertion. Therefore you admit what is imputed in that allegation, to your theory, you do not confute the charge. You also blend, in a confused way, the permission of the Fall, and the permission, by which God allows one to finally fail of blessedness.

For these are not the same, or from the same cause. For all have Fallen by the divine permission, but many do not finally perish in their Fallen condition; and permission of the Fall depends on the divine providence, which is general over the whole human race. And the final permission to remain in that Fallen condition depends on reprobation, and only relates to some persons. Your assertion, also, that "sin is subsequent to the desertion and permission of God," is to be understood as referring to that permission, by which He permits man to Fall into sin, which pertains to providence, not to that permission by which He suffers some to finally fail of blessedness, which pertains to reprobation. For sin is the cause of this latter permission, that is, the meritorious cause, as has now been frequently stated.

We now, examine the testimonies you present. In the remark of Peter Lombard, the phrase "future demerits" is to be understood to refer to what one has different from another.[8] But common demerits, though they may not be the moving cause, yet they are the meritorious cause, and a condition requisite in the object of reprobation. So also the assertion of Jerome is to be referred to the doing good or evil, by which the brothers were distinguished from each other, and not to sin, in which they were both conceived. This is apparent from what he says: "and their election and rejection displayed not the desert of each, but the will of him who elected and rejected." In the remark of Anselm that which I claim is clearly apparent. For he says, "God does justly, if He rejects sinners." The word "miserable," used in another remark of the same father, indicates the same thing. With these Thomas Aquinas and Augustine are in agreement.[9]

For the question is not whether the will of God is the cause of election and reprobation, but whether it has sin as an antecedent, as the meritorious cause of reprobation, and a requisite condition in the object both of election and of reprobation, which is most true, according to the views always held by Augustine. The word "conversion," used by Aquinas, and the word "drawing," used by Augustine, make sin the antecedent to the act of the will which "converts" and "draws." We would examine the testimonies of other Schoolmen, if their authority was of much weight with us. But I make this remark, that there is no one of those testimonies, that excludes the sin of Adam—and that of men in common with him—from the decree of Predestination, and some of them, indeed, clearly the same in that decree. For when the words "grace" and "mercy" are used, there is a tacit reference to sin.

That "the latter act," of destruction, takes place "in reference to sin," is certain, but it is in reference to sin not by any previous decree ordained to take place, but ordained to be punished in some by justice,

8. "Lombard, the Master of all the Schoolmen, saith, that God had rejected whom He would, not for any future demerits which He did foresee, but most righteously, though we cannot conceive the reason thereof." William Perkins, *Works*, II: 612.

9. "Why God hath elected some and reprobate others there is no account to be given, except the divine will, as S. Augustine says—'Why he draweth this man, and draweth not that, desire not to explain, if thou desirest not to err.'" Thomas Aquinas, *Summa Theologica.* i.

and to be remitted in others by grace, when it has been committed. This explanation, however, does not show that "the allegation is a slander," unless you at the same time, show that sin did not necessarily exist from that decree of reprobation or from some other.

Your second answer consists only in words. For if an act is unjust, it is not excused by its end or object. It is unjust to destroy a man apart from sin, and it remains unjust, even if anyone may say that it is done "for the declaration of judgment," or "for declaring judgment." And that which is added seems absurd, that "this is done for declaring judgment in just destruction," as it cannot be just unless it is inflicted on account of sin.

Sound Answer

The statement, that "God pleases to punish, with due destruction, a man, not as he is a man, but as he is a sinner," has the force of a sound answer, on the condition that the man has sinned freely, not of necessity. For the necessity and inevitability of sinning excuses from sin, and frees from punishment, him who commits that act. I say act, and not sin, because an act that one necessarily and inevitably commits, cannot be called sin.

The apparent distinction, by which a man is said to sin freely in respect to himself, but necessarily in relation to the divine decree, has no effect in warding off this blow; since it cannot be that one should do freely that which he does necessarily, or that one act can be performed necessarily, that is, cannot but be performed, and yet contingently, that is, can possibly not be performed. For this is at variance with the first principles of universal truth, in reference to whatever it is proper to make an affirmation or negation. I know that some defend this distinction by referring to the example of God Himself, of whom they assert that He is both freely and necessarily good. But this assertion is incorrect. So false, indeed, is it that God is freely good, that it is not much removed from blasphemy. God is, what He is, necessarily, and if He is freely good, He can be not good, and who has ever said that those things which are in Him, of nature and essence, are in Him freely? The assertion of Cameracensis[10] is indeed partly blasphemous, partly true.

It is blasphemous to say that "God can, without loss or detriment to His justice, punish and afflict eternally His own innocent creature." It

10. Cardinal Camaracensis was a Roman Catholic Church leader of the early fifteenth Century.

is true that "God can annihilate one of His creatures apart from sin." But punishment and annihilation are very different. The latter is to deprive of that, which had been graciously bestowed, the former is to render one miserable, and indeed infinitely miserable, and apart from any demerit on account of sin. Misery is far worse than annihilation, as Christ says:

> "It had been good for that man if he had not been born" (Matt 26:24).

> That it is contrary to the divine justice to punish one, who is not a sinner, appears from very many declarations of Scripture. "That be far from thee to do after this manner, to slay the righteous with the wicked" (Gen 18:25).

> "Whosoever hath sinned against me, him will I blot out of my book" (Exod 32:33).

> "Seeing it is a righteous thing with God to recompense tribulation to them that trouble you, and to you, who are troubled, rest with us" (2 Thess 1:6, 7).

> "For God is not unrighteous to forget your work and labor of love," etc. (Heb 6:10).

The saying of Wisdom (chapter 12), quoted by Cameracensis, likewise teaches the contrary of what he attempts to prove from it. For it treats the perdition of unrighteous nations, and, in plain words, declares in verse 15: "For so much, then, as thou art righteous thyself, thou orderest all things righteously, thinking it not agreeable with thy power to condemn him that hath not deserved to be punished."

I grant, indeed, that the error of Cameracensis was caused by the fault of the old version. But you cannot be excused on the account of this. For you ought to omit the testimony of an author who is led into an error by the fault of a version, since you are acquainted with it from the Greek text itself, and from translations better than that ancient one. It is true that "God is not bound by created laws," for He is a law unto Himself and He is justice itself.

That law, also, according to which no one is permitted to inflict punishment upon the undeserving was not created, or made by men, and it has place not among men only. It is an eternal law, and immovable in the divine justice to which God is bound in the immutability of His nature, and righteousness. It is not universally true, that "whatever is right, is right because God so wills it," as there are many things God wills, because they are right. It is right that God alone should be acknowledged by the creature to be the true God. We affirm that God wills this because it is right, not that it is right because God wills it.

The act of simple obedience is right, not because God wills that it should be performed by the creature, but because it is such in itself, and God cannot but require it of the creature, though it may belong to free will to prescribe in what matter He wills that obedience should be rendered to Him. As far as we are concerned, also, it is truly our duty in reference to laws, divinely enacted for us, not so much to see whether that which they command is just in itself, but simply to obey them, because God prescribes and commands it.

Yet this duty is founded on the fact that God cannot prescribe that which is unjust, because that He is essential justice, and wisdom, and omnipotence.

I had designed to omit a more extended examination of the remarks, quoted by you, from the Scholastic Theologians; but I will say a few words. Franciscus Maro's[11], "four signs necessary" as he affirms "to understand the process of Predestination and reprobation" are of no value, are notoriously false, and are confused in their arrangement. In the sentence from D. Baunes, the "permission by which all nature was permitted to Fall in Adam" is absurdly ascribed to reprobation, as that permission, and the Fall which followed it, extended to the whole human race, without distinction of the elect and the reprobate.

Found in the Reprobate

Those "four things," which, Ferrariensis[12] says, "are found in the reprobate," are not in him, as reprobate, and in respect to the decree of reprobation, but the latter two, only. For "the permission of the Fall and sin," to use his own words, are found in the elect, and pertain to the more general decree of providence, by which God left man to the freedom of his own will, as has been before and frequently said. Therefore, arguments, other than these, should have been presented by you, for the refutation of that charge. I very much wish that you would cite Scripture for the confirmation of your sentiments and the overthrow of those allegations. The writings of the Schoolmen, ought not to have weight and authority,

11. Franciscus Maro was a fourteenth century theologian who had been a pupil of John Duns Scotus (1266–1308).

12. Franciscus Ferraniensis was a sixteenth century Catholic official and author.

especially among us; for our Doctors of Theology with one voice affirm
of them, "that they have changed true theology into philosophy, and the
art of wrangling, and that they endeavor to establish their opinions, by
the authority, not so much of the Sacred Scriptures, as of Aristotle."

ALLEGATION 3

"The Predestination of the Stoics, and the fatalism of the Stoics
has been introduced by us: Because, they say, we assert that all
things are done of the necessary and efficient decree of God.
Also, that the Fall of Adam was, according to our opinion as
they allege, decreed and willed by God."

This is indeed a heavy charge, and yet is set forth in a milder form by
you, than by those who make it. You ought to add those things which
pertain essentially to this allegation, and are charged by them upon you
and your doctrine. Such are these: "It would follow from this, 'that God
is the Author of sin; that God really sins; that God alone sins; and that
sin is not sin,'" which Bellarmine charges against the sentiment of certain
of our doctors, the sentiment also, which you seem to defend. But the
reason that they present all those things, as opposed to your doctrine, is
this: You say that all things happen by the efficacious will of God, which
cannot be resisted, and that events do not occur, because God, by an
absolute decree, has determined that they should not occur.

From this, it follows, also, that sinful acts are performed by the will
of God, cannot be resisted, and that righteous acts are omitted, because
God has simply and absolutely decreed that they shall not be performed.
Therefore, God is the author of sin, and the preventer of righteousness
and of good acts. From this it is inferred that God, truly and properly
speaking, sins; and, since the necessity, from which men perform such
acts, acquits them from sin, it follows that God alone sins, just as He
alone is responsible, who strikes a blow by the hand of another person,
of which he has laid hold.

But since God cannot sin, it follows that sin is not sin. Hence, it
seems to me that no injustice is done to your doctrine by that allegation.
But let us see how you dispose of it. Neglecting the general charge, you
begin your discussion with that part which refers to the Fall of Adam.
You admit that this occurred "not only according to the foreknowledge
of God, but also by His will and decree; yet," as you explain it, "by His

will, not approving or effecting it, yet not prohibiting, but permitting it." This distinction, properly used, indeed, solves the difficulty.

If it is your opinion and the opinion of others, that God did not approve, and did not effect the Fall, did not incite and did not impel Adam to Fall, did not lay upon him any necessity of sinning, either by acting or not acting, but only willed not to prevent, but to permit the Fall of Adam. Then, I acknowledge that all those things are unjustly alleged against your sentiment. You, indeed, make this statement verbally, while in fact you so explain permission or non-prevention, that it amounts to the "efficient decree of God." This I will prove.

You say, "What God does not prevent, occurs, because God does not prevent it, the reason of the non-existence of a fact, or event, is that God does not will that it should exist." I conclude, therefore, that the divine permission or non-prevention, and the event are mutually, and indeed immediately connected, as cause and effect. Thus, also, non-prevention has the relation of energetic performance. Therefore, likewise, the volition of God, and the non-existence or event of a thing are mutually connected as cause and effect, and hence, a volition that a thing shall not be done, has the relation of energetic prevention. This I show, more extendedly, in this manner.

Sin is twofold, of commission and omission: of commission, when that is performed which has been forbidden, of omission when that is not performed which has been commanded. There is, in your opinion, a concurrence in that act which cannot be committed by a man without sin, and indeed such a concurrence that God is the first cause of the act, and man is the second, the former moving man, the latter moved by God, and, indeed, moving, in such sense, that man of necessity follows that motion, and consequently of necessity performs that act which involves transgression.

Not to prevent sin of omission is, in your opinion, not to give that grace without which sin cannot be stopped and the contrary good cannot be performed. But he, who in that manner, concurs, and denies such grace, is absolutely the chief and efficient cause of sin, and indeed, the only cause, as the joint cause of the act: man, since he cannot resist the motion of the first cause, cannot resist sin in following that irresistible motion. But, if you can so explain your sentiment and that of others, that it shall not, in reality, differ from it, then I shall not object to it.

You will not escape by the distinction that "it is one thing to will a thing per se, and another to will it as to the event," unless, by the "event" of a thing, you understand that which results from the prolongation and the existence of the thing itself, which is not your sentiment. For you say that "God wills the event of sin," that is, "that sin should happen, but does not will sin itself;" which distinction is absurd. For the essence of sin consists in the event, for sin consists in action. God, also, wills sin itself, in the mode in which He wills that sin should happen, and He wills that sin should happen in the mode in which He wills sin itself. He does not love sin per se. He wills that sin should happen for His own glory; He wills also sin for His own glory. I speak this in the sense used by yourself. Show, if you can, the difference, and I will acquiesce.

Your Assertion

Your assertion, that "God wills not to prevent sin," is ambiguous, unless it is explained. What! Has not God hindered sin, as far as was suitable, and according to the mode in which it is right for Him to treat a rational creature, namely, by legislation, threatening, promise, the bestowment of sufficient grace, and even the promise of His assistance, if man would consent to have recourse to it? This he could do, or we go infinitely astray.

But He did not hinder sin by any omnipotent or physical action, because that would have been against his nature. He would have thus prevented man from using that primeval liberty in which He had placed him; and, by consequence, as we have elsewhere quoted from Tertullian, "He would have rescinded His own arrangement."

It is rightly said, that God properly and primarily, and we may add, immediately, willed His own permission. But it does not thence follow, that God also willed the event of sin. For it is a non-sequitur: "God voluntarily permits sin, therefore, He wills that sin should happen." The contrary is true: "God voluntarily permits sin; therefore, He neither wills that sin should happen, nor wills that it should not happen." For permission is an act of the will when inoperative which inoperativeness of the will may here be properly ascribed to the Deity, since He endowed man with free will, that He might test his free and voluntary obedience. He could not have done this, if He had imposed an inseparable hindrance upon man. But the cause of the occurrence of that which God permits is not the permission, although it would not happen without that permission. He who performs the act is the proper and immediate cause, with the concurrence of the Deity, which is always prepared for him. But permission cannot be resolved into a cause per se, if we are to treat this subject accurately and truthfully, but only into a cause sine qua non, or one which removes, or rather, does not present a hindrance, and indeed such a hindrance as I have referred to, which cannot be resisted by the creature.

Your statement, "as no good thing can exist or be done, except by the agency of the Deity, so no evil can be avoided, unless God hinders it," is true, if rightly understood.

That is, the agency of the Deity being that by which He may suitably effect what is good by means of a rational and free creature, and the hindrance of God being that, by which He may suitably hinder a free creature from that which is evil. But the limit both of doing and hindering is such that it does not deprive man of freedom, but permits him, also, freely and of his own will, according to the mode of will, to do good and to abstain from evil.

Otherwise good is not performed by man, and evil is not avoided by him, but an act, only is performed or avoided by a necessity either natural or supernatural. Those words also are susceptible of amendment, if anyone should wish to discuss these things with greater accuracy. The statement might have been this: "As no good is, or is done, except by the agency of God, so no evil is avoided, except by the hindrance of God." For by the agency of God, good not only can be but is done, and by His hindrance, evil not only can be, but is hindered.

But if you wish to retain that word "can," you ought to have expressed your ideas in this way: "As nothing good can be, or can be done, unless God wills to do it, or to give to another the power and the will to do it, and to concur with him in doing it, so nothing evil can be avoided unless God wills to give, and actually does give strength sufficient for the avoidance of sin, and wills to call out that strength and to cooperate with it." In this sense, "not even the least thing is done without the will of God, namely, either willing that it should be done, or willing not to prevent, but to permit, that it should be done." It is not true that "providence is inactive" in permission, even explained in such a manner as to coincide neither with that will of God, by which He wills that something shall be done, nor with that by which He wills that something shall not be done. If it coincides with either of these, there is no permission, and the assertion of Augustine: "nothing is done except by the agency or permission of God," is without force.

Examine Some Arguments

I will now examine some arguments you present in favor of your view. The first is deduced from several passages of Scripture. Let us see now what can be proved from these passages. Acts 2:23 teaches not that God willed that the Jews should slay Christ, but, that he was "delivered by the determinate counsel and foreknowledge of God" into the power of those who wished to slay him. Nothing more can be inferred from Acts 4:28. For God predetermined to deliver His own Son into the hands of his enemies, that He might suffer from them that which God had laid upon him, and which the Jews, of their own wickedness and hatred against Christ, had determined to inflict upon him.

God, indeed, "determined before" that death should be inflicted on Christ by them. But in what character did God consider them when He "determined before" that this should be done by them? In that character, surely, which they had at the time when they inflicted death upon Christ, that is, in the character of sworn enemies of Christ, of obstinate enemies and despisers of God and the truth, who could be led to repentance by no admonitions, prayers, threats or miracles; who wished to inflict every evil on Christ, if they could only obtain the power over him, which they had often sought in vain.

It is evident, then, that there was here no other action of God in this case than that He delivered His own Son into their hands, and permitted them to do their pleasure in reference to him. Yet he determined the limit to which He pleased that they should go, regulating and governing their wickedness, in such a manner, yet very gently, that they should inflict on him only that which God had willed that His own Son should suffer, and nothing more.

This is clearly seen in the very manner of his punishment, in preventing the breaking of his legs, in the piercing of his side, in the inscription of the title, and the like. But there appears here no action of God by which they were impelled or moved to will and to do what they willed and did. But He used those who wished, of their own malice and envy, to put Christ to death, in a mode, which, He knew, would conduce to His own glory and the salvation of men.

But the reason that it cannot be said, with truth, that God and Christ, in the delivery of Christ to the Jews sinned, does not consist only or chiefly, in the fact that they were led to this delivery by various motives.

What if Judas had done the same thing with the design that Christ, by his own death, should reconcile the world unto God, would his sin have been less heinous? By no means. It was not lawful for him to do evil that good might come. But the chief reason of the difference is that God had the right to deliver His Son, and Christ also had the right to deliver his own soul to death, and consequently, in doing this, they could not sin. But Judas had no power in this case, and he, therefore, sinned. There is a distinction in actions not only as to their end, but as to their principle and form. Saul was not acquitted of sin because he preserved the herds of the Amalekites for sacrifice (1 Sam 15:9–22).

Again, what is implied by that inference: "Therefore, we may also say that, when Adam ate of the forbidden fruit, he did that which the hand and counsel of God foreordained to be done?" This, indeed, never was the language of the apostles and of the church, and never could be, in matters having so much dissimilarity. For the relation of Adam and of those enemies of Christ is not the same. The former, previous to eating the fruit, was holy and righteous; the latter, before the death of Christ, were wicked, unrighteous, unfriendly, and hostile to Christ.

The latter, in all their desires, sought for and frequently in many ways, attempted to put Christ to death. Adam was disinclined to eat of the forbidden fruit, even when he was enticed to it by his wife, who had already transgressed. The death of Christ was necessary for the expiation of sins, and was, per se, declarative of the glory of God. The Fall of Adam was wholly unnecessary, and, per se, violated the majesty and glory of God. He needed not the sin of man for the illustration of His own glory. What, likewise, can be imagined more absurd than that circular reasoning: "The death of Christ was foreordained by God, that it might expiate the sin of Adam; the Fall of Adam was foreordained, that it might be expiated by the death of Christ."

Where is the beginning and where is the end of that ordination? Nevertheless God ordained the Fall of Adam, not that it should occur, but that, occurring, it should serve for an illustration of His justice and mercy. The passage in 1 Pet 3:17, is to be explained in a similar manner: "God wills that the pious should suffer evils," for their chastening and trial. He wills that they should suffer these evils from other men; but from men of what character? From those, who of their own wickedness and the instigation of Satan, already will to bring those evils upon them, which ill will God already foresaw, at the time when He predetermined that those evils should be inflicted upon the pious. Therefore, they were moved, by no act of God, to will to inflict evils upon the pious.

Not to Inflict Evils

They were moved, also, by no act to inflict evils, unless by an act such as ought rather to move them from that volition, and to deter them from that infliction; such as would, in fact, have moved and deterred them, unless they had been deplorably wicked. The doctrine, life, and miracles of Christ and the Apostles, drew upon them the odium and hatred of the world.

The fact that God is declared, in 2 Sam 16:10, to have said about Shemei's hostility to David, "The Lord hath said unto him, Curse David," also, if rightly explained, presents no difficulty. Let Shimei and David, and the act which may be called "the precept of cursing," be considered. Shimei was already a hater of David, of most slanderous tongue, and bitter mind, impious, and a despiser of God and the divine law, which had commanded: "Thou shalt not curse the rule of thy people" (Exod 22:28).

David, by his own act against God and his neighbor, had rendered himself worthy of that disgrace, and altogether needed to be chastened and tried by it; he was, moreover, endued with the gift of patience to endure that hostility with equanimity. The act of God was the ejection and expulsion of David from the royal city and from the kingdom. In consequence of this occurred the flight of David, the fact that the rumor of that flight came to the ears of Shimei, and the arrangement that David and Shimei should meet together. Thus, by the act of God, David, fleeing and driven before his son, was presented to Shimei "a man of the family of the house of Saul," and an enemy of David, ready to curse him.

Add, if you please, the hardening of the mind of Shimei, lest he should fear to curse David, on account of the attendants of David, that so he might in some way, satisfy his own mind and his inveterate hatred against David. Therefore, that opportunity, by which David, in his flight, was presented to Shimei, and the hardening of the mind of Shimei divinely produced. Also, the direction of that cursing tongue were acts pertaining to that precept of God, apart from which acts, nothing in that precept can be presented, which would not impinge on the justice of God, and make God the author of sin.

A comparison of all these things will show that Shimei, not so much as God, was the author of that malediction. Shimei was alone the author of the volition, yet it is rather to be attributed to God, as He effected that which He willed, not by moving Shimei to the malediction, but by procuring for Shimei the opportunity to curse David, and the confidence to use that opportunity. From this, it appears, most plainly, that God is without blame, and Shimei is involved in guilt. The passages, Jer 34:22, and Lam 3:37, will be explained similarly and will present no difficulty. From an examination of these, it will appear that they have no reference to the Fall of Adam, which was the beginning of sin; and all other evils have place, sin having now entered into the world, and men having become depraved by sin.

We proceed to your second argument, that "God voluntarily permits sin" is certain, and it is equally certain that "the will to permit is the will not to prevent." But pause here. The will to permit or not to prevent, is not the same with "the will not to bestow grace." For He permits that person to Fall, to whom he has given grace sufficient and necessary to enable him to stand. Let us proceed. You say that "He, who does not will to prevent sin, which he foreknows will happen, by confirming grace when he can do it, in fact wills that the same should happen." But I deny that the volition of sin can be deduced from the no-lition of preventing or hindering. For there are three things distinct from each other, no one of which includes another: "to will that sin should not be committed," that is, to will its prevention; "to will that it should occur or be committed," that is, to will its commission; and "to will to prevent or not to prevent it," that is, to will its permission or non-prevention.

The former two are affirmative acts, the last one a negative act. But an affirmative act cannot be deduced from a negative for there is more in an affirmative than in a negative act, and there cannot be more in a conclusion than in the premises.

Further, I say that your argument, on this point, is fallacious. For God wills to permit sin in one respect, and to hinder it in another, to hinder it so far as would be appropriate, which hindrance is not followed of certainty, by the omission of sin, and to not to hinder it, in another mode, which hindrance would, indeed, be followed by the omission of sin. Yet there is no virtue or praiseworthiness in him who omits it, as he cannot do otherwise than omit it on account of that hindrance.

But I may be allowed to argue, in opposition to such a view, that He, who hates sin and by the enactment of law and the bestowment of sufficient grace wishes to hinder, wills, not that sin should happen, but that sin should not happen, which is an affirmative act of the will. You will say that this is a correct conclusion, the will being understood as that "of approval." I answer that God cannot, by any mode of volition, will things which are contradictory.

But "to happen" and "not to happen" are contradictory. Therefore, it cannot be that God, by one mode of volition should will that an event should happen, and, by another mode of volition, should will that it should not happen. It may indeed be true that God, in His will "of good pleasure" as they style it, purposes to permit that which, in His will "of approval" or "that which is revealed," He wills should not be done. Thus your conclusion is faulty, and the remarks of Calvin and Beza, let it be said with due respect to so eminent men, are hardly consistent with the truth.

Your Subjoined Arguments

But examine, I pray you, your subjoined statements, and you will see and acknowledge that you put them on paper, when you did not observe what you said. You say, "Whatever God does not hinder, He does not hinder it, either because He wills it to be done, or because He is altogether unwilling that it should be done, or because He does not will that it should be done." What is the difference between the latter two reasons? "To be unwilling that anything should be done" is "not to will that anything should be done;" the modifying word "altogether" is of no effect, since, in things opposed to each other, the negative cannot receive any increase, as, for instance, in the phrase "not a man."

A wolf is as much "not a man" as is the earth, the air, the sky; but perhaps by the expression: "He is altogether unwilling that it should be done" you mean "He wills that it should not be done," or "because His will does not act." If the first be true, my view is correct. But the second cannot be true, for it is absurd to say "God does not will to prevent anything because He wills that it should not be done." You ought not, in that enumeration of reasons, to have introduced such a statement; for "not to

will to prevent," and "to will that a thing should not be done" are opposites and from this it is certain that one cannot be the cause of the other.

In the investigation and distribution of causes, it is neither usual
nor proper to introduce that which is the opposite of an effect. But let
that pass. You will say then, "that 'not to hinder' must be on account of
one of those three causes." I grant it. "But it is not 'because His will does
not act,' which is Epicureanism, nor 'because He does not will that it
should be done,' therefore, it is, 'because He wills that it should be done.'"
I deny the antecedent. For this is the reason that God does not hinder
an event, because He neither wills that it should occur, nor wills that
it should not occur, as will be more clearly evident, if you consider the
matter in this light. That, which God wills to be done, He efficaciously
brings to pass.

That which He wills not to be done, he efficaciously hinders. That,
which he neither wills to be done, nor wills not to be done, He leaves to
the creature. How is it possible that the human mind should conceive
that God does not prevent, that is, permits anything, because He wills
that it should be done. Indeed the expression "He wills that it should
be done" has too much comprehensiveness to admit that permission or
non-hindrance should be deduced or concluded from it.

Your objection to this argument, namely, that from it the conclusion is drawn that "such things are done, either through the ignorance
or through the negligence of the Deity," is absurd; you cannot defend it,
even against yourself. For you have already made a distinction between
"not to will" and "not to care that a thing should be done." Therefore,
you cannot deduce one from the other. How also, can it be asserted that
a thing is done without the knowledge of God, which is done by the
permission of God, and by His will, the agent of that permission. But,
it will hereafter appear, when we shall have explained, more largely, in
reference to that permission, that what God permits, He does not permit
without knowledge or care. It is, however, to be understood that permission is an affirmative volition, and not one that is merely negative. For
God wills His own permission by an affirmative act. But in reference to
the thing, which He permits, the act of His will is a negative act.

Far be it from anyone to think that any decree of God is contrary
to justice or equity. If God has decreed anything, it is certain that He has
justly decreed it. But it is to be considered whether, and how God has
decreed it. It is not possible that any of His decrees should be at vari-

ance with His justice, as revealed to us in the Scriptures; it is, then, to be understood that it is not sufficient, in order to remove a charge from a decree which we ascribe to God, to add: "He has decreed it but justly." For the addition of that phrase does not make the decree just, but it must be shown that the decree, which we attribute to God, really belongs to Him, and there will, then, be no question concerning its justice.

Your third argument is weak. For, from the event of anything, it cannot be concluded that God willed that it should happen, but that He willed not to prevent it. And this volition, not to prevent, is also an act of the providence of God, which is present to all things and to each, and presides over them, either by effecting them, or by permitting them; yet administering and ordaining all things for just and legitimate ends, and in such a way as to "regard, not only the events of things, but also their commencements, and the principles of things and actions."

Satan and the Wicked

It is known, indeed, that Satan and the wicked cannot only not perfect anything, but cannot even begin it, except by the permission of the Deity. That which you add, "by His will," I do not concede, until you shall prove it by a greater weight of arguments than you have yet adduced. You say truly: "It is impious to affirm that anything exists or is done, unless the holy and just God has decreed it from eternity, and indeed willed either to do or to permit it." For the decree of God is twofold, efficacious and permissive. Neither can take the place of, or intrude upon the other.

Let us consider also your fourth argument: "The decision of the ancient church." Augustine, manifestly makes a distinction between permission and efficiency. And although he says that "nothing is done unless God wills it to be done" he yet explains himself when he says "either by permitting it to be done, or by doing it Himself." Thus, that which He permits is not an immediate object of the will, but permission is the immediate object, while that which God permits is the object of permission. So, also, the statements of Tertullian, Jerome and others, are to be explained, that they may not impinge on the Scriptures, which declares absolutely: "Thou art not a God which hath pleasure in wickedness" (Ps 5:4).

Hence, if I may be permitted to speak freely, I shall affirm that I should prefer that Augustine, Jerome, Catharinus and all others had abstained from phrases of this kind, which are not contained in the

Scriptures, and which need lengthened explanation, that they may not be made the occasion of heresy and blasphemy. That second distinction, according to which God is said "to will that evil may be, and yet not to will evil," has no force. For God hates evil, and hates the existence of evil; and since evil exists in action, its being done is its being, and its being is its nature. Through there may be a subtle distinction between the essence and the existence of evil, it cannot be said that there is so much difference between them that God wills that sin should exist, but does not will sin itself.

For since God hates the essence of evil, if I may so speak for the sake of form, He therefore forbids that evil should be done. The reason that He is unwilling that sin should exist, is the fact that He hates sin itself. But He does not hate the existence of evil, or evil itself, so much that He may not permit evil to be done by a free agent, not because it is better that evil should be, than that they should not be, but because it is better first, that He should permit His rational and free creatures to act according to their own will and freedom, in which consists the trial of their obedience, than that contrary to His own original arrangement, He should take away that freedom from the creature, or even prevent its exercise; secondly, that He should bring good out of evil, rather than not permit evil to be. But the idea that God wills that evil should exist not as such, but as the means of good, needs a more extended explanation, which by the will of God we will hereafter present.

The first objection to which you refer is of great weight. For the will is said to be evil in view of an evil volition and that volition is said to be evil, which is directed to an object to which it ought not to be directed. But evil is an object to which it ought not to be directed. Therefore that volition is evil, by which anyone wills evil, and by which he wills that evil should be done. For there is a verbal distinction, but a real agreement between those ideas. Hence, also, "it belongs to an evil will to will that evils should be done, whether that will delights in the evils, or wills to use them for a good purpose." It is not right that anyone should will that evil should be done, that he may have an opportunity of using that evil to a good end. The rule, which you cite is correct, "Evil is not to be done," or even willed "that good may come." The first wickedness exists in the will or the volition of evil, the second in its perpetration.

Your answer does not remove the difficulty stated in this objection. Of what importance are those "two principles?" Even if their correctness is conceded, the objection is still valid. For, in reference to the first, as there is no evil in the nature of things, the will cannot be directed to evil, per se, and it pertains to universal will, and not only to that, but to universal desire and appetite to tend to good per se. The evil consists in this, not that the will is directed to evil but that it is directed towards an undue good, or in reference to an undue mode and end. As to the second: It is true that "there is no evil which has no good joined with it." There is no supreme evil allowed; for evil exists not except in that which is good.

It does not, however, follow that it is good that sin should happen. For sin is so great an evil that it ought to be avoided, even if it have some good united with it. The act of fornication has this good, it is the sexual intercourse, natural to man and woman, yet it is to be avoided, because it cannot be committed without sin. But the good to which you seem to refer, is not united to sin except incidentally, that is, by the intervention of the Divine will, directing that evil to a good end.

The remark of Augustine, if understood strictly, cannot be admitted, but with suitable explanation it may be tolerated. It is not true that "it is good that evils should exist." For God effects every good. Then it would follow, according to the remark, that He effects the existence of evils. This is at variance with another statement of Augustine, in which he says, "God does some things, but permits other things to be done, as in the case of sin." How can it be said, without a contradiction in terms, of God, "He causes that evils should exist, and permits evils to exist"?

Does Not Prove This

The reason, subjoined, does not prove this. For Almighty God does not, therefore, permit evil, because it is good that evil should exist, but because He knows that, in His own wisdom and omnipotence, He can educe good from the evil, contrary to its nature and proper efficacy, and this of His own pure act, either by way of just punishment or gracious remission. It is not good that evil should exist unless incidentally, namely, on account of the wisdom, omnipotence and will of God. But that, which is incidental, is not under consideration.

But let us, now, look at your answer. You say that "Sin, considered universally in its causes and circumstances, assumes a twofold respect or formality." In the first place, you say that "Sin is considered not under the relation of sin, but as far as it has the relation of good in the mind of God, decreeing it." But I deny that sin has the relation of good in the mind of God decreeing it. For the acts of God, in reference to sin, altogether declare that sin is considered by God not in the relation of good, but in that of evil.

For He permits sin, but effects good. He punishes sin, but He punishes that which is evil, and as it is evil. He remits sin and pardons it; but that which is pardoned is considered as an evil by him that pardons it. But God decrees the permission of sin because He knows that He can produce good results from sin, not in that sin is good, but in that it is evil. Nor is it rightly said: "Sin has the relation of good in the mind of God, who decrees it, because God knows how to make sin an opportunity of good acts."

For He does not produce those acts except with the consideration of sin as sin. It is wonderful, also, that any consideration can be affixed to sin, which is contrary to its definition. The definition of sin is a transgression of the law, and, therefore, it is a violation of the Divine will. Hence it is also evident that it is incorrect to say, "sin has the relation of good, because it exists in that which is good, and because it tends to that which is good." For "good" is affirmed of a subject, in which sin exists as a deforming vice and as corrupting, not of sin existing in that subject.

But how far God wills the subject in which sin exists, that is, the act which cannot be performed by a man without sin, we will perhaps discuss, more largely, hereafter, when we speak of permission in general. Sin likewise tends to good not per se, but incidentally only because God ordains not that it should be done, but that, having been done, it should result in good, and makes, from it an occasion for good. God is not said to will that sin should occur so far as in His wonderful wisdom He knows how to elicit good from it, but He so far wills to permit and not to hinder it. For this is the reason that He permits and does not will to hinder, not that He wills that sin should occur.

You affirm, in the second place, that another relation of sin is "that, in which it is considered formally and properly, that is, as sin." Here, also, you adduce a twofold consideration of sin, either as it is sin in respect to men, or as it is sin to God. But if you will listen to me, those are vain and frivolous distinctions, and invented not to explain the matter, but to involve it more deeply.

"In respect to men," you say, "God does not will, or approve, or effect sin, but wills as to its event, not absolutely, as in the case of those things which are good in themselves, but only by willing to permit that sin should be committed." Be it so, and this, if rightly understood, can be tolerated. I will not examine what you say in reference to a three-fold action of the divine will, since it has no bearing at all on the subject, at least against the sentiment which I defend.

What you say in the margin is true, "God wills that sin should happen, so far as it is possible that it should happen without the efficiency of God." I wish that you had discussed this subject more fully, and it would, indeed, have been evident that you have, thus far, not rightly, set forth the mode in which God wills that sin should happen. You so set it forth as not to acquit God of the efficiency of sin. You say that "sin, as such to God, is neither willed, nor approved, nor affected, nor indeed permitted by Him." I concede the first three, but deny the last, for the proper object of the divine permission is evil, as it is evil, and indeed considered by God as evil; though the reason of His permission of sin, is not the evil itself. A distinction is to be made between the object of permission and its cause.

We have already demonstrated that He permits evil as evil. But you have not rightly stated the cause or reason why God permits evil, for He does not permit evil on account of a conjoined good, but because He can elicit good from evil, which good cannot, on that account, be said to be conjoined to sin, because it is elicited from sin only by the action of God.

But if you understand the phrase "conjoined good" to imply—not in the nature of sin itself, but in the act of God, I do not oppose you.

The words of Beza, which you quote, will not bear a rigorous examination. The former is either false, or equivocal; false, if understood of the permission, of which we now treat, which is opposed not to legal prohibition, but to efficacious prevention. It is true that God by law prohibits sin as sin, and yet permits, that is, does not hinder the same sin as sin. But if it refers to the permission, the opposite of the prohibition, made by law, the discussion is equivocal, for we are not treating of that permission. For who does not know that God cannot, at the same time, strictly require and not strictly require the same thing by law.

Permission has likewise been previously defined or described by yourself as "the denial of confirming grace" not indeed as "the non-imposition of a law." The second statement of Beza is simply false. For punishments of sins are not permitted by the Deity, but inflicted by a just judge, and have God himself for their author. "Shall there be evil in a city, and the Lord hath not done it?" (Amos 3:6). Also, of what sin, I pray, was the first sin the punishment? Yet it was permitted. Therefore, it was not a punishment.

Must Be Understood

The remarks of Calvin, must be understood according to the interpretation already presented by us, otherwise they cannot be defended. But, as it was his aim to overthrow the doctrine of the Schoolmen on this subject, it ought not to be said by one who has undertaken to defend his views, that "the Schoolmen speak correctly when they do not disjoin the will from permission." This you say; they, however, state that there is this distinction between the two, that permission is the immediate object of the will, but sin is the object of permission. All the Schoolmen openly acknowledge that what God permits, He voluntarily permits. Nor is the blasphemy of the Manichees to be charged upon Calvin, because though he sometimes uses unsuitable phraseology, he elsewhere clearly defends himself and his doctrine from that accusation.

The second objection, noticed by you, is this: "God wills contraries, if He wills that to happen, which He, in His law, prohibits." This is, indeed, a valid objection, and your answer does not remove it. For "to will anything to happen," and "to will the same thing not to happen," do not differ "in respects" only, but "absolutely and in their whole essence." Nor is there any respect or mode, according to which God can be said to will that anything should happen, and at the same time to will that it should not happen. For the divine will cannot be engaged in contrary acts about one and the same object, in whatever respects it may be considered.

Nor can one and the same act of the divine will be engaged on two contrary objects, such as "to happen" and "not to happen," in whatever respects those objects may be considered. "God prohibits evil as evil," but He permits the same, not as it puts on the relation of good, for it is false that sin ever puts on the relation of good, but because God knows how, from it, to elicit and produce good. The remark of Thomas Aquinas does not favor your view, and is not opposed to mine.

The third objection you have formed at your own pleasure, that you might be able more easily to overthrow it. For a boy, possessed of very little skill in dialectics, knows that there is a great difference between the cause of the consequence, or conclusion, and the cause of the consequent, or immediate effect. The cause, indeed, can be inferred from the effect. And therefore you, properly, affirm that the major of the syllogism, contained in the objection, "is not general." But your correction added to that major, has no effect as to its truth. For it is not true that "if no middle cause intervenes between the antecedent, on the existence of which the consequent follows, and that consequent, then the antecedent is the cause of the consequent."

Nor does the antecedent, therefore, cease to be the cause of the consequent, even if a middle cause intervenes. For Satan was the cause of the eating of the forbidden fruit, even if man was its proximate and immediate cause. By this, the force of your reply is weakened. If you can show that these two things are mutually consistent, that God can will that sin should happen, and that man still sins of his own free will, you have gained your case. I indeed admit that man can sin certainly, and yet freely; but to sin certainly is not the same as to sin necessarily. For the word "certainly" is used in respect to the divine foreknowledge; but "necessarily" in respect to the decree of God, and the divine will, by which He wills that sin should happen.

Hence, also, you incorrectly attribute certainty to the decree of God, when you ought to attribute it to His foreknowledge, and necessity to His decree. You also, afterwards, yourself acknowledge that God is the author of the sin of man, that is, by a desertion of him, and by the non-bestowment of the aid necessary for the avoidance of sins, from which it follows that man necessarily sinned. For he who makes a law and does not bestow the aid necessary for the fulfillment of the law, is the cause of the transgression of his own law.

Will of Man Comes in

You say, that "in this desertion, the will of man comes in, since he is not deserted, unless he wills to be deserted." I answer, that, if it is so, then the man deserved to be deserted. I ask, however, whether the man could will not to be deserted. If you say that he could, then he did not sin necessarily, but freely. If, on the other hand, you say that he could not, then the fault falls back upon God not less than before, because God is the cause of that volition, by which the man willed to be deserted, since He did not bestow the necessary grace, by which the man could will not to be deserted, and nothing can be conceived, which may intervene between this desertion on the part of God, and the volition of man, by which he willed to be deserted.

Your second answer to this objection is of no greater advantage to you; indeed you twice admit that God, by His own decree, by which He willed that sin should happen, is the cause of sin. First, you say that "sin is the mere consequent of the decree;" whence it follows that the decree is the cause of sin, unless you present some other relation in which sin may be the consequent of the divine decree, which you are wholly unable to do.

You say that "the decree of God is, in such a manner, the antecedent of human sin, that it has no relation of cause, except that of deficiency." But I affirm that, in the use of this second argument, you are convicted of making God the author of sin. If that which was deficient through the influence of the cause, was necessary to the avoidance of sin, then certainly God, by the deficiency of the operation, which was necessary to the avoidance of sin, is the cause of sin. That is, unless you teach that man had previously deserved this deficiency of the divine operation. The words of Augustine do not sustain your opinion. For he only means that sin committed contrary to the precept of God, is not committed when He is unwilling that it shall be committed, and absolutely wills that it shall not be committed, but when He permits it, and by a voluntary permission.

You refer to another objection: "The decree of God is the energetic principle of all things, according to your sentiment; therefore, also, it is the principle of sin." You acknowledge and teach that the antecedent is true.

First, by the authority of the Scripture in Eph 1:11, but in a sense different from that of the Holy Spirit. For all passages in that chapter, refer to salutary gifts and effects which God, in His Son, and by the Holy Ghost, works in the elect, which is what the word *eudokia* signifies. Secondly, by a reason that is sound, for God is the cause of all beings and acts; yet it is to be suitably explained how He produces all acts. You deny the consequence, because sin is a "defect of being—not a real being, but only a being of the reason." It is necessary to explain, more fully, in what sense sin is a "defect" rather than "a real being." Sin is a being of the reason, because it not only has its subsistence in the mind, but also has its origin from the mind, and was produced by the mind, that it might serve to obtain for it the knowledge of things, of good and evil.

But a defect, even if it has no substance or fixed form yet exists in the subject, from which the habitude of sin proceeds and so affects the subject that it is perceived by it. It is not understood by the mind, except in relation to its own habits, by which its limits are also determined. From that it is apparent that sins are not purely beings of the reasons. You allow, indeed, that sin is not a being of the reason, when you say "it follows and exists, immediately and surely, from the removal of original righteousness." But though sin is not a positive being, but a defect, yet if God is the energetic cause of that act, which cannot be committed by man without sin, then He is also the energetic cause of sin. You admit this, when you say that "God is the energetic cause of all acts."

5

An Examination of Predestination and Grace in Perkins' Pamphlet

Part 2

YOU THEN, DO AND must admit the consequence unless you show in what way it can be effected that a man should freely perform the act, which, in respect to himself is sin, if the same act is produced by the energetic decree of God, which no one can resist. But more on this subject hereafter.

Finally, it is objected to your sentiment that it teaches that "God inclines to sin and positively hardens." I admit that this objection is made, and not without cause. It has never happened to me to see an answer, which frees the doctrine you advocate from that objection and charge. You answer, that you "do not approve of a permission, separate from the will."

Who does approve of such a permission? Who has ever denied that what God permits, He voluntarily permits? You say, "I do not attribute to God positive or physical action, as if He would infuse corruption and wickedness into a man." I wish, however, that you would explain how sin is committed, "necessarily in respect to the Divine decree," apart from any physical action of the Deity—whether that physical action be positive or negative—and, indeed, if you please, apart from positive action. You resolve that act, which is not performed without sin, into a first cause, in such a manner as, also, of necessity, to make God the positive cause of sin.

But it is not necessary that He should infuse wickedness or corruption to such a degree that physical, or positive action can be attributed to Him. It is sufficient, if He moves, if He impels to the act, if He limits the liberty of the man, so that He cannot but will and do that, which has been prohibited. You admit that "God effectively hardens;" which, indeed, I do not deny, but it is necessary that there should be an explanation, such that God may not in any way, be made the author of sin. This we shall hereafter see.

I do not disapprove of the threefold action of Divine Providence in reference to human acts, referred to by Suidas. But consider whether that action, *kat eudokian*, according to the good pleasure, "by which God wills, proves, effects, and is thereby pleased," is referred to in a sense different from that, in which you always use *eudokia*. For you have before said, on the authority of Eph. 1:11, that "God does all things according to the good pleasure of His own will;" of which passage, relying on its true interpretation, which you here present from Suidas, I have deprived you.

In reference to the second action, however, which is *kat oikonomian*, "with regard to administration," or "sustentation and conservation," I would have you consider whether it is so much the preservation and sustentation of "motions, actions, and passions" as to existence and faculties. For since the existence of things, and the faculties existing in them are the first acts, and motions, actions, and passions, resulting from them are the second acts, or from second acts, it seems, indeed, that an act of Divine Providence presides over the latter, different from that which presides over the former. It is true, indeed, that God sustains sinful nature.

But it should be carefully explained how far and in what way God concurs with the creature in the performance of an action. But whatever explanation of that matter may be made, there must always be caution that a concurrence, with a second cause, may never be attributed to the first cause, such that the cause of evil can be rightly ascribed to the latter. You say: "the will can do nothing alone, yet it can act in an evil manner," and illustrate it by simile. Let us see how far it is appropriate. It is especially to be considered that it is applicable to a man, in an unfallen state, because "his pipe is not disjointed," therefore that simile is not to be applied to his primitive state.

Again, in "lameness," two things are to be considered, namely, "the walking or motion, and lameness, which is irregularity of motion." You compare walking with the act, and lameness with the irregularity of the act, in which the relation of sin properly consists. But those two things are not present in every act which is evil. For instance, the eating of the forbidden fruit, in which it is not allowable to distinguish between the act and its sinfulness.

For the act itself ought not to have been performed, and the relation of sin consists, not in the fact that he performed the act of eating in a mode, in which it ought not to have been performed, but in that he performed it at all. That illustration would have place in acts good in themselves, but performed in a way in which they ought not to be performed. Thus he, who gives alms, "that he may be seen of men," performs a good act, but in an improper manner: he walks, but is lame. Hence it follows that no one can be impelled to an act, the commission of which is a transgression of the law, without sin, and blame in the impeller and mover. You, also see from this how cautiously the mode, in which God is said to be the cause of an act, but not of the sin existing in the act, is to be explained.

Action of Divine Providence

You say that "the third action of Divine Providence is *kata sugchoresin*, 'according to concession,' by which God in the evil work of man, effects some things holily." It is not doubtful that this may be truly said of the Deity.

In this third action, you make also another three-fold division. You say that the first is "permission," but you explained it in such a manner, that it could not be adapted to Adam in his original state, but to those only who have sinned, and, by their sins, deserved to be left by God to themselves, and given "over to a reprobate mind." For "God did not loose the reins upon Adam. He did not remove the impediments of sinning. He did not free him, previously bound, with cords." I have nothing at all against "the second action" and its explanation, if it be applied to sinners; yet I think that some things, highly necessary, might be added to it.

You do not seem to me to explain, with sufficient distinctness, "ordination," which is the third action. For the word is used in a threefold sense: that of decreeing and determining that something shall be done, that of establishing an order in that which is done, and of disposing and determining to a suitable end, things that are done. This equivocal use of the word should have been avoided, and the different significations of the word should not be confounded, as you do in the same discussion, when you say that "God ordains sin as to its cause and principles," in which case, the word "ordain" is used, in its first signification: again: "He ordains the same thing as to its result and purposes," in which case, it is used in the second signification. The explanation, which you add, from the case of Satan, is only in reference to the ordination, as to the end and the result. If there is not a suitable explanation of the mode in which "God ordains, as to its causes and principles, an act, which cannot be done by a man without sin"—I prefer to use this phraseology rather than the word "sin"—the cause and blame of sin will, by an easy transition, be charged upon God.

The words of Clement of Alexandria[1] can only be understood of an ordination to an end, and I wish that you and all our writers would persist in the use of such language. For it is correct, and explains the action of God, who effects His own work by the evil deeds of wicked persons. In the words of Augustine, there is the most manifest difference between "to make" and "to ordain," and the word ordain is used in its second signification, that of disposing and determining wills, evil by their own fault, to these and those purposes and to certain actions.

But those words of Augustine, "God works in the hearts of men, inclining their wills whithersoever He pleases, even to evil things, according to their demerits," are to be suitably explained, so as not to impinge upon what follows; that "God does not make the wills evil." He, therefore, inclines evil wills to evil things, so that they expend their wickedness upon one object, rather than upon another. If he is said to impel anyone to will that which is evil, it is to be understood that He does this by the instrumentality of Satan, and, in such a way as can be easily reconciled with His justice.

Fulgentius[2] explains the matter most correctly and in a few words. For he sufficiently acquits Him of sin, when he denies that "God is the author of evil thoughts." For thoughts are the first causes in the performance of a work; and he also uses the word "ordain" in the latter signification, as can be clearly seen from his subjoined explanation. For he says that "God works good out of an evil work."

1. Clement says, "It belongs to God's wisdom, virtue, and power, not only to do good, which is the nature of God, but also to bring into some good and profitable end what has been invented by those who are evil, and to use profitably those thing which seem evil." Perkins, *Works*, II: 618.

2. Saint Fulgentius, Bishop of Ruspe (467–532), was considered the greatest North African theologian after Augustine.

Your third answer denies, and with propriety, that the "Fate of the Stoics" is introduced by your doctrine, that is, Fate explained as the Stoics taught concerning it. But it does not remove this difficulty, that on the supposition of that Divine decree, which you suppose, a necessity is introduced with which liberty cannot be consistent. While, therefore, the Fate of the Stoics may not be presented in your doctrine, yet a fate is presented, which places a necessity upon all things, and takes away freedom. You attempt to explain the decree of God in a way such as may not, by the divine decree, take away freedom, though it supposes necessity; to do which is, in my opinion, wholly impossible. But let us see how you present the mode of explaining and of disentangling the matter.

First, you distribute that which is necessary into the simply or absolutely necessary, and the hypothetically necessary. The absolutely necessary—you correctly say—"is that which cannot be otherwise, and whose contrary is impossible." But you do not, in your statement, make any distinction whether you treat of a thing which is noncomplex and simple, or of a complex being. But let that pass. It is certain that there is nothing necessary in that sense, but God, and what pertains to Him. All other things are placed outside of that necessity.

Cannot be Otherwise

You say, "that the necessary, by hypothesis, is that which cannot be otherwise when one, or a number of things, is supposed." You do not here make a distinction in the supposition of things, between that by which a thing is supposed to be, and that by which a thing is concluded; which latter necessity is distinguished into that of the *consequent* and that of the *consequence*. The latter is syllogistic, the former is that of causes producing effects or consequents, causes which neither are necessarily supposed, nor act necessarily as causes. But if they are supposed, and act as causes, the effect necessarily exists. For example, God does not necessarily create a world, but if He creates one, then it exists necessarily, from that action. You consider that "the necessary by hypothesis is of nature, of precept, and of decree."

That which is necessary of nature removes freedom and contingency. So, also, that which is necessary of precept; for that, rendered obligatory by law, is not left to the freedom of the creature, though, from the necessity of nature, an act is necessarily produced unless it be prevented by that which has greater power. But by the necessity of precept, the act is not necessarily produced; there is laid upon the creature a necessity of performing the act, if it wishes to obey God, and to be accepted by Him.

You badly define necessity of decree, as "that which God has foreknown and willed either to effect or at least to permit." For the necessity of foreknowledge, and of the Divine permission is one thing, and that of efficiency is another. Indeed, we may allow that there is no necessity of foreknowledge and of permission, but only of efficiency, or of the Divine will.

For, not the foreknowledge of God, but "His will is the necessity of things," though, the foreknowledge of God being supposed, it may follow that a thing will be, not from foreknowledge as an antecedent, but as sustaining to foreknowledge the relation of conclusion.

We shall hereafter treat of permission, at a greater length. We remark, also, that what is necessary of decree, cannot at the same time, be called free or contingent in respect to the will as efficient.

In the second place, you distinguish necessity into that of compulsion, and that of certainty. This is not well, for these are not opposed, as one and the same thing can be produced, by the necessity of compulsion, and can be certainly foreknown. Again, they are not of the same genus. For the former belongs to the will, effecting something, and is prior in nature, to the thing effected, while the latter is by foreknowledge, and is subsequent in nature, to the thing. The former coincides with the necessity of consequent, the latter with that of the conclusion. Thirdly, there is a necessity which is nearer to the necessity of compulsion, as to relation, cause and genus, and is the opposite of compulsion, and from which as its contrary, the necessity of compulsion ought to have been distinguished. It is the necessity of inevitability, which term, also, indeed, comprehends the idea of compulsion, but an unnamed species may be called by the name of its genus.

That this may be more clearly understood, I explain myself thus: The necessity of inevitability is twofold, one introducing force, in things purely natural, when it is called violence, and in things voluntary, when it is called compulsion; the other, inwardly moving a thing, whether it be nature or will, so smoothly and gently, that it cannot but be inclined in that direction, and will that to which it is moved.

Yet I admit that the will is not carried or moved according to the mode of the will, but according to the mode of nature, as, by the act of moving, freedom is taken away, but not spontaneous assent, while both are taken away by the act of impelling. I pass over your definition of compulsion. That of certainty does not please me; for, in that definition, you conjoin things, which do not belong together. For a thing is said to happen certainly in respect to foreknowledge, but immutably in respect to the thing itself; and immutability does not correspond with certainty.

For certainty is attributed to foreknowledge, which cannot be deceived on account of the infinity of the divine nature and wisdom. You should then, expunge that word "immutably" from your argument. For that which can either happen or not happen, cannot be done immutably, yet it can surely be foreknown by Him who foreknows with certainty, all things even those which are contingent. But you rightly add an axiom to the certainty of necessity; "Everything which is, so far as it is, is necessary."

Thus far, the distinctions of necessity. You will now show how they mutually correspond. "All relations of effects are to their own causes," but either to separate causes, or to concurrent causes, and to joint causes, and to causes which act at the same time. If they are to separate causes, the effects are named from the mode, in which those effects exist from their causes.

Necessary Effects

If necessarily, they are called necessary effects, if contingently, they are called contingent. But if many causes concur to produce one effect, that effect has relation to and connection with, each of its causes. But it does not receive its name, except from the mode in which it exists and is produced from those united causes. If that mode is necessary, the effect is called necessary; if that mode is contingent, it is called contingent.

It cannot however, be that one and the same effect should exist in part contingently, and in part necessarily, in any respect whatever. It is, indeed, true that, if that which is called a second cause, operates alone and of its own will, the thing might be called contingent. But, since the first cause moves the second, so that it cannot but be moved, the whole effect is said to be necessary, since it cannot be that the effect should not be produced, when those first and second causes are in operation.

The position that "the freedom of second causes is not taken away by that necessity," is, here, of no importance. As is also your opinion that "an effect can be called free and contingent in respect to a certain cause, which is said to be necessary in respect to the first cause." For it is absurd to wish to harmonize freedom with necessity, and the latter with the former. All necessity, indeed, is at variance with freedom, and not the necessity of compulsion alone.

This is so true, that even any degree of vehemence cannot be successful in weakening its truth. I grant that it is true, that "the decree of God ordains second causes, and, among them, the freedom of human will," but, in such a manner that freedom is not taken away by that "ordination." But freedom is taken away, when God, either by compulsion (which cannot be, both on account of the divine omnipotence, and on account of the nature of the will), or, by an easy and gentle influence, so moves the will, that it cannot but be moved.

You seem to me not to discriminate between a free movement and one which is spontaneous. A spontaneous movement is so different from one that is free, that the former may coincide with a natural and internal necessity, but the latter can by no means do so. For a man spontaneously wishes to be happy, but not freely. Beasts are spontaneously borne towards those things that are good for them, by natural instinct, but no liberty can be attributed to them.

From these considerations, it is apparent that it can in no manner, be said that "Adam fell necessarily and at the same time freely," unless you introduce the necessity of certainty that belongs not to the Fall, but to the foreknowledge of God, on account of His infinity. But freedom is taken away, if a decree of God is supposed, since "Adam could not resist the will, that is, the decree of God." Your answer that "as he could not, so he also would not," is refuted by the consideration that he could not will otherwise.

This you confess to be true "as to the event," but not true "as to his power." But it is not the subject of disputation, whether the will of Adam was deprived of the power, called freedom, which was not necessary to induce the necessity of the Fall, but whether the event itself, that is, the Fall, occurred necessarily. When you admit this, you must admit also that he did not fall freely. For that power was limited and determined as to the act and event, so that, in the act, he could not will otherwise; else the decree of God was made in vain. Here, also, you unskillfully use spontaneous motion for free motion.

To elucidate the subject, you "distinguish three periods: previous, present, and future to the Fall." But the present and the future are of no importance to this discussion. For the Fall cannot have any necessity from present and future time. Previous time only serves our purpose. You say that "at the present moment, the Fall was necessary, in a two-fold respect." First, "on account of the foreknowledge of God." But foreknowledge is not a cause of necessity, nor can anything be said to be done infallibly, on account of foreknowledge, but foreknowledge is the cause, that a thing "which will occur, contingently, at its own time," is certainly foreknown by God.

And secondly, "on account of the permissive decree of God." But permission cannot be a cause of immutability or of necessity. For it is a negative act, not a prohibition; and from it an affirmative necessity cannot exist. The words of Honorius and Hugo do not aid you, for they treat of something wholly different, and they are not reliable authorities. But the reason you present, is partly begging the question, partly of no reason. The begging the question is, "because an evil permitted, cannot but happen." The no reason, when you say "because it cannot happen otherwise than God decreed."

It does not follow from this, that it therefore happens necessarily; since, though evil cannot happen otherwise than God permits it, yet that permission does not impose a necessity upon the event or sin. For the divine determination is not in reference to sin, that is, shall be committed, but in reference to the same thing, which is about to take place of its own causes, that is, shall not extend further than seems good to God. I do not accede to your definition of "permission" that "it is a negative of that grace, which is sufficient for the avoidance of sin." For, as has often been said, this is not to permit a man to sin freely, but to effect that he should sin necessarily.

I wish also that you had explained, in what way "the necessity of the divine decree, by which He determined that Adam should sin, was evitable in respect to the freedom of the human will, when it was inevitable in respect to the event." I pass over the inconsistency of calling necessity evitable.

Anyone Should Think

You do not wish that anyone should think that "that necessity arose from the decree of God." But you have said so many things in proof of it, that you now express your unwillingness in vain. Explain how that necessity follows the decree, and yet the decree has not the relation of cause, in respect to that necessity. For the decree is the cause of necessity, in the relation of consequent, not in that of consequence. Those are words and phrases, designed to avoid the force of truth, in which there is no truth, and not even the semblance of truth. For it will always remain true that whatever is necessary "of decree" has the cause of its necessity in and from the decree of God. Is not that laborious investigation and use of many distinctions a sign of falsity, when the statement of truth is simple and open? The assertion that "the predestinated are saved necessarily, and the reprobate are damned necessarily," is to be correctly understood. The fact, that anyone is predestinated, is at variance with the fact of damnation, and the fact, that anyone is reprobate, is at variance with the fact of salvation.

But the ability to be saved or damned, is at variance with neither. For the decree is not in respect to the ability, but in respect to the fact of salvation or damnation. But those two acts you mention, namely, that of not showing mercy and that of damning, are subsequent to sin. For mercy is necessary, only to the miserable and the sinner, and it is truly said that "the purpose of damning does not make any necessity of damnation unless by the intervention of sin," but by its intervention, in such a sense, that it is possible that it should not intervene. If, however, God has decreed to make and govern men, that they cannot but sin, indeed, in order that He may declare His own righteousness in mens destruction, that purpose introduces a necessity of sin and of damnation.

It is an absurd assertion that "from foreknowledge that necessity follows in the same way." For what God foreknows, He foreknows because it is to take place in the future. But what He decrees, purposes, and determines in Himself to do, takes place thus because He decrees it. Also, from foreknowledge is concluded the certainty of an event, which is a necessity of the consequence, and from the decree immutability of the same thing is concluded, which is a necessity of the consequent.

You make an objection against yourself, "They who are predestinated to death cannot, if they will, be freed by repentance." That objection is not appropriate to this time and place. But I present you with an objection, that they who are predestinated to death, are also, according to your doctrine, predestinated to sin, that what God has decreed to bring upon them, namely, death that He may be able to bring upon them justly, that is, on account of sin. But indeed, if God can predestinate to sin, that He may be able to bring death upon the sinner. He is able also to bring death upon one who is not a sinner, because he who is a sinner in consequence of the divine Predestination, is in fact not a sinner. It is far worse to predestinate a just man to sin than to predestinate an innocent man to death. Of this we have also previously spoken.

Your effort to charge the same necessity on the opinion "which supposes a permission of evil" is futile. I refer, here, to "permission," when rightly explained, and understood according to its own nature. But you describe permission in such a manner, as really to amount to an act of efficiency.

For if "to permit is to will not to hinder," which it is in fact, and "the will not to hinder is such, that, without that hindrance, sin cannot be avoided," as you assert, then, "to will not to hinder sin" is to effect sin, by a negation of the necessary hindrance. Thus evil also necessarily exists from that permission, but by no means freely on the part of man. From which, it is clearly evident that the decree of God is not more avoidable than a permission of the kind, which you have described. But, unless the distinction of the decree of God into energetic or efficacious and permissive is without foundation, as it certainly is not, then it is necessary that permission should be described so as not to coincide with energetic decree.

The charge of holding the Stoic and Manichean doctrine, which is made by some against you, is not made by them with the idea that your opinions entirely agree with that doctrine, but that you agree with it in this, that you say that all things are done necessarily. You ought to remove this charge from yourself, and free your doctrine from this accusation.

You unite contrary things when you say that "a man cannot abstain from sinning, and yet he sins not necessarily, but freely." Nor is it sufficient to constitute freedom of the will, that it "be capable of being turned in opposite directions, and to choose spontaneously," if it shall be "determined to one direction only, by the Deity." For that determination takes away the freedom of the will, or rather the liberty of volition. For though the will, in other things not determined by God may remain capable of change in any directions and free, yet the volition is not free, since it is determined precisely to one of two contraries.

The remark of Anselm presents the same idea we have often presented, that a distinction is to be made between the necessity of the *consequent*, and that of the *consequence*. The former precedes, the latter follows the action. But your necessity of decree precedes the act and does not follow, while that of Anselm follows it, therefore, they are not the same. In the remark of Gaudentius[3] there is not even a trace of the doctrine which you defend.

In your brief recapitulation, you fail as greatly, of untying the knot. For it will always remain true that a denial of grace, necessary to the avoidance of sin, is a cause of sin, by the mode of the non-bestowment of the necessary hindrance. And it will always be false that he sins freely and voluntarily, who cannot but sin, and that the will acts freely in that direction, to which it is determined by the certain and inflexible decree of God. It is false in the sense that freedom and determination are mutually opposed in the limits of their action.

For the former has respect to two contraries, the latter to one only. You present the example of the "angels who obey God both necessarily and freely," on your own authority, and do not at all prove what you assert. I assert that these two things are mutually inconsistent, so that if you affirm that the angels obey God freely, I shall say, with confidence, that it is possible that the angels should not obey God. If, on the other hand, you affirm that they cannot but obey God, I shall thence boldly infer that they do not obey God freely. For necessity and freedom differ from each other in their entire essence, and in genus.

And I would dare say, without blasphemy, that not even God Himself, with all His omnipotence, cannot effect that what is necessary so that it may be contingent or free, and that what is done necessarily, so it may be done freely. It implies a contradiction, that a thing should not be possible not to be done, and yet be possible not to be done, and it is a contradiction, opposed to the first and most general idea, divinely infused into our minds, in reference to whatever subject the truth is affirmed or denied.

And a thing cannot, at the same time, be and not be, at the same time, be and not be of a given character. For the fact, that God cannot do this, is a mark not of impotence but of invariable power. The fact that a thing exists, depends on the actual power of God. If it should happen, at once and at the same time with the previous fact, that the same thing should not be, then the actual power of God would be either overcome, or have an equal power opposed to itself, so that it would happen that a thing that is by the power of God, at the same time, is not. This is the greatest of all absurdities.

---

3. St. Gaudentius (unknown–410) was Bishop of Brescia, Italy.

Treatise on God's Permission

As frequent mention of the permission of sin has been already made by us, it will be a work, not useless in itself and not displeasing to you, if I shall distinctly set forth what I consider the true view concerning permission, in general, according to the Scriptures. You will read, weigh, and judge, freely and with candor, and if I shall, as to any point, seem to err, you will recall me to the right way, by serious and friendly admonition. I will treat, first, of permission in general, then of the permission of sin.

We know that permission pertains to action, in a generic sense, from the very form of the word, whether in itself or by reduction as they say in the schools. For cessation from act may also be reduced or referred back to the act, but it has, as its proximate and immediate cause, the will, not knowledge, not capability, not power, though these, also, may be requisite in the being, who permits. No one is rightly said to permit, who does not know what and to whom he permits, and is not capable of permitting or preventing, and finally has not the right and authority to permit. If permission is attributed to anyone who is destitute of that knowledge, capability, or power, it is in an unusual and extended sense, which ought not to have a place in an accurate discussion of a subject.

The object of permission is both the person to whom anything is permitted, and the act which is permitted, and, under the act, I would include, also, cessation from the act. In the person, to whom anything is permitted, two acts are to be considered in respect to the person. First, strength sufficient to the performance of an act, unless there is some hindrance; secondly, an inclination to perform the act, for apart from this, the permission would be useless. Strength is necessarily requisite for the performance of an act; even if this is present, unless the person, to whom an act is permitted, has an inclination to the act, it is permitted to no purpose, and in vain.

Indeed it cannot be said correctly, that an act is permitted to anyone, who is influenced by no inclination to the performance of the act. From this it is apparent that permission must be preceded by the foreknowledge or the knowledge of the fact that both sufficient strength and an inclination to perform the act, exist in him, to whom the permission is granted. The mode of permission is the suspension of efficiency, which efficiency is also possible to the being who permits, either according to right, or according to capability, or in both respects, and, when used, would restrain, or in fact prevent the act.

We may, hence, define permission in general. Thus, it is the act of the will by which the being who permits, suspends any efficiency possible to him, which, being used, would restrain or in fact, prevent an act in him to whom the permission is granted, to the performance of which act the same person has an inclination and sufficient strength. These conditions being applied to the Divine permission, by which He permits an act to a rational creature, the definition may be thus arranged: Divine permission is an act of the divine will by which God suspends any efficiency possible to Himself, either by right, or by power, or in both modes, which efficiency, used by God, would either restrain or really prevent an act of a rational creature, to the performance of which act, the same creature has an inclination and sufficient strength. But, since the will of God is always directed by His wisdom, and tends to good, that permission cannot but be instituted to a certain end and the best end.

There are two modes or species of permission, as is manifest in the definition, in which, to efficiency, if used, either the limitation of an act, or its prevention is ascribed. For the will of God is considered, in a twofold respect, either as He prescribes something to His creatures, by command or prohibition, or as He wills to do or to prevent anything. Hence the efficiency under discussion, is twofold, on one hand, as the prescription or enactment of a law by which any act of the creature is restrained, by which restraint or limitation that act is taken away from the freedom of the creature, so that he cannot, without sin, perform it if it is forbidden, or omit it if it is commanded. And on the other, as the interposition of an impediment, by which any act of the creature is prevented.

In the first mode, there was a limit as to the eating of the forbidden fruit of the tree of knowledge of good and evil, and as to the love due to a wife, the former by prohibition, the latter by command. In the second mode, Balaam was prevented from cursing Israel, Ahaziah from the murder of Elijah, Sennacherib from the capture of Jerusalem, and Abimelech from sin with Sarah. But since God, if He pleases, suspends this efficiency, in both modes, when and where it seems good to Him, permission is also twofold. On one hand, as He does not restrain an act by a law, but leaves it to the decision and freedom of the creature, whether this may be on account of the simple nature of the act itself, as in that expression of the apostle "all things are lawful for me" (l Cor. 6:12) or, on account of another forbidden evil, an example of which may be taken from the "bill of divorcement." On the other hand, as He does not, by His own action, interpose an impediment to an act, an impediment, by which the act may be really prevented, not one, by which it can or ought to be prevented. Thus He permitted Adam to eat of the forbidden fruit, and Cain to kill his own brother. Though He used impediments, by which each of those acts could, and ought to have been prevented, yet He did not use impediments, by which the act, in either case, *was* prevented.

Allowed to Divide

We may be allowed to divide also, the latter mode of permission which is by abstaining from the use of an impediment, which would prevent the act, according to the difference of the modes in which God is able, and, indeed, accustomed to prevent an act, to the performance of which a creature is inclined and sufficient. I do not wish, however, that such sufficiency should be ever understood apart from the concurrence of the first cause.

That variety arises from the causes by means of which a rational creature performs an act. Those causes are power or ability, called *dunamis* and will. We, here, speak of voluntary acts, to which the permission, of which we now treat, has reference. Therefore, the impediment is placed either upon the capability or the will of the creature. That is, God effects that the creature should be either not able, or not willing to produce that act. In the former mode He prevented Adam from remaining in Paradise. In the latter, He prevented Joseph from polluting himself with adultery with the wife of his master.

More particularly, we must consider in how many ways God may prevent the creature from being able or willing to perform the act, to which he has an inclination and sufficient strength, that is, apart from this impediment.

We consider prevention as applied, first to the capability, secondly, to the will. That the creature may be able to effect anything, it is necessary that he should have capability; that no greater or equal power should act against him; finally, that he should have an object on which his capability can act.

From this it is evident that an impediment may be placed on the capability in a four-fold manner: first, by the taking away of being and life that are the foundation of capability; secondly, by the deprivation or diminution of the capability itself; thirdly, by the opposition of a greater, or, at least, an equal power; fourthly, by the removal of the object; either of which ways is sufficient for prevention. We will adduce examples of each mode.

In the first mode, the capture of Jerusalem attempted by Sennacherib, was prevented by the slaughter of "a hundred fourscore and five thousand" men, by one angel (2 Kings 19:35, 36). Thus, also, the effort to bring Elijah before Ahaziah was prevented by the fire, twice consuming fifty men, who were sent to take him.

In the second mode, Samson was prevented from freeing himself from the hands of the Philistines, after his hair was cut off (Judges 16:19, 20), the strength of the Spirit, by which he had formerly been so mighty, having been taken away or diminished.

In the third mode, Uzziah was prevented from burning incense to the Lord by the resistance of the priests (2 Chron. 26:18), and the carrying of Lot and the Sodomites into captivity was prevented by Abram with his servants, attacking the victorious kings (Gen. 14:15, 16).

In the fourth mode, Ahab was prevented from injuring Elijah (1 Kings 19:3), and the Jews, who had sworn to slay the apostle Paul, were prevented from effecting their design (Acts 23:10). God removed Elijah, and Paul was rescued from the Jews by the chief captain. Thus, also, Christ often removed himself out of the hands of those, who wished to take him; of those, also, who wished to make him a king.

The permission, which is contrary to this prevention, also subsists by four modes, contrary to those just exemplified, but united together. For a complete cause is required to the production of an effect, the absence of a single necessary cause, or element of the cause, being sufficient to prevent the effect. Thus it is necessary that, when God permits any act to the capability of a creature, that creature should be preserved as it is, and should live; that its capability should remain adapted to the performance of the act; that no greater or equal power should be placed in opposition; finally, that the object, to be operated upon, should be left to that capability.

Divine Permission

It appears, from this, that this divine permission is not inactive, as so many actions of the providence of God are requisite to that permission, the preservation of being, of life, and the capability of the creature, the administration and government, by which a greater or an equal power is opposed to the creature, and the presentation of the object. We may be allowed, also to adduce similar examples of permission. Thus God gave His Son into the power of Pilate and of the Jews. "This is your hour and the power of darkness" (Luke 22:53). Thus He gave Job into the hands of Satan (Job 1:12), Zachariah into the hands of his murderers (2 Chron. 24:21), and James into the hands of Herod (Acts 12:2).

Let us now consider how God may prevent a creature from a volition to perform an act, to which he has an inclination and sufficient strength. An impediment is placed by the Deity, upon the propensity and the will of a rational creature, in a twofold mode, according to which God can act on the will. For He acts on the will either by the mode of nature, or according to the mode of the will and its freedom. The action, by which He affects the will, according to the mode of nature, may be called physical impulse; that, by which He acts on the same, according to the mode of the will and its freedom, will be suitably styled suasion.

God acts, therefore, preventively on the will either by physical impulse or by persuasion, that it may not will that, to which it is inclined by any propensity. He acts preventively on the will, by physical impulse, when He acts upon it, by the mode of nature, that, from it may necessarily result the prevention of an act, to which the creature is inclined by any propensity. Thus the evil disposition of the Egyptians towards the Israelites seems, in the judgment of some, to have been prevented from injuring them. God acts, preventively, on the will by persuasion, when He influences the will by any argument, that it may not will to perform an act, to which it tends by its own inclination, and to effect which the creature has, or seems to himself to have, sufficient strength. By this, the will is acted upon preventively, not of necessity, indeed, but of certainty.

But since God, in the infinity of His own wisdom, foresees that the mind of the rational creature will be persuaded by the presentation of that argument, and that, from this persuasion, a prevention of the act will result, He is under no necessity of using any other kind of prevention. All the arguments, by which the reason can be persuaded to the performance of an act, can be reduced to three classes: that which is easy and practicable; that which is useful, pleasant, and delightful; and that which is honest, just and becoming.

Hence, also, God, by a three-fold persuasion, prevents a person from the will to perform any act. For He persuades the mind that the act is either difficult to be performed, or even altogether impossible; or useless and unpleasant; or dishonest, unrighteous and indecorous. By the argument from the difficult and impossible, the Pharisees and chief priests were often prevented from laying violent hands on Christ. For they knew he was considered a prophet by the multitude, who seemed prepared to defend him against the efforts of his enemies. The Israelites, pursuing the king of Moab when they saw that he had offered his eldest son as a burnt offering, and, from this fact, knew that he was strengthened in his own mind, departed from him, thinking that they could not take the city without very great difficulty and much slaughter (2 Kings 3:23–27). Sanballat and Tobiah, and the other enemies of God's people, endeavoring to hinder the building of the walls of Jerusalem, were prevented from accomplishing their design when they heard that their plots were known to Nehemiah (Neh 4:15).

For they despaired of effecting anything, unless they could take the Jews by surprise. By the argument from the useless, the soldiers who crucified Christ, were prevented from breaking his legs (John 19:33), because he was already dead, and it would have been useless to break his legs, as this was designed, and usually done to hasten death. And at this time the Jews desired that their bodies should be taken down from the cross before sunset. But God had declared, "a bone of him shall not be broken" (John 19:36). By the same argument of inutility Pilate was prevented from releasing Christ: "If thou let this man go, thou art not Caesar's friend" (John 19:12).

Thus, also, Pharaoh did not wish to let the people of God go. (Exod 5–7) By the argument from the unrighteous or dishonest, David was prevented from slaying Saul, when he had fallen into his hands; "The Lord forbid that I should stretch forth my hand against the anointed of the Lord" (1 Sam. 24:6).

It is sufficient, for the prevention of an act by the argument of persuasion, that the act should seem to be impossible, useless, or unrighteous to those, by whom God wills that it should not be performed, even if it is not so in reality. Thus the Israelites were prevented from going up into the promised land, when they learned, from the spies, the strength of the nations, and the defenses of the cities, thinking that it would not be possible for them to overcome them (Num 13 and 14). Thus David was prevented from fighting for the Philistines, against Saul and the Israelites; for the Philistines said to their king—"let him not go down with us to battle, lest, in the battle, he be an adversary to us" (1 Sam 22:4).

Asking a Sign

Thus, Ahaz was prevented from asking a sign of the Lord, at the suggestion of Isa, the prophet; for he said, "I will not ask, neither will I tempt the Lord" (Isa 7:12). To this last argument pertain the revelations of the Divine will, whether they are truly such, or are falsely so esteemed. Thus David was prevented from building the temple of the Lord, by the Divine prohibition in the mouth of Nathan (2 Sam 7:5, etc.), though he had purposed, in his own mind, to do this for the glory of God. Thus Laban was prevented from speaking "to Jacob either good or bad," for, he said, "it was in the power of my hand to do you hurt" (Gen 31:29).

The king of Babylon being prevented by the oracle of his own gods he consulted, from attacking the Ammonites, marched against the Jews, whom God wished to punish. Each of these is not always used separately from the others by God to prevent an act which He wishes should not be performed. But they are sometimes presented, two or three together, as God knows may be expedient, to the prevention of an act which He wishes to prevent.

We do not in this place professedly discuss what that action is by which God proposes persuasive arguments designed to act preventively on the will, to the mind of the creature, inclined to the act and having strength adequate to its performance. Yet it is certain, whatever that act may be, that it is efficacious for prevention, and will certainly prevent, which efficacy and certainty depends not so much on the omnipotence of the divine action as, on the foreknowledge of God. He knows what arguments, in any condition of things or at any time, will move the mind of man to that, to which He desires to incline him, whether on account of His mercy or of His justice.

Yet, in my judgment, it is lawful so to distinguish that action as to say that, on the one hand, it is that of the gracious and particular providence of God, illuminating by His Holy Spirit, the mind of the man who is regenerate, and inclining his will, that he may will and not will that which God purposes that he should will and not will, and that, indeed, of a pure inclination to obey God. On the other hand, it is that of more general providence, by which He acts on men as men, or as only morally good, that they may not will, and may will, as God purposes that they should not will and should will, though not with this event and purpose, that they should, in their nolition or volition, obey God.

We now deduce, from this, the modes of permission, the opposite of prevention, which are not to be separated like those of prevention, but are to be united. For, as a single argument can act preventively on the will, that it may not will what God purposes to prevent. So it is necessary that all those arguments should be absent by which the will would be persuaded to an act of nolition, otherwise, there would be no permission. Therefore, the permission by which God permits a rational creature to perform an act, to the performance of which he has inclination and adequate strength, is the suspension of all those impediments, by which the will was to have been persuaded, and in fact moved to a nolition.

For it can be that God, being about to permit an act to the will of the creature, should so administer the whole matter, that not only some arguments of dissuasion, but all conjoined, may be presented to the will of a rational creature. Yet, as persuasion can but result from that presentation of arguments which is also known to God, it is from this fact that the presentation of arguments, is most consistent with the permission of that thing to dissuade from which they were used.

Let us illustrate the subject by examples. God permitted the brethren of Joseph to think of slaying him (Gen 37:18) and at length they sold him, not caring that he was their brother, and that they were forbidden, by the laws of God, to commit murder, or to sell a free person into slavery.

So, also, He permitted the enemies of His Son to condemn him, though innocent and unheard, and finally to slay him, setting at naught their own law, which not only had been imposed on them by the Deity, but was called to their remembrance by Nicodemus, Joseph and others, in the inquiry, "Doth our law judge any man before it hear him?" They obtained false witnesses, and found that "their witness agreed not together" (Mark 14:56). Yet they did that, which their envy and hatred against Christ dictated. Thus God likewise permitted Saul to persecute David (1 Sam 23 and 24), making no account of the fact that he had been taught and convinced of David's innocence by his own son, and by personal experience.

From this discussion, it is apparent that a difference must be made between a sufficient and an efficacious impediment, and that the permission of which we here treat, is a suspension of efficacious impediment. A sufficient impediment is used by God partly to declare that the act, to prevent which He takes care that those arguments should be proposed, and presented, is displeasing to Himself, partly that they may be more inexcusable, who do not permit themselves to be prevented; and even that He may the more, on account of their iniquity, incite them to the act which is so eagerly performed.

Three-Fold Permission

Then we have this three-fold permission of the Deity, first, that by which God leaves any act to the decision of a rational creature, not restraining it by any law; secondly, that by which He permits an act, in respect to the capability of the creature; third, that by which He permits the act, in respect to the inclination and will of the creature. The last two cannot be disjoined in a subject, though they can and ought to be suitably distinguished from each other. For it is necessary that an act God does not will to prevent, should be permitted both to the capability and the will of the creature, since, by the sole inhibition, either of the capability, or of the will, an impediment is presented to the act such that it is not performed.

Some may say that the species or modes of prevention are not sufficiently enumerated, as no act is prevented in its causes only, but also, in itself. It is necessary to an act, not only that God should bestow both the power and the will, that he should produce the effect itself, and without the intervention of means. It must follow, therefore, that an act will not be certainly produced, even if God should bestow the power and the will, and hence it is possible that an act should be prevented, even if God does not present an impediment to the capability or the will. That is, if He withholds from the creature his own concurrence, either active or motive, which is immediately necessary to produce the act. From this, it can be deduced, also, that an act is not fully permitted, even if it is left by God to the capability and will of the creature, unless God has determined to unite immediately to produce the same act, by his own act, motion, or concurrence. I reply, that I do not deny the necessity of that concurrence or immediate act of God to the production of an act.

But I say that it has once been determined by God not to withhold from His creatures His own concurrence, whether general or special, for producing those acts, to perform which He has given to His creatures the power and the will of which He has left to the power and will of His creatures. Otherwise, He has in vain, bestowed the power and the will, and He has without reason, left the act to the capability and the will of the creature. I add that an example of an impediment of that kind cannot be given, that is, an impediment placed by God in the way of an act permitted to the capability and will of a creature, by withholding from the creature His own immediate concurrence.

I, therefore, conclude that the modes or species of prevention, and therefore, of permission, have been sufficiently enumerated. I grant that not only much light, but also completeness, will be added to the doctrine of the divine permission, if it not only may be shown how God prevents acts, for which rational creatures have an inclination and sufficient strength, but may be explained, with accuracy, how God produces and effects His own acts and His own works, through His rational creatures, whether good or bad. In which investigation, many learned and pious men have toiled, and have performed labor, not to be regretted; yet I think that so many things remain to be solved and explained, that no genius, however surpassing, can be sufficient for all of them, and so it can be truly said that the mine of this truth is not only deep and profound, but also inexhaustible.

Yet, if we descend into it with soberness and, following the thread and guidance of the Holy Scriptures, there is no doubt that it will be granted unto us to draw thence so much as God, the only fountain and giver of the truth, knows will conduce to the salvation of the church, and to the sanctification of His name in this world, to whom be glory for ever, through Jesus Christ. Amen.

Having thus discussed the subject of permission in general, let us now consider the permission of sin. At the outset, it must be understood that sin is not permitted in the first mode of permission, for it is sin in that it is forbidden by the law. Therefore, it cannot be permitted by the law; else, the same thing is sin and not sin; sin in that it is forbidden, and not sin, in that it is permitted, and not forbidden. Yet, since it is said truly that sin is permitted by God, it is certain that it is permitted in some way, which will generally considered, be a suspension of all those impediments by the interposition of which sin could not be committed by the creature. But the impediments by which sin, so far as it is sin, is prevented, are the revelation of the divine will, and an act moving or persuading to obedience to the divine will. From which it is evident that permission of sin is a suspension of that revelation, or of that suasion, or of both.

It may be stated, here, from the general definition of permission, that revelation, motion, or persuasion have so much efficacy, that if they are used and applied, the sin would not, in fact, be committed. I say this, then: Let no one think that God performs no act sufficient to prevent sin, when sin is not, in fact, prevented, and thence conclude that God wills sin. Again, let no one judge that, when God performs one or more acts, sufficient to prevent sin, that He unwillingly permits sin. In the latter of which remarks, we see that they are frequently mistaken, who do not consider the subject with sufficient accuracy.

Efficacious Prevention

For the sole consideration of efficacious prevention, by the suspension of which permission is properly and adequately defined, effects that we should understand that God does not will sin, even through inefficacious impediments, nor yet that he permits it unwillingly. He has, in addition to those sufficient impediments, also efficacious ones in the storehouse of His wisdom and power, by the production of which sin would be certainly and infallibly prevented.

That what has been thus said by us, in general terms, may be more evident, let us explain, with a little more particularity, in reference to differences of sin. Sin is either of omission or of commission. Sin of omission is a neglect of an act, prescribed and commanded by law; sin of commission, is a performance of that, which is forbidden and prohibited by law. But since, in a preceptive law, not a good act only, is enjoined, but its cause, mode and purpose, also in a prohibitive law, not a bad act only, are forbidden, but also the cause and purpose of the omission. It is apparent that sin, both against a preceptive law, and against a prohibitive law, is twofold: against a preceptive law if the enjoined act is omitted, and if it is performed unlawfully as to manner and purpose; and against a prohibitive law, by performing an action, and by not performing, but omitting it with an unlawful reason and purpose. The examples are plain.

He who omits to bestow alms on the poor, sins in omitting a prescribed act. He, who bestows alms on the poor that he may be seen of men, sins in omitting the due reason, and purpose of the bestowal. He who steals, sins in committing a forbidden act. He who abstains from theft, that his iniquity may be covered for the time and may afterwards more deeply injure his neighbor, sins in omitting the forbidden act with a wrong purpose. The divine permission is to be accommodated to each of the modes both of mission and of commission.

Sin is distributed, in respect to its causes, into sin of ignorance, of infirmity, and of malice. By some, an additional distinction is made, namely sin of negligence or thoughtlessness, as different and separate from the former, while others think that this is embraced in the three species previously mentioned.

The divine permission is also adjusted to these differences. It would be an endless work to present all the divisions and differences of sin, and to show how the divine permission is related to each class. But we must not omit that, in sin, not it alone but the act also blended with it, is to be considered, as in sin there is the transgression of the law, and the act, that is the act simply as such, and the act, as forbidden or prescribed, the omission of which prescript is sin. But permission can be considered, either in respect to the act, or to the transgression, for sin is prevented in the prevention of the act, without which sin cannot be committed.

Again, the act is prevented in the prevention of the sin, which necessarily inheres and adheres to the act, so that the act itself cannot be performed without sin. For one may abstain from an act, towards which he is borne by his inclination, because it cannot be performed without sin. Another, on the contrary, abstains from sin because he is not inclined to the act itself.

When he abstains from the act because it is sin, he abstains from sin per se, from the act incidentally. But when he abstains because the act is not pleasant to him, he abstains from the act per se, from sin incidentally.

When also an act, is permitted as an act, it is permitted per se, sin is permitted incidentally. When sin is permitted as sin, it is permitted per se, the act is permitted incidentally. All of which things are to be diligently considered in reference to the subject of permission, that it may be understood what efficiency God suspends in that permission, and what efficiency He uses to no purpose in relation to the event, in that sin is not omitted, not to no purpose in relation to the objects which God has proposed to Himself, the best and the most wisely intended, and most powerfully obtained. But though we have already discussed the permission of acts in general, it will not be superfluous to treat here of the same, so far as those acts are blended with sin, and sin with them; though, in the meantime, the principal reference in this discussion, must be to the permission of sin, as such.

For, as these two are so connected, that they cannot be separated in an individual subject, the very necessity of their coherence seems to demand that we should speak of the permission of both in connection, though of the permission of sin per se, and of the act incidentally. But the relation of sin appears most plainly in an act committed against a prohibitive law, as omission of good may be often comprehended under it by synecdoche, as in the definitions of sin: "it is that which is done contrary to the law"; also, "a desire, word, or deed against the law." It will not be irrelevant to show, in the first place, how God permits that sin, whether as it is a sin, or as it is an act He permits, or in both relations.

Modes of Permission

We will present the modes of permission corresponding to the contrary modes of prevention, as before. The murder Ahab and Ahaziah intended to perpetrate on the prophet Elijah, was an act, which, if performed would have taken away the life of Elijah, and was a sin against the sixth commandment of God. God prevented that murder, not as a sin, but as an act. This is apparent from the mode of prevention, for in one instance, he took Elijah out of the hands of Ahab, and in another He consumed, with fire sent down from heaven, those who had been sent to take the prophet (2 Kgs 1:10).

The former case was according to the fourth mode, heretofore mentioned; the latter was, according to the first mode, in opposition to the power of Ahaziah and in this case prevented the effect. David, being instigated by his followers to slay Saul, his persecutor and enemy, refused, being restrained from that act, not as an act, but as a sin. He said "The Lord forbid that I should stretch forth my hand against him, seeing he is the anointed of the Lord" (1 Sam 24:6).

The mode of prevention was by a revelation of the divine will, and by a persuasion to obedience, and was suitable to the prevention of sin as such. The defilement of Sarah, the wife of Abraham when she was brought to Abimelech, would have been an act, by which, as the violation of Sarah's chastity, would have caused great grief to Abraham, and would have been a sin against the seventh precept of the Decalogue. It was divinely prevented, if you consider the mode of prevention, as far as it was sin. For God, in a dream, revealed to him that she was "a man's wife" (Gen 20:3), and he could not, without sin, have carried out his design.

If you examine the design and reason of the prevention, it was both in respect to the act and to the sin; as an act, because it would have caused indelible grief to Abraham, and from this God wished to spare his servant; as sin, because God knew that Abimelech would have done this "in the integrity of his heart" (verse 6). He therefore, withheld him from sin, in adultery with the wife of his friend.

Let us look at the opposite modes of permission in examples, also selected from the Scriptures. The sale of Joseph, made by his brethren (Gen 37), was an act and a sin; also, the affliction by which Satan tried Job, the man of God (Job 1 & 2). Both were permitted by God. Was this in respect to the act or to its sin? This cannot be gathered from the mode of the permission, for God abstains from all modes of restraint when He permits anything, and if He did not so abstain, He would prevent, and then there would, consequently, be neither the act nor sin.

But, from the end and the mode of effecting the permitted act and sin, a judgment may be formed of the respect according to which God has permitted the act of sin. From the sale of Joseph resulted his removal to Egypt, his elevation to the highest dignity, in that land from which, food, necessary for his father's family, could be procured in a time of most direful famine. God declares that He sent him into Egypt for this purpose. All this resulted from the sale, not as it was a sin, but as an act. In the affliction of Job, God desired that the patience and constancy of His servant should be tried, and it was tried by the affliction not as a sin but as an act.

On the other hand, God permitted David to number the people (2 Sam 24:1), and Ahab to slay Naboth (1 Kgs 21:13–14), in which cases the numbering of the people, and the murder were acts, but were permitted as sin. For God purposed to punish Israel, and that Ahab should fill up the measure of his crimes. It is, indeed, true that God also wished to take pious Naboth from this vale of sorrows to the heavenly land; this was effected by the murder, not as it was a sin, but as an act. Yet the proper, immediate, and adequate reason that God permitted Ahab to perpetrate that murder, is that of which I have spoken: the measure of his crimes was to be filled.

For God could, in some other way, without human sin, have called Naboth to Himself. Again, God permitted Absalom to pollute by incest the wives or concubines of his father, and this was done in respect to both. For it was permitted both as an act, and as sin. As an act, it served for the chastisement of David who had adulterously polluted the wife of Uriah. As a sin, it was permitted, because God wished that Absalom, by his crime, should cut off all hope of reconciliation with his offended father, and, in this way, hasten his own destruction, the just punishment of rebellion against his father.

In both respects, also, God permitted Ahab to go up to Ramoth-Gilead contrary to the word of the Lord; as a sin, because God wished to punish him; as an act because God wished that he should be slain in that place, to which he came by the act of going up. From these examples a judgment may be formed of similar cases. Thus far, we are referring to permission of sin, which consists in the perpetration of an act, prohibited by law.

Let us now consider sin, as it is committed when an act, forbidden by law, is not performed, but omitted not from a due reason and purpose. Here the act is prevented, but sin is not prevented. There is, then, in this case, the permission of sin only, as such, and the mode of permission is a suspension of the revelation of the divine will, or at least of -persuasion and motion to obedience to the known will of God. For the creature omits the act, not because God has forbidden it, but for some other reason.

Brothers of Joseph

Thus the brothers of Joseph omitted to slay him, as they had determined to do, not because they began to think that this crime would displease God, but because, from the words of Judah, they thought it useless, and that it would be better to sell him into bondage (Gen 37:21–28). Absalom, after thousands of followers had been collected, omitted to pursue his fleeing father as Ahithophel counseled him, not because he considered it wrong to pursue his father, for he was wholly hostile to him. But he followed the counsel of Hushai, because he considered that the curse, advised by Ahithophel, would be dangerous for himself and the people.

In this and similar examples, we see that God restrained an act, which had been forbidden and therefore was sin, and yet did not prevent sin, which was committed by those who omitted that forbidden act; but he permitted them to sin in the mode of omitting the forbidden act. The reason is manifest, as by the act, a person, whom God purposes to spare would be injured, but no one but the sinner himself is injured by sin committed in an undue omission of an act, as is just. Indeed by the prevention of an act, there is prepared for the persons who have omitted an act, the punishment due to them both on account of this sin of undue omission, and for other reasons, as happened to Absalom.

We now proceed to the permission of sin, which is committed in the mere omission of an act, which has been commanded. This is permitted by God, as it is an omission of an act, and as it is sin. God, I assert, permits that act, which the law commands to be omitted either as it is an act or as it is sin. God permitted the sons of Eli to disobey the admonitions of their father (1 Sam 2:25); Saul, to spare the king of the Amalekites, (1 Sam 15:8); the Israelites, when the statement of the spies had been made, to refuse to go up into the promised land, (Num 14:4), the citizens of Succoth and Penuel, to deny bread to the army of Gideon, (Judg 8:6, 8); Ahab, to send away Benhadad alive, a man devoted to death by the Lord, (1 Kgs 20:34:); Festus, before whom Paul was accused, not to pronounce sentence against him, and in favor of the Jews, (Acts 25:12); etc.

He permitted all these things partly as they were omissions of acts, partly as they were sins, that is, omissions contrary to a preceptive law, which imposed commands, partly in both respects. In reference to the sons of Eli, the Scripture says—"they hearkened not unto the voice of their father, because the Lord would slay them" (1 Sam 2:25). The permitted omission of obedience thus far was sin. The omission by Saul of the slaughter of those, whom God willed and commanded to be slain, was permitted as it was a sin, not as it was the omission of an act, by the performance of which they would have been deprived of life.

For God had determined to take away the kingdom of Saul from him, and had already denounced this against him, by the mouth of Samuel, because he had sacrificed, not waiting for Samuel (1 Sam 13:9–14). Agag, also, was afterwards hewed in pieces before the Lord by the prophet Samuel. The fact that the Israelites omitted to go up into the promised land, as they had been commanded by the Lord, occurred because God purposed that their bodies should fall in the wilderness, as they had so often tempted God, and murmured against Him. Then that omission was permitted as a sin. God permitted the citizens of Succoth and Penuel to withhold bread from the army of Gideon, partly that He might test the constancy of those, who were "pursuing after Zebah and Zalmunna," partly that He might prepare punishment for the citizens of Succoth and Penuel.

In this case then, the omission of the act was permitted as it was such, and as it was sin. For as, being provided with food, they would have been strengthened, who were pursuing the Midianites, so the omission of the act, as such, on their part was grievous and to be worthy of punishment. The sending away of Benhadad, or his release from death was permitted by God, as a sin committed against an express command, for God purposed that Ahab should heap up wrath against the day of wrath, on account of his heinous sins, also as an act. He purposed that Benhadad, in the prolongation of his life, by the omission of an act commanded by God, might fight afterwards with Ahab, and, after his death, with the Israelites, and besiege Samaria to the great injury of its inhabitants. Festus was permitted by God, to refrain from acquitting Paul, according to law and right as he could be convicted of no crime, in respect to the act as such and not as sin. For, from that omission resulted a necessity for the appeal of Paul to Caesar, which was the occasion of his departure to Rome, where God willed that he should bear testimony concerning His Son.

In respect to sin, when a prescribed act is performed unduly as to manner and design, it is certain that it is permitted as such, for in it nothing is permitted except the omission of a due mode and purpose, which omission is purely sinful. This is evident from the mode of permission, which in this case, is certain; namely, the suspension of efficiency by which sin, as sin, is permitted. Joab performed many distinguished deeds and those prescribed by God, in fighting bravely, against the enemies of the people of God, in behalf of Israel, that it might be well for the people of God. But God did not incline his mind to do this from a right motive.

It is apparent that he sought his own glory in those deeds from the fact that he, by wicked treachery, destroyed men equal to himself in bravery and generalship, that he might be alone in honor. For the man who defends any cause, only that it may be defended, and for the glory of God, will not be vexed that as many as possible endued with skill and bravery should be united in its defense. Indeed, he would most deeply rejoice and be glad on this account.

Differences of Sin

As to the differences of sin in view of its causes: ignorance, infirmity, malice, negligence, there is in respect to these a clear distinction in their permission. For the permission of a sin of ignorance arises from the suspension of the revelation of the divine will: of malice, from the suspension of the act by which the perversity of the heart is corrected and changed; of infirmity, from the withholding of strength to resist temptation, of negligence, from the suspension of the act by which a serious and holy care and anxiety is produced in us to watch our faculties, and to walk in the law of the Lord. For God knows, when it seems good to him to perform a work by the acts of rational creatures, which cannot be committed by them without sin, how to suspend His own efficiency, so as to permit His creatures to perform their own acts. He willed that His church should be proved and purged by persecutions, and indeed by the act of Saul, a man zealous for the law, who from inconsiderate and preposterous love towards his own religion, wished that the sect of the Nazarenes, so called should be extirpated.

That this might be effected through him, He suffered him to be some time in ignorance, without which, as he was then constituted, he would not have persecuted the church. For he says that he "did it ignorantly" (1 Tim 1:13). In the case of Julian the apostate, a most foul persecutor of the church, God did not correct his willful and obstinate hatred of Christ and his church. For when he was convinced of the truth of the Christian doctrine, he could have persecuted it only through willful malice. God's procedure, in not correcting that hatred, was deserved by him, who, willingly and of his own fault, had apostatized from Christ.

God purposed that Peter, presuming too much on himself, should come to a knowledge of himself. He suffered him to deny his Master, from fear of death, not affording him such support of His Spirit, as to move him to dare to profess Christ openly, despising the fear of death. David, being freed from his enemies, and having conquered many neighboring kings and nations, began to guard his steps with too little care, and heedlessly gave himself up to negligence, especially because he had Joab, a distinguished general and skilled in military duties, in whom, on account of consanguinity, he could trust. From this it happened that he fell into that shameful adultery with the wife of Uriah. But God permitted him to fall into that negligence, and on that occasion to commit sin, that he might be more diligently watchful over himself, mourn on account of his own sin for an example to others, afford a distinguished specimen and example of humility and repentance, and rise more gloriously from his sin.

It would be tedious to remark the same thing in each kind of sin. But let these suffice, as exhibiting the means and mode of forming a correct judgment in reference to permission. But though the whole complex matter, made up of acts and transgression, may be permitted by God through a suspension of all divine acts, by the use of which on the part of God, the act either as an act or as sin, would have been prevented. Yet it is useful to consider distinctly, in what respect that permission may be given by God, and what efficiencies, and of what kind, He suspends, that He may not hinder the commission or omission of an act prescribed or forbidden.

For in this the divine goodness, wisdom and power, and even justice is seen as distinctly as possible, and it is most clearly proved how God in all his own action, restraint and permission, is free from blame, without sin, and by no means to be considered the author of sin. In showing which, it is so much the more evident how easily they may fall into absurdity and blasphemy, who refer, indeed, to a providential acting, restraining, permitting, but not with sufficient distinctness, accuracy, and diligence, bringing together and comparing them, and distinguishing each from the others.

The individual causes of permission, in its variety and in that of the permitted acts, and of sins, are at the same time various and manifold and not generally explicable. They can, perhaps in some way be demonstrated by those who have their senses exercised in divine things, and are accustomed to consider them with earnest study. Two general or universal reasons can be presented for the fact that God permits events in general, and why He permits any particular event. One is the freedom of the will, which God bestowed on rational creatures, and which He designed as the mistress and the free source of their actions.

The other is the declaration of the divine glory, which is of such a character as not only to effect and prevent that which can be effected and prevented, for his own glory, but also to reduce to order the acts of rational creatures that are permitted, and which frequently deviate from the order prescribed to them. From it the praise of the divine goodness, mercy, patience, wisdom, justice and power may shine forth and be revealed. To which pertains that, which is beautifully said by Augustine, "God has judged that it belongs to His own omnipotent goodness to bring good out of evil rather than not to permit evil to exist."

The creature is likewise to be considered, to whom is granted the permission of an act of commission or of omission, which cannot without sin, be committed or omitted; namely, as to his character at the time when that act is permitted to him, whether as only created, and remaining in his primeval integrity, or as fallen from that state. Again, this is whether a partaker of grace, or invited to a participation of grace; whether brought to that state, or resisting grace, or not sufficiently solicitous to receive it, and to continue in it, and the like.

For God can deny to any creature, considered as such, action, motion, efficiency, concurrence, either general or special, of nature or of grace, of providence or Predestination. However, I do not dare to make a confident assertion in reference to the act of Predestination—which act and concurrence, which motion and efficiency He could not without injustice, deny to the same creature considered in a different relation. But a permission of sin depends, as we have before seen, on a suspension of the divine act, motion, efficiency, etc.

Wishes to Discuss

He, however, who wishes to discuss fully and thoroughly the subject of permission must of necessity, treat of the general providence of God, and of that special providence that preserves, governs, rules, effects, prevents and permits. For, as permission is opposed to prevention, by the mode either of privation or of contradiction, so it is opposed to efficiency by negation. And it is the nature of permission to have, antecedent to itself, various acts of God concerning the same creature to which permission is granted and concerning that act which is permitted.

If these acts of God are not accurately explained, it cannot be understood what that efficiency is, in the suspension of which, permission properly and immediately consists. This also, is the reason that many, when they hear anything concerning permission, immediately in their own minds, conceive of inactive quiet and abstinence from all effort on the part of providence. Others, considering the power and efficacy of that providence, present in and presiding over all things and acts, either reject the idea of permission, or acknowledge it only in word, in the mean time, so explaining it as to resolve it into a certain act of God, and into the efficiency of providence. But these errors are both to be avoided, lest we should take away from the divine providence, acts which belong to it, or should attribute to it things foreign to it, and unworthy of His justice.

In reference to the remarks already made, someone will object that I attribute to permission not only the illegality and the irregularity of the act, but also the act itself, and thus remove from the operation of the divine will and efficiency, not only the illegality of the act, but the act itself. He will say that in this he perceives a double error: first, because I attribute sin, simply and taken in any respect, to permission, and remove it from the divine efficiency and will; when it ought in a certain respect to be attributed to the divine efficiency and will; secondly, because I take away, from the efficiency and the will of God, the act that is the first and supreme cause of all being. Let us examine a little more closely both objections.

We explain the former by the sentiments of the objector himself. In sin there are three aspects: first, guilt; second, punishment; third, the cause of other sins. Indeed God is not, they say, the cause of sin in respect to its guilt, but to its punishment, and to its being the cause of other sins. They affirm that God is, without controversy, the cause of punishment, because that is an act of justice, by which sin, deviating from the law of the prescriptive justice of God, is brought under the rule of divine punitive justice. That sin is of God, as it is the cause of other sins, they also, prove from the acts of blinding, hardening, giving over to a reprobate mind, which are acts of God and are causes of sins.

I answer: to the first, that the objection is not valid against all sins. For the first sin, committed by a creature, cannot be the punishment of another sin. There are also many sins that are not, in fact, the causes of other sins. For God may so administer and dispense the Fall and the sins of His creatures, as that they may result in good that is a greater odium against sin, and a more diligent solicitude and anxiety to guard their own steps. Therefore many sins, contrary to this objection, come to partake of an opposite character by the permission of God and in no respect by His efficiency. It will be said, in reply, that there are, nevertheless, many sins that must be considered in those three aspects. Of these at least, it may be proper to say, that in the last two aspects they have God as their cause and author. I answer secondly, that there is no act or sin, which has at the same time, the relation of guilt, of punishment, and of the cause of another sin, if these things may be correctly and strictly considered. I confess that this is usually said, and is common with many who treat of this subject.

First by Argument

I will prove my assertion, first by argument, then by presenting examples of blinding and hardening. That no act is at the same time, sin and punishment, is certain, since sin is voluntary, punishment is involuntary; sin is action, punishment is passion. By punishment sin is brought into subjection, but sin is not brought into subjection by sin, but by punishment, I say, differing from sin or guilt, not in relation only, but in the thing and subject which is the act. When this is said by learned men, a reason ought to be assigned for this opinion. I acknowledge it, but let us consider the sense in which this is said and understood by them.

They say that sin is the punishment of sin, because on account of previous sin, God permits the sinner to commit another sin, and, indeed, suspends some of His own acts, and performs others in which case the creature will sin of his own wickedness, and will commit other sins. On account of this he deserves greater punishment and condemnation, and thus, as sin deserves greater punishment, it is said to be the punishment of sin by a metonymy of cause and effect. In this sense they understand their own declaration, or it cannot be sustained. But that no sin is, at the same time, guilt and the cause of another sin, is also true, if it may be rightly understood; that is, a proximate and immediate cause. It is indeed the meritorious cause of another sin, that is it deserves that God should afterward suspend some act, and perform other acts, which being performed, he will, of his own wickedness, as said before, commit some sin. It is also the preparatory cause of the perpetration of other sins, for by sin the conscience is wounded, desire for prayer, and confidence in it are destroyed. A habit of sinning is prepared, a power over the sinner is granted to Satan, from which an easy lapse into other sins readily follows. Yet it is not the proximate and immediate cause of another sin.

"It is nevertheless a cause," some may say, "though remote and meritorious." What then? By this very distinction the whole force of the objection is destroyed. By it, God is made the cause of some acts, the creature will, of His own wickedness, deservedly add another sin to the former, and God is absolved from the charge of being the cause of sin, which deserved that He should perform those acts of sin, as it is the cause of another sin. For the action of the Deity intervenes between the sin, which is the cause of another sin, and that consequent sin. In that objection, however, it was inferred that God is the cause of sin, in that He is the occasion of the second sin.

That error arises from the confusion and the inaccurate consideration of those acts. Sin, in the relation of guilt, is first in order then follows demerit or conviction to punishment, from the justice of God, which is the act of God who punishes that sin by merited desertion, and blindness. But "blindness," you say, "is sin or guilt, and the punishment of previous sin, and the cause of subsequent sin, and God is the cause of blindness." The truth of what has been previously said may be demonstrated in this example.

That blindness judicially produced by God is correctly said to be the punishment of previous sin, and can, if rightly understood, be said to be the cause of consequent sins, that is, by a removal of restraining grace, and by the performance of some acts, from which it will follow that the creature, thus blinded and left, will of his own wickedness, commit sin. But that blindness is not sin or guilt. A distinction is to be made between the blindness as the act of God to which man is judicially subjected, and the blindness of man himself by which he renders his own mind hard and obstinate against God, which is the act of man, produced by wickedness and obstinate pertinacity. These acts indeed concur, but do not coincide, nor are they one single action made up of the efficiency of those concurrent actions, which together make up one total cause of that act, which is called blindness.

Learned men often speak in such a manner, I grant, but not with sufficient distinctness; and perhaps in a sense which agrees with my explanation, and is not contrary to it. For they use the term *blindness* in a complex and indistinct manner, for the act and its result, or the work and its effect, which is thereby, produced in the person made blind, which may be called passive blindness, produced by that active blindness. Of blindness, thus confusedly and indistinctly considered, it may be said that it is sin, the punishment of sin, and the cause of sin, but this is not at variance with my opinion, for I deny that God is the cause of that blindness, so far as it is sin and guilt.

Active blindness, as we now term it, by way of distinction, produced by a man, making himself blind, is sin, for it is a great crime to harden one's own mind against God. Active blindness, which proceeds from God, is the punishment of previous sin, by which the sinner has merited to himself desertion, and privation of grace. The active blindness, from man, and that, which is from God, concur to the same effect, which is passive blindness, which is properly, punishment. Finally, the active blindness of man, blinding himself, and that of God blinding man, is the cause of the accumulation of other sins with those previously committed, by the blinded sinner, but in the mode of which I have spoken.

Sin or Guilt

I answer, that if it is true that one and the same act is sin or guilt, the punishment of sin, and the cause of subsequent sin, then it cannot be true that God is its cause, according to the last two relations, and not according to the first, for a twofold reason. First, this distinction of relation cannot effect that God should be the cause of one thing and not of another in fact joined to it, unless in that mode, which will be hereafter explained, which they exclude from this subject, who say that blindness, produced by God, is sin, and the cause of sin.

These aspects are useful to a mind, intelligent and able to discriminate between things most intimately connected, which constitutes actually and numerically, one thing, but considered in different relations, they cannot have place in actual efficiency, the limit of which is real existence. God inflicts punishment on a person who is a sinner, and His creature. The act of infliction does not distinguish the creature from the sinner, but the mind of Him, who punishes, makes the distinction, for it knows how to punish the creature, not as such, but as sinful. This error is frequently committed, that relations are carried further than their nature may permit.

Secondly, because of those three relations, order, nature, and causality, the former is that in which sin is considered as guilt, the latter two are those in which it is considered as punishment, and the cause of consequent sin. God is the first cause of all effects, which He produces with or by His creatures. But in this case, He will be a subsequent cause, for He will produce, in the relation of subsequent respects, an act the creature produces in the relation of prior respect, which is absurd, and inverts the order of causality and efficiency, which exists between first and second causes. There may, indeed, be supposed to exist a concurrence, which we shall hereafter explain. But they, who say that the blindness, inflicted by the Deity, is the cause of consequent sins, and at the same time a sin, deny that this concurrence has any place here. These things, indeed, I have thought, ought to be explained somewhat fully on account of the difficulty of the subject itself, and of preconceived opinions.

Let us proceed to the second objection, which we thus set forth, according to the meaning of its authors: "In sin there are two things, the act and its illegality, or violation of law. As an act, it is positive; as a violation of law, it is privative: the latter has the will of the creature for its cause. The former must necessarily be referred back to the first cause, and, in this relation, God is the cause of that act which, in respect to man, or as it proceeds from man, is sin. Therefore it is wrong to remove the act, which is not performed by a man without sin, from the divine will and efficiency, and attribute it to the divine permission, since that act as such belongs to efficiency, but as it violates law, it belongs to the divine permission."

I reply, first, that it cannot be said truly and universally of all sin, that in it there are these two things, namely, the act and the violation. For, sometimes, it is the act itself that is prohibited, and sometimes, not the act itself but some circumstance in reference to the act. Thus the eating of the fruit of the tree of knowledge of good and evil was prohibited, not any circumstance connected with it; and, therefore, the act of eating, itself, was undue, unlawful and inordinate. It was indeed, in itself a deviation from the rule, that is, from the law which forbade the eating. That act, of and in itself, apart from the law, is a natural act and has, in itself, no inordinacy.

But after the enactment of a law that prohibits eating, that act cannot be considered as good, agreeably to its natural relations, as there is added to it the fact of inordinacy, on account of which it ought to be omitted. For it is then to be omitted, of itself and on its own account, because it is forbidden by the divine law, and because to eat is to sin. The whole inordinacy consisting in the fact that the act of eating referred to has a place in the number and series of human actions, which place it ought not, on any account to have, and the number of which ought not to increase. But it ought to be wholly omitted, and be kept under restraint, and never be carried into effect.

The simile of a lame horse, which many adduce to illustrate this matter, is not applicable to an act prohibited by law. For in lameness there is the gait, and there is the limping or irregular gait. A defect is added to the gait or motion on account of weakness or injury of a leg, which defect, though it may not in fact be separated from the gait itself, can nevertheless be readily distinguished from it. Hence it may occur that the same horse, after the cure has been effected, can walk properly, and so lameness will be separated from his gait. But in the eating of the forbidden fruit, it was not the eating and the defect of eating that was forbidden. But the eating itself, wholly and solely, had the relation of sin, because it was committed contrary to the law.

That simile would be applicable in sin, which is committed against a law that prescribes the act itself, but prohibits some circumstance of the act. Such a sin consists in the fact that an act, good, according to and prescribed by the law, is performed in a manner that is not right, as when alms are given to a poor man, from ambition and pride, that he, who bestows them, may appear unto men to be liberal and a lover of the poor, and even religious. That act is good and may be illustrated by the gait, but the defect in it is like the lameness produced by disease or injury, and causes the act to limp, and to be displeasing to God. Yet it is not to be omitted, but to be performed only in a due and right manner, all defectiveness being avoided and omitted, which, rightly and in fact, can and ought to be separated from it.

Question or Objection

I acknowledge that the question or objection is not satisfied by that answer. For someone may affirm, that, "eating is nevertheless, a positive act, and, therefore, has an existence, though forbidden, and since all existence has God as its cause, God also is the cause of that act of eating. And so, also, of other positive acts, though they may be committed against a prohibitory law; and consequently, sin, as an act cannot be removed from the efficiency of God."

I reply that I by no means take from the efficiency of God an act that is not perpetrated by the creature without sin. Indeed, I openly confess that God is the cause of all acts perpetrated by His creatures, but I desire this only that the efficiency of God should be so explained as not to derogate anything from the freedom of the creature, and not to transfer the fault of his sin to God. That is to show that God may, indeed, be the effecter of the act, but only the permitter of the sin; and that God may be at once the effecter and permitter of one and the same act. This subject is of most difficult explanation, yet we may make some effort towards its elucidation.

I remark then, that God is either mediately or immediately the cause of an act that proceeds from a creature. He is the mediate cause, when He exerts an influence upon the cause and moves it to cause the act. He is the immediate cause, when He exerts an influence on the act and, with the creature is the whole cause of that act. When God moves the creature to cause anything, since the creature, as the second and subordinate cause, is determined by the first moving cause to a particular act, which has its form from the influence and motion of the Deity, that act, whatever may be its character, cannot be imputed, as a fault to the creature. But if the act can be called sin, God is necessarily the cause and the author of that sin. But since the latter idea can never be true, it is certain that the explanation cannot be found in that mode of the mediate action of the Deity, how God is the cause of the act, which is not performed by man without sin, and the permitter of the sin.

When God is the immediate cause of an act proceeding from a creature, then the second cause, if it is free, and we are now treating of free agents, has it in its own power either to exert its influence in the act, or suspend that influence so that the act may not take place, and to exert its influence so that one act, rather than another, may be performed. Hence it follows, that, when a second cause has freely exerted its influence to produce an act, and when, by its particular influence, it has determined the general influence of God to this particular act, and has disposed the form of the act, the second cause is responsible. Thus the act may be deservedly called "sin" in respect to the second cause; but God is free from responsibility, and in respect to Him, the act cannot be called sin.

The concurrence and influence of the Deity bestows nothing upon the free will of the creature, by which he may be either inclined, or assisted, or strengthened to act, and it does not in the first act, but in the second, disposes the will. It therefore presupposes, in the will, whatever is necessary for acting, even without the exception of the concurrence of the Deity itself. Though the will of the free creature may not in reality, have that concurrence, except when he puts forth activity, yet he has it in his own power before he performs that which is prepared for, and imposed upon him. If this is not so, the will cannot be said to have the act in its own power, or in its proximate capability; nor can the cause of that act be called moral but natural only, and therefore necessary, to which sin can, by no means, be attributed.

In this way that difficulty is solved, and it is shown how God can be the cause of an act, which cannot be performed by the creature without sin, so that neither He may be the author of sin, nor the creature be free from sin. He, indeed, may be only the permitter of sin, but the creature may be the proper cause of sin. For God leaves to the choice of a free second cause the disposition of its own influence to effect any act, and when the second cause is in the very movement and instant of exerting its influence, God, freely and of His own choice, joins His influence and universal concurrence to the influence of the creature, knowing that, without His influence, the act neither could nor would be produced.

Nor is it right that God should deny His concurrence and influence to the creature, even if He sees that the influence of the creature, exerted to effect an act, which he is just ready to perform, is joined to sin, and is committed contrary to His law. For it is right that the act, which He left to the freedom of man when the law had not yet been enacted by which that act was afterwards forbidden, should be left to the freedom of the same creature, after the enactment of the law.

Imposed in Vain

A law would be imposed in vain on an act, for the performance of which God should determine to deny His own concurrence. In that case, it could not be performed by the creature, and therefore no necessity would exist that its performance should be forbidden to the creature by a law. This is besides God, in His legislation, designed to test the obedience of His creature. But this He could not do, if He determined to deny, to the creature His concurrence to an act forbidden by law; for apart from that concurrence, the creature cannot perform that act. Why should God, in reference to an act, to which, as naturally good, determined not to deny His concurrence, deny that same concurrence, when the act has been made morally evil by the enactment of law; when He declares and testifies in His own legislation that He wills that the creatures should abstain from that act, in that it is morally evil, and not in that it is an act in its natural relations?

But He wills that the creature should abstain from the act as evil, when He imposes upon him a prohibitory law, to which he is bound to yield obedience. When, however, He determines to deny His concurrence, He wills that in its natural relations, it shall not be performed by the creature.

For the former is a kind of moral hindrance, the latter is a natural hindrance. The former, by the enactment of law; the latter, by the denial of concurrence by the enactment of law, in view of which that act cannot be committed without sin, and by denial of concurrence, in view of which the act cannot be committed at all. If the latter impediment, that of the denial of concurrence, exists, there is no necessity that the other, that of the enactment of law, should be interposed.

It is apparent from this explanation, that the creature committing sin, commits it in the full freedom of his will, both as to its exercise, and as to the form of the action, to which two things the whole freedom of the will is limited. Freedom, as to its exercise, is that by which the will can put forth, and suspend volition and action. Freedom, as to the form of action is that, by which it wills and performs this rather than that action. We will show that freedom in both respects exists in another manner in the act of sin, which the creature performs with the general concurrence of God. In the act of sin, its existence and its essence are to be considered. The existence of the act depends on the freedom of the will, as to its exercise.

That its essence should be of this rather than of that character, that it should be rather a forbidden act than one not forbidden, against this precept rather than against that, depends on the freedom of the will as to the form of action. That the act should exist, the creature effects by its own free influence, by which it wills to do rather than not to do, though not without the influence of the divine concurrence, uniting itself freely to the influence of the creature at its very first moment and instant. But that the act should be of one character rather than of another, the second cause effects, freely determining its own act to a certain direction, to this rather—than to that—that it should be one thing rather than another.

If anyone says that, on this supposition the divine concurrence is suspended on the influence of the creature, I reply that this does not follow from my statements. Though God may not concur unless the creature wills to exert his influence, yet the exertion of that influence depends purely on his own freedom; for he can omit that exertion. It may be clear from this, how God is both the permitter of sin, and the effector of an act, without which the creature cannot commit sin. He is the permitter of sin, in that He leaves to the creature the free disposition of His own influence; the effector of an act, in that He joins His own concurrence to the effort of the creature, without which the act could not be performed by the creature.

If anyone takes exception to this distinction, on account either of the difficulty of the subject or of the defect of my explanation, and so contends that efficiency in sin is in some respect to be ascribed to God, because He is the effecter of that act, I wish that he would consider that God can, on the same principle, be called the permitter of the act. This is because He is the permitter of the sin and indeed far more justly, since in His own prohibition, He declares that He is unwilling that the act, already permitted, not only to the freedom and the ability of the creature, but also to its right and power, should be performed by the creature. By such prohibition, that act is removed from the divine efficiency, only so far as that ought to avail to deter the will of the creature from performing the act. On the other hand, the efficiency of that act is, so much the more, to be ascribed to the freedom of the will, as it can be understood to have more vehemently willed that which is forbidden by the divine law.

But, in whatever way that subject may be explained, it is carefully to be observed both that God be not made the author of sin, and that the act itself be not taken away from the efficiency of God; that is, that the whole act both as an act merely and as sin, may be rightly made subject to the providence of God, as an act to efficient providence, as a sin to permissive providence. If, however, there shall still be an inclination in the other direction, there will be less error, if the act is taken away from the divine efficiency, as an act, than if sin is attributed to the efficiency of God, as a sin. For it is better to take away an act from the Deity, which belongs to Him, than to attribute to Him an evil act that does not belong to Him. So a greater injury is charged on God, if He is said to be the cause of sin, than if He is regarded as an unconcerned spectator of an act.

ALLEGATION 4:

"We Teach that the Greatest Part of the Human Race are Left Without Christ and Without Any Saving Grace."

The meaning of this allegation, is that God, by His own eternal and immutable decree, has determined of His will to elect some, but to reprobate others, and those are the more numerous. Since the elect cannot be brought unto salvation, as having become sinners in Adam, unless satisfaction to the justice of God and expiation for sin should have been made, therefore God determined to give his own Son to them as Mediator, Reconciler, and Redeemer, who should assume human nature for them only, should die for their sins only. Also that He should reconcile them only to the Father, should meritoriously obtain the Holy Spirit and eternal redemption for them only, should offer, according to His purpose grace to them only, should call them only, to faith, and should bestow, by an internal vocation, faith on them, only, etc. This is to the exclusion, from all these things, of those whom He reprobated, so that there should be to them no hope of salvation in Christ, because God had willed from eternity that Christ should not be made man for them or die for them apart from any consideration of their unbelief.

And when He arranged that the gospel should be preached also to them, it was not done for their benefit, but because the elect were intermingled with them, who, by that preaching, were according to the decree of God, to be led to faith and salvation. You should indeed have answered whether you admitted that allegation as made truly against your doctrine, or whether you think your doctrine to be not amenable to it. You seem to admit that this is truly your sentiment. It ought indeed to be admitted by you, if you wish to be consistent with yourself, and to speak in harmony with your doctrine.

You answer, then, that what is charged against your doctrine in that allegation, is not a crime, but let us see how you show and prove this. First, you say that "it is not hard that they should be left without Christ," because "they might at the first, in Adam, have received saving grace, righteousness, and a life of blessedness, together with the ability to persevere in the same, if they had only willed it." I affirm that very many persons are absolutely left without Christ, who never were, and never will be partakers of the saving grace of Christ. For the grace, bestowed on Adam and on all his posterity in him, was not the grace of Christ, which was not at that time necessary.

But "God could," you say, "without injustice, at that time, have condemned all, and not have bestowed, on a single individual, grace through Christ." Who denies it? The point in dispute is not whether God, when man with all his posterity, sinned of his own fault: and became obnoxious to eternal death, was obligated to give His own Son to the world as a mediator. It is whether it can be truly said that, when God willed His own Son should become a man and die for sins, He willed it with this distinction, that he should assume, for a certain few only, the human nature he had in common with all men; that he should suffer for only a few the death which could be the price for all the sins of all men, and for the first sin, which all committed alike in Adam.

The issue is whether God purposed to proceed according to the rigor of His justice, and to the strictness of the law, and the condition made requisite in the law, with the largest part of the human race, but according to His mercy and grace with a few, according to the gospel and the righteousness of faith, and the condition proposed in the gospel; whether He proposed to impute, even to a certain few, the sin they had personally committed in Adam, without any hope of remission. This, I assert, is the question: you reply affirmatively to this question and therefore confess that the allegation is made, with truth, against your doctrine, nor can you escape by the plea, that "it is not wonderful that they should be left without Christ, since they had rejected the grace offered in Adam." Your answer has reference to the justice of the act, and the question is concerning the act itself; your answer has reference to the cause, and the question is concerning the existence of the thing, the cause of which you present.

That your answer may not, to some, seem too horrible, you present secondly, another answer, namely, "Christ may be said to have died for all." But you subjoin an explanation of this kind, which perverts the interpretation, and absolutely nullifies your apparent and verbal confession. For you add that "he did not die for all and for each equally in reference to God, in the same sense for the lost and for the elect, or efficiently on the part of God." Let us linger here, and weigh well what you say. The Scripture declares explicitly, and in plain terms, that Christ died even for those who are lost (Rom 14:15; 2 Peter 2:1).

Not equally, you say, in respect to God. But what is the meaning of the phrase "in respect to God"? Is it the same as "according to the decree of God?" Indeed, Christ "was crowned with glory and honor; that he by the grace of God should taste death for every man" (Heb. 2:9). By the command of God, Christ laid down his life "for the life of the world" (John 6:51), and "for the sheep" (John 10:15). He cannot, indeed, be said to have died for any man, except by the decree and the command of the Father. You will say that you do not now refer to the decree, by which God the Father, imposed upon His Son the office and duty of expiating sins by his own death; but to the decree, by which He determined to save the elect through Christ. But I assert that the latter decree is, in its nature, subsequent to the death of Christ, and to the merit obtained by that death.

Died Not Equally

You add then, that "he died not equally for the reprobate" (you ought to use that word, and not the word "lost") "and for the elect." You consider these things in the wrong order. For the death of Christ, in the order of causes, precedes the decree of election and reprobation, from which arises the difference between the elect and the reprobate. The election was made in Christ as dead and risen, and having meritoriously obtained grace and glory. Therefore, Christ died for all, without any distinction of elect and reprobate. For that twofold relation of men is subsequent to the death of Christ, pertaining to the application of the death and the resurrection of Christ, and of the blessings obtained by them. The phrase, "Christ died for the elect," does not signify that some were elected before Christ received the command from God to offer his life, as the price of redemption for the life of the world, or before Christ was considered as having died (for how could that be, since Christ is the head of all the elect, in whom their election is sure?). But it means the death of Christ secures for the elect only the blessing bestowed through an application of Christ and his benefits.

Hence, also, the phrase used by the Schoolmen, is to be understood thus, that "Christ died for all men sufficiently, but, for the elect and believers only, he died efficaciously." Your phrase, "efficiently on the part of God," is, in my judgment, irrelevant. What is the meaning of the statement, "Christ died efficiently, on the part of God for the elect, and not for the reprobate"? This phraseology cannot be used in any correct sense. I know that you wished to give the idea that the efficacy of Christ's death is applied to some and not to others. If you mean this, you ought to speak so that this might be understood to be your meaning. If your affirmation and that of the Schoolmen, be rigidly examined, it will be seen that they cannot be used without injury to the death of Christ and its merit. For they attribute sufficiency to the death of Christ, but deprive it of efficacy when indeed, the death of Christ is a sufficient price for the life of the world, and was efficacious for abolishing sin and satisfying God. We do not speak, you say, of the efficacy of his death, but of that of its application. The contrary, however, is clearly manifest. For you deprive of efficacy that to which you attribute sufficiency and you attribute sufficiency to the death of Christ. If this also is examined rigidly, it will be seen that you do not even attribute sufficiency to the death of Christ.

For how shall that be a sufficient price which is no price? That is not a price, which is not offered, not paid, not reckoned. But Christ did not offer himself except for a few only, namely, the elect. Certainly, my friend, those are words and evasions sought for the purpose of avoiding the stroke of truth.

You, then, bring some passages of Scripture to prove your proposition.

"Christ says to the reprobate, "I never knew you" (Matt. 7:23). Therefore, He never acknowledged them for his own. What then? Did he, therefore, not die for them? That certainly is an inconclusive argument. For it is necessary that, by his own death, he should redeem unto himself those whom he was to have for his own: but those whom he has not as his own, he did not know as his own, or acknowledge for his own. But, as he acknowledges some for his own, it is not sufficient that he should die for them, and, by the right of redemption, prepare them for himself, but also should make them his own in fact, by an efficacious application of blessings. Hence, it is apparent that there are, here, the Fallacies of *ignoratio elenchi* and of "the cause for the non-cause."

The other argument you adduce is not more valid. "If all and each are efficaciously redeemed, all and each are also reconciled to God. But all are not reconciled, nor do all receive the remission of their sins. Therefore, not all and each are efficaciously redeemed." What if I should say that I concede all this, if it is only correctly understood, and that your conclusion does not belong to the question? You confound the result with the action and passion, from which it exists. For the offering of Christ in death, is the action of Christ, by which he obtained redemption.

You then confound the obtaining of redemption with its application: for to be efficaciously redeemed, means to be a partaker of the redemption, made and obtained by the death of Christ. You confound also reconciliation made with God by the death and sacrifice of Christ, with the application of the same, which are plainly different things. For "God was, in Christ, reconciling the world unto himself, and hath committed unto us the word of reconciliation" (2 Cor. 5:19). We are said to have been "reconciled to God, when we were enemies" (Rom 5:10), which cannot be understood of the application of reconciliation. But your statement, "remission of sins and satisfaction belong together," is not, in all respects true.

Death and Obedience

For satisfaction precedes, as consisting in the death and obedience of Christ, but remission of sins consists in the application of that satisfaction by faith in Christ, which may possibly, not actually follow the satisfaction which has been rendered. Christ, indeed, obtained eternal redemption and the right to remit sins, but sin is not remitted except to those who really believe in Christ. The remark of Prosper[4] is entirely in accordance with these statements. For, by the word "redemption," he understands the act both in its accomplishment and in its application. This, your second argument, therefore, aside from the purpose, and on account of confusedness and equivocation, proves nothing.

Your third argument is also inconclusive. For, even if the antecedent is granted, the consequent does not follow. It is true that "Christ gave himself, that he might obtain, from the Father, the right of sanctifying those who should believe in him," and these are thus immediately joined.

But, as he obtained the right, he also in fact used that right, by his Spirit and the application and sprinkling of his own blood, sanctifying to himself a peculiar people, and redeeming and freeing them from their own depraved condition, which right pertains to the application of the benefits, obtained for us by the death of Christ. But it does not thence,

---

4. "Very well therefore saith Prosper, 'As it is not sufficient for the renewing of men that Christ Jesus was born man, unless they be renewed also in the same spirit whereof He was born; so it is not sufficient for man's redemption that Christ Jesus was crucified, unless we die together and be buried with Him in baptism.'" Perkins, *Works*, 2:621.

follow that because all do not in fact become partakers of that sanctification, therefore, Christ did not give himself for them as the price of redemption. For the action of Christ is confounded with its result, and the application of benefits with their obtainment.

The fourth argument labors under the same fault: that of confusion. It is true that "the redemption, which has been accomplished, and therefore sonship, are destined for those who believe in Christ." But it is necessary that the act should precede, by which Christ must obtain for us redemption and sonship. But it must precede the act by which it behoved Christ to merit redemption and sonship for us; which act in the order of causes precedes all destination of God respecting the application of redemption.

In the fifth argument, you commit the same fallacy. For the point in dispute, is, "Did Christ die for all without any distinction of elect and reprobate?" And you present, as an argument, the assertion—"his death and the benefits of his death are not applied to all without distinction."

You say, "We may grant that they are, on the part of God, freed from condemnation; yet they are not so far the recipients of grace as that sin no longer reigns in them." I reply that if you grant the former, the latter must also be conceded. For these two benefits, obtained for us by the death and resurrection of Christ, freedom from the condemnation of sin, and from its dominion, are conjoined. One cannot be bestowed without the other, on any person.

You lastly, produce some testimonies from the old writers, but they all, if rightly explained, agree with these things which we have said. For Ambrose plainly speaks of the advantage resulting from the application of Christ's passion, when he says "he did not descend for thee, he did not suffer for thee," that is, "not for thy benefit." Whence also, I pray, does faith come to us? Is it not from the gift of the Spirit which Christ has merited for us? Therefore, the passion and the descent of Christ must have preceded our faith, and, therefore, they cannot be limited by that faith.

But faith is the instrument of that application. Augustine, also, treats of "deliverance" not as obtained, but as applied. Thus also, Bernard, Haimo, and Thomas Aquinas. If any of the fathers or Schoolmen seem at any time to speak differently, their words must be so explained as not to impinge the truth revealed to us in the Scripture.

Let us now look at some of the objections to your doctrine which you notice. The first is this: "The Scriptures assert that Christ redeemed the world." Why did you not use the phrase "suffer for" rather than the word "redeem," so as to avoid ambiguity; especially, when the question has reference not to the application of Christ's passion, but to that passion itself, and the death of Christ. But let us consider the objection, as it is presented by yourself. I say that a distinction is to be made between redemption obtained and redemption applied, and I affirm that it was obtained for the whole world, and for all and each of mankind; but that it was applied only to believers, and to the elect.

First, I show that if it was not obtained for all, faith in Christ is, by no right required of all, and if it was not obtained for all, no one can be rightly blamed, on account of rejecting the offer of redemption. For he rejects that which does not belong to him, and he does it with propriety. If Christ did not die for all, then he cannot be the judge of all. The latter idea is conceded, on both sides. But I say that, in the remark of Augustine, the subject discussed is the application of reconciliation, and actual salvation.

All Men to be Saved

The second objection is, God "will have all men to be saved, and to come unto the knowledge of the truth." But you do not subjoin the conclusion. It may indeed, be deduced from the antecedents. But it is of much importance how that conclusion is formed. For one concludes, "therefore all men universally, will be saved, and will come to the knowledge of the truth. For who hath resisted his will?" Another infers "then there is no Predestination, according to which God wills that some should believe and be saved, and that some, being alien from the faith, should be condemned, and this, also, from His decree."

A third deduces this conclusion: "Therefore, there can be no will of God by which He absolutely and without reference to sin in man, wills that any should be condemned and not come to the knowledge of the truth." The first conclusion is not legitimate. For they are not always saved, whom God wills to be saved. The second, also, cannot be deduced from the text. But of the third, I think that it can be said with truth that it can and must be deduced from those words. I give a plain and perspicuous reason. No one can be condemned for rejecting the truth unless he has been called to it, either in his own person, or in the person of his parents, grand-parents, great grand-parents, etc. No one is called to it if God does not will that he should come to it. And all men who shall be condemned, will be condemned because "light has come into the world, and men loved darkness rather than light" (John 3:19).

Let us consider your reply. You present this in a four-fold manner. The first is this: "The word 'all' does not embrace all the descendants of Adam, but is used in reference to men in the last age of the world." This indeed, is truly said, the circumstance of this passage being considered, which treats of the amplitude of the grace exhibited, in the New Testament, in Christ. But the truth of the same words extends itself even further. For that is the perpetual will of God, and had its beginning in the first promise of the blessed Seed, made in paradise. That God did indeed suffer the Gentiles to walk in their own ways, does not contravene this declaration.

For they were alienated from the covenant of God, and deprived of the promises by their own fault, committed either in themselves or their ancestors. It ought then, to have been conceded by you that God willed through all ages that all men, individually, should come to the knowledge of the truth and be saved, so far as they were embraced in the divine covenant, not indeed, when they had in themselves or their parents, departed from it.

Your second answer is, "God willed that all men should be saved who are saved," which, indeed, does open violence to the phraseology, and holds up to ridicule the apostle, who if that explanation is correct, presents so foolish an argument. The design of the apostle is to exhort that "prayers should be made for all men, and for all that are in authority" (1 Tim 2:1–2). This reason is "this is good and acceptable in the sight of God, who will have all men to be saved, and to come to the knowledge of the truth" (1 Tim 2:3–4). It is here apparent that the word "all" is used, in the same sense, in the statement of the reason, as in the exhortation. Otherwise, the connection of the parts is destroyed, and there are four terms in the syllogism. But if it is intended in the statement of the reason to refer to all who will be saved, then it must be taken in the same sense in the exhortation also, and then the exhortation of the apostle must be understood in this sense: "I exhort that prayers and supplications be made for all who are to be saved, for God wills that all, who are to be saved, shall be saved."

What is doing violence to the meaning of the apostle, if this is not? "But Augustine so explains it: "What then? We do not rest in his authority." Also, we prove this by a collation of a similar passage: "This I deny. For the passage in 1 Cor 15:22, "in Christ shall all be made alive," is not similar. For the emphasis may here be placed on the words "in Christ," and then it will read thus: "all, who are made alive, will be made alive in Christ, and no one out of Christ." The emphasis indeed belongs on those words, as is apparent from the contrast of the other member, "as in Adam all die."

But in 1 Tim 2:4, there is nothing similar to this. For it says, "God wills that all men should be saved," in which that repetition and reduplication cannot have any place. Does not the Scripture teach that we must pray for all, even for those who are not to be partakers of salvation? So far at least, as it is not evident to us whether they have or have not sinned unto death; for those of the former class, and them only, prayer is not to be made.

Your third answer is that "the phrase means not single individuals of classes, but classes of single individuals;" as if the apostle had said "God wills that some of all classes, states and conditions of men should be saved." This answer you defend from the diverse use of "all," which is taken, at one time distinctively, at another collectively, which is indeed true although you have interchanged the distributive and collective use of the word. For all the animals were, in a distributive sense, in Noah's ark, and all men, in a collective sense. Even if the use of that word is twofold, it does not thence follow that it is used in one and not in the other sense, for it can be used in either.

Classes of Individuals

In this passage, however, it is used not for classes of single individuals, but for single individuals of classes. For the will of God goes out towards single individuals of classes, or to single human beings. For he wills that single men should come to the knowledge of the truth and be saved, that is, all and each, rich and poor, noble and ignoble, male and female, etc. As the knowledge of the truth and salvation belong to single human beings, and is in fact prepared by Predestination, for the salvation of single individuals not for classes, and is denied by reprobation, to single individuals not to classes.

So also, in the more general providence of God, antecedent, in the order of nature, to the decree of Predestination and reprobation, the divine will has reference to single individuals of classes, not to classes of single individuals. For providence, having reference to classes of single individuals, pertains to the preservation of the species, but that which refers to single individuals of classes, pertains to the preservation of individuals. But that providence that ministers salvation and the means necessary for salvation, pertains to the preservation and salvation of individuals. Besides, if this passage is to be understood to refer to classes, then the apostle would not have said "for all in authority," but "for some, at least, in eminent positions," but he openly says that prayers should be made for single individuals in that relation.

Nor is there any necessity of any other acceptation of that word, for there is no need of that plea to avoid this consequence, "therefore, all and each are saved." For the salvation of all would not follow from the fact that God wills that anyone should be saved by his will approving and desiring the salvation of all and of each, but it would follow, if He by an efficacious volition, saves all and each. To this effect also is the distinction made by Damascenus, which we will examine at somewhat greater extent.

Your fourth answer is, "Paul here speaks according to the judgment of charity, not according to the judgment of secret and infallible certainty." This is really absurd, unless you refer to the charity of God. For Paul here treats of the will of God to which he attributes this volition, that He wills the salvation of all men, not of His will according to which He earnestly desires the salvation of all. But it is in the meantime true that God does not will this infallibly or certainly, so that it cannot, or at least will not happen otherwise. This however is not said by those who use this passage to sustain a positive contrary to your sentiment. It is settled, then, that from this passage it is a fair inference that "God cannot be said, without reference to sin in men, to will that any should err from the truth, or should not come to the truth, and should be condemned."

We may now consider the distinction, made by Damascenus[5], in which He regards the will of God, as antecedent and consequent. It is of special importance to observe, when the antecedent and consequent wills are spoken of relatively, in what relation they receive those appellations. This relation is that of the will to the will, or rather that of the

5. Saint Johannes Damascenus (675–749) was a priest and scholar of the Eastern Church whose pursuits included law, theology, philosophy and music.

divine volition, to the divine volition, the former as antecedent, the latter
as consequent, for God puts forth one volition before another, in the
order of nature, though not of time.

Or it is that of the divine volition to the preceding or subsequent
volition or act of the creature. In respect to the latter, the divine will is
called antecedent; in respect to the former, consequent. But these two
relations do not greatly differ, though I think the relation to the volition and act of the creature, either subsequent to or preceding the divine
volition, was the cause of the distinction. If we consider the order of volitions, which God wills previous to any act or volition of the creature, we
shall see in that order, that there are some antecedent, some consequent
volitions, yet all previous to any act and volition of the creature.

And, since that volition, which exists of some cause in us, may be
called consequent, it is certain that the distinction was understood by
Damascenus, its first author, in the sense that it was in relation to the act
or volition of the creature. The will of God, then, may be called antecedent, by which He wills anything in relation to the creature (in our discussion, a rational creature) previous to any act of the creature whatever, or
to any particular act of it.

Thus He willed that all men and each of them should be saved. The
consequent will of God is that, by which He wills anything in reference
to a rational creature after any act or after many acts of the creature. Thus
He wills that they who believe and persevere in faith, shall be saved,
but that those who are unbelieving and impenitent shall remain under
condemnation. By His antecedent will, He willed to confirm and establish the throne of King Saul forever; by His consequent will, He willed
to remove him from the kingdom, and to substitute in his place a man
better than he (1 Sam 13:13, 14). By his antecedent will Christ willed to
gather the Jews as a hen gathers her chickens. By his consequent will, he
willed to scatter them among all nations.

Examine the Reasons

You indeed, approve this distinction, but do not approve the example of
antecedent will presented by Damascenus himself. Let us examine the
reasons, in view of which you form this decision.

First you say, "It would follow from this that there is in the Deity
weakness and limited power." I deny this sequence, for the divine power
is not the instrument of the divine inclination, or desire, or wish, but of

free volition, following the last decision of the divine wisdom, though God may use His power to obtain what He desires within proper limits. Nor is it true that, if one desires or seriously wills anything, he will effect the same in anyway whatever, but he will do it in those ways in which it is suitable that he should effect it.

A father may desire and seriously propose that his son should obey him, but he does not violently compel him to obedience, for it would not be obedience. A father seriously wills that his son should abstain from intoxication, yet he does not confine him in a chamber, where he cannot become intoxicated. A father seriously wills to give the paternal inheritance to his son; and by a consequent volition, namely one that follows the contumacious and obstinate wickedness of the son, wills to disinherit him, nor yet does he do all things within the scope of his power, that his son may not sin. For, it was possible for the father to keep his son bound and lettered with chains, that he might not be able to sin. But it was as suitable that the father should not use that mode of restraint, as it was to will the patrimony to his son.

The illustration taken from the merchant desiring to save his goods, yet throwing them into the sea, is well adapted to its purpose. God seriously wills that all men should be saved. But compelled by the pertinacious and incorrigible wickedness of some, He wills that they should suffer the loss of salvation, that they should be condemned. If you say that the analogy fails because God could correct their wickedness, but the merchant cannot control the winds and the waves, I reply that it may indeed, be possible to absolute omnipotence, but it is not suitable that God should in that way correct the wickedness of His creatures. Therefore God wills their condemnation because He does not will that His own righteousness should perish.

They, who object that this will may be called conditional, do not say all which might be said, yet they say something. Not all, because this inclination by which God desires the salvation of all men and of each, is simple, natural, and unconditional in God. Yet they say something, since it is true that God wills the salvation of all men, on the condition that they believe. For no will can be attributed to God, by which He may will that any man shall be saved in a sense, such that salvation will certainly and infallibly, come to him, unless he is considered as a believer and as persevering in faith even to the end.

Since, however, that conditional volition may be changed into an absolute one, in this manner: God wills that all believers should be saved, and that unbelievers should be condemned, which, being absolute, is always fulfilled, this volition may be said not to pertain to this distinction of the will. For in that volition, He wills nothing to His creature but He wills that these things, faith and salvation, unbelief and condemnation, should indissolubly cohere. Yet, if it seems proper for anyone to consider this an example of antecedent volition, I will not contradict him, yet the application is only by a volition consequent on the act of faith and perseverance, of unbelief and impenitence.

Your conclusion that "the will of God must be in suspense until the condition is fulfilled, and that the first cause is dependent on second causes," is not valid. For, concerning the former part, I remark that inclination in God is natural towards His own creature, whether the man believes or not. For that inclination does not depend on faith, and uncertainty cannot be attributed to the will of Him who, in His infinite wisdom has all things present to himself, and certainly foreknows all future events, even those most contingent.

Nor is the first cause, consequently, dependent on second causes, when any effect of the first cause is placed, in the order of nature, after an effect of the second cause, as that effect, consequent in order, belongs to the mere will of the first cause. It is absurd to say that the condemnation of those who perish, depends on themselves, even if they would not perish unless by their own demerit. For they willed to merit perdition, and not to perish, that is, they willed to sin and not to be punished.

Therefore that punishment depends on the mere free will of God, yet it can inflict it only on sinners, the operation of power being suspended by justice, agreeably to which that power ought to be exercised. It is no more a valid conclusion that, by this distinction, the free choice of faith or unbelief is attributed to men. For it is in entire harmony with that condition that no one has faith except by the gift of God, though there can be no doubt that man has the free choice not to believe.

You say secondly, "this conditional will of God is inactive because it belongs to infinite power, and because He can do whatever He will." But it is not suitable that He should use His infinite power to effect that, to which He is borne by natural desire, and it is useful for man, that this will of God should be presented to him as conditional, indeed, rather than as absolute. As was previously said, for it seems as an argument to persuade him to believe. For if he wishes to be saved he must believe, because God has appointed that men shall be saved only through faith.

Your third reason, referring to angels, can be made doubtful by the relation of the antecedent, and even if this is conceded, the consequent does not follow. For the relation of angels and of men is not the same. I am indeed, fully of the opinion that it is most true that God by antecedent volition willed that all and each of the angels should be saved, but only in a due mode and order. Three divine volitions in reference to angels may be laid down in order: the salvation of angels, the obedience of angels, and the condemnation of angels.

Love for His Creatures

God wills the first from love for His creatures; the second from love for righteousness and the obedience due to Him from His creatures, and, indeed, in such a sense, that He more strongly wills that the second should be rendered to Himself, than the first to His creatures. The third He wills from the same love for justice, whose injury He cannot leave unpunished, since punishment is the sole mode of correcting disorder.

Your statements, under your fourth reason, are correct: "and God might will that all sinful men as such should be condemned," if He had not from love towards men determined to lay their sins on His Son, to this end that all who should believe in him, being freed from their sins, should obtain the reward of righteousness. It may indeed be said that God willed that all sinners, as such, should be condemned. But not all sinners are in fact condemned, because believers, though they have sinned, are considered not as sinners, but as righteous in Christ.

Fifthly, you say that "the antecedent will of God is absolute." What then? I do not wish to hinder you from regarding the antecedent will in your own way, different from the sentiment of Damascenus. You should, however, consider that you are not then arguing against him. But who has ever defined absolute will, "that which cannot be resisted"? Absolute will is that which is unconditional. For example, God willed absolutely that Adam should not eat of the forbidden tree; yet he did eat of that tree. The will, which cannot be resisted, is called efficacious. It is not allowable to arrange things defined, and their definitions, according to our own choice.

"But," you may say, "it is not possible to resist the antecedent will." I deny it. You assert, as proof, that "the will, referred to in Rom 9, is antecedent will, and that it cannot be resisted." It is for you to prove that assertion. The very statement declares, since the subject in that passage is the will of God, by which He hardens, and has mercy, which are divine effects, following acts of the creature which are sinful, called sin, that the will here spoken of is consequent not antecedent.

Another method you use to prove the same thing, is equally weak. For, it is not true that "God, simply and absolutely, wills that some should believe and persevere, and others be deserted, either not believing or not persevering." He does not will to desert them, unless they desert themselves; and He is even gracious to those, who do not think of Him.

The argument from the event is futile. For some things occur by the will and the efficiency of God, some by His permission. Therefore it cannot be concluded from any event that God willed it. But it has been previously shown how an event may take place, not because God may be unwilling to prevent it; though it would not happen, if God should will efficaciously to prevent it. Therefore that conclusion cannot be thus deduced. It is, indeed, true that the reason cannot be given why God should afford to one nation the means of salvation, and not to another, why he should give faith to one man, and not to another, which facts may not be resolved into his will. Yet it is not thence concluded, and it is not true, that the will, in that case, is antecedent, even though it precedes all causes in men.

Sixthly, you say that the foundation being destroyed, the edifice falls. But the foundation of that opinion in reference to the antecedent will, which desires the salvation of all men and of each, is the passage in 1 Tim 2, which has been already discussed by us, and that is incorrectly understood by Damascenus. I reply, first, not only that passage, but many others, most clearly sustain that distinction of the will into antecedent and consequent. "How often would I have gathered you together," is an example of antecedent, and "your house is left unto you desolate" of consequent will (Matt 23:37–38). "And sent forth his servants to call them that were bidden to the wedding," is a case of antecedent will, "they which were bidden were not worthy" and were destroyed, of consequent will. He also was invited, according to antecedent will, who, being afterwards found, not having on a wedding garment, was cast out, according to consequent will (Matt. 22:3, 7, 8, 12, 13).

According to antecedent will, the lord commanded his servants to reckon their talents, and to use them for gain for their master; by consequent will, the talent, which he had received, was taken from the wicked and slothful servant (Matt 25). By antecedent will, the word of God was first offered to the Jews; by consequent will, the same word was taken from them and sent to others (Acts 13). The same distinction is proved by a consideration of the attributes of God; for since God is good and just, He cannot will eternal death to His own creature, made in His image, without reference to sin. He cannot but will eternal salvation to His creature.

Immutability of God

The immutability of God necessarily requires the same thing. For since His providence He has given to all His creatures means, necessary and sufficient, by which they can attain their designed end. But that end of man, made in the image of God, is eternal life; it hence follows that all men are loved by God unto eternal life by antecedent will. Nor can God, without a change of His own arrangement, deny eternal life unto men, without reference to sin; which denial, being consequent on the act of man, pertains to consequent will.

The views of Augustine are not opposed to Damascenus. Augustine, indeed, denies that this passage refers to efficacious will. But Damascenus makes no such assertion. He even concedes the very same thing with Augustine: "God does not will efficaciously to save all and each of mankind." The second interpretation of Augustine is rejected by us on sure grounds. Nor is Prosper opposed to Damascenus. For he, who says that "God wills antecedently that all men should be saved," does not deny that He can, by a consequent will, pass by many men to whom He does not impart the grace of vocation. Thomas Aquinas, also, is no more than the others, opposed to Damascenus, for he, in commenting on this passage, speaks of efficacious and of consequent will. Elsewhere he approves of the distinction of Damascenes, and makes use of it in explaining the passage, which is in controversy. Hugo clearly agrees with Damascenus, if his views are suitably explained.

The third objection is this: "Whatever anyone is bound to believe is true. But everyone is bound to believe that he has been efficaciously redeemed by Christ. Therefore, it is true that everyone has been efficaciously redeemed by the death of Christ; and, therefore, even the reprobate have been redeemed, since they also are bound to believe this."

Since this objection is of great importance, and alone sufficient, if it is true it is necessary that we should examine it with diligence, and at the same time your answer to it. The truth of the major is manifest, for truth is the foundation of faith, nor can one be in any way, bound to believe what is false. But you make a distinction in reference to truth and say, that "what is true, is either: true, as to the intention of God, who obligates us to believe, or as to the event."

But that distinction is of no importance. I affirm that what is true, according to the intention of God, must be believed according to that intention. What is true, according to the event, must be believed according to the event. And the intention of God cannot obligate anyone to believe anything to be true according to the event, which is not true according to the event. In general, it is true that we are bound to believe that which is true in that mode in which it is true, not in any other mode. Otherwise, we should be bound to believe what is false.

You see, then, that there is no need of that distinction in the major; indeed it is most clearly evident that you, lest you should say nothing, wished, by that minute distinction, to avoid this effective blow.

Let us consider the minor. Its phraseology is bad, because the efficacy of redemption pertains to its application, which is made through faith.

Therefore faith is prior to efficacious application, and the object of faith is prior to faith itself. We may correct it, and it will read thus, "But everyone is bound to believe in Christ the Savior, that he died for his sake, and obtained for him reconciliation and redemption before God." This is, indeed, most true. For they cannot be condemned, for want of faith, who were not bound to believe this. But here also you use a distinction, but one which is irrelevant and ridiculous—pardon my freedom of speech—and you do great injustice to yourself, and your own genius, when you endeavor to disguise the plain truth, by so puerile distinctions.

You say that the elect are obligated to believe, so that by faith, they may be made partakers of election, the reprobate are obligated to believe, so that, by neglecting to do so, they may be without excuse, even in the intention of God. But what is the difference whether one is bound to believe to this or that end, provided he is only bound to believe? From which obligation to believe, the truth of that which anyone is bound to believe may afterwards be inferred.

The expression, "that they may be made partakers of election," is absurd. It should be corrected thus, "that they may be made partakers of the blessings prepared for them in election," or, if we wish to confine ourselves to the limits of the objection, "that they may in fact be made partakers of the redemption prepared for them by Christ." But the reprobate are also bound to believe for the same reason. If it be said that they absolutely cannot be made partakers, I will say that for this very reason, the reprobate are not obligated to believe.

Exercise of Faith

For the end of the exercise of faith is the application of redemption, and of all the blessings, obtained for us by the merit of Christ. The end of the command and the requirement of faith is that the application may be possible. But how absurd is the declaration that the reprobate are under obligation to believe, so that they may, by not believing, be rendered inexcusable. Unite, if you can, these things, so inconsistent, and widely distant as heaven and earth.

This, however, has been before referred to. You proceed with your distinctions, and say, "one command has reference to obedience; another, to trial." But what relation has this to the present matter? For whether God commands with the purpose that man should in fact obey, or with the purpose only, of testing his obedience in the effort to execute the command, the man is always obligated to perform what God commands, as is apparent in the offering of Isaac by Abraham.

Nor has this command, in the relation of trial, any analogy with what you subjoin, "God does not mock men, even if He, by the preaching of the word, calls those whom He does not purpose to save." Indeed we have already said enough in reference to those and similar evasions. I will say, in a word, that no one can confess that he is guilty for rejecting a promise made verbally, if the mind of the promise maker has determined that the promise does not belong to the person addressed; or rather if he, who verbally promises, has by a fixed decree, determined that the promise may not and cannot belong to the other person.

You present an objection, as an adversary to yourself, thus, "but you will say that it could not belong to him." Not only may that objection be urged, but also another: "How do you confute that statement, so that it may not follow from it that he is without blame, who could not receive the salvation offered to him?" You will say that such inability is voluntary and born with us and therefore undeserving pardon. You err here, and confound inability to keep the law, propagated in us from Adam, with inability to believe in Christ and to accept the grace of the gospel, offered us in the word. By what deed have we brought this inability upon ourselves? Not by a deed preceding that promise. Then it was by a deed following it, that is, by a rejection of the promise of the gospel, which rejection also cannot be imputed to us as a fault, if we were unable to receive it at the time when the promise was first presented to us. The answer, then, amounts to nothing, because the two kinds of inability are confounded, in which is the Fallacy of *ignoratio elenchi*, and of equivocation.

You reply in the second place, that "what anyone is obligated to believe is true, unless he may have placed before himself an obstacle by not believing." Is this correct? Can anyone place before himself an obstacle by his own unbelief, that what he is bound to believe may not be true? Absurd. One can, by his own unbelief, place before himself an obstacle, so as not to be able afterwards to believe, that is, to deserve hardening in unbelief on account of rejecting the truth offered to him. One can also, by his own unbelief, deserve that God should change that good will, by which He offered His Son as the redeemer, into wrath, by which He may will to punish him without remission or pardon.

Thirdly, you reply that "the argument twice depends on assertion, in both parts." But who compelled you to so reduce that argument into an illogical syllogism, when it might have been put in a legitimate form and mode, in this way, "That which everyone is bound to believe, is true: That Christ is his redeemer, who by his own death, meritoriously obtained the divine grace, and the pardon of his sins, is what everyone, called in the gospel, is bound to believe. Therefore it is true, that Christ is the redeemer of all, who are called by the gospel and commanded to believe.

"But among them are many reprobate persons. Therefore it is true that Christ is the redeemer of many reprobate persons. If we consider vocation to be that by which anyone is called, either in himself or in his parents, then all men, universally, are or have been partakers of that vocation, and therefore all have been redeemed by Christ."

But the form, also, in which you have put it is the same in effect, though you have so arranged the words, that they seem to have a different meaning. I see, O Perkins, that you wrote those things with a hurried pen, without an examination of the syllogism as you have proposed it.

The fourth objection, from the fathers, is valid against you, nor do you reply in accordance with the terms of the sentiment hostile to you. The amount of the objection is this, "Christ died for all sufficiently, both as to the common nature of the human race, and as to the common cause and sufficient price of redemption." You have introduced efficacy into the argument or objection, while they who make this objection against you, know that there is the clearest distinction between the death of Christ itself and its application. You say, "and thus far in reference to the extent and efficacy of Christ's death," when the discussion has been hitherto in reference not to its efficacy, but to its sufficiency, and its oblation and the universality of that oblation. You, now, proceed to treat of the amplitude of grace, but what you present does not much affect the point at issue.

All and Each of Human Race

The question is not, whether all and each of the human race are in fact, regenerated and renewed, but whether God has reprobated any man, without respect to sin as a meritorious cause; or whether He has determined absolutely to deny to any man the grace of remission and of the renewal of the Holy Spirit without reference to unworthiness, in that he has made himself unworthy of that grace: unworthy, not resulting from original sin, but from the rejection and contempt of that offered grace. The distinction of sufficient and efficacious grace might have been well adapted to this subject, as we have also previously demonstrated.

Yet there is one thing of which I may admonish you. You seem to me not correctly to deprive, of supernatural grace, the image of God, consisting of righteousness and holiness. For though the former gift was bestowed on man at his creation and at the same time with nature itself, I now consider it. Yet it is supernatural, and surpasses the nature of man itself, as I prove from the act of regeneration, which belongs to supernatural grace.

For, since there is need of regeneration for the recovery of that righteousness and holiness, of which regeneration is a supernatural act, it is necessary that the same should, originally, have been bestowed on man by a supernatural action. I wish also to know what those supernatural things are which man is said to have lost in the Fall, his natural qualities having become corrupt. Thus far, in reference to these things, I think, indeed, that it is sufficiently evident from what we have thus far discussed that the view of Predestination which you have presented cannot be proved by the Scriptures. It cannot be defended against strong objections and cannot be acquitted of manifold absurdity. It ought then to be abandoned by you, and another should be sought from the Scriptures, which may harmonize with them, and may be able to sustain without injury the onset of assailant objections.

In the first part of our treatise, we have examined, most learned Perkins, your sentiment concerning Predestination, and have proved that it is, by no means, consistent with the Holy Scriptures. Another labor now remains, to consider how you refute the opinion which you say is different from yours.

You, briefly, set forth that opinion, diligently gathered from the writings of others, consisting of four parts: First, "God created all and each of mankind in Adam unto eternal life."

Secondly, "He foresaw the Fall."

Thirdly, "Since He is good by nature, He seriously wills that all men, after the Fall, should be saved, and come to the knowledge of the truth; and therefore He wills to bestow, on all men, all the aids both of nature and of grace that they might be saved, but indefinitely, that is if they should believe. This will of God" (they say) "is Predestination, and is the same with that embraced in the gospel. The rule of this will is, 'He that believeth shall be saved, but he that believeth not, shall be damned.'"

Fourthly, "Election is according to foreknowledge of future faith, to fail of which is possible, wholly, as some, or finally, as others claim, and Reprobation is according to foreknowledge of unbelief or contempt of the gospel."

I cannot speak with certainty, in reference to the statement of that theory, whether it agrees with the views of its authors or not, because you are silent concerning the authors from whom you have taken it. Yet, with your permission, I may say that it does not seem to me to have been staged by you with sufficient correctness. Omitting the first two propositions, that precede Predestination itself, in enunciating the third, you make an *adoleschia, a* frivolous statement, which will, I believe, be scarcely admitted by those whose sentiment you profess to present. For what is the meaning of this: "God wills that all men should come to the knowledge of the truth, but indefinitely, if they should believe"?

Is not faith itself the knowledge of the truth? Therefore the enunciation is deceptive and ridiculous: "God wills that all men should come to the knowledge of the truth, but indefinitely, if they shall have believed." Is not faith that knowledge of the truth? Alternative versions are equally ridiculous: "God wills all men to come to a knowledge of the truth, but if they shall have come to the knowledge of the truth," or "wills all to come to faith, if they shall have believed." The next sentence is of a similar character: "God wills to bestow, on all men, all the aids both of nature and of grace, that they may be saved, but indefinitely, if they should believe," when faith itself holds a distinguished place, among the aids of grace by which salvation is obtained.

From the passage of the gospel, which is quoted, "Whosoever shall believe, shall be saved," it is apparent that they, whose sentiment you present, would, in this third proposition, have stated not that which you do. They would say, "God determined to save, from the Fallen human race, only those who should believe in His Son, and to condemn unbelievers."

Expressed Sufficiently

The fourth proposition is not, I think, expressed sufficiently in accordance with the views of those authors. For, if I am not mistaken, their sentiment is this: "Election to salvation is according to foreknowledge of future faith, which God has determined to bestow of His own grace upon them by the ordinary means ordained by Himself. But Reprobation is according to foreknowledge of unbelief or contempt of the gospel, the fault of which remains, entirely, in the reprobate themselves." I admit that there may be need of some explanation of that sentiment, but you do not seem to have explained it correctly.

You should have considered not one view only, adverse to your own view, but the others also opposed to it. And you should have refuted all of them, that in this way, it might be evident that no view, other than yours, is true.

We may now, consider in what way you refute that theory. You enumerate very many errors you think result from it, which we will examine in their order:

The first error: This either is not an error, or cannot be deduced from that theory. It is not an error, if its hypothesis be correctly understood.

For it is universally true that "God wills that all men should be saved if they believe, and be condemned if they do not believe." That is, God has made a decree for electing only believers, and for condemning unbelievers. "But this," you say "is an error because it makes Election universal, and from it universal Reprobation is inferred, that is, by the added condition."

But that sentiment makes neither Election nor Reprobation universal, which cannot be done. But it establishes the particular Election of believers, and the particular Reprobation of unbelievers. Innumerable passages of Scripture present this Election and Reprobation. "He that believeth on the Son hath everlasting life," etc. (John 3:36) "If ye believe not that I am he, ye shall die in your sins" (John 8:24). "To him give all the prophets witness" etc. (Acts 10:43). "Seeing ye put it from you," etc. (Acts 13:46). "He, that hath the Son, hath life; and he, that hath not the Son of God, hath not life" (1 John 5:12).

Election and Reprobation are, therefore, evidently proved by many passages of Scripture. It does not follow, from this, that; "God always acts in the same manner towards all men." For though He may seriously will the conversion and salvation of all men, He does not equally effect the conversion and salvation of all. "For what nation is there so great, who hath God so nigh unto them," etc. (Deut 4:7). "The Lord thy God hath chosen thee to be a special people unto himself," etc. (Deut 7:6) "He hath not dealt so with any nation . . ." (Ps 147:20).

"Because it is given unto you to know the mysteries of the kingdom of heaven," etc. (Matt 13:11). "Who in times past suffered all nations to walk in their own ways" (Acts 14:16). But you have not distinguished, as you ought to have done, between the decree of God, by which He determined to save those who should believe in His Son, and to condemn unbelievers, and that by which He arranged with Himself, in reference to the dispensation of means, ordained by Him to faith and conversion. For those decrees "I will to give life to him who believes," and "I will to give faith to this man" are distinct. Faith, in the former, holds the place of subject, in the latter, that of attribute. If you had made this distinction, you would not have laid the burden of such an absurdity on that theory.

The second error: I remark that the highest and absolute design of the counsels of God "is not regarded by the authors of that theory to be the communication of the divine goodness in true happiness, to be made to all men." For they say that God destined salvation for believers alone; and, though He may not impart his goodness, and life eternal to a large number of persons, as unbelievers, yet they do not say this "without reference to the divine purpose." For they assert that one part of the divine purpose is that by which He determined to deny eternal life to unbelievers. Therefore this is alleged in vain against that opinion. "But" you say "the ultimate design of the counsels of God either has an uncertain event, or is proposed in vain," which ideas coincide, and should not have been expressed distinctly, if "the theory is received." Its supporters will deny that conclusion. For the ultimate design of the divine counsels is not the life of one and the death of another, but the illustration of the goodness, justice, wisdom and power of God, which He always secures.

Yet allow that the eternal life of these, and the death of those is the ultimate design of those counsels: it will not follow that it has an uncertain event, or is proposed in vain, if the former is bestowed upon no one, apart from the condition of faith, and the latter awaits no one, apart from unbelief. For God by His own prescience, knows who of His grace will believe, and who of their own fault, will remain in unbelief. I wish that you would consider, that certainty of an event results properly from the prescience of God.

Omnipotent and Irresistible

But its necessity results from the omnipotent and irresistible action of God, which may indeed be the foundation of the prescience of some events, but not of this event, because He has determined to save believers by grace; that is, by a mild and gentle persuasion, convenient or adapted to their free will. It would not be by an omnipotent action or motion, which would be subject neither to their will, nor to their ability either of resistance or of will. Much less does the damnation of some proceed from an irresistible necessity, imposed by the Deity.

The third error: You ought, here, first to have explained what is meant when it is said that "the will of God depends on the will of man." It may be that you extend that phrase further than is proper. It is indeed certain that the will of God, since He is entirely independent—or rather His volition—cannot depend on the will of man, if that phrase be correctly understood, as signifying "to receive its law or rule from the volition of man." On the other hand, it is certain that God does will some things, which He would not will, if a certain human volition did not precede. He willed that Saul should be removed from the throne. He would not have willed it if Saul had not willed to be disobedient to God.

God willed that the Sodomites and their neighbors should be destroyed. He would not have willed it if they had not willed to persevere obstinately in their sins. God willed to give His own Son as the price of redemption for sinners. He would not have willed it, if men had remained in obedience to the divine command. God willed to condemn Judas. He would not have willed it unless Judas had willed to persist in His own wickedness.

It is not true, indeed, that "the will of God depends on the will of man." Man would if he could, effect that the volition of God should not follow his own antecedent volition, that punishment should not follow sin. Indeed God is purely the author of His own volition. For He has determined in His own free will to follow a volition of His creature, by His own volition of one kind and not of another: the faith of His creature by the remission of sins and the gift of eternal life; the unbelief of the same, by eternal damnation. This is the meaning of that opinion you undertake to refute, and you therefore, with impropriety charge this absurdity upon it.

You, however, make an allegation of much greater weight, against this sentiment, that "by it the creature is raised to the throne of God, the Omnipotent Creator." How do you sustain that allegation? "It is claimed" you say "that God wills that all men should be saved through Christ, and that many of them are not saved because they, of themselves, refuse." But, good sir, does that doctrine say "God wills that all men should be saved through Christ, whether they will or not?" It does, indeed, assert, "God wills that they should be saved and come to the knowledge of the truth" which cannot be done, apart from their free will. For no one can, if he is reluctant or unwilling, come to the knowledge of the truth, that is to faith. If God should will, absolutely and apart from any condition, that all men should be saved, and yet some should not be saved because they refused, then it would follow that the divine will was overcome by the human will, and the creature was raised to the throne of the Creator.

But as God wills that His own volition, joined in due order and mode, with the volition of man, should precede salvation, it is not wonderful that a man who should deny his own assent unto God should be excluded from salvation, by that same determination and purpose of the divine will. "But God," you say, "ordains and disposes the action of the second cause; the divine will is not ordained by the will of the creature." Who denies these statements? That is not the doctrine you here oppose. Therefore, here also, you attempt in vain, to overthrow it by this absurdity. You add another absurdity, as consequent on this opinion. "If that sentiment is true, then men elect themselves, by accepting the grace of God, which is offered to them by the common aid of grace, and are reprobated by themselves, by rejecting offered grace." Let us examine this.

Even if a man should, by accepting common grace, through the aid of common grace, make himself worthy of Election, and another, by rejecting the same, should make himself worthy of Reprobation, it would not follow that Election and Reprobation belong to the man, but to God, who judges and rewards worthiness and unworthiness. It is also entirely true, in reference to Reprobation, that man is the meritorious cause of his own damnation, and therefore of Reprobation which is the purpose of damnation. Wherefore he may be called the maker of his own damnation, in reference to its demerit; although God can, if He will, remit to him this demerit. But the relation of Election is different, for it is merely gratuitous, not only unmerited, but even contrary to the demerit of man.

Grace Offered to Man

Whether the grace offered to man may be also received by him by the aid of grace, which is common to him with others who reject the same grace, or by grace peculiar to him, is perhaps in controversy. I do not indeed see that the sentiment you have presented, has given any prejudgment concerning that matter. It is a strange assertion that "God would not be extolled, if men should obtain his blessing merely by the aid of common grace." Who has deserved that a blessing should be offered to him? Who has deserved that grace of any kind should be bestowed on him to the obtainment of that blessing?

Do not all these things pertain to gratuitous divine favor? If so, is not God to be extolled on account of them, with perpetual praises by those who, having been made partakers of that grace, have received the blessing of God? Of what importance to this matter is it, whether he may have obtained the offered blessing by the aid of common or of peculiar grace, if the former as well as the latter, has obtained the free assent of man, and it has been foreknown by God that it certainly would obtain it? You will say that, if he has apprehended the offered grace by the aid of peculiar grace, it is then, evident that God has manifested greater love towards him than towards another to whom He has applied only common grace, and has denied peculiar grace. I admit it, and perhaps the theory you oppose, will not deny it. But it will assert that peculiar grace is to be so explained as to be consistent with free will, and that common grace is to be so described, that a man may be held worthy of condemnation by its rejection, and that God may be shown to be free from injustice.

The fourth error: The knowledge of God, as it has relation to his creatures, may be regarded in two modes. In one, as God knows that He can make those creatures, and at the same time that they can be made in this or in that mode, that they may not only exist, but may also be able to serve this or that purpose. This knowledge, in the Deity, is natural and precedes the act or the free determination of the will by which God has determined in Himself to make the same creatures at such a time. In the other mode, as God knows that those creatures will exist at one time or another and, regarded in this light, it depends on the determination of the divine will. This knowledge can be referred to the acts of the creatures themselves, which God has determined either to effect or to permit.

Knowledge, considered in the former mode, refers to all acts in general, which can be performed by the creatures whether God is efficient in them, or only permits them. From this follows the decree to effect these and those acts, and to permit them, which decree is followed by the knowledge by which God foreknows that those acts will occur, at any particular time. This latter knowledge, rightly called prescience, is not properly the cause of things or acts. But the former knowledge, with the will, is the cause of things and acts. For it shows the mode of operating, and directs the will. The will, however, impels it to execution. It is therefore, certain that there is no determinate or definite prescience in reference to culpable evil, unless it has been preceded by a decree to permit sin.

For without this, sin will not exist. Prescience has also reference to things future and certainly future. Otherwise, either it is not prescience or it is uncertain. These things are rightly said by you, and the order you have made in prescience and decree, is correct. But it is not contrary to the hypothesis of the doctrine you oppose, but is so consistent with it that it cannot be defended without this order. For it states that God from eternity knew that it was possible that man, assisted by divine grace, should either receive or reject Christ; also, that God has decreed either to permit a man to reject Christ, or to cooperate with him that he may accept Christ by faith, then, that God foreknows that one will apprehend Christ by faith, and that another will reject him by unbelief. From this follows the execution of that decree by which he determined to justify and save believers and to condemn unbelievers, which is an actual justification of the former, and a condemnation of the latter. It is, therefore, apparent that you improperly allege such absurdity against that doctrine.

Your statement that "God permits evil, always, with respect to or on account of a conjoined good," deserves notice. Those words can be understood to mean that God would permit an evil on account of a good, conjoined with the evil, which sentiment cannot be tolerated. For the good that comes out of evil is not conjoined with the evil but is wonderfully brought out of evil as its occasion by the wisdom, goodness and omnipotence of God. For He knows how to bring light out of darkness. The knowledge also by which God knows he can use evil to a good end, is also the cause of the permission of evil. For, as Augustine well says, "God, in His goodness, never permits evil unless, in His omnipotence, He can bring good out of the evil."

The fifth error: Here, three things must be properly distinguished. The acts and sufferings of Christ, the fruits and results of those acts and suffering, and the communication and application of those fruits. Christ, by the sacrifice of his own body, by his obedience and passion, reconciled us unto God, and obtained for us eternal redemption without any respect or distinction of elect and reprobate, of believers and unbelievers, since that distinction is later in order. That reconciliation and redemption are applied to us, when we, having faith in the word of reconciliation, believe in Christ, and in him are justified, or regarded as righteous, and are in fact, made partakers of redemption.

According to Theory

Hence it appears, according to that theory, "that not many of those, to whom reconciliation and redemption are, in fact applied by faith, are lost." Therefore, it will not follow, from this, that "sin, Satan, the world, death, hell, are more powerful than Christ the Redeemer." For, they could not in the first place prevent Christ from offering himself to the Father in sacrifice, obeying the Father, and suffering death. And, in the second place, that he should not thereby obtain reconciliation and eternal redemption before God.

In reference to the application of these blessings, it is true that sin, Satan, the world, and the flesh, prevent many from believing in Christ, and being made partakers of them. Yet God is not overcome by these, both because it has seemed good to God not to use His omnipotent and irresistible power to cause men to believe, and because God has determined that no one shall be a partaker of those blessings who does not believe in Christ.

It is not true that "God is mutable, according to this hypothesis." For the theory does not state that God, absolutely and simply, wills to save all men, but conditionally: and according to His own prescience, He has determined to condemn, eternally, those who will not incline themselves to this counsel. This is also, finally, performed in fact without any charge. It is not sufficient to charge absurdity on any doctrine; it must be proved, by fair inference, to be a consequence of that doctrine.

The sixth error: I am very certain, from the Scriptures, "that saving grace is" not "universal" in the sense that it can be said to have been bestowed on all and each of mankind in all ages. But you ought to have said that "saving grace is stated to be universal" by that doctrine. You neglect to do that, and are much engaged in proving something else. I do not, indeed, object to this but the other thing was equally necessary to reach the object, which you had proposed to yourself. But also at this point there are some things deserving consideration. You do not with sufficient accuracy regard the distinction between "the ability to believe, if one wills," and "the ability to will to believe." For each of these, the latter as well as the former must and indeed does pertain to those who will continue in unbelief.

For unless they have the ability to believe, and indeed, the ability to will to believe, they cannot rightly be punished for their unbelief. Besides one includes the other, for no one can believe, unless he can will to believe. No one believes, without the exercise of his will. But the actual exercise of the will to believe is a different thing from the ability to will to believe. The latter belongs to all men, the former to the regenerate only, or rather to those enlightened by the grace of the Holy Spirit. Hence, you see that you ought to make corrections in many particulars, and that in place of "the ability to will to believe," should be substituted "the will to believe," which is most closely connected with the act of faith, while the other is removed to the greatest distance from actual faith.

The distinction between the ability, the will, and the act, is here especially necessary. But not only is it to be suitably explained, but also the causes are to be referred to, by which it may be given to men to be able to will and to act.

In your third argument, in which you prove the specialty of grace, you use the disjunctive correctly in your expression, "who had not the knowledge of faith, or did not retain it." There is a greater emphasis in that disjunctive than one would, perhaps, at first, think. For, if they did not "retain it," they lost it by their own fault; they rejected it, and are therefore to be punished for the rejection of the gospel. If they are to be punished for this, they were destined to punishment on this account. For the cause of the decree is not different from that of its execution.

You present an objection to your own doctrine, deduced from the usual saying of the Schoolmen, "A man cannot be excused for a deficiency of supernatural knowledge, from the fact that he could, and indeed would, receive it from God, if he would do so according to his own ability, and since he does not do this, he is held guilty of that deficiency." You reply to this objection, but not in a suitable manner. For it is not a sufficient distinction that "grace is given either of merit or of promise:" nor, indeed, does it agree with the contrary or opposite parts. For God can give this, without either merit (I should have preferred the word "debt"), or promise, but of unpromised grace, since He does and gives many things of grace, which He has not promised.

Let us look at that promise, which was made immediately after the Fall. It was made neither of debt nor of promise, but of grace preceding the promise. For God gives life "to him that worketh," of promise and of debt (Rom 4:4). But consider whether a promise is not contained in that declaration of Christ, "Unto everyone which hath shall be given," by which God pledges himself to illuminate with supernatural grace, him who makes a right use of natural grace, or at least uses it with as little wrong as is possible for him. The argument, from idiots and infants, is wholly puerile.

Idiots and Infants

For who dares to deny that many idiots and infants are saved? Yet this, indeed, does not happen to them, apart from saving grace. Some remark is to be made in reference to the passages you cite, though it may perhaps be irrelevant. In Rom 9:16, where it is said "not of him that willeth, nor of him that runneth, but of God that showeth mercy," the word "righteousness" is understood.

For the discussion in that place is in reference to those to whom righteousness is properly imputed, not to them that work but to them that believe, that is, righteousness is obtained not by him that willeth or that runneth, but by him to whom "God showeth mercy," namely, to the believer. Matt 13:11 proves that grace is not given equally and in the same measure to all, and indeed, that the knowledge of "the mysteries of the kingdom of heaven" is not divinely bestowed on all. In the other passages, the things that are opposed, do not belong in this relation. "The wind [Holy Spirit] bloweth where it listeth . . ." (John 3:8). We discern that the Spirit breathes not upon all, but on whom He wills.

What if He wills to breathe upon all? From the idea that He breathes where he wills, it does not follow that he does not breathe on anyone, unless it is proved that he does not will to breathe upon him. So, also, "No man knoweth who the Son is, but the Father; and who the Father is but the Son, and he to whom the Son will reveal him" (Luke 10:22). What if the Son wills to reveal the Father, as well as himself, to all? Not all believe, but those who are "drawn" (John 6:44). But, what if all are drawn? You see that those things are not rightly placed in opposition, though it may be true that the Spirit does not breathe upon all, that Christ does not reveal the Father to all, that all are not drawn by the Father.

I wish also, that your remarks in reference to the disparagement of efficacious grace, had been more extended. First, indeed, the nature of grace itself and its agreement with the free will of man, then its efficacy, and the cause of that efficacy, ought to have been more fully explained. For I consider nothing more necessary to the full investigation of this subject. Augustine, because he saw this, treats in very many places the agreement of grace and of free will, and of the distinction between sufficient and efficacious grace. I remark here, in a word, that by efficacious grace is meant not that grace is necessarily received and cannot be rejected, when certainly it is received, and not rejected by all to whom it is applied. I add that it is not to the disparagement of grace that the wickedness and perversity of most men is so great that they do not suffer themselves to be converted by it unto God.

The author of grace determined not to compel men by his grace to yield assent, but to influence them by a mild and gentle persuasion, which influence, not only does not take away the free consent of the free will, but even establishes it. Why is this strange, since God, as you admit, does not choose to repress the perverse will, that is, otherwise than by the application of grace, which they reject in their perversity. I do not oppose those things you present from the fathers, for I think that most of them can be reconciled with the theory you here design to confute.

You also present certain objections, which can be made against you and in favor of that doctrine, and you attempt to confute them. The first is, "the promise, in reference to the Seed of the woman, was made to all the posterity of Adam, and to each of the human race, in Adam himself." This indeed is true, nor do those things stated by you avail to destroy its truth. For the idea that the promise pertained to all men, considered in Adam, is not at variance with the idea that the Jews were alone the people of God. These ideas are reconciled by the fact that the people of other nations were alienated from the promise by their own fault or that of their parents, as may be seen from the whole tenor of the Holy Scriptures.

The second and third objections are made by those who do not think that historical faith in Christ is necessary to salvation. Your refutation of these pleases me, and those objections are of no moment. You also meet with a sufficient reply the objection from the fathers. But that objection is not presented oppositely to the views of those, whom in this treatise, you oppose. For they admit that the grace, by which anyone is enabled to will to be converted and to will really to believe in Christ, is not common to all men, which idea they do not regard as opposed to their own sentiment concerning the election of believers, and the reprobation of unbelievers.

The seventh error: Should I say that this dogma is falsely charged upon that doctrine, you will be at a loss, and indeed will not be able to prove your assertion. For they acknowledge that the rule of Predestination is "the will and the decree of God." This declaration: "Believers shall be saved, and unbelievers shall be condemned," was made apart from any prescience of faith or unbelief by God, of His own mere will, and they say that it is comprehended in the definition of Predestination and Reprobation. But when Predestination of certain individuals is discussed, then they premise the foreknowledge of faith and of unbelief, not as the law and rule, but as properly antecedent. To which view, the passage in Eph 1 is not opposed.

Predestined According to

For believers are "predestinated according to the purpose of Him who worketh all things after the counsel of His own will" (Eph 1:11). The purpose, according to which Predestination is declared to have been made, is that of adopting believers in Christ to sonship and eternal life, as is apparent from many passages of Scripture, where that purpose is discussed including Rom 8 and 9. From this, it is also evident that your first argument against those who hold that opinion, amounts to nothing.

In the second place, you assert, that "divine Election is rule of giving or withholding faith. Therefore Election does not pertain to believers, but faith rather pertains to the elect, or is from the gift of Election." You will allow me to deny this, and to ask for the proof, while I plead the cause of those whose sentiment you here oppose. Election is made in Christ. But no one is in Christ, except he is a believer. Therefore no one is elected in Christ, unless he is a believer. The passage in Rom 11:5, does not serve to prove that thesis. For the point there discussed is not the election of grace, according to which faith is given to some, but that according to which righteousness is imputed to believers. This may be most easily proved from the context, and will be manifest to any one who will more diligently inspect and examine it. For the people, "which he [God] foreknew" (Rom 11:2), that is He foreknew according to His grace, were the people who believed, not those who followed after righteousness by the works of the law. (Rom 9:31) This people God "hath not cast away" (Rom 11:2).

For thus is to be understood from Rom 11:5, "there is a remnant according to the election of grace," that is, they only are to be esteemed as the remnant of the people of God, who believe in Christ. They alone are embraced in the election of grace, the children of the flesh, who followed after righteousness by the law, being excluded. That, which follows (11:6), teaches the same thing: "And if by grace, then is it no more of works." What is that which is "by grace?" Is it election to faith? By no means; but it is election to righteousness, or righteousness itself.

For it is said to be "by grace" not "by works." For it is not here inquired whether faith, but whether righteousness belongs to anyone by works. Consider also the next verse "What then? Israel hath not obtained that which he seeketh for, but the election hath obtained it, and the rest were blinded" (11:7). What is that which Israel had sought for, and had not obtained? Not faith, but righteousness. See the end of the 9th and the beginning of the 10th chapters. They rejected faith in Christ, and endeavored to obtain righteousness by the works of the law, and this is the reason that they did not attain "to the law of righteousness." It is the same thing, also, which the elect are said to have obtained, not faith, but righteousness.

You will ask, "Is not faith, then, given according to Election?" I answer faith is not given according to that election, there discussed by the apostle, and therefore that passage does not conduce to your purpose. But is there, then, a twofold Election on the part of God? Certainly, if that is Election, by which God chooses to righteousness and life, that must be different, by which He chooses some to faith, if indeed he does choose some to faith. I will not now discuss that issue, because it is my purpose only to answer your arguments. Your third argument is equally weak, for prescience of faith and of unbelief has the same extent as Predestination. In the first place, unbelief is a negative idea, that is want of faith, and it was foreseen by God, when He decreed unto damnation. Secondly, the infants of believers are considered in their believing parents, and are not to be separated from the people of believers.

Your fourth argument is answered in the same way as the second. Faith is not the effect of that election, by which some are elected to righteousness and life. But it is this election to which they refer, in the examination of whose doctrine you are now engaged. The passage, in Eph 1, regards faith, as presupposed to Predestination. For no one but a believer is predestinated to adoption through Christ: "as many as received him, to them gave he power to become the sons of God" (John 1:12). The passages, adduced from the fathers, sustain the idea that faith is the effect of election, but, without doubt, that election is referred to by which God makes a distinction among men in the dispensation of means by which faith is attained. That will perhaps not be denied by those with whom you are now engaged, if it may only be correctly explained according to the Scriptures.

The fifth argument amounts to this: "Election is not according to the foresight of faith, since the cause of the divine foresight of faith in one, and not in another, is the mere will of God, who purposes to give faith to one, and not to another." Your opponents would reply that faith is in such a sense of the mere will of God, that it does not use an omnipotent and irresistible influence in producing faith in men, but a mild persuasion and one adapted to incline the will of man, according to the mode of the human will. Therefore the whole cause of the faith of one, and the unbelief of another, is the will of God, and the free choice of man.

To the sixth argument, he, who acknowledges that faith can be wholly lost will reply that the rule or rather the antecedent condition of election is not faith, but final perseverance in faith: of that election, I mean, by which God chose to salvation and eternal life.

True and Saving

The eighth error: That true and saving faith may be totally and finally lost, I should not at once dare to say: though many of the fathers frequently seem to affirm this. Yet the arguments, by which you prove that it can be, neither wholly nor finally lost are to be considered. Your first proof is deduced from Matt 16:18: "upon this rock I will build," etc. You argue in favor of your doctrine in a three-fold manner from that passage. Your first proof is equivocal on account of the double meaning of the word "faith." For it means either the confession of faith made by Peter concerning Christ, or trust resting in that confession and doctrine of faith.

Faith, understood in the former sense, is the rock, which remains unshaken and immovable, and is the foundation of the church. But faith, understood in the latter sense, is inspired in the members of the church, by the spirit and the word, by which they are built upon the rock as their foundation. Therefore the word "faith" is used in the antecedent in a sense, different from that in which it is used in the consequent.

Your second proof is this: "Those that are built upon the rock never fall away entirely." Answer: The major of this proposition is not contained in the words of Christ, for he says not that "those built on the rock shall not fall from the rock," but "the gates of hell shall not prevail against it [the rock, or the church]" (Matt. 16:18). It is one thing that the gates of hell should not prevail against the rock, but another that those who are built upon the rock shall not fall from it. A stone, built upon a foundation, may give way and fall from it, while the foundation itself remains firm. If Christ referred to the Church, I say, even then, that to assert that those who are built upon the rock shall not fall from it, is not the same as to declare that the gates of hell shall not prevail against the church. For the act of falling pertains to the free will of the person who falls. But if the gates of hell should prevail against the church, this would occur on account of the weakness of the rock on which the church is founded.

The minor does not repeat the same idea as was contained in the major. For, in the minor it is stated that believers are built, not having been built completely on the rock, on account of the continuation and confirmation of the work of building, which must necessarily, continue while they are in this world. But while that continuation and confirmation lasts, believers do not seem to be out of danger of falling. For as any person may be unwilling to be built upon the rock, so it is possible that the same man, if he begins to be built, should fall, by resisting the continuation and confirmation of the building.

But, it is not probable that Christ wished to signify by those words that believers could not fall, as such an assertion would not be advantageous. Since it is necessary that they should have their own strength in the rock, and therefore, that they should always bear upon and cling to the rock, they will give less earnest heed in temptations, to adhere firmly to the rock, if they are taught that they cannot fall from it. It may be sufficient to animate them, if they know that no force or skill can throw them from the rock, unless they willingly desert their station.

As to your third proof, even if it should be evident that Christ declared, that the gates of hell should not prevail against the church, yet it would not follow that no one could fall away from the faith. If anyone should fall, nevertheless the church remaineth unshaken against the gates of hell. The defection of an individual, as was before said, is not caused by the power of hell, but by the will of him who falls, in reference to the inflexibility of whose will the Scripture says nothing. The use of argument presenting such consolation would not be useful for the confirmation of the faithful.

In reference to the sentiments of the fathers, you doubtless know that almost all antiquity is of the opinion that believers can fall away and perish. But the passages you present from the fathers, either treat faith in the abstract, which is unshaken and immutable, or concern predestinated believers on whom God has determined to bestow perseverance, who are always to be distinguished, according to the opinion of the fathers, and especially of Augustine, from those who are faithful and just, according to present righteousness.

Your second argument proves nothing, for though it is true that he that asketh may be confirmed against temptations, and may not fall away, yet it is possible that he may not ask, and thus may not receive that strength, so that defection may follow. Hence arises the constant necessity of prayer, which does not exist if one obtains that assistance from God, without daily prayers. Nor is it here declared that believers may not intermit the duty of prayer, which must necessarily be presupposed to that conclusion, which you wish to deduce from prayer.

Confess the Elect

That Christ undertakes to confess the elect before the Father (Matt. 10:32) is true. But "elect" and "believers" are not convertible terms according to the view of the fathers, unless perseverance is added to faith. Nor is it declared, by Christ in Matt. 24:24, that the elect cannot depart from Christ, but that they cannot be deceived, by which is meant that though the power of deception is great, yet it is not so great as to seduce the elect. This serves as a consolation to the elect against the power and artifices of false Christs, and false prophets.

Your third argument can be invalidated in many ways. First, "entire defection from true faith would require a second engrafting, if indeed he, who falls away, shall be saved." It is not absolutely necessary that he who falls away should be again engrafted. Indeed some will say, from Heb 6 and 10, that one who wholly falls away from the true faith cannot be restored by repentance. Secondly, there is no absurdity in saying that they may be engrafted a second time, because in Rom 11:23, it is said of branches that had been cut or broken off, that "God is able to graft them in again."

If you say that the same individuals are not referred to here, I will ask the proof of that assertion. Thirdly, It does not follow from the second engrafting that "a repetition of baptism would be necessary" because baptism, once applied to an individual, is to him a perpetual pledge of grace and salvation, as often as he returns to Christ. And the remission of sins, committed even after baptism, is given without a repetition of baptism. Hence, if it be conceded that "baptism is not to be repeated," as they with whom you now contend willingly admit, yet it does not follow that believers cannot wholly fall away, either because those who wholly fall away may not be entirely restored, or because if they are restored, they do not need to be baptized a second time.

It does not seem that your fourth argument from 1 John 3:9, can be easily answered. Yet Augustine affirms that here they only are referred to who are called according to the divine purpose and are regenerated according to the decree of the divine Predestination. If you say that it is here said of all who are born of God that they do not sin, and that the seed of God remains in them, I will reply that the word "remain" signifies inhabitation, but not a continuance of inhabitation, and that so long as the seed of God is in a person, he does not sin unto death. But it is possible that the seed itself should, by his own fault and negligence, be removed from his heart, and as his first creation in the image of God was lost, so the second communication of it may be lost. I admit, however, that this argument is the strongest of those which have been hitherto referred to.

To the fifth, I reply that the seed of the word of God is immortal in itself, but it can be removed from the hearts of some who have received it (Matt 13:19, etc.).

The sixth argument: So long as the members abide in Christ as the branches in the vine, they cannot indeed perish, as the vivifying power of Christ dwells in them. But if they do not bear fruit, they shall be cut off (John 15:2). It is possible that the branches, even while abiding in the vine, may not bear fruit, not from defect of the root or of the vine, but of the branches themselves. Rom 6, is also an exhortation of the apostle to believers, that they should not live any longer in sin, because they, in Christ, are dead to sin. This admonition to Christians would be in vain, if it were not possible that they should live in sin, even after their liberation from its dominion.

It is to be considered that the mortification of the flesh is to be effected through the whole life, and that sin is not, in a single moment, to be so extinguished in believers that they may not at some time bear the worst fruit, provoking the wrath of God, and deserving the destruction of the individual. But, if a person commit sins, deserving the divine wrath and destruction, and God remits them only on condition of contrition and serious repentance, it follows that those, who thus sin, can be cut off, and indeed finally, if they do not return to God. That they should return, is not made necessary by the efficacy of their engraftment into Christ, although that return will certainly occur in those whom God has determined, by the immutable decree of His own Predestination, to make heirs of salvation.

The seventh argument: "All who are members of Christ attain the stature of a perfect man." This is true, if they do not depart from Christ. This they can do, but it is not included in the internal and essential definition of members, that they should not be able to recede and fall away from their head. It is declared in John 15 that the branches that do not bear fruit are taken away; and in Rom 11, some branches are said to have been broken off on account of unbelief.

You then inquire as if you had fully proved that faith cannot be wholly lost, "What is the reason that faith may not utterly fail?" and reply, "It is not from the nature of faith, but from the gift of grace, which confirms that which is promised to believers." You here incorrectly contrast faith itself and confirming grace, when you ought to contrast a man endued with faith on one hand, and the gift of grace on the other. The reason that faith cannot wholly perish, or rather that the believer cannot wholly lose his faith, is found either in the believer himself, or in grace, which confirms or preserves faith, that the believer may not lose it. It is not in the believer himself, for he as a human being obnoxious to error and fall, can lose his faith.

Not Lose Faith

But if God has determined that he should not lose his faith, it will be preserved through the grace by which He strengthens him, that he may not fall. "Simon, I have prayed for thee, that thy faith fail not" (Luke 22:32). The faith, then, of Peter could have failed, if we consider his strength. But Christ, by his intercession, obtained for him that grace, by which its preservation was secured. The covenant of God mentioned in Jer 32:40, does not contain in itself an impossibility of departure from God. But it mentions a promise of the gift of His fear, by which, so long as it shall continue in their hearts, they shall be restrained from departing from God.

But the Scripture nowhere teaches that it is not possible to shake off that gift of fear, nor is it profitable that promises of such a type should be made to those in covenant with God. It is sufficient that they should be sustained by the promises against all temptations of the world, the flesh, sin and Satan, and that they may be made strong against all their enemies, if they will only be faithful to themselves and to the grace of God.

You add another question: "How far can believers lose grace and the Holy Spirit?" You reply that this question can be solved by a twofold distinction, both in believers and in grace. In the distinction you make among believers, those whom you mention first do not at all deserve to be called believers. For hearing and understanding the Word, if approbation of the same is not added, do not constitute a believer. They who occupy the second order, are called believers in an equivocal sense. For true faith cannot but produce fruit, convenient to its own nature, confidence in Him, love towards Him, and fear of Him who is its object.

You distinguish believers of the second and third order in such a manner as to make the latter those who "apprehend Christ the redeemer by a living faith unto salvation" which you deny in reference to the former in the meantime, conceding to both not only an approbation of evangelical truth, heard and understood, but also the production of certain fruits. This is when you ought, indeed, to have considered the declaration of Christ: "As the branch cannot bear fruit of itself, except it abide in the vine, no more can ye, except ye abide in me . . . for without me ye can do nothing" (John 15:4, 5).

Can anyone indeed abide in Christ, unless he apprehends him as a redeemer, by a living faith unto salvation? Therefore that whole distinction among believers is futile, since the last class only ought to receive this name. If you can prove that these cannot fall away and perish, you fully accomplish your purpose. The other classes cannot be said to lose grace and the Holy Spirit, but rather to reject grace and to resist the Holy Spirit, if they do not make further progress. Hearing, understanding and approbation of the word may tend to this end, that they should apprehend Christ Jesus as their Redeemer, by a living faith unto salvation.

Let us now come to your distinction of grace, and see how you from this distinction meet the question above presented. You say that "Grace is of a twofold character. Primary grace is the gratuitous favor of God, embracing his own in Christ unto eternal life." Be it so. You also say that "some fall from this grace, in a certain manner, that is, according to some effects of that grace of which they must be destitute and the contrary of which they must experience, when they commit any grievous sin; not according to that grace, when God always preserves His paternal feelings towards them, and does not change His purpose concerning their adoption, and the bestowment on them of eternal life."

But these things need more diligent consideration. The effect of grievous sin committed against the conscience is the wrath of God, the sting of conscience, and eternal damnation. But the wrath of God cannot be consistent with His grace in reference to the same thing at the same time and in respect to the same person, so that he should, in reference to him with whom He is angry, in that very wrath, yet will eternal life. He can will to bestow on him certain effects of grace, by which he can be brought back to a sound mind, and, again to bestow on him, thus restored, that grace of God unto eternal life. An accusing conscience, one really accusing, cannot be consistent with grace and the gratuitous favor of God unto eternal life. For, in that case, the conscience would not really accuse. God does not will to bestow eternal life on one whom His own conscience testifies, and truly, to be unworthy of eternal life unless repentance shall intervene, which, of the gracious mercy of God, removes unworthiness.

God does not will to bestow eternal life on him who has by his sin merited eternal damnation, and has not yet repented while he is in that state. Therefore he truly falls from that grace that is designed to embrace him unto everlasting life. But since God knows that such a man will, by those means He has determined to use for his restoration, rise from the death of sin, he cannot be said to wholly fall from the Divine grace. But a distinction is to be made here in relation to the various blessings God wills to bestow on such.

Believing and Penitent

He wills eternal life only to the believing and penitent. He wills the means of faith and conversion to sinners not yet converted, not yet believers. And it does not seem to be a correct statement that "God regards sin, but not sinners with hatred," since the sin and the sinner are equally odious to God. He hates the sinner on account of his sin, of which he (the sinner) is the author, and which, except by him, would not be perpetrated. In the description of that primary grace, there is that which weakens the answer itself. "It is the favor by which God embraces in Christ his own."

He embraces no one in Christ, unless he is in Christ. But no one is in Christ except by faith in Christ, which is the necessary means of our union with Christ. If any one falls from faith, he falls from that union, and, consequently, from the favor of God by which he was previously embraced in Christ. From this it is also apparent, that in this explanation there is a begging of the question. For the question is this, "Can believers fall from this primary grace, that is, from the favor of God, by which he embraces them in Christ?" It is certain that they cannot while they continue to be believers, so long they are in Christ. But if they fall from faith, they also fall from that primary grace. Hence the question remains: "Can believers fall from faith?" But you concede that believers do fall so far as themselves are concerned. I conclude then that God does not remain in them, and that neither the right of eternal life nor sonship belongs to them according to the declaration, "as many as received him, etc." (John 1:12).

Hence, if you had wished to make your statements consistent, it was necessary to deny that believers fall from faith or, if you concede this, to concede at the same time that they can fall from the favor of God by which He embraces them in Christ unto eternal life. But as I said, this whole subject may be elucidated, if the grace of God is suitably distinguished from its various effects.

Let the passages of Scripture you cite, be examined. "Neither shall any man pluck them out of my hand" (John 10:28). Who will deny this? But some say: "The sheep cannot be taken out of the hands of the shepherd, but can, of their own accord, depart from him." You affirm that "this is a weak statement." By what argument? "Because when they fall, they are taken by the Devil." Truly indeed, they are taken when they fall, and it is not possible that it should be done in any other way.

For unless the sheep are in the hands of the shepherd, they cannot be safe against Satan. But the question is: Does not the act of departure and defection in its nature, precede their seizure by Satan? If this be so, your answer is vain and futile. You argue again in this manner, "If ye continue in my word, ye are my disciples indeed" (John 8:31). Therefore, he who continues to be one of the flock and does not fall, is truly one of the flock."

Answer: In the first place, there is ambiguity in the word "continues." It signifies either present observance of Christ's word, or continuous observance without defection from that word. Present observance, if it is sincere, makes one a disciple of Christ, or rather proves that one is a true disciple of Christ. Otherwise one can never be truly called a disciple of Christ unless when he has passed the limit of this life, when defection will be no longer to be feared, which is absurd. In the second place, I affirm that in the phrase "my disciples indeed" there is a twofold sense. It signifies either that one who at anytime falls away from the word of Christ, was never a disciple indeed, though he may, at some time, have kept his word in sincerity. Or it can indicate one who at anytime has kept the word of Christ and then obtained the name of disciple, if he yet falls away, is afterwards unworthy of the name of disciple.

Therefore, if the relation of his present state is considered, He is "a disciple indeed" if in the relation of his subsequent state, he is not a disciple indeed, or does not deserve that name, because he at some time deserts it, unless one may say that no one has ever sincerely observed the word of Christ, who falls from it. This assertion needs proof.

The passage in Rom 8:35, "Who shall separate us from the love of God?" is wholly irrelevant. For it is the consolation by which believers are strengthened against all present and assailing evils.

None of these can at all effect that God should cease to love those, whom He has begun to love in Christ. Rom 11:29 is not better adapted to your purpose. For though "the gifts of God are without repentance" yet one can reject the gifts of God that he receives. Your quotation from (2 Tim 2:19), "The Lord knoweth them that are His," does not favor your design. The Lord knoweth His own, even if some believers do fall away from faith. For it can be said that God has never known them as His own by the knowledge that is the handmaid of Predestination now under consideration. The distinction of Augustine may be applied here: "Some are children according to present justification, some according to the foreknowledge and Predestination of God."

Imputed or Inherent

Secondary grace, you say, is either imputed or inherent. The phrase imputed grace does not sound well in my ears. I have heretofore thought that grace is not imputed, but imputes, as in Rom 4:4, "the reward is not reckoned of grace, but of debt." Righteousness is said, in the same chapter, to be imputed of grace without works. But, passing by this, let us examine the subject. The question proposed was, "How far may believers lose grace and the Holy Spirit?" You answer, in respect to imputed grace, which consists in justification, a part of which is the remission of sins, "The remission of sins is not granted in vain." Be it so. But believers may, after remission of some sins has been obtained, commit sin and grievously backslide.

If then, they should not repent of that act, will they obtain remission? You answer in the negative. I conclude from this, that they can lose that grace of the remission of their sins. But you reply, "It cannot be that they should not repent." I know that this is asserted, but I desire the proof, not that the elect indeed cannot depart hence without final repentance, but that they who have once been believers cannot die in final impenitence. When you shall have proved this, it will not be necessary to recur to this distinction of grace, for then you would be permitted to say that the believer never finally loses his faith and dies in impenitence.

You make a distinction in inherent grace, as "faith" and "the consequent gift of faith." In faith you consider "the act and the habit of faith." From this distinction, you answer the proposed question, thus: "Faith, considered in respect to habit and ability, cannot be lost, on account of confirming grace (though it can per se be lost) but faith, in respect to any particular act, can be lost." First, I ask proof of your assertion. "Faith, in respect to habit, cannot be lost, on account of confirming grace." I also inquire: "Is that act of faith, in respect to which faith can be lost, necessary or not, that anyone may apprehend Christ? If it is, then a man can fall from grace if he loses, as you say, the act of apprehension of Christ, or rather, if he does not apprehend Christ by that act. If it is not necessary, then it was indeed of no importance to have considered that act, when the loss of grace was under discussion.

You attempt to prove, both by the example of David and by the opinions of the fathers, that the habit of faith and love cannot be lost. The example of David proves nothing. For, should it be conceded that David, when he was guilty of adultery and murder, had not lost the Holy Spirit, it does not follow from this that the Holy Spirit cannot be lost. For another might sin even more grievously, and thus lose the Holy Spirit. If, however, I should say that David had lost the Holy Spirit when he committed that adultery and murder, what would you answer? You might reply that it is evident that it was not so from Psalm 51.

That Psalm, I reply, was composed by David after he had repented of those crimes, having been admonished by Nathan. God, at that time, according to the declaration of Nathan, restored the Holy Spirit to David (2 Sam 12:13). In reference to the assertions of the fathers, I consider that the case of Peter is not to the prejudice of the opinion that states that faith can be destroyed. For Peter sinned through infirmity, which weakens faith, but does not destroy it. I pass over Gratian. It would be proper to discuss, at some length, the sentiment of Augustine, if it had been proposed to present it fully.[6] From these passages, it will, in my judgment,

6. For more information concerning Augustine on this matter, we recommend: *De Praedestinatione Sanctorum*, Lib. 1, Cap. 14; *De Bono Perseverantiae*, Lib. 2, Cap. 1, 6,

be apparent that Augustine thought that some believers, some justified and regenerate persons, some, on whom had been bestowed faith, hope and love, can fall away and be lost, and indeed will fall away and be lost, the predestinate alone being excepted. You quote some objections to the foregoing explanation. The first is: "Sin and the grace of the Holy Spirit cannot subsist together." You reply, that "this is true of reigning sin, or sin with the full consent of the will." But you deny that the regenerate sin with the full or entire consent of the will. I answer, first, that "reigning sin" is not the same as that which has the full consent of the will. For the former belongs, generically to quality or habit, the latter pertains generically to action, and by the latter is prepared a way for the former. From this, it is clearly manifest that reigning sin cannot subsist with the grace of the Holy Spirit.

It is also true that sin does not reign in the regenerate. For, before this can take place, it is necessary that they should reject the grace of the Holy Spirit, which mortifies sin and restrains its power. We must then, examine the other mode of sin and see whether some of the regenerate may sin or not with the full consent of the will. You deny this and deduce the reason for your denial from the beginning and successive steps of temptation. You consider the beginning of temptation to be concupiscence or native corruption, and you say that "it exists alone in the unregenerate man, who is entirely carnal. But in the renewed man, there is flesh and Spirit together, but in various degrees, so that he is partly carnal, partly spirit." You conclude that "concupiscence can subsist with the grace of the Holy Spirit, but not reign." I reply that though I have but little objection to that conclusion, I cannot altogether approve those things which precede. For some of them are not true, and the statement is imperfect.

It is not true that "an unregenerate man is wholly carnal," that is, that there is in him only the flesh. For by what name shall that truth be called that the wicked are said to "hold in unrighteousness"? (Rom 1:18). What is that conscience which accuses and excuses? (Rom 2:15). What is the knowledge of the law by which they are convinced of their sins? (Rom 3:20). All these things cannot be comprehended under the term

---

8) and *De Corruptione et Gratia*, Cap. 13, 16, 22, 23. Let some passages be added from Prosper, who defends the opinions of Augustine, e.g. *Ad Capitula Gallorum Respons.* 7; *Ad Objectiones Vincentainas Respon.* 16; *De Vocatione Gentium*, Lib. 2, Cap. 8, 9, and 28.

"flesh." For they are blessings, and are adverse to the flesh. Yet I admit that the Holy Spirit does not dwell in the unrenewed man.

The statement is imperfect, because it omits the explanation of the proportion, which exists between the flesh and the Spirit in the renewed man, as the Spirit predominates in the regenerate person, and because, from the predominating element, he receives the name of spiritual man, so that he cannot come under the term carnal. But observe moreover, that your conclusion has reference to concupiscence, which is in the predicament of a quality, while the question should have been: "Can actual sin consist with the grace of the Holy Spirit?"

You Concede

You refer to "five steps, of temptation." You concede that the first step may pertain to the regenerate, also the second, and it is indeed, true. But it can never be proved that Paul, for such a reason, "complained of his own captivity, because he could delight in sorrowful meditation in reference to the commission of sin." For he is treating there sin already committed. "The evil which I would not, that I do" (Rom 7:19).

The third step, which is "the consent of the will to the perpetration of sin," you attribute also to the regenerate, "but a more remiss consent, according to which they will, in such a sense, that they are even unwilling to commit sin." You think that this can be proved from the example of Paul in Rom 7. I wish you to consider here, how these things harmonize, that in reference to one and the same act, the will or volition may be twofold, and, indeed contrary to itself, even at the very moment when the act is performed. Before the act, while the mind is yet in doubt, and the flesh is lusting against the Spirit, and the Spirit against the flesh, this might be affirmed. But, when the flesh carries out its concupiscence into action, that is, does that which it has lusted against the Spirit, then, indeed the Spirit has ceased to lust.

The position must then be assumed, that the renewed man commits sin from the concupiscence of the flesh, the Spirit in vain lusting against it, that is, the flesh is stronger than the Spirit, and the desire of the Spirit is overcome by the flesh. This is contrary to the declaration of Scripture: "greater is he that is in you, than he that is in the world" (1 John 4:4), and contrary to the condition of the regenerate, in whom the Spirit predom-inates over the flesh, nor does it occur that the flesh should conquer, unless when the Spirit is quiet and intermits the contest.

"But the Scripture affirms (Rom 7) that the renewed man would do good, yet does it not, and would not do evil, yet does it." I answer, in that passage reference is made not to a regenerate person, but to a man under the law. But even if this point be conceded, I affirm that it is not possible that there should be volition and nolition, at the same time, concerning the same act. Hence, that volition, which is followed by an act, is a pure and efficacious volition. The other is not so much volition as desire, which is produced not by the Holy Spirit striving against the flesh, but by the conscience, or the law of the mind existing in man that ceases not to struggle against the flesh, until it is seared and deprived of all feeling.

That struggle of the conscience does not effect that the man should not sin with his full consent. It rather aggravates the sin, and declares how vehement is the consent of the will to a sin, presented by the concupiscence of the flesh, when not even the conscience, exclaiming against it, has power to restrain the will from that consent.

It is, then, an injurious and most dangerous opinion, which holds that the renewed man does not sin with full consent, when he feels the sting of conscience, opposing the sin which the will is about to perpetrate. As this happens to all who are affected by any sense of right and wrong, it will be very easy for them to persuade themselves that, as they do not sin with the full consent of the will, they have a certain indication of their own regeneration.

Therefore, if the full consent of the will to sin cannot consist with the grace of the Holy Spirit, it is certain that the regenerate sometimes lose the grace of the Holy Spirit because they sin with the full consent of the will when they sin against the conscience. You consider the fourth step to be "the carrying out of an evil work into an act." This is correct, but the distinction which you make, cannot be proved from the Scriptures.

When the regenerate person commits sin, he commits it by being overcome by the concupiscence of the flesh, while the Spirit of regeneration is quiescent and not testifying against the sin, unless before the sin, when the consent of the will has not yet been gained by the persuasion of concupiscence, and after the sin when the Spirit has begun to revive. But the "testifying," of which you speak is nothing else than the act of the conscience accusing the person both before and after the commission of sin. The whole man then, sins, but "not according to that principle by which he is renewed." This was unnecessarily added; for who would ever call this in question? This also can be said of a man placed under the law, as he does not sin according to the law of his mind, that is, of his conscience approving the law, but only according to the flesh.

Distinction in This Case

Hence, you see that the distinction in this case, ought to have been of another character. Nor does it seem necessary to concede, "that an action, performed by a regenerate person, may be less sinful than if performed by him in whom sin reigns."

For the fault and sinfulness of an action is to be judged from the strong consent of the will to the sin. But he is borne more vehemently towards sin who rejects the act of the Holy Spirit striving in the contrary direction, and follows the concupiscence of the flesh, than he who, opposing the concupiscence of the flesh by his conscience alone, at length yields. Thus the sin of David, committing adultery and murder was far more heinous than that of a heathen man committing the same sins. The inhabitants of Bethsaida and Chorazin sinned more grievously than the citizens of Tyre and Sidon because the former committing their sins resisted more influences, adapted to restrain from the commission of sin, than the latter. You say that the last step is "when a sin, confirmed by frequent repetition, becomes a habit." That step or degree was called, you remark, by the Greeks *to apotelein* ["completion" or "persuasion"]. But you will allow me to deny that the Greeks used that word, in that sense. For your fourth step was *apotelian*, the same as to commit sin. But this last step is a degree not so much in sin, as in sinners, of whom some advance further than others.

You deny that this step can happen to the regenerate. This needs proof. In all those distinctions, there is a continual assumption of the point to be proved. For they who say the regenerate can lose the grace of the Holy Spirit, say also that the regenerate may not only sin, but may persevere in sin and contract the habit of sin.

The second objection you adduce, is: "Adam, being yet pure, fell wholly, therefore, much more may they fall, who, having been born and renewed after the Fall of Adam, have believed." The force of the argument depends on the parity or equality of the conditions of the parties: that of Adam, in respect to which he was created in righteousness and true holiness; and that of his descendants, in respect to which they have been renewed in righteousness and true holiness. You attempt to solve the difficulty by showing the dissimilarity of the cases. But the dissimilarity, which exists between the two conditions, does not effect that the regenerate may not be able altogether to fall away. Nor, indeed, is this affirmed in the passage you cite from Augustine.

For, though the regenerate may have the will to do according to their ability, of which gift Adam was destitute, according to the sentiment of Augustine, yet it does not follow that they cannot repudiate and willingly reject this gift. You were permitted to add other things, in which the condition of believers in Christ differs from the original state of Adam in righteousness. Among other things, this is peculiar that the latter state had not the promise of the remission of sins, if it should happen that Adam should ever once commit sin. But that of believers is rendered more blessed by the promise: "their sins and their iniquities will I remember no more" (Heb. 8:12). Hence it is that the faith of God is not made "without effect," even if those in covenant with him do sin (Rom 3:3).

For the covenant is one of grace and faith, not of righteousness and works. Yet make whatever differences you please between the two states, it will be always necessary to admit that perseverance, voluntary, free, and liable to change, was necessary to salvation in both states. Man does not persevere, either in the former or the latter state, unless freely and willingly. This is so far true "that God does not take away even from those, who are about to persevere, that liability to change, by which they may possibly not choose to persevere."[7] You refer to a third objection: "This member of a harlot is not a member of Christ. But the believer, who is a member of Christ, can become the member of a harlot. Therefore, the believer may cease to be a member of Christ." You reply to this objection by making distinctions in the term "member." But those distinctions are unnecessary. First, the subject of discussion is a member not in appearance, but in truth. An apparent member is in an equivocal sense a member, and therefore does not belong to the definition; and there would be four terms to the syllogism.

Discussion a Member

Nor is the subject of discussion a member, which is such in its destination, for we know that all men, who are in destination members of

---

7. St. Augustine, *De Vocatione Gentium*, Lib. 2, Cap. 28.

Christ, are universally members of Satan before they are in fact brought to Christ and united to him. Since therefore, members who are really such, are referred to in the objection, to what purpose are these niceties of distinction sought? "In reference to those who are really members," you say, "some are living, others are half dead. But both are members, according to election." If this be so, you attain your object; for who is so foolish as to say that the elect may finally be lost? But they whom you consider your opponents, will deny that all true members of Christ are such by Predestination. They will affirm that some are such according to their present state, their righteousness and present engraftment in Christ.

Let us however, consider your answer, in the supposition of the truth of that distinction. You assert that "a true and actual member, and one that remains such cannot be a member of a harlot." That, indeed, is not strange. For it is an identical proposition, and therefore amounts to nothing. The member of Christ who remains such, is not a member of a harlot, but this does not answer the question: Will a living member of Christ always remain alive?

It was affirmed in the objection that a living member of Christ may become a member of a harlot, and may, therefore, not remain a member of Christ. The point, to be proved is again assumed in your answer to that argument. But you say that "the half dead may, as far as they are concerned, at any time, lose the Holy Spirit." But, from what state do they become half dead? Is it not from being wholly alive? You would not indeed say that anyone is half dead at the time he is engrafted in Christ. You see that such an assertion is absurd. The state of the case, according to those who argue against you, is like this. At the beginning of faith in Christ and of conversion to God, the believer becomes a living member of Christ.

If he perseveres in the faith of Christ and maintains a good conscience, he remains a living member. But if he becomes indolent, has no care for himself, gives place to sin, he becomes, by degrees half-dead. Proceeding in this way he at length wholly dies, and ceases to be a member of Christ. You ought to have refuted these statements, which, so far from refuting, you rather confirm by your distinctions. You have indeed treated this subject, with less care than its dignity and your learning deserved.

The ninth error: That, which is so styled by you, is erroneously charged on the sentiment adverse to you, for they do not say this, nor can it in any way, be deduced from their sentiment. This is their opinion. "A man, by his own freewill, receives the grace divinely offered to him, whatever it may be." For as grace preserves, so the free will is preserved, and the free will of man is the subject of grace. Hence it is necessary that the free will should concur with the grace, which is bestowed to its preservation, yet assisted by subsequent grace, and it always remains in the power of the free will to reject the grace bestowed, and to refuse subsequent grace. This is because grace is not the omnipotent action of God, which cannot be resisted by the free will of man.

And since the state of the case is such, those same persons think a man can reject grace and fall away. From which you see that you have undertaken a futile task, when you refute the error you charge on that sentiment. Yet we may consider, also, those same things. Perhaps an opportunity will be afforded to note something, which will not be unworthy of knowledge.

"This sentiment," you affirm, "attributes a free will, flexible in every direction, of grace, to all men." Do you deny that the free will is "flexible in all directions," I add, even without grace? It is flexible by its own nature, and as it is addicted to evil in its sinful state. So it is capable of good, which capability grace does not bestow upon it; for it is in it by nature. But it is, in fact, only turned to good by grace, which is like a mold, forming the ability and capacity of the material into an act, though it may be of itself sufficiently evil. Augustine says, "It belongs to the nature of man to be able to have faith and love, but it pertains to the grace of believers to actually have them."[8]

But you may be dissatisfied that this is said "to exist in all men," but that dissatisfaction is without cause. Their meaning is not that grace is bestowed on all men, by which their free will may be actually inclined to good; but that in all there exists a will that may be flexible in every direction by the aid of grace. But they teach, you say, that "it is in the will of man to apply itself to the grace bestowed by the aid of universal grace, or to reject the same by the inability of corrupt nature." What do you desire at this point? You will answer "that for the phrase 'universal grace' should be substituted 'particular grace.'"

8. St. Augustine, *De Praedest. Sanctorum*, Cap. 5.

But who has ever said that "a man can apply himself to particular grace by the force of universal grace"? I think that no one can be so foolish: for the man is led to the use of particular grace, offered to him by the free will, assisted by particular grace. The expression, "to reject the same by the inability," etc., is ineptly used; for inability does not reject. A passive non-reception pertains to it, while it is the province of depravity to reject. When, therefore, you have introduced according to your own judgment, the phrase "universal grace," you fight against your own shadow.

Ability to Believe

For it is evident that "the ability to believe is not carried out into action, unless by the aid of other subsequent grace, which we call particular or special, since it does not happen to all and to each of mankind." The passages of Scripture you adduce,[9] do not answer your purpose. For the former two are adapted to prove that the faithful do not fall away from Christ; and let it be remembered that, according to Augustine and the author of *De Vocatione Gentium*,[10] that perseverance pertains only to believers who are predestinated to life. The passages from Augustine show that the grace, prepared for the predestinated, will certainly incline their hearts and will not be rejected by them because God uses such persuasions with them, as He knows to be suitable to them and adapted to persuade them.

This he calls efficacious grace, and always distinguishes it from efficient grace. You however, in quoting Augustine, with sufficient superciliousness, repudiate that distinction. But what arguments do you use? You say that no grace is sufficient for conversion, which is not efficacious. I deny it, and nature itself exclaims against your assertion, while she distinguishes sufficiency from efficacy. God is sufficient for the creation of many worlds, yet He does not efficaciously perform it. Christ is sufficient for the salvation of all men, yet he does not efficaciously accomplish it.

But you perhaps understand by efficacious cause that which can effect anything, and so make it identical with efficient cause. But they who distinguish between sufficient and efficacious define the latter as that which really produces the effect. You do not prove that which you

9. Jer 32:40; 1 Cor. 1:8, 9; John 6:45.

10. The author's identity is uncertain. The work has variously been attributed to Prosper, Ambrose, Leo the Great and others.

intend, when you say that "man has not free will in spiritual things." Granted. But if grace may restore the freedom of the will, is it not then in the exercise of free will, that he either can do sufficiently, or really does efficaciously?

Nor is it to the purpose to say that "ye are dead," (Col. 3:3) and that "our sufficiency is of God" (2 Cor. 3:5). This is not denied by those who speak of sufficient grace. Nor does that three-fold inability do away with sufficient grace. They who make the distinction say that sufficient grace is able to remove that three-fold inability, and to effect that a man should receive offered grace, should use it when received, and should preserve it.

You endeavor to prove in the next place, as the necessary consequence of "the five-fold nature of grace, preeminent, preparative, operative, cooperative, and persevering," that no single grace can be sufficient, because "no one of those five kinds of grace is alone sufficient for salvation, since all joined together are necessary." It is not a sound conclusion, that there is no sufficient grace because no one of those five kinds of grace is sufficient alone. The reasoning here is from a particular case to a general conclusion, and therefore is not valid. There is here also the Fallacy of Composition.

But the first two kinds of grace, namely prevenient and preparative, are either sufficient or efficacious. For God precedes (by His grace) sufficiently and efficaciously. He also *prepares* sufficiently and efficaciously. It may be questioned also whether the same cannot be said of operative and cooperative grace. Yet let us concede that those terms properly pertain to efficacious grace. Nevertheless they who defend the use of the term "sufficient," will say that these latter kinds of grace are prepared for and offered to all who have suffered to be moved by prevenient and preparative grace, which is sufficient in its character, in the direction intended by that grace; and afterwards the gift of perseverance is also bestowed.

Hence you have not by that argument disproved sufficient grace so far as it is distinguished from efficacious grace. But we will not examine the definitions of that five-fold grace, because this does not pertain to the scope of this discussion. You also endeavor to refute the same distinction by a simile. But in it there is a great want of analogy. For an inert mass is moved, naturally and necessarily, by the application of forces that exceed the force of its gravity. But we, as human beings, are moved according to the mode of freedom, which God has bestowed on the will, from which it is called free will.

At this point, the simile Cardinal Contarini uses in his treatise on Predestination[11], in a way that is the opposite of yours. He supposes a twofold gravity in a stone, one natural, the other internal. The strength that is sufficient to raise a stone tending downwards by natural gravity alone, will not be sufficient if that internal gravity shall be added, and the efficiency of sufficient strength will be hindered by the supplemental gravity. We see this clearly in athletes engaged in wrestling.

One endeavors to raise the other from the earth, and to prostrate him, thus raised up. Either of them would be able in a moment to effect this in reference to his antagonist, if the latter should only offer the resistance of the native weight of his body. But because he does not wish to be raised, he depresses himself and his adversary as much as he can by using the strength of his nerves and bones, which far exceeds the weight of his body alone. So there is in man by derivation from the first sin of the first man a weight that is, or may be called, native. There is in addition to this another produced in each person by his own wickedness, which does not so much exist in him as is present with him, hindering the power of that grace that is sufficient to overcome the native gravity, from effecting what it would avail to do if that hindrance were not put there.

Flexibility of our Will

Nor is the flexibility of our will, nor our power of choice taken away by the concurrence of those five gifts. But by that concurrence, it is effected that the will, which by its own nature is flexible in every direction, and the choice, which is able to elect freely between two different things, should incline certainly and infallibly in that direction, towards the motion the five-fold grace impels it.

Hence, I also wish that instead of "inflexible inclination," you had said "certain and infallible inclination." For, if we do not say that the mind of a man may possibly be inclined in another direction, even at the time when it is inclined in a given direction by efficacious grace, it follows that the will of man acts not according to the mode of liberty, but according to the mode of nature. Thus, not the free will, but the nature of man, will be saved. But the free will, at least as to its exercise, will be in

11. Cardinal Gasparo Contarini (1484–1542), referring to his *De libero Arbitrio de Praedestinatione*.

that case destroyed by grace, while it belongs to grace not to take away, but to correct nature itself, wherein it has become corrupt.

Nor is what is said concerning the promised Spirit opposed to these views. For the "Spirit, who causes us actually to walk," does not take away the freedom of the will and of human choice, but He acts upon the free will in such a manner as He knows will be suitable and adapted to it, that it may be certainly and infallibly inclined. I wish that the same thing may be understood of the phrase, "the Father which hath sent me draw him" (John 6:44). Those things that follow, have not the effect of weakening this doctrine.

For, by the supposition of "efficacious grace acting in those, concerning whom God, certainly and infallibly, wills their conversion and salvation," the existence of sufficient grace is not denied. Nor indeed is that, which you infer, included in that supposition, namely that they who are truly believers, cannot but persevere. We may be permitted to infer from it the certain, but not the necessary existence of an effect. Ignorance of this distinction is the cause of your idea that you must deny sufficient grace.

Next follows the explanation of some passages of Scripture, which they who hold to sufficient grace are accustomed to use in proof of it. You seem to have selected them from Bellarmine[12], who presents them in the same order as you use. We will consider your refutation. The first passage is from Isa 5. Bellarmine deduces from that passage a twofold argument in proof of sufficient grace. The first is like this, when put in a syllogistic form: "He, who did all things for his vineyard which were necessary that it might be able to bear fruit, used sufficient culture for producing fruit; But God: . . . Therefore . . ." etc. The truth of the Major is plain from its very terms. It consists in a definition, and is itself a definition. For "sufficient culture" is that in which all things necessary for fruitfulness are used. The truth of the minor is contained in the text. For "he who has done all things which he might do for fruitfulness, has used all necessary means."

God could not with justice, speak in such terms if He had not used all necessary means. Therefore the conclusion is a correct one. You reply by making a twofold distinction in sufficiency, and in the nature of the vineyard; the sufficiency of external means, and that of internal grace;

12. Cardinal Robert Bellarmine (1542–1621) was one of the most important cardinals of the Catholic Reformation.

also of a good and bad vineyard. In the first part of this reply, you concede what is proved in the passage under consideration. For, if the external means are of such a character that men would be sufficiently invited and led by them unto salvation, unless their minds were so perverse and depraved, as you say, then it follows that those means would have been sufficient.

For is it necessary, in order that sufficiency by those means may be attributed to grace, that internal grace changing the bad vine into a good one, should be added. Indeed it can be said that so much internal grace as would be sufficient for a change of heart, was not wanting, or at least would not have been wanting, if they had not, in their perversity, rejected the external means. The distinction between the good and the bad vineyard is of no importance in this place. For this is the very thing, concerning which God complains that His vineyard was so perverse, that it would not respond to the sufficient culture bestowed upon it.

The second argument of Bellarmine is like this. If God had not bestowed on that vineyard all things necessary for the production of grapes, then He would have said absurdly that He "looked that it should bring forth grapes." But He said, *well and justly*, that He "looked that it should bring forth grapes." Therefore he had bestowed on it all things necessary for the production of grapes. The truth of the major is certain.

For God knew that a vineyard could not produce fruit, which was destitute of any of the means necessary for fructification. If He knew this, He knew also that it would be futile, nay, foolish to look for grapes from a vineyard that could not bear grapes.

Conclusion is Valid

The minor is contained in the text. Therefore the conclusion is valid, that sufficient grace was not wanting for the vineyard. It is worth the while to consider what is the meaning of that divine looking for or expectation, and how it may be correctly attributed to the Deity. An expectation by which an act is looked for from anyone, depends on a proper knowledge of the sufficiency necessary for the performance of the act, which either exists in Him or is present with Him on whom the act is incumbent, else, the expectation would be unreasonable. No one looks for figs from thistles, or roses from a thorn bush. This divine expectation, therefore, if we do not wish to call it unreasonable, which would be blasphemy, depends on the same knowledge.

Nor does the fact that, in the infinity of His knowledge, God knows that no effect will follow from the sufficiency of those forces to prevent us from attributing that expectation to Him. For that knowledge does not at all interfere with the sufficiency of causes on which depends the justness and reasonableness of the expectation. It is, indeed, true that the divine knowledge effects that God cannot be deceived. But he who looks for fruit in vain, and to whose expectation the event does not correspond, is deceived. From this, it is easy to infer that expectation is attributed to God only by the figure of *anthropopathy*, the possession of human passions and feelings.

But if even this be conceded, it will nevertheless follow from the consideration that expectation is attributed, with this appropriate qualification to the Deity, that sufficient strength was present with the individual from whom something was expected. But if, in that expectation, we consider not only the knowledge referred to, but also the highest desire with which he to whom expectation is attributed, demands the production of fruits. In that respect, expectation is most properly attributed to God. For he desires nothing so much from men, so in nothing is He equally delighted. This also is most plainly expressed in that parable.

Let us now return from this digression. To that second argument you make no reply, but propose another case you think will be more easily managed. But let us examine this also, with your answer. The case is this: "If he did not bestow grace to bear fruit, which could not be had except by His gift, then God had no just cause of expostulating with the Jews." The reply consists in a denial of the consequence, for the denial of which, a three-fold reason is assigned. The first is this: "As He did not owe that grace, He was under obligation to no one."

Secondly, "because they rejected it when offered to them in their parents." Thirdly, "because they did not, after having rejected it, seek it anew, or have any care concerning it." Indeed to one who carefully considers the matter, the reason is a single one, though consisting of three parts. For the reason assigned that God could rightly expostulate with those who do not bear fruit in this, that "they had grace sufficient for this purpose but rejected it." To confirm and strengthen this reason, it is added that God would not be obligated to give grace a second time, and that, even should He be obligated, He would not deny it to those desiring it. But He would not give it to those not desiring it, and not having any care whatever concerning that grace.

That reason for just expostulation is to be examined, and even so much more diligently, as it is more frequently used. It is asked, then, "Could God rightly expostulate with them because they do not bear good fruit, who have rejected the grace received in their first parents, which is necessary for the production of those fruits, or rather who have lost it, by a judicial removal of it, on the part of God?" For the discussion of this question, it is necessary to consider, first, "whether God could demand fruit from those who have, as a punishment from God, lost the grace necessary for that production, which was received in their first parents," that is, who are destitute of necessary grace, though by their own demerit. From this will readily follow the answer of the question whether He can justly expostulate with such persons, if they do not produce fruit. We remark, then, every divine demand by which He requires anything from a creature, is prescribed by law. But a law consists of two parts, command and sanction.

The command, by which an act is prescribed or forbidden, ought not to exceed the strength of him on whom the command is laid. The sanction contains a promise of reward to the obedient, and a denunciation of punishment against the transgressor. Hence it is evident that the demand of the law is twofold, of obedience and of punishment.

That of obedience is prior and absolute; that of punishment is subsequent, and has no place except when obedience is not yielded. Hence also, there is a twofold satisfaction of the law: one, in which the obedience prescribed by the law is rendered; the other, in which the punishment required by the law is inflicted. He who satisfies the claim of the law in one way, is free from its demands, in the other. He therefore, who pays the penalty laid down in the law, is entirely free from obligation to render obedience. This is true universally of every kind of punishment.

If the punishment of disobedience comprehends within itself a privation of that grace without which the law cannot be obeyed, then indeed, by a twofold right he seems to be entirely free from obligation to obedience, both because he has suffered due punishment and because he is deprived of that strength without which the law cannot be obeyed. He is deprived punitively by God Himself, the enacter of the law, which fact is of much importance. For thus is excluded that argument, which some present, saying the servant is bound to render obedience or servitude, even if he has cut off his own hands, without which he cannot render it.

The case is not analogous. For the fault and sin of the servant consists in the fact that he has cut off his hands, but in the other case God, himself the lawgiver, takes away the strength because it has not been used by him who had received, according to the declaration, "to him that hath shall be given, etc." That servant indeed deserved punishment for that crime, and if he should suffer it, his master could not afterwards demand from him service he could not render without hands. Therefore it seems necessary to conclude that God cannot demand fruit from those whom he has deprived, though on account of their own demerit, of the strength necessary for producing fruit. Let us take the illustration of a tree. The tree, which does not bear fruit, deserves to die, but when that punishment has been inflicted upon it, no one can, by any right demand fruit from it.

God Cannot

Hence, therefore it follows, secondly: "God cannot justly expostulate with those, who do not bear fruit if they are destitute of grace necessary for this, even by the punishment of God." It is of no consequence that God is not obligated to restore grace to them. For as He is not obligated to bestow grace, so He cannot demand the act of obedience. And, if He wills to demand an act, He is obligated to restore that grace, without which the act cannot be performed. Thus also it is not to the purpose that they do not seek the grace, which they have lost.

For thus they twice deserve not to receive grace, both because they have lost it of their own fault, and because they do not seek it when lost. On this very account, God has not the right to demand an act, not susceptible of performance. These things are in reply to your answer to the case proposed. The second passage is in Matt. 23:37: "How often would I have gathered thy children together . . . and ye would not." From this passage Bellarmine, to prove that there is sufficient grace, thus argues, "If Christ did not desire that the Jews should be able to will, then he could not justly complain that they would not. But he did justly complain that they would not. Therefore he desired that they might be able to will. This reasoning is based on the supposition that no one can justly complain of any person who he has not performed an act, for the performance of which he had not sufficient strength." Your reply to that argument is twofold. The former part, which refers to the distinction of the will into that of good pleasure, and that of sign or revelation, has nothing whatever to do with the subject of the argument.

For Bellarmine does not say Christ wished to gather them according to his good pleasure, but he openly denies it, and affirms that he can sustain that position from the passage itself. For a gathering, which is made according to the will of good pleasure is not only sufficient but also efficacious. Let the gathering together here referred to, be according to the will, which is styled that of sign or revelation, and from it what Bellarmine deduced still follows.

For, in no mode of the will, does he wish to gather them unless he assists or is ready to assist, that they also, whom he wishes to gather, may be able to will. Thus it is a false assertion, that "God can, by the will of sign, will to gather the Jews together, though He may not aid them to be able to will." For the necessary consequences or effect of this will is sufficient aid, by which also the Jews themselves might be able to will. It is a contradiction in terms, though indirectly, to assert that "He wills to gather, and wills not to give sufficient aid by which the Jews may be able to will to be gathered, who cannot, except by their own will, be gathered." You add to this reply that which has also been said in reference to the first argument, and its repetition is unnecessary.

The latter part of your reply is, "Christ does not here speak as God, but as the minister of the circumcision." Granted. Then he wished to gather them together as the minister of the circumcision, and as a minister who had power to baptize with the Holy Ghost. Therefore, in that declaration of his will he showed that he either had given or was ready to give sufficient grace to them, without which they could not be gathered together. But in Isa 5, God Himself speaks, who is able efficaciously to soften and convert hearts, and says, "What could have been done more to my vineyard?" Who would reply, according to the meaning of your answer, "Thou mightest have softened their hearts and have converted them and it was suitable that thou shouldst do this. For thou art God, and speakest there as God." Therefore that distinction is absurd and not adapted to solve that objection. We see indeed on how weak foundations, that opinion rests, which cannot present other answers to meet those arguments.

The third argument is from Acts 7:51: "Ye do always resist the Holy Ghost." From this passage, Bellarmine argues in a twofold manner: First: "Those, in whom good desires are not inspired, cannot be said to resist

the Holy Spirit. But the Jews are said to have resisted. Therefore good desires were inspired in them, by which they could have been converted."
Secondly: "They, who cannot but resist, cannot be justly accused on account of their resistance. But the Jews were justly accused by Stephen.
Therefore they were able to resist."

Two syllogisms Deduced

From these two syllogisms can be deduced as a consequence: "They had
grace sufficient to enable them not to resist and even to yield to the Holy
Spirit." The latter argument is the stronger. Though something may be
said against the former, yet a small addition may also give to it strength
to withstand any opposition. Let us examine your reply. It seems to us
not at all pertinent and in part very ridiculous. For Bellarmine concedes
that this is not said of "the efficacious operation of the Spirit." For he
clearly distinguishes between sufficient and efficacious grace or operation. Indeed he does this very thing by quoting passages to show that
there must be a division of special grace into sufficient and efficacious.

"But this passage," (Acts 7:51), you say "refers to the external
ministration of the prophets." True, but that ministration was one by
which the Spirit chose to work; otherwise the man who opposed that
ministration could not be said to resist the Holy Ghost. These things are
coordinated and conjoined so far that the Spirit wills to work at least sufficiently through that ministration. The interpretation of Peter Lombard
is truly worthy of the parent of the Scholastic Theology, and unworthy of
an introduction to the light by you, without stern reprehension. I do not
add a refutation of it, because its perversity appears, on its very front, to
those who examine it.

The fourth passage, which you have made third in order, is from
Rev. 3:20: "Behold. I stand at the door and knock." On this Bellarmine
remarks: "He, who knocks at a door, knowing with certainty that there is
no one within who can open; he knocks in vain, and indeed is a foolish
person. Far from us be such an idea in reference to the Deity. Therefore
when God knocks, it is certain that the man can open, and consequently
he has sufficient grace." Your answer does not touch this argument of
Bellarmine, for he does not wish to infer the universality of grace but
that there is such a thing as sufficient grace, and this you do not, in your
answer, contradict.

Whether indeed that sufficient grace is universal that is, it is bestowed on all and each of mankind universally, is discussed in another place, by Bellarmine, whose defense, indeed, I have not undertaken and I am not desirous to do so. Yet it is necessary to love the truth, by whatever person it may be spoken.

The tenth error: This, in your estimation, is that "the hypothesis, which you oppose, is at variance with itself." This is indeed a valid mode of confutation. But how do you prove the liability of that theory to the charge of self contradiction? You very injuriously charge it with the opinion that "God determined to bestow all natural and gracious aids upon all men." Who can hold such an opinion, when he acknowledges that there is an "efficacious grace which God does not impart to all?"

Indeed you are not consistent with yourself in the statement of their doctrine. For you say that it affirms that "God bestows all aids upon all men," and afterwards say that it asserts: "God does grant to all not actual perseverance, but the ability to persevere or to will to persevere." Is not the gift of actual perseverance one among all aids? How shall both these assertions be made without contradiction? Correct your error, and when you have corrected it, you will see that you ought to have made the remark "without which no one actually obtains salvation," as explanatory of efficacious grace.

Yet God is not wanting to those to whom He gives the grace, by which they can be saved, though He may not give the grace by which they will actually be saved. Those words "by persevering, to obtain salvation," should have been arranged thus "to persevere and obtain salvation." You erroneously confound act with ability and efficacy with sufficiency.

The eleventh error: In this, you allege against this doctrine that "it introduces heresies long condemned," namely, those of the Pelagians.

This assertion you indeed afterwards seem to soften down, because the Pelagians attribute the faculty of doing well either wholly to nature, or only in part to grace, while the doctrine attributes it wholly to grace. You however, find fault with it because "it makes grace universal, and thus involves itself in yet greater difficulty." Something has been heretofore said on this point. Yet of what weight is your refutation? For what if any one should say that all men universally have the power of believing and obtaining salvation, if they will, and that this very power is bestowed divinely upon the nature of mankind? By what argument will you disprove the assertion? It does not follow from this statement that nature and grace have an equally wide extent.

For the ability to believe pertains to nature, actual belief is of grace. So with the ability to will and actual volition, "It is God, which worketh in you," etc. (Phil 2:13). "For unto you it is given on behalf of Christ . . . to believe on him" (Phil 1:29). You seem to do injury to the truth, when you say that it is a Pelagian idea that "a man can, by the opposition of his will, resist grace." There is no page in Scripture, where this is denied. Is a man a mere log that, by pure necessity of nature, he must yield to grace? If this is not true, then a man consents freely and therefore has the ability not to consent, that is, to resist. Otherwise to what purpose are threats and promises? The opinion that "a man has ability in the exercise of the will, to yield to the grace of God, when explained to refer to remote ability, and which may, otherwise, be called capacity to receive active and immediate ability, by which any one can will to yield to grace," is not Pelagian.

Dogma of Predestination

I wish that who now holds the dogma of Predestination, might prove that it does not introduce by fair inference the idea of "fatal necessity." You say also that the "Catholics" formerly held these views. The fact that a similar crime is charged on both does not prove a similarity in other respects. It is possible that they whom you oppose may differ from the Papists, and that the latter defend a doctrine obnoxious to your objections.

The last error: You affirm that "this doctrine is in harmony with the Popish view of Predestination." If that should be conceded, is the doctrine therefore false? You indeed present a statement of it but do not refute it. You think that it is so absurd that it may be sufficient to have presented it that the statement itself will be a sufficient refutation. But, if someone should undertake to defend that doctrine, how would you refute it? We may make the attempt, "God foresaw from eternity the natures and the sins of men; this foresight preceded the decree by which he gave Christ to be the Savior of the world." I should say: "The foresight of most sins," for He did not foresee the sin of the crucifixion of Christ, until after that decree was made.

You have given a careless statement of that doctrine, as you have not made that necessary distinction. Then God decreed "to give, for the sake of Christ, sufficient grace, by which men might be saved." To all? The Papists do not assert this. Then, "He predestinated to life those whom He foresaw would finish their life in the state of grace, which was prepared for them by the Predestination of God;" this is indeed not very far from the doctrine of Augustine.

Your theory is "God did not reveal Christ for all and each of mankind." This theorem is not of much service to you in proving the particularity of Predestination and of grace, since those with whom you contend, even on the supposition of its truth, meet you with a twofold argument. First: the reason that God did not reveal Christ to all and to each of mankind was the fact that their parents rejected the word of the gospel. On which account He permitted both the parents and their posterity to go on in their own ways, and this, for so long a time, as the divine justice and their sins seemed to demand.

The second argument is, that in the meantime, while they were destitute of the knowledge of Christ, God "left not himself without witness" (Acts 14:17). But even then revealed to them some truth concerning His power and goodness, and the law also, which He kept inscribed on their minds. If they had made a right use of those blessings, even according to their own conscience, He would have bestowed upon them greater grace, according to that declaration, "to him that hath shall be given." But by abusing, or not using, those blessings they made themselves unworthy even of the mercy of God, and therefore were without excuse. Not having the law, they were condemned, their own thoughts accusing them (Rom 2:14, 15).

But that God concealed the promise of the Messiah from any man before that, rejection cannot be proved from the Scriptures. Indeed, the contrary can be proved from those things narrated of Adam and his posterity, and of Noah and his children in the Scriptures. The defection from the right way gradually progressed, and God is not bound at any particular time to send a new revelation to men who do not rightly use the revelation they already have.

From this, it is manifest what judgment must be passed on those deductions. To the first: The reason that the promise of the blessed seed was not revealed to all men is both the fault of their parents in rejecting it, and of themselves in holding the truth, which they now have, in unrighteousness.

To the second: The answer is the same.

To the third: All men are called by some vocation, namely, by that witness of God, by which they may be led to feel after God that they may find him (Acts 17:27). Also, by that truth, which they hold in unrighteousness, that is whose effect in themselves they hinder; and by that inscription of the law on their hearts, according to which their thoughts accuse one another. But this vocation, although it is not saving in the sense that salvation can be obtained immediately from it, yet it may be said to be antecedently saving, as Christ is offered for them. Salvation will, of the divine mercy, follow that vocation if it is rightly used.

To the fourth: It is stated that no one has said that "the prescience of faith or unbelief is the rule of Predestination," and this charge is futile. But that some may be condemned by the law alone is most true, and on account of their impenitence, though not on account of their rejection of Christ, if they had not heard the Gospel message.

6

A Defense Against Several Theological Articles
Extensively Distributed

These articles accuse both James Arminius and Adrian Borrius, a minister of Leyden, of novelty and heterodoxy, error and heresy on the subject of religion.

CERTAIN ARTICLES RELATING TO the Christian Religion are now in a course of circulation. In a paper recently delivered into my hands, the number of them is distinguished into two series, one consisting of twenty articles and the other of eleven. Some of them are attributed to me, others to Adrian Borrius, and several both to him and me.

Those persons by whom they were first disseminated, attempt in them to render us suspected of having introduced into the Church and the University of Leyden novelties and heretical instructions, and to accuse us of error and heresy—that both the students of Divinity and the common people may stand on their guard against us, who have this black mark imprinted on us, lest they become infected with the same envenomed disorder. And that those persons who enjoy the supremacy both in Church and State, may seasonably interpose their authority to prevent the evil from extending any further, or rather to extinguish it in its very commencement. If they neglect to do, "they will be instrumental in producing the greatest detriment to Divine Truth, and to the Political and Ecclesiastical concord of these Provinces."

The dispersion of some of these articles is not a very recent circumstance. For, above two years ago, seventeen out of these thirty-one came into my hands, expressed exactly in the same words as those that occur in the writing that is the subject of my present remarks. But I was silent and concealed my regret; for I thought, that those articles would in their very infancy die a natural death, since part of them were destitute of the truth of historical narration, by not being attributed to those who had been the authors of them; and part of them were void of all real theological sense, by the strange intermixture of truth and falsehood. But the issue did not answer my expectation. For they not only remained without diminution, but gained an increase, by the addition of another fourteen to the former seventeen Articles, and by a far wider dispersion of the whole than had at first been made.

This unexpected result had the effect of inducing me to think, that I ought to oppose their progress by a moderate answer, lest my continued silence should be interpreted as tantamount to a confession. If this is the interpretation which on many occasions is given to silence, it is an easy matter thus to construe it respecting any doctrine aspersed as a heresy, "under which imputation," it is said in a vaunting tone, "St. Jerome would have no man to remain patient." In this reply I will use candor and conscience. Whatever I know to be true, I will confess and defend: On whatever subjects I may feel any hesitation; I will not conceal my ignorance. And whatever my mind dictates to be false, I will deny and refute. May the God of truth and peace direct my mind and my hand by his Holy Spirit! Amen.[1]

Faith, that is justifying faith, is not peculiar to the elect. It is possible for believers finally to decline and fall from faith and salvation.

Answer: The connection between these two articles is so intimate, that when the first of them is granted, the second is necessarily inferred. In return, when the latter is granted the former is to be inferred, according to the intention of those persons who framed these articles. For if "faith be not peculiar to the elect," and if perseverance in faith and salvation belong to the elect alone, it follows, that believers not only can, but that some of them actually do, "fall away from faith and salvation."

And, on the contrary, if it be "possible for believers finally to fall away from faith and salvation," it follows that "faith is not peculiar to the elect," they being the individuals concerning whom the framers of these articles assert, that it is impossible for them not to be saved. The reason of the consequence, is, because the words *faith* and *believers*, according

---

1. This chapter addresses several of these accusations received by Arminius. The alleged statements are in italics, followed by Arminius' reply.

to this hypothesis, have a wider signification than the words *election* and *the elect*. The former comprehend some persons that are not elect, that is, "some who finally fall away from faith and salvation." No necessity therefore existed for composing both these articles.

It was quite sufficient to have proposed one. And if the authors of them had sought for such amplification, as had no real existence, but consisted of mere words, it was possible to deduce the second from the first in the form of a consectary [that which logically follows]. Thus it is evident, that the multitude of the articles was the great object to be attempted for the purpose of making it appear as if those persons erred in very many points, whom the too sedulous curiosity of the brethren is desirous, without cause, of rendering suspected of heresy.

I. But, to treat each article singly, I declare, respecting the first, that I never said either in public or in private, "Faith is not peculiar to the Elect." This article therefore is not attributed to its proper author; and thus is committed a historical error.

I add, Even if I had made such a declaration as this, a defense of it would have been ready. For I omit the scriptures, from which a more prolix discussion of this subject might be formed. And since the Christian Fathers have with great semblance of truth defended their sentiments from that Divine source, I might employ the consent of those Fathers as a shield to ward off from myself the charge of novelty. And the Harmony of Confessions, severally the composition of those Churches that have seceded from Popery and come under the denomination of "Protestants" and "the Reformed," I might adopt for a polished breast plate, to intercept or turn aside the dart of heresy that is hurled against me. Neither should I be much afraid of this subject being placed for adjudication in the balances of the Belgic Confession and the Heidelberg Catechism.

1. Let St. Augustine, Prosper, and the author of the books, *The Vocation of the Gentiles*,[2] be brought forward to bear testimony respecting "the Consent of the Fathers."

(a.) Augustine says, " It is wonderful, and indeed most wonderful, that God does not bestow perseverance on certain of his sons, whom He has regenerated in Christ, and to whom he has given faith, hope and love;

---

2. This two-book set, a polemic against Pelagianism, was authored anonymously by one or more Catholic theologians—editor.

while he pardons such great acts of wickedness in sons that are alienated from him, and, by imparting his grace, makes them his children."[3]

(b.) Prosper says, "It is a lamentable circumstance which is proved by many examples, that some of those persons who were regenerated in Christ Jesus, have relinquished the faith, and, ceasing to preserve their former sanctity of manners, have apostatized from God, and their ungodly course has been terminated under, his displeasure and aversion."[4]

(c.) The author of *The Vocation of the Gentiles* says, "God bestows the power of willing to obey him, in such a manner as not to take away, even from those who will persevere, that mutability by which it is possible for them to be unwilling [to obey God]. If this were not the case, none of the believers would have departed from the faith."[5]

2. *The Harmony of Confessions*[6] might in the following manner contribute to my defense: This dogma states, that "faith is the peculiar property of the elect," and that "it is impossible for believers finally to decline from faith and salvation." Now, if this be a dogma necessary to salvation, then that Confession which does not contain it, or which asserts something contradictory to it, cannot be considered as harmonizing with the rest on the subject of religion. For wherever there is harmony, it is proper that there should be neither defect nor contradiction in things pertaining to salvation. But the Augustinian [or Lutheran] Confession says, that "it condemns the Anabaptists, who deny that those persons who have once been justified can again lose the Holy Spirit." Besides, Philip Melancthon with his followers, and the greater portion of the Lutheran Churches, are of opinion, that "faith is bestowed even on the non-elect." Yet we are not afraid of acknowledging these Lutherans for brethren.

3. The Belgic Confession does not contain this dogma [that "faith is peculiar to the elect"]; and without controversy, it cannot be deduced from our catechism. For when it is said, in the article on the Church, "I believe that I shall perpetually remain a member of the Church" and, in the first question, "God keeps and preserves me in such a manner, as to make all things necessarily subservient to my salvation," those ex-

3. St. Augustine, *De Corrept. et Gratia*, Cap. 8.

4. Prosper, *Ad Capita Gal. Resp. 7*.

5. Lib. 2, Cap. 9.

6. Jean Francois Salvard, ed., *Harmonia Confessionum Fidei, Orthodoxarum, & Reformatarum Ecclesiarum*. This was an early work of comparative dogmatics in defense of Protestant theology.

pressions are to be understood of a believer, in reference to his actual believing. For he who is truly such a one, answers to the character of a Christian. But no man is such, except through faith. Faith is therefore presupposed in both the expressions.

II. With regard to the Second Article, I say, that a distinction ought to be made between power and action. For it is one thing to declare, "it is possible for the faithful to fall a way from faith and salvation," and it is another to say, that "they do actually fall away." This distinction is of such extensive observance, that even antiquity itself was not afraid of affirming, concerning the elect and those who were to be saved, "that it was possible for them not to be saved," and that "the mutability by which it was possible for them not to be willing to obey God, was not taken away from them." However, this was the opinion of the ancients, "that such persons never would in reality be damned." On this very subject, too, the greater part of our own doctors lay down a difference. For they say, "that it is possible for such persons to fall away, if their nature, which is inclined to lapses and defection, and if the temptations of the world and Satan, be the only circumstances taken into consideration: but that they will not finally fall away, because God will bring back to himself his own elect before the end of life."

If anyone asserts, "that it is not possible for believers, in consideration of their being elect persons, finally to fall away from salvation, because God has decreed to save them," I answer, the decree concerning saving does not take away the possibility of damning, but it removes damnation itself. For "to be actually saved," and "a possibility of not being saved," are two things not contrary to each other, but in perfect agreement.

I therefore add that in this way I have hitherto discriminated these two cases: And at one time I certainly did say, with an explanation subjoined to it, "that it was *possible* for believers finally to decline or fall away from faith and salvation." But at no period have I asserted, "that believers *do* finally decline or fall away from faith or salvation." This article therefore is ascribed to one who is not its author; and it is another offence against historical veracity.

I subjoin, that there is a vast difference between the enunciation of these two sentences:

1. "It is possible for believers to decline from the *faith*;" and 2. "It is possible for believers to decline from *salvation*." For the latter, when

rigidly and accurately examined, can scarcely be admitted, it being impossible for believers, as long as they remain believers, to decline from salvation. Because, were this possible, that power of God would be conquered which he has determined to employ in saving believers. On the other hand, if believers fall away from the faith and become unbelievers, it is impossible for them to do otherwise than decline from salvation, that is, provided they still continue as unbelievers. Therefore, whether this hypothesis is granted or not, the enunciation cannot be accurately expressed. For if this hypothesis (their perseverance in faith) be granted, they cannot decline; but if it be not granted, they cannot do otherwise than decline.

But that first enunciation includes no hypothesis; and therefore an answer may be given to it simply, either that it is possible, or that it is impossible. For this cause, the second article ought to be corrected in the following manner: "It is possible for believers finally to fall away or decline from the faith;" or rather, "Some believers finally fall away and decline from the faith." This being granted, the other can be necessarily inferred,—"therefore they also actually decline from salvation."

Respecting the truth of this article, I repeat the same observations which I made about the First. For the following expressions are reciprocal to each other, and regular consequences: "Faith is peculiar to the elect," and "Believers do not finally fall away from the faith." In like manner, "Faith is not peculiar to the elect," and "Some believers finally decline from the faith."

It is a matter of doubt, whether the faith by which Abraham is said to be justified, was a faith in Jesus Christ who was still to come. No proof can be adduced of his having understood the promises of God in any other manner, than that he should be the heir of the world.

Answer: There are two members in this article, or rather, those members are two distinct articles, each of which presents itself to be separately considered by us. I have observed that in this passage no affirmation or negation, each of which properly constitutes a heretic, is attributed to us. But it is a mere doubt alone, that betokens a consciousness of ignorance and infirmity, which those who arrogate to themselves the knowledge of all these things, ought to endeavor to remove by a mild course of instruction, and not to make it a subject of reviling or provocation.

I. To the first member I reply:

First: I never uttered this expression, but have, on more occasions than one, taught both in public and private a contrary doctrine. Yet I remember, when a certain minister at Leyden had boasted of the clearness of this article and was astonished how any persons could be found who entertained a different opinion about it I told him that the proof of it would not be a very easy occupation to him if he had to encounter a powerful adversary. And I challenged him to make a trial, which challenge I now repeat. I wish him to prove this assertion by such plain arguments, as will not leave a man just reasons for doubting any longer about the matter. This is a point on, which the labors of a divine will be more profitably expended, than on publishing and magnifying the doubts of the infirm, whose confidence in themselves is not equal to that which he manifests.

Secondly: "Faith in Christ" may be received in two acceptations: Either according to promise, which was involved in the types, figures and shadows of words and things, and proposed in that manner. Or, it is according to the gospel, that is clearly manifested. The difference between these two is so great, that with regard to it the Jews are said "to have been detained or kept under the law before faith came, concluded or shut up unto that faith which should afterwards be revealed" (Gal 3:23). And the Apostle says, "the children of Israel were prevented, by the veil placed over the countenance of Moses, from steadfastly looking to the end of that which is abolished" (2 Cor 3:13), that is, to the end of the law, as is evident from the whole chapter, and from Rom 10:5, where Christ is said to be "the end of the law for righteousness to everyone that believeth." Let the whole description of the faith of Abraham, which the Apostle gives at great length in Rom 4 be attentively considered, and it will appear, that no express mention of Jesus Christ is made in it. But it is implied in such a way as it is not easy for anyone to explain.

Let it be added that faith in Jesus Christ seems to some persons to be used by metonymy, for "that faith which is concerning the types and figures which adumbrate and prefigure Jesus Christ," although it has not united with it an understanding of those types, unless it be a very obscure one, and such as appears suitable to the infant Church, according to the economy of the times and ages which God in his wisdom employs. Let a comparison be instituted between that servitude under which the heir, so long as he is a child, is said by the Apostle to be held (Gal 4:1–3), and that bondage from which the Spirit of the Lord is declared to liberate the man whose heart is converted to Him (2 Cor 3:16–18). This doubting will then be considered ascribable to the proper fear of a trembling [scrupulous] conscience, rather than to a disposition that has a powerful propensity towards heresy.

II. To the Second Member of this Article I answer:

First, I never made such an assertion.

Secondly, even if I had, it would not have called for any deserved reprehension, except from a man that was desirous by that very act to betray at once the weakness of his judgment and his want of experience 1. It is a sign of a judgment not the most accurate, to blame any man for saying that which it is possible to prove has been written by the Apostle himself in so many words. For if the heir-ship of the world was promised to Abraham in these words, "Thou shalt be the father of many nations," what wonder is there if Abraham understood the promises in no other manner than as they had been divinely pronounced? 2. It is a mark of great inexperience in the men who framed these articles, to suppose that the heir-ship of the world promised to Abraham, appertained to this animal life and to carnal benefits; because the world of which mention is made in that passage is that future world to which belongs the calling of the Gentiles, by which vocation Abraham was made the father of many nations.

This is apparent from the consideration, that he is said to have been made the heir of the world by the righteousness of faith, of which the Apostle Paul (Rom 4:13) proves the Gentiles likewise to be partakers; and in Eph 3:1–11, the Apostle addresses the vocation of the Gentiles, and says, it belongs to "the grace of the gospel, and to the fellowship of the mystery which from the beginning of the world hath been hidden in God and is now brought to light by Christ, by whom God created all things." I repeat it, that vocation does not belong to the wisdom by which God formed the world, but to that by which he constituted Christ *His* wisdom and power to salvation to them that believe; and by which he founded the Church, which will endure forever. See 1 Cor 1:21–23; 2:6–8; Eph 3:1–11. If the forgers of this article say, "that they have likewise perceived this, but had supposed that my opinion was different," I reply, it is not the part of a prudent man to frame a foolish adversary for himself.

Faith is not an effect of election, but is a necessary prerequisite foreseen by God in those who are to be elected: And the decree concerning the bestowing of faith precedes the decree of election.

Answer: Of this article also there are two entire members:

I. In the first of them, three assertions are included: 1. "Faith is not an effect of election." 2. "Faith is a necessary prerequisite in those who are to be elected or saved." 3. "This prerequisite is foreseen by God in the persons to be elected."—I confess, all these, when rightly understood and correctly explained, agree entirely with my opinion, on the subject. But the last of the members is proposed in terms too odious, since it makes no mention of God, whose benefit and gift I acknowledge faith to be.

I will now proceed to explain myself on each of these assertions:

With regard to the first, the word "election" is ambiguous. For it either signifies "the election by which God determines to justify believers, while those who are unbelievers or workers are rejected from righteousness and salvation." Or it signifies "the election by which he determines to save certain particular persons, as such, and to bestow faith on them in order to their salvation, other particular persons being also rejected, merely in reference to their being such particular individuals." Election is received according to this latter signification, by those who charge me with these articles. I take it in the former acceptation, according to Rom 9:11: "For the children being not yet born, neither having done any good or evil, that the purpose of God according to election might stand, not of works, but of Him that calleth. It was said unto her, The elder shall serve the younger."

I will not now enter in to a prolix disputation, whether or not the sense in which I receive it, be the correct one. It is evident, at least, that there is some decree of God by which he determines to justify believers; and which, since it excludes unbelievers from righteousness and salvation, is appropriately called "the decree according to election" or "with election," as being that which does not include all men within its embrace. This decree I consider as the foundation of' Christianity, of man's salvation, and of his assurance of salvation. And it is this of which the Apostle treats in Rom 8 to 9 and Eph 1.

But I have not yet declared what my sentiments in general are about that decree by which God is said "to have determined absolutely to save certain particular persons, and to bestow faith upon them in order to their salvation, while others are reprobated from salvation and faith." I have confessed, though, that there is a certain decree of God, according to which he determines to administer the means to faith and salvation, as he knows them to be suitable and proper to his righteousness, mercy and severity. From these premises it is deduced as a most manifest consequence, that faith is not an effect of that election by which God determines to justify those who believe.

With regard to the second assertion, from the particulars thus explained it is concluded, that "faith is a necessary prerequisite in those who shall be partakers of salvation according to the election of God;" or, that "it is a condition prescribed and required by God, to be performed by those who shall obtain his salvation." And: "This is the will of God, that whosoever believeth in the Son hath eternal life; he that believeth not, shall be condemned." The propositions contained in this passage cannot be resolved into any other than this brief one, which is likewise used in the Scripture, "Believe on the Lord Jesus Christ and thou shalt be saved" (Acts 16:31). The word " believe" has the force of a demand or requirement; and the phrase "thou shalt be saved" has that of a persuasion, by means of a good that is promised. This truth is so clear and perspicuous, that the denial of it would be a proof of great perversity or of extreme unskilfulness. If anyone says, "It is a condition, but yet an evangelical" one, which God may himself perform in us, or (as it is better expressed) which He may by his grace cause us to perform" the man who speaks thus, does not contradict this truth, but confirms it when he adds this explanation, "of what description soever that condition may be."

With regard to the third, I say, that we must distinguish between the condition by which it is *required*, that by which it is *performed*, and that by which it is *seen* or *foreseen* as performed. This third member therefore is proposed in a manner much too confused. Yet when this confusion is corrected by the distinction which we have stated, nothing of absurdity will be apparent even in that member. Because foreseeing or seeing, in the very nature and order of things, follows the performance itself. The performance has its own causes into which it is to be resolved; and the efficiency of those causes is not necessary, unless faith be prescribed and required by the law of faith and the gospel.

Since therefore faith is said "to be foreseen by God in those who are to be saved," those causes, without the intervention of which there could be no faith, are not removed but are rather appointed. Among those causes I consider the preventing, accompanying and succeeding [subsequent] grace of God, as the principal: And I say, with Fulgentius, "Those persons will be saved," or "they have been predestined and elected, who, God foreknew, would believe by the assistance of his preventing [prevenient] grace (I add, and of his accompanying grace), and would persevere by the "aid of his subsequent grace." In this first member, then, there is nothing except truth of the greatest purity.

II. The second member is, "The decree concerning the gift of faith, precedes the decree of election" in the explanation of which I employ the same distinction as in the former, and say: The decree of election, by which God determines to justify and save believers, precedes the decree concerning the bestowment of faith. For faith is unnecessary, nay it is useless, without this previous decree. And the decree of election, by which God resolves to justify and save this or that particular person, is subsequent to that decree according to which He determines to administer the means necessary and efficacious to faith, that is, the decree concerning the gift of faith.

If anyone says, "God wills first absolutely to save some particular person; and, since he wills that, he also wills to bestow faith on him, because without faith it is not possible for him to be saved," I tell him, that he lays down contradictory propositions that God wills absolutely to save someone without regard to faith, and yet that, according to the will of God, he cannot be saved without faith. Through the will of God it has been revealed to us: Without faith it is impossible for any man to please God, or to be saved. There is therefore in God no other will, by which he wills anyone to be absolutely saved without consideration of faith. For contradictory wills cannot be attributed to God.

God Wills the End

If any person replies, "God wills the end, before he wills the means leading to the end; but salvation is the end, and faith the means leading to the end," I answer, first, salvation is not the end of God; but salvation and faith are the gifts of God, bound and connected together in this order between themselves through the will of God, that faith should precede salvation, both with regard to God, the donor of it, and in reality.

Secondly, faith is a condition required by God to be performed by him who shall be saved, before it is a means of obtaining that salvation.

Since God will not bestow salvation on anyone, except on him who believes, man is on this account incited to be willing to believe because he knows that his chief good is placed in salvation. Man therefore tries, by faith as the means, to attain to salvation as the end, because he knows that he cannot possibly obtain salvation except through that means. And this knowledge he does not acquire, except through the declaration of the Divine Will, by which God requires faith from those who wish to be saved, that is, by which he places faith as a condition in the object, that is, in the person to be saved.

Things contingent cannot be said to be done in respect to the Divine decree.

Answer: My opinion concerning Necessity and Contingency is, that they can never be applicable at once to one and the same event. But I speak of the necessity and contingency that are both of the same kind, not those which are different in their genus. The Schoolmen state, that there is one necessitas consequentis [an absolute necessity], and another necessitas consequentiae [a hypothetical necessity]. The former is, when the necessity arises from a cause antecedent to the thing itself. But necessitas consequentiae [a hypothetical necessity] arises from certain premises [or principles] antecedent to the conclusion.

A consequent [or absolute] contingency cannot consist with a consequent [or absolute] necessity, nor can they meet together in one event. In the same manner, one conclusion cannot be both necessary and contingent in regard to its consequence [that is, it cannot have at the same time a necessity and a contingency that are hypothetical]. But the cause why one thing cannot be necessary and contingent at the same time is this: that what is necessary and what is contingent divide the whole amplitude of being. For every being is either necessary or contingent. But those things that divide the whole of being, cannot coincide or meet together in any single being. Otherwise they would not divide the whole range of being. What is contingent and what is necessary, likewise differ in their entire essences and in the whole of their definition. For that is necessary which cannot possibly not be or not be done [or in the old English way, which cannot but be or be done].

And that is contingent which is *possible* not to be or to be done. Thus contradictorily are they opposed to each other; and this opposition is infinite and therefore always dividing truth from falsehood. As, "this thing is either a man or not a man," it is not possible for anything to be both of these at once, that is, it is impossible for anything of one essence. Otherwise [in another sense] "Christ is a man," as proceeding from his mother Mary. "He is not a man," in reference to his having been begotten of the Father from all eternity; but these are two things and two natures.

But they say, "It is possible for one and the same event to be necessary and contingent in different respects, necessary with regard to the First Cause, which is God, and contingent in respect to second causes." I answer, first, those things that differ in their entire essences, do not coincide in respects. Secondly, the necessity or contingency of an event is to be estimated, not from one cause, but from all the causes united together. For after ten causes have been fixed, from which a thing is produced, not necessarily, but contingently if one be added from which the thing may be necessarily completed, the whole of that thing is said to have been done not contingently but necessarily. Because when all these causes were together appointed, it was impossible for that thing to hinder itself from being produced and from being brought into existence.

That thing, I confess indeed, when distinctly compared by our mind with each of its causes, has a different relation to them respectively. But since none of those causes is the total cause of that event, and since all of them united together form the total cause, the thing ought itself to be accounted and declared to have been done from that total cause, either necessarily or contingently.

It is not only a rash saying, but a false and an ignorant one, "that a thing which in regard to second causes is done contingently is said to be done necessarily in regard to the Divine decree." For the Divine decree itself, being an internal action of God, is not immediately the cause of the thing; but, whatever effects it may produce, it performs them by power, according to the mode of which a thing will be said to be either necessary or contingent. For if God resolves to use an irresistible power in the execution of his Decree, or if He determines to employ such a quantum of power as nothing can resist or can hinder it from completing his purpose, it will follow that the thing will necessarily be brought into existence: Thus, "Wicked men, who persevere in their sins, will necessarily perish" for God will by an irresistible force cast them down into the depths of hell. But if he resolves to use a force that is not irresistible, but that can be resisted by the creature, then that thing is said to be done, not necessarily, but contingently, although its actual occurrence was certainly foreknown by God, according to the infinity of his understanding, by which He knows all results whatever, that will arise from certain causes laid down and whether those causes produce a thing necessarily or contingently.

From whence the Schoolmen say, "all things are done by a necessity of infallibility," which phrase is used in a determinate sense, although the words in which its enunciation is expressed are ill-chosen. For infallibility is not an affection of a being, which exists from causes; but it is an affection of a mind that sees or that foresees from what causes it will transpire. But I readily endure a catachrestic metalepsis [an improper expression], when it is evident concerning a thing, although it is my wish that our enunciations were always the best-accommodated to the natures of the things themselves.

But the inventors of these articles try to prove by the examples they produce, that "one and the same thing, which with respect to second causes is done contingently, is in respect to the Divine Decree done necessarily."

Bones of Christ

They say, "It was possible for the bones of Christ to be broken, or not to be broken. It was possible for them to be broken, if any person considers the nature of bones; for they were undoubtedly fragile. But they could not be broken, if the decree of God be taken into the account." In answer to this, I deny that in respect of the Divine Decree they could not be broken. For God did not decree, that it was *impossible* for them to be broken, but that they *should* not be broken. This is apparent from the manner in which the transaction was actually conducted. For God did not employ an irresistible power by which he might prevent the bones of Christ from being broken by those who approached to break them; but by a mild kind of persuasion he caused that they should not will to break the bones of Christ, by an argument drawn from its inutility. For since Christ had already given up the ghost, before those who broke the legs had arrived at the cross, they were not at all inclined to undertake a vain and fruitless labor in breaking the legs of our Savior.

Because the breaking of legs, with a design to hasten death, was only done lest the bodies should remain suspended on the cross on a festival or sacred day, contrary to the Divine law. Indeed if the Divine Wisdom knows how to effect that which it has decreed, by employing causes according to their nature and motion, whether their nature and motion be contingent or free, the praise due to such Wisdom is far greater than if it employ a power which no creature can possibly resist. Although God can employ such a power whensoever it may seem expedient to his Wisdom, I am therefore of the opinion, that I committed no offence when I said, "No contingent thing, that is, nothing which is done or has been done *contingently*, can be said to be or to have been done with regard to the Divine decree."

All things are done contingently.

Answer: This article is expressed in such a stupid and senseless manner, that they who attribute it to me, declare by this very circumstance, that they do not perceive under how many falsities this expression labors. Nay, they do not understand the meaning of the words they employ. For if that is said to be done contingently which it is possible *not to do* [or which may not be done] after all the causes required for i.e. being done have been fixed; and, on the other hand, if that is said to be done necessarily which cannot be left undone, [which cannot *but* be done] after all the causes required for its performance have been fixed, and if I grant, that, after some causes have been fixed, it is impossible for any other event to ensue—than that the thing shall be done and exist,— how then can I be of the opinion, that "all things are done [or happen] contingently"? But they have deceived themselves by their own ignorance, from which it would be possible for them to be liberated, if they would bestow a becoming and proper attention on sentiments that are more correct, and would in a friendly manner obtain from the author a knowledge of his views and opinions.

I have declared and taught, that "necessity, in reference to its being said to be or to happen necessarily, is either absolute or relative." It is an absolute necessity, in relation to a thing being said simply "to be or to happen necessarily," without any regard being had to the supposition [or laying down] of any cause whatever. It is a relative necessity, when a thing is said "to be or to happen necessarily," after some cause had been laid down or fixed. Thus, God exists by an absolute necessity; and by the same absolute necessity, he both understands and loves himself. But the world and all things produced from it, are, according to an absolute consideration, contingent, and are produced contingently by God freely operating.

But it being granted that God wills to form the world by his Infinite Power, to which *nothing itself* must be equal to matter in the most perfect state of preparation, and it being likewise granted, that God actually employs this power, it will then be said, "It was impossible for the world to do otherwise than exist from this cause." [or, "From this cause the world could not but exist."] And this is a relative necessity, so called from the hypothesis of an antecedent cause being laid down or fixed.

I will explain my meaning in a different manner: Two things in this place come under our consideration—the cause and the effect. If both of them are necessarily fixed, that is, if not only the effect is fixed necessarily when the cause is fixed, but if the cause also necessarily exists and is necessarily supposed to operate, the necessity of the effect is in that case simple and absolute. In this manner arises the absolute necessity of the Divine effect, by which God is said to know and love himself; for the Divine understanding and the Divine Will cannot be inoperative [cannot but operate]. This operation of God is not only an internal one, but it is also *ad intra* [inwards], tending towards an object, which is himself.

But whatever God may do *ad extra* [externally], that is, when acting on an object which is something beside himself [or, something different from himself]—whether this object is united to him in understanding and he tends towards it by an internal act, or whether it is in reality separated from him and towards which he tends by an external act— the whole of this he does freely. The whole of it is therefore said to be absolutely contingent. Thus God freely decreed to form the world, and did freely form it. And, in this sense, all things are done contingently in respect to the Divine decree; because no necessity exists why the decree of God should be appointed, since it proceeds from his own pure and free [or unconstrained] Will.

Simple and Absolute

Or, to express it in another form: That is called the simple and absolute necessity of any effect, "when the cause necessarily exists, necessarily operates, and employs that power through which it is impossible jar the thing not to exist," [or through which it cannot but exist]. In the nature of things, such an effect as this cannot be contemplated. For the intellect of the Deity, by which he understands himself, proceeds from a cause that necessarily exists and that necessarily understands itself. But it does not proceed from a cause that employs a power of action for such an understanding.

Under this consideration, the relative necessity of any event is two-fold:—*First*: When a cause that necessarily exists, but does not necessarily operate, uses a power of action that cannot be resisted. Thus, it being fixed, that "God, who is a Necessary Being, wills to create a world by his Omnipotence," a world must in that case necessarily come into existence. *Secondly*: When a cause that does not necessarily exist and yet necessarily operates, acts with such efficacy as is impossible to be resisted by the matter or subject on which it operates. Thus, straw is said to be necessarily burnt [or consumed] by the fire, if it is cast into the flame. It is impossible either for the fire to restrain its power of burning so as not actually to burn, or for the straw to resist the fire. But because God can prevent the fire from burning any combustible matter that is brought near it or put into it, this kind of necessity is called partial in respect to the cause, and only according to the nature of the things themselves and the mutual affection [or relation] between them.

When these matters have been thus explained, I could wish to see what can possibly be said in opposition. I am desirous, that we should in preference contend for the necessity of God alone, that is, for his necessary existence and for the necessary production of his ad infra [internal] acts, and that we should contend for the contingency of all other things and effects. Such a procedure on our part would conduce far more to the glory of God, to whom by this method would be attributed both the glory of his necessary existence, that is, of his eternity, according to which it is a pure act without [the exercise of] power,—and the glory of his free creation of all other things, by which also his Goodness becomes a supreme object of our commendation.

God has not by his eternal decree determined future and contingent things to the one part or the other.

Answer: A calumny that lies concealed under ambiguous terms is capable of inflicting a deep injury with the greatest security; but after such equivocal expressions are explained, the slander is exposed, and loses all its force among men of skill and experience.

The word "determined" is of this ambiguous description: For it signifies, first, "the determination of God by which he resolves that something shall be done; and when such a determination is fixed (by an action, motion and impulse of God, of whatever kind it may be), the second cause, both with regard to its power and the use of that power, remains free either to act or not to act, so that, if it is the pleasure of this second cause, it can suspend [or defer] its own action." Or it signifies, "Such a determination, as, when once it is fixed, the second cause (at least in regard to the use of its power), remains no longer free so as to be able to suspend its own action, when God's action, motion and impulse have been fixed. But by this determination, it [the second cause] is necessarily bent or inclined to one course or the other, all indifference to either part being completely removed, before this determined act is produced by a free and unconstrained creature."

1. If the word "determined," in the Article here proposed, is interpreted according to this first method, far be it from me to deny such a sort of Divine determination. For I am aware that it is said, in Acts 4:27–28 that "both Herod, and Pontius Pilate, with the Gentiles and the people of Israel, were gathered together," against Jesus "to do whatsoever thy hand and thy counsel determined before (or previously appointed) to be done." But I also know, that Herod, Pontius Pilate, and the Jews, freely performed those very actions; and (notwithstanding this "foredetermination of God," and though by his power every Divine action, motion and impulse which was necessary for the execution of this "foredetermination," were all fixed). Yet it was possible for this act (the crucifixion of Christ), which had been "previously appointed" by God, not to be produced by those persons, and they might have remained free and indifferent to the performance of this action, up to the moment of time they perpetrated the deed. Let the narrative of the passion of our Lord be perused, and let it be observed how the whole matter was conducted, by what arguments Herod, Pontius Pilate and the Jews were moved and induced, and the kind of administration [or management] employed in the use of those arguments. It will then be evident, that it is the truth which I here assert.

2. But if the word "determined" is received according to the second acceptation, I confess that I abominate and detest that axiom (as one that is false, absurd, and preparing the way for many blasphemies) which, declares "God by his eternal decree has determined the one part or the other of future contingent things." By this last phrase understand "those things which are performed by the free will of the creature."

(a.) I execrate it as a falsehood. Because God in the administration of his Providence conducts all things in such a manner that when he is pleased to employ his creatures in the execution of his decrees. He does not take away from them their nature, natural properties or the use of them, but allows them to perform and complete their own proper motions. Were it otherwise, Divine Providence, which ought to be accommodated to the creation, would be in direct opposition.

(b.) I detest it as an absurdity. Because it is contradictory in the adjunct, that "something is done contingently," that is, it is done in such a manner as makes it possible not to be done. Yet this same thing is determined to the one part or the other in such a manner, as makes it impossible to leave undone that which has been determined to be done. What the patrons of such a doctrine advance about "that liberty not being taken away which belongs to the nature of the creature," is not sufficient to destroy this contradiction. It is not sufficient for the establishment of contingency and liberty, to have the presence of a power that can freely act according to nature. But it is requisite that the use and employment of that power and liberty should on no account be impeded. What insanity therefore is it [according to the scheme of these men], to confer at the creation a power on the creature of acting freely or of suspending its action, and yet to take away the use of such a power when the liberty comes at length to be employed. That is, to grant it when there is no use for it but, when it becomes both useful and necessary, then in the very act to prevent the exercise of its liberty. Let Tertullian be examined[7] where he discusses this matter in a most erudite and nervous manner: I yield my full assent to all that he advances.

I never yet saw a refutation of those consequences which have been deduced from this dogma by some other persons. I wish such a refutation was prepared, at least that it would be seriously attempted. When it is completed, if I am not able to demonstrate even then that these objections of mine are not removed, I will own myself to be vanquished, and will ask pardon for my offence. Although I am not accustomed to charge and oppress this sentiment [of theirs] with such consequences before other people, yet I usually confess this single circumstance (and this, only when urged by necessity), that "I cannot possibly free their opinion from those objections."

---

7. Tertullian, *Against Marcion*, Lib. 2, Cap. 5, 6, 7.

Sufficient grace of the Holy Spirit is bestowed on those to whom the gospel is preached, whosoever they may be; so that, if they will, they may believe: Otherwise, God would only be mocking mankind.

Answer: At no time, either in public or in private, have I delivered this proposition in these words, or in any expressions that were of equivalent force, or that conveyed a similar meaning. This assertion I confidently make, even though a great number of persons might bear a contrary testimony. Unless this Article receives a modified explanation, I neither approve of it at present, nor has it at any time obtained any portion of my approval. Of this fact it is in my power to afford evidence, from written conferences I have had with other people on the same subject.

In this Article there are three topics concerning which I am desirous of giving a suitable explanation.

First: Concerning the difference that subsists among the persons to whom the gospel is preached. Frequent mention of this difference is made in the scriptures, and particularly in the following passages.—"I thank thee, O Father, Lord of heaven and earth, because thou hast hid these things from the wise and prudent, and hast revealed them unto babes" (Matt 11:25). The explanation of these words may be discovered in the following: "And into whatsoever city or town ye shall enter, inquire who in it is worthy; and there abide till ye go thence. And when ye come into a house, salute it: And if the house be worthy, let your peace come upon it; but if it be not worthy, let your peace return to you" (Matt 10:11–13).

The Jews of Berea "were more noble than those in Thessalonica, in that they received the word with all readiness of mind," &c. (Acts 17:11). "Finally, brethren, pray for us, that the word of the Lord may have free course, and be glorified, even as it is with you: and that we may be delivered from unreasonable and wicked men: for all men have not faith. But the Lord is faithful," &c. (2 Thess 3:1–3).

Secondly: Concerning the bestowing of sufficient grace, what is to be understood by such a gift? It is well known, that there is habitual grace, and [the grace of] assistance. Now the phraseology of the Article might be understood according to this acceptation, as though some kind of habitual grace were infused into all those to whom the gospel is preached, which would render them apt [or inclined] to give it credence [or believe the gospel]. But this interpretation of the phrase is one of which I do not approve. But this sufficiency, after all that is said about it, must, in my opinion be ascribed to the assistance of the Holy Spirit, by which he assists the preaching of the gospel, as the organ [or instrument] by which He [the Holy Spirit] is accustomed to be efficacious in the hearts of the hearers. But it is possible to explain this assistance, in a manner so modified and appropriate, and such sufficiency may be ascribed to it, as to keep at the greatest possible distance from Pelagianism.

Thirdly: Concerning the expression, "By this sufficient grace they may believe, if they will." These words, when delivered in such a crude and undigested form, are capable of being brought to bear a very bad interpretation, and a meaning not at all agreeable to the scriptures, as though, after that power had been bestowed, the Holy Spirit and Divine Grace remain entirely quiescent, waiting to see whether the man will properly use the power which he has received, and will believe the gospel. When, on the contrary, he who wishes to entertain and to utter correct sentiments on this subject, will account it necessary to ascribe to Grace its own province, which indeed is the principal one, in persuading the human will that it may be inclined to yield assent to those truths which are preached.

This exposition completely frees me from the slightest suspicion of heresy on the point here mentioned; and proves it to be a report not entitled to the least credit, that I have employed such expressions, as I am unwilling to admit, except with the addition of a sound and proper explanation.

In reference to the reason appended to this proposition that otherwise God would only be mocking mankind, I confess it to be a remark several adversaries employ against the opinion entertained by many of our Divines, to convict it of absurdity. And it is not used without just cause, which might easily have been demonstrate had it pleased the inventors of these Articles (instead of ascribing them to me) to occupy themselves in openly declaring on this subject their own sentiments, which they keep carefully concealed within their own bosoms.

The temporal afflictions of believers are not correctly termed "chastisements," but are punishments for sins. For Christ has rendered satisfaction only for eternal punishments.

Answer: This Article is attributed to me by a double and most flagrant falsehood. The first will be found in the Article itself, and the Second in the Reason appended.

Concerning the first: Those who are mere novices in Divinity know that the afflictions and calamities of this animal life, are either punishments, chastisements, or trials. That is, in sending them, God either intends punishment for sins, in regard to their having been already committed, and without any other consideration. Or, He intends chastisement, that those who are the subjects of it may not afterwards fall into the commission of other or similar offences. Or, in sending afflictions and calamities, God purposes to try the faith, hope, charity, patience, and like conspicuous virtues and graces of his people. What man would be so silly as to say, when the Apostles were called before the Jewish Council and were beaten with rods, "It was a punishment!" although "they departed from the presence of the council, rejoicing that they were counted worthy to suffer shame for his name" (Acts 5:41). Is not the following expression of the Apostle familiar to everyone?

"For this cause many are weak and sickly among you, and many sleep. For if we would judge ourselves, we should not be judged. But when we are judged, we are chastened (reproved or instructed, *paideuometha*) of the Lord, that we should not be condemned with the world" (1 Cor 11:30–32). By not reflecting on these and similar passages of scripture, the persons who attributed these articles to me betrayed their ignorance, as well as their audacity. If they had bestowed the least reflection upon such texts, by what strange infatuation of mind has it happened, that they ascribe to me a sentiment thus confuted by plain and obvious quotations from the word of God ?

On one occasion, the subject of discussion was the calamities inflicted on the house of' David on account his criminal conduct towards Uriah. When the passages of scripture adduced tended with great semblance of truth to prove that those calamities bore some relation to punishment, I stated, that "no necessity whatever existed for us to allow ourselves to be brought into such straits by our adversaries the Papists, from which we could with difficulty escape; since the words appear to make against the opinion which asserts that they have by no means any reference to punishment. And because sin merits both an eternal punishment corresponding with its grievous enormity, and a temporal punishment (if indeed God be pleased to inflict the latter, which is not always his practice even with respect to those who persevere in their transgressions, as may be seen in Ps 73 and Job 21), it might not unseasonably be said, that after God has pardoned the guilt so far as it is meritorious of eternal punishment, he reserves or retains it in reference to temporal punishment." And I showed, that, "from these premises, no patronage could be obtained for the Popish dogma of a Purgatory" which was also the subject of that discussion.

With regard to the reason appended, it is supported by the same criminal falsehood as the preceding part of the Article, and with no less absurdity of object, as I will demonstrate. For I affirm, in the first place, that this expression at no time escaped from my lips, and that such a thought never entered my imagination. My opinion on this subject is: "Christ is our Redeemer and Savior from sins, which merit both temporal and eternal death; and He delivers us not only from death eternal, but from death temporal, which is the separation of the soul from the body."

But it is amazing, that this opinion ["Christ has rendered satisfaction only for eternal punishments"], could possibly have been attributed to me by men of discretion, when the scriptures expressly declare, Christ was also a partaker of flesh and blood, "that, through death, he might destroy him that had the power of death, that is, the devil" (Heb 2:14). By the term "death" in this place must be understood either "the death of the body alone," or "that in conjunction with eternal death." Let us recall that "the Son of God was manifested, that he might destroy the works of the devil" (1 John 3:8). Among those works to be destroyed, we must reckon death temporal: For "by the envy of the devil, death entered into the world." In another passage it is said, "For since by man came death, by man came also the resurrection of the dead" (1 Cor 15:21). This man is Christ, "who shall change our vile body, that it may be fashioned like unto his glorious body, according to the working whereby he is able even to subdue all things unto himself" (Phil 3:21). The greatest necessity exists for that man to become conversant with the scriptures. Who denies, that by the death of Christ we are redeemed from temporal death, and obtain a right and title to a happy resurrection?

Affirmation I Have Made

The following is an affirmation I have made: "We are not actually delivered from temporal death, except by the resurrection from the dead, through which our last enemy, death, will be destroyed. These two truths, therefore, are, in my judgment, to be considered and taught: 1. Christ, by his death, immediately took away from death the authority or right which he had over us, that of detaining us under his power, even as it was not possible that Christ himself should be held by the bonds [pains] of death (Acts 2:24). But 2. Christ will in his own time deliver us from its actual dominion, according to the administration [or appointment] of God, whose pleasure it is to concede to the soul an early period liberation and to the body one that is later."

But, I confess, that I cannot with an unwavering conscience assert, and therefore dare not do it as if it were an object of certain knowledge, that "temporal death, which is imposed or inflicted on the saints, is not a punishment, or has no regard to punishment," when it is styled "an enemy that is to be destroyed " by the omnipotence of Christ.

The contrary opinion to this is not proved by the argument, that "our corporeal death is a passage into eternal life." It is the passage of the soul, and not of the body, the latter of which, while it remains buried in the earth, is held under the dominion of death. Nor is it established by the remark of Paul "having a desire to depart, and to be with Christ, which is far better" (Phil 1:23). For when Christians have a desire to so depart, that desire is according to the soul, the body in the meantime remaining under the dominion of death its enemy, until it likewise (after being again united to its own soul) be glorified with it. The address of Christ to Peter may also be stated in opposition: "When thou shalt be old, thou shalt stretch forth thy hands, and another shall gird thee and carry thee, whither thou wouldest not. This spake he, signifying by what death he should glorify God" (John 21:18–19).

The framers of these Articles, therefore, have imputed this opinion to me, not only without truth, but without a sufficient sanction from their own discretion. Of this weakness of their judgment I observe, in this Article, other two tokens:

First: They do not distinguish between the magnitude of each error in a proper manner. For he falls into a far greater error who denies, that "Christ has rendered satisfaction for corporeal punishments," that is, for the punishment of death temporal, than is he who asserts, that "the death of the body has regard to punishment, since it is inflicted even on holy persons." But they have placed the latter error as the proposition; and the firmer one is brought, as a reason, for its confirmation. They ought to have adopted an opposite mode of stating them, according to the relative estimate of each of these errors thus: "Christ has rendered satisfaction for eternal punishments alone. Therefore, the temporal afflictions of believers are not correctly called chastisements, but punishments for sins."

Secondly: Because they make me employ an argument, which I cannot discover to be possessed of any force towards proving the proposition. For I grant, that Christ has rendered satisfaction even for temporal punishments; and yet I say, "It may likewise be true, that temporal death has a reference to punishment, even when it is inflicted on believers."

Thirdly: From these considerations, a third mark of an inconsistent and wavering judgment discovers itself. For when they employ this mode of argumentation: "Christ has liberated us from temporal punishments. Therefore our death cannot have any respect to punishment," they do not perceive, that I might with equal facility draw from the same premises the following conclusion: "Therefore it is not equitable that the saints should die a temporal death." My method of reasoning is [direct] *a re ad rem*, from subject to subject: "Because Christ has borne the death of the body, it is not to be borne by us." Their method is [relative] *a re ad respectum rei*, from the subject to its relation, thus: "Because Christ has borne the death of the body, it is indeed inflicted on us, but not so as to have any reference to punishment."

God will himself approve and verify this argument *a re ad rem*, from subject to subject, by the effect He will give to it at some future period. But the argument will be prepared and stated in a legitimate form. Thus, "Christ has borne the death of the body; and (secondly) has taken it away, which fact is apparent from his resurrection: Therefore, God will take away death from us in his own good time."

Christ has died for all men and for every individual.

Answer: This assertion was never made by me, either in public or private, except when it was accompanied by such an explanation as the controversies that are excited on this subject have rendered necessary. For the phrase here used possesses much ambiguity. Thus it may mean either that "the price of the death of Christ was given for all and for every one," or that "the redemption, obtained by means of that price, is applied and communicated to all men and to every one."

1. Of this latter sentiment I entirely disapprove, because God has by a peremptory decree resolved, that believers alone should be made partakers of this redemption.

2. Let those who reject the former of these opinions consider how they can answer the following scriptures, that declare Christ died for all men; that He is the propitiation for the sins of the whole world (1 John 2:2); that He takes away the sin of the world (John 1:29); that he gave his flesh for the life of the world (John 6:51); that Christ died even for that man who might be destroyed with the meat of another person (Rom 14:15); and that false teachers make merchandize even of those who deny the Lord that bought them, and bring upon themselves swift destruction (2 Pet 2:1, 3). He therefore who speaks thus, speaks with the Scriptures. While he who rejects such phraseology, is a daring man, one who sits in judgment on the Scriptures and is not an interpreter of them. But he who explains those passages agreeably to the analogy of faith, performs the duty of a good interpreter and prophesier [or preacher] in the Church of God.

All the controversy therefore lies in the interpretation. The words themselves ought to be simply approved, because they are the words of Scripture. I will now produce a passage or two from Prosper of Aquitaine, to prove that this distinction was even in his time employed: "He who says that the Savior was not crucified for the redemption of the whole world, has regard, not to the virtue of the sacrament, but to the case of unbelievers, since the blood of Jesus Christ is the price paid for the whole world. To that precious ransom they are strangers, who, either being delighted with their captivity, have no wish to be redeemed, or, after they have been redeemed, return to the same servitude."[8]

In another passage he says: "With respect both to the magnitude and potency of the price, and with respect to the one [general] cause of mankind, the blood of Christ is the redemption of the whole world. But those who pass through this life without the faith of Christ, and without the sacrament of regeneration, are utter strangers to redemption." Such is likewise the concurrent opinion of all antiquity. This is a consideration to which I wish to obtain a little more careful attention from many persons, that they may not so easily fasten the crime of novelty on him who says anything which they had never before heard, or which was previously unknown.

8. Prosper, Sent. 4, super cap. *Gallorum*.

Original Sin will condemn no man. In every nation, all infants who die
without [having committed] actual sins, are saved.

Answer: These articles are ascribed to Borrius. To augment their
number, they have made them two, when one would have been sufficient,
from which the other necessarily follows, even according to their own
opinion. For if "original sin condemns no one," it is a necessary consequence that "all those will be saved who have not themselves committed
actual transgressions." Of this class are all infants without distinction,
unless someone will invent a state between salvation and damnation,
by a folly similar to that by which, according to St. Augustine, Pelagius
made a distinction between salvation and the kingdom of heaven.

But Borrius denies having ever publicly taught either the one or the
other. He conferred indeed in private on this subject, with some candi-
dates for Holy Orders. And he considers that it was not unlawful for him
to do so, or to hold such an opinion, under the influence of reasons he
willingly submits to the examination of his brethren; who, when they
have confuted them, may teach him more correct doctrine, and induce
him to change his opinion. His reasons are the following:

1. Because God has taken the whole human race into the grace of
reconciliation, and has entered into a covenant of grace with Adam, and
with the whole of his posterity in him. In which, he promises the remission of all sins to as many as stand steadfastly, and deal not treacherously,
in that covenant. But God not only entered into it with Adam, but also
afterwards renewed it with Noah, and at length confirmed and perfected
it through Christ Jesus. And since infants have not transgressed this covenant, they do not seem to be obnoxious to condemnation, unless we
maintain that God is unwilling to treat with infants, who depart out of
this life before they arrive at adult age. On that gracious condition under
which, notwithstanding, they are also comprehended [ut faederati] as
parties to the covenant. Therefore their condition is much worse than
that of adults, to whom is tendered the remission of all sins, not only of
that which they perpetrated in Adam, but likewise, of those which they
have themselves personally committed.

The condition of infants however is, in this case, much worse by
no fault or demerit of their own, but because it was God's pleasure thus
to act towards them. From these premises it would follow, that it was
the will of God to condemn them for the commission of sin, before He
either promised or entered into a covenant of grace. This is as though

they had been excluded and rejected from that covenant by a previous decree of God, and as though the promise concerning the Savior did not at all belong to them.

2. When Adam sinned in his own person and with his free will, God pardoned that transgression. There is no reason then why it was the will of God to impute this sin to infants, who are said to have sinned in Adam, before they had any personal existence, and therefore before they could possibly sin at their own will and pleasure.

3. Because, in this instance, God would appear to act towards infants with far more severity than towards the very devils. For the rigor of God against the apostate angels was extreme, because he would not pardon the crime which they had perpetrated. There is the same extreme rigor displayed against infants, who are condemned for the sin of Adam. But it is much greater, for all the [evil] angels sinned in their own persons, while infants sinned in the person of their first father Adam. On this account, the angels themselves were in fault, because they committed an offence which it was possible for them to avoid, while infants were not in fault, only so far as they existed in Adam and were by his will involved in sin and guilt.

These reasons are undoubtedly of such great importance, that I am of opinion those who maintain the contrary are bound to confute them, before they can affix to any other person a mark of heresy. I am aware, that they place Antiquity in opposition, because [they say] its judgment was in their favor. Antiquity, however, cannot be set up in opposition by those who, on this subject, when the salvation of infants is discussed, are themselves unwilling to abide by the judgment of the Ancients. But our brethren depart from Antiquity, on this very topic, in two ways:

Antiquity maintains, that all infants who depart out of this life without having been baptized, would be damned, but that such as were baptized and died before they attained to adult age, would be saved. St. Augustine asserts this to be the Catholic doctrine, in these words: "If you wish to be a Catholic," be unwilling to believe, declare, or teach, that infants who "are prevented by death from being baptized, can attain to the "indulgence of original sins."[9] To this doctrine our brethren will by no means accede; but they contradict both parts of it.

---

9. St. Augustine, *De Anima et ejus Orig.*,Lib. 3,Cap. 9.

Antiquity maintains that the grace of baptism takes away original sin, even from those who have not been predestined; according to this passage from Prosper:

"That man is not a Catholic who says, that the grace of baptism [percepta], when received, does not take away original sin from those who have been predestinated to life."[10] To this opinion also our brethren strongly object. But it does not appear equitable, that, whenever it is agreeable to themselves, they should be displeased with those who dissent from them because they dissent from the Fathers; and that, whenever it is their good pleasure the same parties do themselves dissent from the Fathers on this very subject.

Respect to Sentiments

But with respect to the sentiments of the Ancient Christian Fathers about the damnation of the unbaptized solely on account of original sin, they and their successors seem to have mitigated, or at least to have attempted to soften down such a harsh opinion. For some of them have declared, "that the unbaptized would be in the mildest damnation of all;" and others, "that they would be afflicted, not with the punishment of [sensus] feeling, but only with that of loss." To this last opinion some of them have added, "that this punishment would be inflicted on them without any stings from their own consciences."

Though it is a consequence of not being baptized that the parties are said to endure only the punishment of loss and not that of feeling, this feeling exists wherever the stings or gnawings of conscience exist, that is where the gnawing worm never dies. But let our brethren consider what species of damnation is inflicted on account of sin, and from which no gnawing remorse proceeds.

From these observations thus produced it is apparent what opinion ought to be formed of the Fourteenth Article. It is at least so dependent on the Thirteenth, that it ought not to have been composed as a separate article by those who maintain there is no cause why infants should perish, except original sin which they committed in Adam, or which [*propagatum est in ipsos*] they received by propagation from Adam. But it is worth the trouble to see, on this subject, the sentiments of Dr. Francis Junius, who a few years ago was Professor of Divinity in our University.

---

10. Prosper, *Ad Cap. Gallorum*, Sent. 2.

He affirms, that "all infants who are of the covenant and of election, are saved." But he presumes, in charity, that "those infants whom God calls to himself, and timely removes out of this miserable vale of sins, are rather saved."[11] Now, that which this divine either "affirms according to the doctrine of faith,'" or "presumes through charity," may not another man be allowed, without the charge of heresy, to hold within his own breast as a matter of opinion, which he is not in the least solicitous to obtrude on others or persuade them to believe? Indeed, this "accepting of men's persons" is far too prevalent, and is utterly unworthy of wise men. And what inconvenience, I pray, results from this doctrine? Is it supposed to follow as a necessary consequence from it, that if the infants of unbelievers are saved, they are saved without Christ and his intervention? Borrius, however, denies any such consequence and has Junius assenting with him on this subject.

If the brethren dissent from this opinion, and think the consequences they deduce are agreeable to the premises, then all the children of unbelievers must be subject to condemnation, the children of unbelievers, I repeat, who are "strangers from the covenant." For this conclusion no other reason can be rendered, than their being the children of those who are "strangers from the covenant." From this it seems, on the contrary to be inferred that all the children of those who are in the covenant are saved, provided they die in the age of infancy. But since our brethren deny this inference, behold the kind of dogma which is believed by them: "All the infants of those who are strangers from the covenant are damned; and of the offspring of those parents who are in the covenant, some infants that die are damned, while others are saved." I leave it to those who are deeply versed in these matters, to decide whether such a dogma as this was ever obtained in any church of Christ.

If the Heathen, and those who are strangers to the true knowledge of God, do those things which by the powers of nature they are enabled to do, God will not condemn them, but will reward these their works by a more enlarged knowledge by which they may be brought to salvation.

Answer: This was never uttered by me, nor indeed by Borrius, under such a form, and in these expressions. Nay, it is not very probable that any man, how small his skill might be in sacred things, would deliver the apprehensions of his mind in a manner so utterly confused

11. Francis Junius, *De Natura et Gratia*, R. 28.

and indigested, as to beget the suspicion of a falsehood in the very words in which he enunciates his opinion. For what man is there, who, as a stranger to the true knowledge of God, will do a thing that can in any way be acceptable to God? It would necessitate that the thing which will please God, be itself good, at least in a certain respect. It is further necessary, that he who performs it knows it to be good find and agreeable to God.

"For whatsoever is not of faith, is sin," that is, whatsoever is done without an assured knowledge that it is good and agreeable to God. Thus far, therefore, it is needful for him to have a true knowledge of God, which the Apostle attributes even to the Gentiles (Rom 1:18–21, 25, 28; 2:14, 15). Without this explanation there will be a contradiction in this enunciation: "He who is entirely destitute of the true knowledge of God, can perform something which God" considers to be so grateful to Himself as to remunerate it with "some reward." These our good brethren either do not perceive this contradiction; or they suppose that the persons to whom they ascribe this opinion are such egregious simpletons as they would thus make them appear.

Then, what is the nature of this expression, "If they do those things which the powers of nature enable them to perform?" Is "nature," when entirely destitute of grace and of the Spirit of God, furnished with the knowledge of that Truth said to be "held in unrighteousness," by the knowledge of "that which may be known of God, even his eternal power and Godhead," which may instigate man to glorify God, and which deprives him of all excuse, if he does not glorify God as he knows Him? I do not think that such properties as these can, without falsehood and injury to Divine Grace, be ascribed to "nature," which, when destitute of grace and of the Spirit of God, tends directly downward to those things that are earthly.

If our brethren suppose that these matters exhibit themselves in this [foolish] manner, what reason have they for so readily ascribing such an undigested paragraph to men, who, they ought to have known, are not entirely destitute of the knowledge of sacred subjects? But if our brethren really think man can do some portion of good by the powers of nature, they are themselves not far from Pelagianism, which yet they are solicitous to fasten on others. This Article, enunciated thus in their own style, seems to indicate that they think man capable of doing something good "by the powers of nature," but that, by such good performance, he will "neither escape condemnation nor obtain a reward."

For these attributes are ascribed to the subject in this enunciation; and because they do not in their opinion agree with this subject, they accuse of heresy the thing thus enunciated. If they believe, that "a man, who is a stranger to the true knowledge of God," is capable of doing nothing good, this ought in the first place to have been charged with heresy. If they think, that no one "by the powers of nature" can perform anything that is pleasing to God, then this ought to be reckoned as an error, if any man does affirm it. From these remarks it obviously follows, either that they are themselves very near the Pelagian heresy, or that they are ignorant of what is worthy, in the first instance or in the second, of reprehension, and what ought to be condemned as heretical.

It is apparent therefore, that it has been their wish to aggravate the error by this addition. But their labor has been in vain, because by this addition they have enabled us to deny that we ever employed any such expression or conceived such a thought; they have at the same time afforded just grounds for charging them with the heresy of Pelagius. Thus the incautious hunter is caught in the very snare he had made for another. They would therefore have acted with far more caution and with greater safety, if they had omitted their exaggeration, and had charged us with this opinion, which they know to have been employed by the Scholastic Divines, and which they afterwards inserted in the succeeding Seventeenth Article, but enunciated in a manner somewhat different, "God will do that which is in Him, for the man who does what is in himself." But, even then, the explanation of the Schoolmen ought to have been added, "that God will do this, not from [the merit of] good works, but from [that of] congruity; and not because the act of man merits any such thing, but because it is befitting the great mercy and beneficence of God."

Saying of the Schoolmen

Yet this saying of the Schoolmen I should myself refuse to employ, except with the addition of these words: "God will bestow more grace upon that man who does what is in him by the power of Divine Grace already granted to him, according to the declaration of Christ, 'To him that hath shall be given,' in which he comprises the cause why it was "given to you (the disciples) to know the mysteries of the kingdom of heaven," and why "to (others) it was not given" (Matt 13:11). In addition to this passage, and the first and second chapters of Rom that have already been quoted, peruse what is related in the Acts 10, 16, and 17 about Cornelius the Centurion, Lydia the seller of purple, and the Bereans.

The works of the unregenerate can be pleasing to God, and are (according to Borrius) the occasion, and (according to Arminius) the impulsive cause by which God will be moved to communicate to them his saving grace.

Answer: About two years ago seventeen articles were circulated and attributed to me. The fifteenth is thus expressed: "Though the works of the unregenerate cannot possibly be pleasing to God, yet they are the occasion by which God is moved to communicate to them his saving grace." This difference induces me to suspect, that the negative of "cannot" has been omitted in this Sixteenth Article, unless, since that time, having proceeded from bad to worse, I now positively affirm this, which as I was a less audacious and more modest heretic, I then denied. However this may be, I assert that these good men neither comprehend our sentiments, know the phrases we employ, nor, in order to know them, do they understand the meaning of those phrases. In consequence of this, it is no matter of surprise that they err greatly from the truth when they enunciate our sentiments in their words, or when they affix other (that is, their own) significations to our words. Of this transformation they afford a manifest specimen in this Article.

1. For the word, "the unregenerate," may be understood in two senses, (a.) Either as it denotes those who have felt no [*actum*] motion of the regenerating Spirit, or of its tendency or preparation for regeneration, and who are therefore destitute of the first principle of regeneration; (b.) Or it may signify those who are born again, and who feel [*actus*] those motions of the Holy Spirit that belong either to preparation or to the very essence of regeneration, but who are not yet regenerated. That is, they are brought by it to confess their sins, to mourn on account of them, to desire deliverance, and to seek out the Deliverer who has been pointed out to them. But they are not yet furnished with that power of the Spirit by which the flesh, or the old man, is mortified and by which a man, being transformed to newness of life, is rendered capable of performing works of righteousness.

2. A thing is pleasing to God, either as an initial act belonging to the commencement of conversion, or as a work perfect in its own essence

and as performed by a man who is converted and born again. Thus the confession, by which anyone acknowledges himself to be "wretched, and miserable, and poor, and blind and naked," is pleasing to God. And the man therefore flies to Christ, to "buy . . . gold tried in the fire, that thou mayest be rich; and white raiment, that thou mayest be clothed, and that the shame of thy nakedness do not appear, and anoint thine eyes with salve, that thou mayest see" (Rev 3:17–18). Works proceeding from fervent love are also pleasing to God.

Distinction Calvin Draws

See the distinction which Calvin draws between "initial and filial fear" and that of Beza, who is of opinion that "sorrow and contrition for sin do not belong to the essential parts of regeneration, but only to those which are preparatory." But he places "the very essence of regeneration in mortification, and in vivification or quickening."

3. "The occasion," and "the impulsive cause, by which God is moved," are not generally received in the same manner, but variously. It will answer our purpose if I produce two passages from a comparison of which a distinction may be collected at once convenient and sufficient for our design. The king says, "I forgave thee all that debt, because thou desiredst me" (Matt 18:32). And God says to Abraham, "Because thou hast done this thing, and hast not withheld thy son, thine only son: That in blessing I will bless thee" (Gen 22:16, 17). He who does not perceive, in these passages, a difference [impulsionis] in the impelling motives, as well as [placentiae] in the pleasure derived, must be very blind with respect to the Scriptures.

4. "The saving grace of God" may be understood either as primary or secondary, as [praeveniente] preceding or subsequent, as operating or cooperating, and as that which knocks or opens or enters in. Unless a man properly distinguishes each of these, and uses such words as correspond with these distinctions, he must of necessity stumble, and make others appear to stumble whose opinions he does not accurately understand. But if a man will diligently consider these remarks, he will perceive that this Article is agreeable to the Scriptures, according to one sense in which it may be taken, but that, according to another, it is very different.

Let the word "unregenerate" be taken for a man who [jam renascitur] is now in the act of the new birth, though he be not yet actually born again. Let "the pleasure" [which God feels] be taken for an initial act. Let "the impelling cause" be taken by the mode of final enjoyment. And let secondary, subsequent, cooperating and entering grace be substituted for "saving grace;" and it will instantly be manifest, that we speak what is right when we say: " Serious sorrow on account of sin is so far pleasing to God, that by it, according to the multitude of his mercies, He is moved to bestow grace on a man who is a sinner."

From these observations, I think, it is evident with what caution persons ought to speak [*ubi*] on subjects, on which the descent into heresy, or into the suspicion of heresy, is so smooth and easy. And our brethren ought in their prudence to have reflected, that we are not altogether negligent of this caution, since they cannot be ignorant that we are fully aware how much our words are exposed and obnoxious to injurious interpretations, and even to calumny. But unless they had earnestly searched for a multitude of Articles, they might have embraced this and the preceding, as well as that which succeeds, in the same chapter.

God will not deny his grace to anyone who does what is in him.

Answer: This Article is so naturally connected with those preceding it, that he who grants one of the three, may by the same effort affirm the remainder. And he who denies one, may reject all the others. They might therefore have spared some portion of this needless labor, and might with much greater convenience have proposed one article of the following description, instead of three: "It is possible for a man to do some good thing without the aid of grace; and if he does it, God will recompense or remunerate that act by more abundant grace." But we could always have fastened the charge of falsehood upon an article of this kind. It was therefore a much safer course for them to play with equivocations, that the fraud of calumny might not with equal facility be made known to all persons.

But with respect to this article, I declare, that it never came into our minds to employ such confused expressions as these, which, at the very first sight of them, exclude grace from the commencement of conversion. We on all occasions make this grace to precede, to accompany and to follow, and without which, we constantly assert no good action whatever can be produced by man. Nay, we carry this principle so far as not to dare to attribute the power here described even to the nature of Adam himself, without the help of Divine Grace both infused and assisting.

It thus becomes evident, that the fabricated opinion is imposed on us through calumny. If our brethren entertain the same sentiments, we are perfectly at agreement. But if they are of opinion that Adam was able by nature, without supernatural aid, to fulfill the law imposed on him, they seem not to recede far from Pelagius, since this saying of Augustine is received by these our brethren: "Supernatural things are lost, natural things are corrupted." Whence it follows, what remnant soever there was of natural things, just so much power remained to fulfill the law, what is premised being granted, that Adam was capable by his own nature to obey God without grace, as the latter is usually distinguished in opposition to nature. When they charge us with this doctrine, they undoubtedly declare that in their judgment it is such as may fall in with our meaning; and, therefore, that they do not perceive so much absurdity in this article as there is in reality; unless they think that nothing can be devised so absurd that we are not inclined and prepared to believe and publish.

We esteem this article as one of such great absurdity, that we would not be soon induced to attribute it to any person of the least skill in sacred matters. For how can a man, without the assistance of Divine Grace, perform anything acceptable to God, and which He will remunerate with the saving reward either of further grace or of life eternal ? But this article excludes primary grace with sufficient explicitness, when it says, "To him who does what is in himself." For if this expression is understood in the following sense, "To him who does what he can by the primary grace already conferred upon him," then there is no absurdity in this sentence, "God will bestow further grace upon him who profitably uses that which is primary." And, by the malevolent suppression of what ought to have been added, the brethren openly declare that it was their wish for this calumny to gain credence.

God undoubtedly converts, without the external preaching of the Gospel, great numbers of persons to the saving knowledge of Christ, among those [ubi est] who have no outward preaching; and He effects such conversions either by the inward revelation of the Holy Spirit, or by the ministry of angels(Borrius & Arminius)

Answer: I never uttered such a sentiment as this. Borrius has said something like it, though not exactly the same, in the following words: "It is possible that God, by the inward revelation of the Holy Spirit or by the ministry of angels, instructed [Magi] the Wise Men, who came from the East, concerning Jesus, whom they came to adore."

But the words "undoubtedly" and "great numbers of persons" are the additions of calumny, and this of a most audacious character, charging us with that which, it is very probable, we never spoke and of which we never thought. We have learned that this audacity of boldly affirming anything whatsoever, under which the junior pastors generally labor, and those who are ignorant of the small stock of knowledge that they possess, is an evil exceedingly dangerous in the church of Christ.

1. Is it probable, that any prudent man will affirm that "something is undoubtedly done in great numbers of persons," of which he is notable, when required, to produce a single example? We confess that we cannot bring an instance of what is here imputed to us. For, if it were produced by us, it would become a subject of controversy; as has been the fate of the sentiments of Zwinglius concerning the salvation of Socrates, Aristides, and of others in similar circumstances, who must have been instructed concerning their salvation by the Holy Ghost or by angels. For it is scarcely within the bounds of probability, that they had seen the Sacred Scriptures and had been instructed out of them.

2. Besides, if this saying of Christ to Paul had occurred to the recollection of our brethren: "speak and hold not thy peace: . . . for I have much people in this city" (Acts 18:9, 10), they would not so readily have burdened us with this article, who have learned from this saying of Christ, that God sends the external preaching of his word to nations, when it is his good pleasure for great numbers of them to be converted.

3. The following is a saying in common and frequent use: "The ordinary means and organ of conversion is the preaching of the Divine word by mortal men, to which therefore all persons are bound. But the Holy Spirit has not so bound himself to this method, as to be unable to operate in an extraordinary way, without the intervention of human aid, when it seemeth good to Himself." Now if our brethren had reflected, that this very common sentence obtains our high approval, they would not have thought of charging this article upon us, at least they would not have accounted it erroneous. For, with regard to the first, what is *extraordinary* does not obtain among "great numbers of persons."

For if it did, it would immediately begin to be ordinary. With regard to the second, if "the preaching of the word by mortal men," be "the ordinary means," by which it is also intimated that some means are extraordinary, and since the whole of our church, nay, in my opinion, since the whole Christian world bears its testimony to this, then indeed it is neither a heresy nor an error to say, "Even without this means [without the preaching of the word] God can convert some persons."

To this might likewise be added the word "undoubtedly." For if it is doubtful whether anyone be saved by any other means (that is, by "means extraordinary"), than by human preaching; then it becomes a matter of doubt, whether it is necessary for "the preaching of the Divine word by mortal men," to be called "the ordinary means."

4. What peril or error can there be in any man saying, "God converts great numbers of persons, by the internal revelation of the Holy Spirit or by the ministry of angels" provided it be at the same time stated, that no one is converted except by this very word, and by the meaning of this word, which God sends by men to those communities or nations He hath purposed to unite to himself? The objectors will perhaps reply, "It is to be feared that if a nation of those who have been outwardly called should believe this, rejecting external preaching, they would expect such an internal revelation or the address of an angel."

Truly, this would be as unnatural a subject of fear, as that a man would be unwilling to taste of the bread laid before him, because he understands, "It is written, Man shall not live by bread alone, but by every word that proceedeth out of the mouth of God" (Matt 4:4). But I desist, lest, while instituting an examination into the causes of this fear, I should proceed much further, and arrive at a point to which our brethren might be unwilling for me on this occasion to advance. A word is sufficient for the wise.

It is the summit of blasphemy to say, that God is freely good.

Answer: In this article likewise our brethren disclose their own disgraceful proceedings, which I would gladly allow to remain buried in oblivion. But, because they recall this affair, to my recollection I will now relate how it occurred.

In a Disputation it was asked, "Can Necessity and Liberty be so far reconciled to each other, that a person may be said necessarily or freely to produce one and the same effect?" These words being used properly according to their respective strict definitions, are here subjoined: "An agent acts necessarily, who, when all the requisites for action are laid down, cannot do otherwise than act, or cannot suspend his acting. An agent acts freely, who, when all the requisites for action are laid down, can refrain from beginning to act, or can suspend his acting."

I declared, "that the two terms could not meet in one subject." Other persons said, "that they could," evidently for the purpose of confirming the dogma which asserts, "Adam sinned freely indeed, and yet necessarily. Freely, with respect to himself and according to his nature. Necessarily, with respect to the decree of God."

Of this their explanation I did not admit, but said, Necessarily and Freely differ not in respects but in their entire essences, as do Necessity and Contingency. Or what is Necessary and what is Contingent, which, because they divide the whole amplitude of being, cannot possibly coincide together, no more than can Finite and Infinite. But Liberty appertains to Contingency.

To disprove this, my opinion, they brought forward an instance, or example, in which Necessity and Liberty met together. That was God, who is both necessarily and freely good. This assertion of theirs displeased me so exceedingly, as to cause me to say that it was not far removed from blasphemy. At this time, I entertain a similar opinion about it. In few words I thus prove its falsity, absurdity, and the blasphemy [contained] in the falsity.

1. Its Falsity. He who by natural necessity, and according to his very essence and the whole of his nature, is good,—nay, who is Goodness itself, the Supreme Good, the First Good from which all good proceeds, through which every good comes, in which every good exists. And by a participation of which what things soever have any portion of good in them are good, and more or less good as they are nearer or more remote from it. He is not *freely* good. For it is a contradiction in an adjunct, or an opposition in an apposition. But God is good by natural necessity, according to his entire nature and essence, and is Goodness itself, the supreme and primary Good, from which, through which, and in which is all good, &c. Therefore, God is not freely good.

2. Its Absurdity. Liberty is an affection of the Divine Will, not of the Divine Essence, Understanding, or Power. Therefore it is not an affection of the Divine Nature considered in its totality. It is indeed an effect of the Will, according to which it is borne towards an object that is neither primary nor adequate, and that is different from God himself. This effect of the Will therefore is posterior in order to that affection of the Will according to which God is borne towards a proper, primary and

adequate object, which is himself. But Goodness is an affection of the whole of the Divine Nature, Essence, Life, Understanding, Will, Power, &c. Therefore, God is not freely good; that is, he is not good by the mode of Liberty, but by that of natural Necessity.

I add, that it cannot be affirmed of anything in the nature of things, that it is freely, or that it is this or that freely, not even then when man was made what he is by actions proceeding from free will. As no man is said to be "freely learned," although he has obtained erudition for himself by study which proceeded from free will.

3. I prove that blasphemy is contained in this assertion. Because, if God be freely good, (that is, not by nature and natural necessity) he can be or can be made not good. As whatever anyone wills freely, he has it in his power not to will. And whatever anyone does freely, he can refrain from doing. Consider the dispute between the Ancient Fathers and Eunomius and his followers, who endeavored to prove that the Son was not eternally begotten of the Father, because the Father had neither willingly nor unwittingly begotten the Son. But the answer given to them by Cyril, Basil, and others, was this: "The Father was neither willing nor unwilling; that is, He begat the Son not by will, but by nature. The act of generation is not from the Divine Will, but from the Divine Nature."[12] If they say, "God may also be said to be freely good, because He is not good by co-action or force" I reply, not only is co-action repugnant to liberty, but nature is likewise; and each of them, nature and co-action, constitutes an entire, total, and sufficient cause for the exclusion of liberty.

Nor does it follow, "Co-action does not exclude liberty from this thing; therefore it is *freely* that which it actually is. A stone does not fall downwards by co-action; it therefore falls by liberty: Man wills not his own salvation by force, therefore he wills it freely." Such objections as these are unworthy to be produced by men; and in the refutation of them shall I expend my time and leisure? Thus therefore the Christian Fathers justly attached blasphemy to those who said, "The Father begat the Son wittingly, or by his own will;" because from this it would follow, that the Son had [*principium*] an origin similar to that of the creatures. But with how much greater equity does blasphemy fasten itself upon those who declare, "that God is freely good!" For if He is freely good, He likewise freely knows and loves himself, and besides does all things freely, even when He begets the Son and breathes forth the Holy Spirit!

12. St. Cyril, *Thess. contra Haeret*, Lib. 1, Cap. 8.

It frequently happens, that a creature who is not entirely hardened in evil, is unwilling to perform an action became it is joined with sin; unless when certain arguments and occasions are presented to him, which act as incitements to its commission. [Administratio] The management of this presentation also is in the hand of the Providence of God, who presents these incitements that He may accomplish his own work by the act of the creature.

Answer: Unless certain persons were under the excitement of a licentious appetite for carping at those things that proceed from me, they would undoubtedly never have persuaded themselves to create any trouble about this matter. Yet I would pardon them this act of officiousness, as the rigid and severe examiners of truth, provided they would sincerely and without calumny relate those things I have actually spoken or written, That is, that they would not corrupt or falsify my sayings, either by adding to or diminishing from them, by changing them or giving them a perverted interpretation.

But some men seem to have been so long accustomed to slander, that, even when they can be openly convicted of it, still they are not afraid of hurling it against an innocent person: Of this fact they afford a luminous example in the present article. For those things I advanced in the thesis *On the Efficacy and Righteousness of the Providence of God concerning Evil*, and which was disputed May 1605, is here quoted, but in a mutilated manner, and with the omission of those things which are capable of powerfully vindicating the whole from the attacks of slander. The following are the words I employed in the Fifteenth Thesis of that Disputation:

"But since an act, though it be permitted to [*potentiae*] the ability and the will of the creature, may yet be taken away [*potestati*] from his actual power, by legislation; and since therefore it will very frequently happen, that a creature, who is not entirely hardened in evil, is unwilling to perform an act because it is connected with sin, unless when some arguments and occasions are presented to him, which resemble incitements to its commission. [*Administratio*] The management of this presenting [of *arguments and occasions*] is also in the hand of the Providence of God, who presents these incitements; both that He [*exploret*] may fully try whether the creature be willing to refrain from sinning, even when urged on, or provoked, by incitements; because the praise of abstaining from sin is very slight in the absence of such provocatives; and that, if the creature wills to yield to these incitements, God may effect his own work by the act of the creature."

These are my words; from which the brethren have extracted what seemed suitable for establishing the slander, but have omitted and quite taken away those things which, in the most manifest manner, betray and confute the calumny. For I laid down two ends of that administration by which God [*dispensat*] manages the arguments, occasions, incitements, and irritations to commit that act that is joined with sin. And these two ends were neither collateral, that is, not equally intended, nor were they connected together by a close conjunction.

Exploration or trial

The first of them, which is the exploration or trial of his creature, God primarily, properly, and of himself intends. But the latter, which is that God may effect his own work by the act of the creature, is not intended by God, except after He has foreseen that his creature will not resist these incitements, but will yield to them, and that of his own free will, in opposition to the command of God, which it was his duty and within his power to follow, after having rejected and refused those allurements and incitements of arguments and occasions. But this article of theirs propounds my words in such a way, as if I had made God to intend this last end only and of itself, omitting entirely the first. It thus omits the previous condition under which God intends this second end through the act of his creature, that is, when it is the will of the creature to yield to these incitements.

This calumny therefore is two-fold, and evidently invented for the purpose of drawing a conclusion from these my words, that I have in them represented God as the author of sin. A certain person, having lately quoted my expressions in a public discourse, was not afraid of drawing from them this conclusion.

But this was purely through calumny, as I will now prove with the utmost brevity.

The reason by which it can be concluded, from the words quoted in this article from my Theses, "that God is the Author of the sin which is committed by the creature" when God incites him by arguments and occasions, is universally three-fold:

The first is that God absolutely intends to effect his own work by the act of the creature, which act cannot be performed by the creature without sin. This is resolvable into two absolute intentions of God, of which the first is that by which He absolutely intends to effect this his work.

The second reason is: that by which He absolutely intends to effect this work in no other way than by such an act of a creature, as cannot be done by that creature without sin. The creature being invited by the presenting of these allurements and provocations to commit that act, cannot do otherwise than commit it. That is, such an excitation being laid down, the creature cannot suspend that act by which God intends to effect his work, otherwise God might be frustrated of his intention. Hence arises:

The third reason, which has its origin in these two, that God intends by these incentives to move the creature to perform an act joined to sin, that is, to move him to the commission of sin.

All these things seem with some semblance of probability, to be drawn as conclusions from the words thus placed, as they are quoted in this their article, because it is represented as the sole and absolute end of this administration and presenting that God effects his work by the act of the creature. But those words I have inserted, and which they have omitted, meet these three reasons, and in the most solid manner confute the whole objection which rests upon them:

1. My own words meet the first of these reasons thus. For they deny that God absolutely intends to effect his own work by the act of the creature. They say that God did not intend to employ the act of the creature to complete his work, before He foresaw that the creature would yield to those incitements, that is, would not resist them.

2. They meet the second, by denying that after assigning this presentation of incitements, the creature is unable to suspend his act; since they say likewise, that if it be the will of the creature to yield to these incitements, then God effects his own work by the act of the creature. What does this mean, if it be hit will to yield? Is not the freedom of the will openly denoted, by which when this presenting of arguments and occasions is laid down, the will can yet refuse to yield ?

3. For they deny that God intends by those incitements to move the creature to the commission of an act joined to sin, that is to commit sin, because they say God intends the trial of his creature, whether he will obey God even after having been irritated by these incitements. And when God saw that the creature preferred to yield to these incitements rather than to obey Him, then He intended not the act of' the creature.

For that is unnecessary because, his intention being now to try, He obtains the issue of the act performed by the will of the creature. But God intended to effect his own work by an act [positum] founded on the will and the culpability of the creature.

It is apparent therefore, that these words my brethren have omitted, most manifestly refute the calumny, and in the strongest manner solve the objection. This I will likewise point out in another method, that the whole iniquity of this objection may be rendered quite obvious.

That man who says, "God tries his creature by arguments and occasions of sinning, whether he will obey Him even after he has been stirred up by incitements," openly declares, that it is in the power of the creature to resist these incitements, and not to sin. Otherwise, this [act of God] would be, not a trial of obedience, but a casting down and an impelling to necessary disobedience. Then, the man who says, "God, by these provocatives and incitements, tries the obedience of his creature," intimates by these expressions, that those occasions and arguments presented by God when He intends to try, are not incitements and irritations to sin through the end and aim of God. But they are incitements, first, by capability according to [affectum] the inclination of the creature, who can be incited by them to commit an act connected with sin. They are also incitements, secondly, in their issue, because the creature has been induced by them to sin, but by his own fault. For it was his duty, and in his power, to resist this inclination, and to neglect and despise these incitements.

Most Wonderful Indeed

It is wonderful, therefore, and most wonderful indeed, that any man at all expert in theological matters, should have ventured to fabricate from my words this calumny against me. Against me, I say, who dare not accede to some of the sentiments and dogmas of my brethren, as they well know, for this sole reason—because I consider it flows from them, that God is the author of sin! And I cannot accede to them on this account, because I think my brethren teach those things from which I can conclude by good and certain consequence, that God absolutely intends the sin of his creature, and thence that He so administers all things, as, when this administration is laid down, man necessarily sins, and cannot in the act itself and in reality omit the act of sin.

If they show that the things I say do not follow from their senti-ments, on this account at least I shall not suffer myself to be moved by their consent in them. Let the entire Theses be read, and it will be evident how solicitously I have guarded against saying anything from which by the most distant probability this blasphemy might be deduced. Yet, at the same time, I have been careful to subtract from the Providence of God nothing, which according to the Scriptures, ought to be ascribed to it. But I scarcely think it necessary, for me now to prove at great length that the fact of God's Providential efficacy respecting Evil is exactly as I have taught in those words, especially after I have premised this explana-tion. I will, however, do this in a very brief manner:

Eve was not only "a creature not entirely hardened in evil," but she was not at all evil. She willed to abstain from eating the forbidden fruit because "it was connected with sin," as is apparent from the answer which she gave to the serpent: "God hath said, Ye shall not eat of it." Her compliance with this command was easy, in the midst of such an abun-dance of fruit; and the trial of her obedience would have been very small, if she had been solicited with no other argument by the tempter. It hap-pened therefore, that, in addition to this, the serpent presented to Eve an argument of persuasion, by which [*irritaret*] he might stimulate her to eat, saying, "Ye shall not surely die, but ye shall be as gods." This argu-ment, according to the intention of the serpent, was an incitement to commit sin. Without it, the serpent perceived, she would not be moved to eat, because he had heard her expressing her will to abstain from the act because it was "connected with sin."

I ask now, Is [*administratio*] the whole management of this tempta-tion to be ascribed to God, or not? If they say, "It must not be attributed to Him," they offend against Providence, the Scriptures, and the opin-ion of all our divines. If they confess that it should be ascribed to Him, they grant what I have said, But what was the end of this management? An experiment or trial, whether Eve, when solicited by arguments, and stimulated by Satan, [*vellet*] would resolve to refrain from an act, that she might obtain from her Lord and Creator the praise of obedience. The instance of Joseph's brethren, quoted in the Fifteenth Thesis of my Ninth Public Disputation, proves this in the plainest manner, as I have shown in that Thesis.

Let the case of Absalom be inspected, who committed incest with his father's concubines. Was not this the occasion of perpetrating that act that God gave his father's concubines into his hands, that is, he permitted them to his power? Was not the argument inducing him to commit that act, from which nature is abhorrent, furnished by the advice of Ahithophel, whose counsels were considered as oracles? (2 Sam 16:20–23) Without doubt, these are the real facts of the case. But that God himself managed the whole of this affair, appears from the Scripture, which says that God did it (2 Sam 12:11, 12).

Examine what God says in Deut 13:1–3: "If there arise among you a prophet, or a dreamer of dreams, and giveth thee a sign or wonder, And the sign or the wonder come to pass, whereof he spake unto thee, saying Let us go after other gods, which thou hast not known, and let us serve them; Thou shalt not hearken unto the words of that prophet or dreamer of dreams . . ."

Prediction of 'the sign'

Is not the prediction of "the sign," [by this false prophet] when confirmed by the event itself, an argument which may gain [*authoritatem*] credit for him ? And is not the credit, thus obtained, an incitement or an argument to effect a full persuasion of that which this prophet persuaded? And what necessity is there for arguments, incitements, and incentives, if a rational creature has such a propensity to the act, which cannot be committed without sin, that he wills to commit it without any argument whatsoever?

Under such circumstances, the grand tempter will cease from his useless labor. But because the tempter knows that the creature is unwilling to commit this act unless he be incited by arguments, and opportunities be offered, he brings forward all that he can of incentives to allure the creature to sin. God, however, presides over all these things, and by his Providence administers the whole of them, but to an end far different from that to which the tempter directs them. For God manages them in the first place for the trial of his creature, and afterwards (if it be the will of the creature to yield), for Himself to effect something by that act.

If any think, that there is something reprehensible in this view, let them so circumscribe the right and the capability of God, as to suppose Him unable to try the obedience of his creature by any other method, than by creating that in which sin can be committed, and from which He commanded him by a law to abstain. But if He can try the obedience of his creature by some other method than this, let these persons show us what that method is beside the presenting of arguments and occasions, and why God uses the former method more than the preceding one which I have mentioned. Is it not because he perceives, that the creature will not, by the former, be equally strongly solicited to evil, and that therefore it is a trivial matter to abstain from sin, to the commission of which he is not instigated by any other incentives ?

Let the history of Job be well considered, whose patience God tried in such a variety of ways, and to whom were presented so many incitements to sin against God by impatience; and the whole of this matter will very evidently appear. God said to Satan: "Hast thou considered my servant Job . . . a perfect and an upright man, one that feareth God and escheweth evil? Then Satan answered the Lord and said: Doth Job fear God for nought? . . . thou hast blessed the work of his hands, and his substance is increased in the land. But put forth thine hand now, and touch all that he hath, and he will curse thee to thy face. And the Lord said unto Satan, Behold, all that he hath is in thy power; only upon himself put not forth thine hand" (Job 1:8–12).

What other meaning have these words than, Behold, incite him to curse me! I grant thee permission, since thou thinkest small praise is due to that man who abounds with blessings, and yet fears me. Satan did what he was permitted, and produced none of the effects [*which he had prognosticated*]; so that God said, Job "still holdeth fast his integrity, although thou movedst me against him" (2:3). This trial being finished, when Satan asked permission to employ against him greater incentives to sin, he obtained his request; and, after all, effected nothing. Therefore God was glorified in the patience of Job, to the confusion of Satan.

I suppose these remarks will be sufficient to free the words of my Theses from all calumny and from sinister and unjust interpretations. When I have ascertained the arguments our brethren employ to convict these words of error, I will endeavour to confute them ; or if I cannot do this, I will yield to what may then be deemed the truth.

The Righteousness of Christ is not imputed to us for Righteousness ; but to believe [or the act of believing], which justifies us.

Answer: I do not know what I can most admire in this article—the unskillfulness, the malice, or the supine negligence of those who have been its fabricators!

1. Their negligence is apparent in this, that they do not care how and in what words they enunciate the sentiments they attribute to me; neither do they give themselves any trouble to know what my sentiments are, which yet they are desirous to reprehend.

2. Their unskillfulness, because they do not distinguish the things which ought to be distinguished, and they oppose those things which ought not to be opposed.

3. The malice is evident, because they attribute to me those things I have neither thought nor spoken; or because they involve matters in such away, as to give that which was correctly spoken the appearance of having been uttered in perverseness, that they may discover some grounds for calumny. But, to come to the affair itself:

Though in this article there seem to be only two distinct enunciations, yet in potency they are three, which must also be separated from each other to render the matter intelligible. The first is, "The righteousness of Christ is imputed to us." Second, "The righteousness of Christ is imputed for righteousness." Third, "The act of believing is imputed for righteousness." For thus ought they to have spoken, if their purpose was correctly to retain my words, because the expression, "justifies us," is of wider acceptation than, "is imputed for righteousness." For God justifies (in a different sense), and it is not imputed for righteousness. Christ, "the righteous servant of God, justifies many by his knowledge." But that by which He thus does this, is not "imputed for righteousness."

With regard to the first, I never said, "The righteousness of Christ is not imputed to us." Nay, I asserted the contrary in my *Nineteenth Public Disputation on Justification*, Thesis 10: "The righteousness by which we are justified before God may in an accommodated sense be called imputative, as being righteousness either in the gracious estimation of God, since it does not according to the rigor of right or of law merit that appellation, or as being the righteousness of another, that is, of Christ, it is made ours by the gracious imputation of God."

I have, it is true, placed these two in alternation: By this very thing I declare, that I do not disapprove of that phrase. "The righteousness of Christ is imputed to us, because it is made ours by the gracious estimation of Christ," is tantamount to, "It is imputed to us," for "imputation" is "a gracious estimation." But lest anyone should seize on these expressions as an occasion for calumny, I say that I acknowledge, "The righteousness of Christ is imputed to us," because I think the same thing is contained in the following words of the Apostle, "For he (God) hath made him (Christ) to be sin for us, who knew no sin, that we might be made the righteousness of God in Him" (2 Cor 5:21).

I have said that I disapprove of the second enunciation, "The righteousness of Christ is imputed to us for righteousness." And why may not I reject a phrase which does not occur in the Scriptures, provided I do not deny any true [*sensum*] signification which can be proved from the Scriptures? But this is the reason of my rejection of that phrase: "Whatever is imputed for righteousness, or to righteousness, or instead of righteousness, it is not righteousness itself strictly and rigidly taken. But the righteousness of Christ, which He hath performed in obeying the Father, is righteousness itself strictly and rigidly taken. Therefore, it is not imputed for righteousness. "For that is the signification of the word "to impute," as Piscator against Bellarmine, when treating on Justification (Rom 4:4), has well observed and satisfactorily proved.

The matter may be rendered clearer by an example. If a man who owes another a hundred florins, pays this his creditor the hundred he owes, the creditor will not speak with correctness if he says, "I impute this to you for payment." For the debtor will instantly reply, "I do not care anything about your imputation!" because he has truly paid the hundred florins, whether the creditor thus esteems it or not. But if the man owe a hundred florins and pays only ten, then the creditor, forgiving him the remainder, may justly say, "I impute this to you for full payment; I will require nothing more from you." This is the gracious [*aestimatio*] reckoning of the creditor, which the debtor ought also to acknowledge with a grateful mind.

Such an Explanation

It is such an estimation as I understand as often as I speak about the imputation of the righteousness revealed in the Gospel, whether the obedience of Christ be said to be imputed to us, and to be our righteousness before God, or whether faith be said to be imputed for righteousness. There is therefore a crafty design latent in this confusion. For if I deny this their enunciation, they will say I deny that the righteousness of Christ is imputed to us. If I assent to it, I fall into the absurdity of thinking that the righteousness of Christ is not righteousness itself. If they say, that the word "impute" is received in a different acceptation, let them prove their assertion by an example; and when they have given proof of this (which will be a work of great difficulty to them), they will have effected nothing. For "the righteousness of Christ is imputed to us by the gracious estimation of God." It is imputed therefore, either by the gracious estimation of God for righteousness; or it is imputed by [*non gratiosia*] his non-gracious estimation. If it be imputed by His gracious estimation for righteousness (which must be asserted), and if it be imputed by His non-gracious estimation, then it is apparent, in this confusion of these two axioms, that the word "impute" must be understood ambiguously, and that it has two meanings.

Faith, or the act of believing, is imputed for righteousness," which are my own words. But omitting my expressions, they have substituted for them the phrase, "The act of believing justifies us." I should say, "They have done this in their simplicity," if I thought they had not read Rom 4, in which this phrase is used eleven times, "Faith, or the act of believing, is imputed for righteousness." Thus it is said in the verse 3, "Abraham believed God, and it was imputed unto him for righteousness" that is, *his believing* was thus imputed. Our brethren therefore do not reprehend me, but the Apostle has employed this phrase so many times in one chapter, and who does not refrain from the use of the other phrase, "to be justified *by* faith and *through* faith," in the third and fifth chapters of the same epistle. They ought therefore to have reprehended, not the phrase itself, but the signification which I attach to it, if I explain it in a perverted manner.

Thus incorrectly should I seem to have explained the Apostle's phrase if I had said, "The righteousness of Christ is not imputed to us or does not justify us, but Faith or the act of believing does." But I have already replied, that this assertion concerning me is untrue, and I have declared that I believe both these expressions to be true: "The righteousness of Christ is imputed to us," and "Faith is imputed for righteousness." When they place these phrases in opposition to each other, they do this, not from the meaning which I affix to them, but from their own. Therefore, according to the signification which they give to them severally, they fabricate this calumny, which is an act of iniquity. But they will say, that I understand this phrase, "Faith is imputed for righteousness," in its proper acceptation, when it must be figuratively understood. This they ought therefore to have said, because this alone is what they were able to say with truth. Such in fact are my real sentiments on this subject, and the words make for the proper acceptation of the phrase. If a figure lies concealed under it, this ought to be proved by those who make the assertion.

The whole of that in which we appear before God, justifies us: But we appear before God, not only by Faith, but also by Works. Therefore we are justified before God, not only by Faith, but likewise by Works.

Answer: A man who is ignorant of those things which [*aguntur*] are here the order of the day, and who reads this article, will undoubtedly think, that, in the point of Justification, I favor the party of the Papists, and am their professed defender. Nay he will suppose, that I have proceeded to such a pitch of impudence, as to have the audacity to maintain a conclusion directly contrary to the words of the Apostle, who says, "We therefore conclude, that a man is justified by faith, without the deeds of the law" (Rom 3:28). But when he shall understand the origin of this article and why it is charged to me, then it will be evident to him that it arises from calumny and from a corruption of my words. I deny therefore, that I made that syllogism, or ever intended to draw that conclusion, or to propound those things from which such a conclusion might be deduced.

This brief defense would suffice for all upright minds, to give a favorable interpretation, if perchance anything had been spoken which could give occasion to unjust suspicion. But it will be labor well bestowed, for me to transcribe my own words from a certain Disputation on Justification, from which this article has been taken; that it may appear with what kind of fidelity they have made their extract. The Ninth Thesis in it is thus expressed:

"From these things, thus laid down according to the Scriptures, we conclude, that Justification, when used for the act of a Judge, is either purely the imputation of righteousness, [*factam*] bestowed, through mercy from the throne of grace in Christ the Propitiation, on a sinner, but on one who believes; or that man is justified before God, of debt, according to the rigor of justice, without any forgiveness. Because the Papists deny the latter, they ought to concede the former. And this is so far true, that, how highly soever any one of the Saints may be endowed with Faith, Hope and Charity, and how numerous soever and excellent may be the works of Faith, Hope, and Charity which he has performed. Yet he will not obtain from God the Judge a sentence of Justification, unless He quits the tribunal of His severe Justice, and places Himself in the throne of Grace, and out of it pronounces a sentence of absolution in his favor, and unless the Lord of his Mercy and Pity graciously accounts for righteousness the whole of that good with which the Saint appears before Him. For woe to a life of the greatest innocence, if it be judged without mercy! This truth even the Papists seem to acknowledge, who assert, that the works of the Saints cannot stand before the judgment of God, unless they be "sprinkled with the blood of Christ." (Public Disput. 19)

Thus far my Thesis: Could any person imagine that the major issue in this article can, according to my sentiments and design, be deduced from it? "The whole of that in which we appear before God, justifies us!" How can this be deduced when I say, "that not even this good, which the Papists are able or know how to attribute to the most holy men, can obtain from God a sentence of Justification, unless He through mercy from the throne of grace reckon this graciously for righteousness!" Who does not perceive, that I grant this through sufferance and concession?, "God considers and esteems for righteousness all this good in which, the Papists say, the Saints appear before God." I yield this, that I may the more firmly confute them. I thus obtain, "that not even that total can be accounted for righteousness except graciously and through mercy."

Real Malignity

This conduct is real malignity and a violent distortion of my words, on account of which I have indeed no small occasion given to me of complaining before God of this injury. But I contain myself, lest my complaint to God should be detrimental to their souls; I would rather beseech God to be pleased to grant them a better mind.

The matter [with regard to me] stands thus, as if anyone should say to a monk or a Pharisee, boasting of his virtues and works, of his faith, hope, love, obedience, voluntary chastity, and similar excellences: "O man ! Unless God were to omit the severity of his [*judicii*] Justice, and unless from the throne of Grace He were to pronounce a sentence of absolution concerning thee, unless He were graciously to reckon all that good of thine, however great it may be, and thus to account it for righteousness, thou wouldst not be able to stand before Him or to be justified."

I declare, and before Christ I make the declaration, that this was my [*mentem*] meaning. And every man is the best interpreter of his own expressions. But let it be allowed, that I have said these things from my own sentiments. Was this proposition [of their fabrication] to be deduced from my words?

If it was, they ought to have proceeded thus according to scientific method. They ought to have briefly laid down the enunciation I employed, and which might be in this form: "Unless God graciously account for righteousness the whole of this good in which a saint appears before Him, that saint cannot be justified before God."

From which will be deduced this affirmative proposition, "If God graciously accounts for righteousness this good in which a holy man appears, then this holy man can be justified before God." Or "He will then be justified before God." The word "the whole" has a place in the negative proposition because it conduces to the exaggeration. But it ought not to have a place in that which is affirmative. Let this question, however, have a place here: Why have my brethren omitted these words: "The Lord graciously of his Mercy, from the throne of his Grace, having omitted the severity of Judgment, accounts that good for righteousness."

And why have they proposed only these? "The whole of that in which we appear before God, justifies us." This is, indeed, not to deny the fact, but a pretext is thus sought for calumny, under the equivocation of the word "justifies," as Justification may be either of grace, or of debt or severe judgment. But I have excluded that which is of debt or severe Judgment from my expressions, and have included only the Justification which is of grace. Let these remarks suffice for the major proposition.

I now proceed to the assumption that they have subjoined to this Proposition, which is theirs and not mine. It reads thus: "But we appear before God, not only by Faith but also by Works." Then is it your pleasure, my brethren, to appear thus before God? David was not of this opinion when he said: "And enter not into judgment with thy servant: For in thy sight shall no man living be justified," or "shall justify himself" (Ps 143:2), which is thus rendered by the Apostle Paul, "For by the works of the law shall no flesh be justified" (Gal. 2:16). But perhaps you will say, that you do not appear before God "by the works of the law, but by works produced from faith and love!"

I wish you to explain to me, what it is to appear by faith, and what to appear by works; and whether it can possibly happen, that a man may appear both by faith and works. I know, the Saints who will be placed before the tribunal of the Divine Justice, have had Faith, and through

Faith have performed good Works. But, I think, they appear and stand before God with this Confidence or Trust, "that God [*proposuit*] has set forth his Son Jesus Christ as a propitiation through Faith in his blood, that they may thus be justified by the Faith of Jesus Christ, through the remission of sins." I do not read, that Christ is constituted a Propitiation through works in his blood, that we may also be justified by Works!

My desire indeed is, to appear before the tribunal of God thus [with this Confidence or Trust in Christ, as a Propitiation through Faith in his blood] and "to be graciously judged through mercy from the throne of grace." If I be otherwise judged, I know I shall be condemned; which sore judgment may the Lord, who is foil of clemency and pity, avert according to his great mercy, even from you my brethren, though you thus speak, whether the words which you use convey your own meaning, or whether you attribute this meaning to me. I also might thus draw wonderful conclusions from this assumption which is laid down, if an accusation were to be set aside by retaliation or a recriminating charge, and not by innocence. But I will not resort to such a course, lest I seem [*paria referre*] to return evil for evil; though I might do this with a somewhat greater show of reason.

Faith is not the instrument of Justification.

Answer: In the enunciation of this Article is given another proof of desperate and [*profligatae*] finished negligence. What man is so utterly senseless as universally to deny, that Faith can be called "an instrument," since it receives and apprehends the promises God has given, and does also in this way concur to justification? But who, on the other hand, will venture to say, that, in the business of justification, Faith has no other relation than that of an instrument? It should therefore be explained, how faith is an instrument, and how, as an instrument, it concurs to justification.

It is, at least, not the instrument of God, not that which He uses to justify us. Yet this is the meaning first intended to be conveyed by these words, when rigidly taken. For God is the primary cause of justification. But since justification is an estimate of the mind, although made at the command of the Will, it is not performed by an instrument. For it is when God wills and acts by his Power, that He employs instruments. Then, in these words, "Believe in Christ, and thy sins shall be forgiven thee," or, which is the same thing, "and thou shall be justified." I say, that Faith is the requirement of God, and the act of the believer when he answers the requirement. But they will say, "that it is the act of apprehending and accepting, and that therefore this Faith bears relation to an instrument." I reply, Faith as a quality has in that passage relation to the mode of an instrument. But the acceptance or apprehension itself is an act, and indeed one of obedience yielded to the gospel. Let that phrase likewise which is so often used by the Apostle in Rom 4, be seriously considered: "Faith is imputed for righteousness." Is this faith as an instrument, or as an act? St. Paul resolves the question, by a quotation from Gen. 15:16, when he says, "Abraham believed God, and it was imputed to him for righteousness."

The thing itself, as it is explained by our brethren, also solves the question: "Faith is imputed for righteousness on account of Christ, the object which it apprehends." Let this be granted. Yet the apprehending of Christ is nearer than the instrument which apprehends, or by which He is apprehended. But apprehending is an act. Therefore, Faith, not as it is an instrument, but as it is an act, is imputed for righteousness, although such imputation is made on account of Him whom it apprehends. In brief, [*potentia*] the capability or the quality by which anything is apprehended, and the apprehension itself, each have relation to the object to be apprehended, the former a mediate relation, the latter an immediate.

The latter, therefore, is a more modest metonymy, as being derived from that which is nearer, even when it is granted that this phrase, "it is imputed for righteousness," must be explained by a metonymy. The man, then, who says, "The act of faith is imputed for righteousness," does not deny that faith as an instrument concurs to justification. It is evident, therefore, from this answer, that our brethren fabricate and "get up" articles of this kind without the least care or solicitude, and charge me with them.

This, I think, will be acknowledged even by themselves, if they examine how they manufactured those Nine Questions which, two years ago, by the consent of their Lordships, the Curators of our University, they endeavored to offer to the Professors of Divinity, that they might obtain their reply to them. Gravity and sobriety are highly becoming in Divines, and serious solicitude is required to the completion of such great matters as these.

Faith is not the pure gift of God, but depends partly on the grace of God, and partly on the powers of free Will; that, if a man will, he may believe or not believe.

Answer: I never said this, I never thought of saying it, and, relying on God's grace, I never will enunciate my sentiments on matters of this description in a manner thus desperate and confused. I simply affirm, that this enunciation is false, "Faith is not the pure gift of God;" that this is likewise false, if taken according to the rigor of the words, "Faith depends partly on the grace of God, and partly on the powers of Free Will." And that this is also false when thus enunciated, "If a man will, he can believe or not believe."

If they suppose, that I hold some opinions from which these assertions may by good consequence be deduced, why do they not quote my words? It is a species of injustice to attach to any person those consequences, which one may frame out of his words, as if they were his sentiments. But the injustice is still more flagrant, if those conclusions cannot by good consequence be deduced from what he has said. Let my brethren, therefore, make the experiment, whether they can deduce such consectaries as these from the things which I teach. But let the experiment be made in my company, and not by themselves in their own circle. For that sport will be vain, equally void of profit or of victory; as boys sometimes feel, when they play alone at chess with their own dice.

For the proper explanation of this matter, a discussion on the concurrence and agreement of Divine Grace and of Free Will or of the human Will, would be required. But because this would be a labor much too prolix, I shall not now make the attempt. To explain the matter I will employ a simile, which yet I confess, is very dissimilar, but its dissimilitude is greatly in favor of my sentiments. A rich man bestows, on a poor and famishing beggar, alms by which he may be able to maintain himself and his family. Does it cease to be a pure gift, because the beggar extends his hand to receive it? Can it be said with propriety, that "the alms depended partly on the liberality of the donor, and partly on the liberty of the receiver," though the latter would not have possessed the alms unless he had received it by stretching out his hand?

Can it be correctly said, because the beggar is always prepared to receive, that "He can have the alms, or not have it, just as he pleases ?" If these assertions cannot be truly made about a beggar who receives alms, how much less can they be made about the gift of faith, for the receiving of which far more acts of Divine Grace are required! This is the question it will be requisite to discuss, "What acts of Divine Grace are required to produce faith in man?" If I omit any act which is necessary, or which concurs, [in the production of faith], let it be demonstrated from the Scriptures, and I will add it to the rest.

It is not our wish to do the least injury to Divine Grace, by taking from it any thing that belongs to it. But let my brethren take care, that they themselves neither inflict an injury on Divine Justice by attributing that to it which it refuses, nor on Divine Grace, by transforming it into something else, which cannot be called grace. That I may in one word intimate what they must prove, such a transformation they effect when they represent "the sufficient and efficacious grace, which is necessary to salvation, to be irresistible," or as acting with such potency that it cannot be resisted by any free creature.

The grace sufficient for salvation is conferred on the Elect, and on the Non-elect; that, if they will, they may believe or not believe, may be saved or not saved.

Answer: Our brethren here also manifest the same negligence. They take no pains to know what my sentiments are; they are not careful in examining what truth there is in my opinions; and they exercise no discretion about the words in which they enunciate my sentiments and their own.

They know that I use the word "Election" in two senses: For the decree by which God resolves to justify believers and to condemn unbelievers, and which is called by the Apostle, "the purpose of God according to election" (Rom 9:11). And for the decree by which He resolves to elect these or those nations and men with the design of communicating to them the means of faith, but to pass by other nations and men. Yet, without this distinction, they fasten these sentiments on me, when, by its aid, I am enabled to affirm, not only, "Sufficient Grace is conferred on, or rather is offered to, the Elect and the Non-elect;" but also, "Sufficient Grace is not offered to any except the Elect":

"It is offered to the Elect and the Non-elect," because it is offered to unbelievers, whether they will afterwards believe or not believe.

"It is offered to none except the Elect," because, by that very thing which is offered to them, they cease to be of the number of those of whom it is said He "suffered all nations to walk in their own ways" (Acts

14:16); and, "He hath not dealt so with any nation" (Ps 147:20). And who shall compel me to use words of their prescribing, unless proof be brought from scripture that the words are to be thus and in no other way received?

I now proceed to the other words of the article: "That, if they will, they may believe or not believe, be saved or not saved." I say, in two different senses may these words be received, "If they will, they may believe," that is, either by their own powers, or as they are excited and assisted by this grace. "Or they may not believe," while rejecting this grace by their own free will, and resisting it. "They may be saved or not saved," that is, saved by the admission and right use of grace, or not saved by their own [*malatia*] wickedness, rejecting that without which they cannot be saved.

To the whole together I reply, that nothing is declared in these words, in whatever manner they may be understood, which St. Augustine himself and his followers would not willingly have acknowledged as true. I say, in these words are enunciated the very sentiments of St. Augustine. Yet he was the chief champion against the Pelagian heresy, being accounted in that age its most successful combatant.

St. Augustine speaks thus: "Since He is everywhere present, who, by many methods through the creature that is subservient to Him as his Lord, can call him who is averse, can teach a believer, can comfort him who hopes, can exhort the diligent man, can aid him who strives, and can lend an attentive ear to him who deprecates; it is not imputed to thee as a fault, 'that thou art unwillingly ignorant, but that thou neglectest to enquire after that of which thou art ignorant; not that thou dost not collect and bind together the shattered and wounded members, but that thou despisest Him who is willing to heal thee."[13]

Another work has the following: "On all men has always been bestowed some measure of heavenly doctrine, which, though it was of more sparing and " hidden grace, was yet sufficient, as the Lord has judged, to "serve some men for a remedy, and all men for a testimony."[14] It continues: "The Grace of God has indeed [*principaliter*] the decided pre-eminence in our justifications, persuading us by exhortations, admonishing us by examples, affrighting us by dangers, exciting us by

13. St. Augustine, *On Nature and Grace*, Cap. 67.

14. *Vocation of the Gentiles*, Lib. 2. Cap. 5. Authorship is uncertain, but it is attributed to either Prosper or St. Ambrose.

miracles, by giving understanding, by inspiring counsel, and by illuminating the heart itself and imbuing it with the affections of faith.

"But the will of man is likewise subjoined to it and is united with it, which has been excited to this by the before-mentioned succors, that it may co-operate in the Divine work within itself, and may begin [*exercere ad meritum*] to follow after the reward which, by the heavenly seed, it has conceived for the object of its desire, ascribing the failure to its own mutability, and the success (if the issue be prosperous) to the aid of grace. This aid is afforded to all men, by innumerable methods both secret and manifest; and the rejection of this assistance by many persons, is to be ascribed to their negligence; but its reception by many persons, is both of Divine Grace and of the human will."[15]

I do not produce these passages, as if I thought that either my brethren or I must abide by the sentiments of the Fathers, but only for the purpose of removing from myself the crime of Pelagianism in this matter.

Believers can perfectly fulfill the Law, and live in the world without sin.

Answer: This is what I never said. But when a certain person once, in a public disputation on the Baptism of Infants, was endeavoring by a long digression to bring me to the point, either to declare that believers could perfectly fulfill the law of God, or that they could not, I declined an answer.

I instead quoted St. Augustine. That passage I will here transcribe, that I may defend myself against the charge of Pelagianism, because I perceive, that the men with whom I have to do consider even these sentiments to be Pelagian, though they can on no account whatever be reckoned such.

St. Augustine says: "We must not instantly with an incautious rashness oppose those who assert, that it is possible for man to be in this life without sin. For if we deny the possibility of this, we shall derogate both from the free will of man, which desires to be in such a perfect state by willing it; and from the Power or Mercy of God, who effects it by the assistance which He affords. But it is one question whether it be possible, and another whether such a man actually exists. It is one question: If such a perfect man is not in existence when it is possible, why is he not?

"And it is another, not only whether there is anyone who has never had any sin at all, but likewise, whether there could at anytime have been such a man, or that it is now possible? In this fourfold proposal of questions, if I be asked 'Is it possible for a man to exist in the present life without sin?,' I shall confess, that it is possible by the grace of God, and by man's free will."[16]

In another of his works, St. Augustine says: "Pelagius disputes correctly, that they confess it not to be impossible, by the very circumstance of either many or all persons wishing to do it [perfectly to fulfill the law of God]; but let him confess whence it is possible, and peace is instantly established. For the possibility arises from the grace of God through Christ Jesus," &c.[17] And in a subsequent passage: "For it may be made a question among true and pious Christians, Has there ever been, is there now, or can there be, in this life, any man who lives so Justly as to have no sin at all ? Whosoever doubts about the possibility of the existence of such a person after this lift, he is destitute of understanding: But I am unwilling to enter into a contest, about this possibility even in the present life."

See the paragraphs that immediately succeed in the same chapter. And in the 69th chapter of that work, he says: "By the very thing, by which we most firmly believe that a just and good God could not command impossibilities, we are admonished both of what we may do in things easy of accomplishment, and of what we may ask in matters of difficulty; because all things are easy to Charity," &c.

I do not oppose this opinion of St. Augustine; but I do not enter into a contest about any part of the whole matter. For I think the time may be far more happily and usefully employed in prayers to obtain what is lacking in each of us, and in serious admonitions that everyone endeavor to proceed and to press forward towards the mark of perfection, than when spent in such disputations.

Questions of our Catechism

But my brethren will say, that in the 114th Question of our Catechism this very subject is treated, and that it is there asked, "Can those persons who are converted to God, perfectly observe the Divine Commands?"

16. St. Augustine, *On the Demerits and Remission of Sins Against the Pelagians*, Lib. 2, Cap. 6.

17. St. Augustine, *On Nature and Grace, Against the Pelagians*, Cap. 59, 60.

The answer subjoined is[*minime*'], "By no means." To this observation I reply, that I do not say anything against it; but that the reason of the negative answer [or scriptural proof added] is about the act, when the question itself is about the possibility; and that therefore, from this, nothing is proved. It is also well known, that this answer had been rejected by some persons and that it was only by the intervention of the brethren, who added an explanation to it, that it afterwards obtained the approbation of the same individuals. But I shall be perfectly willing to enter into a conference with my brethren about this matter, whenever it shall be convenient; and I hope we shall easily agree in opinion.

It may admit of discussion, whether Semi-Pelagianism is not real Christianity.

Answer: In a certain Lecture I said that it would be easy, under the pretext of Pelagianism, to condemn all those things of which we do not approve, if we may invent [*semi*] half, quarter, three quarters, four fifths Pelagianism, and so upwards. I added, that it might admit of discussion, whether Semi-Pelagianism is not real Christianity. By these remarks it was not my wish to patronize Pelagian doctrine. But I was desirous to intimate, that something might be accounted as Semi-Pelagianism which does not depart from the truth of Christian doctrine.

For as, when a departure is once made from the truth, the descent towards falsehood becomes more and more rapid. So, by receding from falsehood, it is possible for men to arrive at truth, which is often accustomed to stand as the mean between two extremes of falsehood. Such indeed is the state of the matter in Pelagianism and Manicheism. If any man can enter on a middle way between these two heresies, he will be a true Catholic, neither inflicting an injury on Grace as the Pelagians do, nor on Free Will as do the Manichees. Let the refutations be perused which St. Augustine wrote against both these heresies, and it will appear that he makes this very acknowledgment.

For this reason it has happened, that, for the sake of confirming their different opinions, St. Augustine's words, when writing against the Manichees, have been frequently quoted by the Pelagians; and those which he wrote against the Pelagians, have been quoted by the Manichees. This therefore is what I intended to convey, and that my brethren may understand my meaning, I declare openly, "that it will be quite as easy a task for me to convict the sentiments of some among them of Manicheism, and even of Stoicism, as they will be really capable of convicting others of Pelagianism, whom they suspect of holding that error."

But I wish us all to abstain from odious names of this description, as they are employed without producing any benefit. For he who is accused will either deny that his sentiments are the same as those of Pelagius; or, if he acknowledges the existence of a similarity, he will say that Pelagius was wrongly condemned by the Church. It would be better then to omit these epithets, and to confer solely about the matter itself, unless, approaching to the opinion of the Papists, we hold that what has once been determined by the Church cannot be drawn into controversy.

7

A Letter to Hippolytus A. Collibus

Hippolytus A. Collibus was an ambassador from the most illustrious Prince, the elector, Frederick Palatine IV, to the Seven United Dutch Provinces. Arminius more fully declares his sentiments on the principal Articles of Christian Doctrine in response to the ambassador's inquiries.

M OST HONORABLE SIR:
When I was lately admitted to a conversation with you, you had the kindness to intimate to me the reports you understood had been circulated at Heidelberg about my heterodoxy in certain articles of our faith. You gave me this information, not only that you might yourself hear from me personally the whole truth about the matter, but, much more, that by the intervention of your good offices, the suspicions concerning me which have been so unhandsomely conceived and propagated, might be removed from the minds of other persons, since this is a course which truth requires.

I endeavored in that interview with diligence and seriousness to comply with your obliging request and by returning a frank and open reply to each of those questions your Excellency proposed. I instantly disclosed my sentiments about those several Articles. For, in addition to my being bound to do this by my duty as a Christian man, and especially as a divine, such a course of conduct was demanded from me by the great candor, condescension and benevolence you exhibited towards me.

But my explanation was so agreeable to your Excellency (which I ascribe to an act of the divine Benignity towards me) as to induce you on that occasion to think it requisite that those propositions of mine should be committed to writing and transmitted to you. This would be not only for the purpose of being thus enabled the more certainly and firmly to form your own judgment about the matter when you had maturely reflected upon it, but also with the design of communicating my written answers to others, that they might confute the calumny and vindicate my innocence.

Having followed the counsel of your prudence, and firmly relying on the same hope, I now accede to your further wishes, in this letter. I entreat your Excellency to have the goodness to peruse its contents with the same candor and equanimity as you displayed when you listened to their delivery. Unless my mind greatly deceives me, your Excellency will find in this letter that which will not only be able to obliterate, but also completely to eradicate, every unjust suspicion concerning me from the minds of those good men who know that everyone is the best interpreter of his own sentiments, and that the utmost credit is to be given to him who sacredly, and in the presence of God, bears testimony to his own meaning.

The articles of doctrine about which your Excellency made inquiries, were as far as my memory serves me, the following: The Divinity of the Son of God, Providence, Divine Predestination, Grace and Free Will, and Justification. Beside these, you inquired about the things which concerned our opinions, in answer to the interrogatories of the States of Holland, concerning the mode of holding the proposed synod. But as the latter relate to that most eminent man, the Reverend John Uytenbogard, minister of the church at The Hague, as much as to me, I leave them to be explained by him, whose residence is much nearer to that of your Excellency.

With regard to all these doctrinal articles, I confidently declare that I have never taught anything, either in the church or in the university, which contravenes the sacred writings that ought to be with us the sole rule of thinking and of speaking, or which is opposed to the Dutch Confession of Faith, or Heidelberg Catechism, that are our stricter formularies of consent. In proof of this assertion I might produce, as most clear and unquestionable testimonies, the theses I have composed on these several articles, and which have been discussed as public disputations in the university. But as those theses are not entirely in readiness for everyone, and can be with difficulty transmitted, I will now treat upon each of them specially, as far as I shall conceive it necessary.

I. THE DIVINITY OF THE SON OF GOD

Concerning the divinity of the Son of God, I have taught and still teach, that the Father has never been without his Word and his Spirit, but that the Word and the Spirit are not to be considered in the Father under the notion of properties, as wisdom, goodness, justice, or power. But they are in the category of really existing persons, to whom it belongs to be, to live, to understand, to will, to be capable, and to do or act, all of which, when united, are indications and proofs of a person. But they are so in the Father as to be also from the Father, in a certain order of origin, not through collaterality, to be referred to the Father, and that they are from the Father neither by creation nor by decision but by a most wonderful and inexplicable internal emanation, which, with respect to the Son, the ancient church called *generation.*

With respect to the Holy Spirit, He was denominated *spiration or breathing,* a term required [linguistically] by the very word *spirit.* But about this breathing, I do not interpose my judgment—whether it is from the Father and the Son, as the Latin Fathers express themselves, or from the Father through the Son, as the Greek Fathers prefer to define it. This matter, I confess, far surpasses my capacity. If, on any subject, we ought to think and speak with sobriety, in my opinion, it must be on this.

Since these are my sentiments on the divinity of the Son of God, no reason could exist why, on this point, I should endure the shafts of calumny. Yet this slander was first fabricated and spread through the whole of Germany by one in whom such conduct was exceedingly indecorous; because he was my pupil, and ought to have refrained from that course, having been taught by his own painful experience that he either possessed an unhappy memory, or was of doubtful credit. For he had previously been convicted of a similar calumny, and had openly confessed his fault before me, and requested my forgiveness. But, as I learned from a certain manuscript transmitted to Leyden out of Germany, and which the same youth had delivered to the Heidelberg divines, he took the groundwork of his calumny from those things which I had publicly taught concerning the economy of our salvation, as administered by the Father through the Son and the Holy Spirit.

In the explanation of this economy, I had said "that we must have a diligent regard to this order, which the Scriptures in every part most religiously observe; and that we must distinctly consider what things are attributed as peculiar to the Father in this matter, what to the Son, and what to the Holy Spirit."

After this, some other persons seized upon a different occasion for the same calumny, from my having said that the Son of God was not correctly called *Autotheon* "very God," in the same sense that word signifies "God from himself." This audacious inclination for calumniating was promoted by the circumstance of my having explained in a different manner, certain passages of the Old and New Testament, which have been usually adduced to establish the consubstantiality or the coessentiality of the Trinity. But I can with ease in a moment show, from the books of the Old and New Testament themselves, from the whole of antiquity, and from the sentiments of the ancient church, both Greek and Latin, as well as from the testimony of our own divines, that nothing can be deduced from those alleged misinterpreted passages that are with the least semblance of probability, adverse to the sound and orthodox faith.

In his able defense of Calvin, against the treatise of Hunnius, entitled "Calvin Judaizing," the learned Paraeus has taught that this last occasion was seized upon in vain; and he has liberated me from the necessity of this service.

To spend any time in confuting the first slander, which was circulated by the young student, would not repay my trouble. Those who know that the Father in the Son hath reconciled the world unto himself, and administers the word of reconciliation through the Spirit, know, likewise, that, in the dispensation of salvation, an order must be considered among the persons of the Trinity, and their attributes must not be confounded, unless they be desirous of falling into the heresy of the Patripassionists.

Respecting the second occasion, concerning the word *Autotheon*, "very God," an answer somewhat more labored must be undertaken, because there are not a few persons who are of a contrary opinion. Yet our church does not consider such persons as holding wrong sentiments concerning the Trinity. This is the manner in which they propound their doctrine: "Because the essence of the Father and of the Son is one, and because it has its origin from no one; therefore, in this respect, the Son is correctly denominated *Autotheon* that is, God *from himself.*"

But I reply, "The essence of the Son is from no one, or is from himself," is not the same as "The Son is from himself, or from no one." For, to speak in a proper and formal manner, the Son is not an essence, but having his essence by a certain mode *Uparxeos* of being or existence.

They rejoin—"The Son may be considered in two respects, as He is the Son, and as he is God. As He is the Son, He is from the Father, and has his essence from the Father. But as He is God, he has his essence from himself or from no one." But the latter of these expressions is the most correct; for to have his essence from himself implies a contradiction.

Admit This Distinction

I reply, I admit this distinction, but it is extended much further than is allowable. For as He is God, He has the divine essence. As He is the Son, He has it from the Father. That is, by the word "God," is signified, generally, that which has the divine essence without any certain mode of subsistence. But, by the term "the Son," is signified a certain mode of having the divine essence, which is through communication from the Father, that is, through generation. Let these double ternaries be taken into consideration, which are opposed to each other, in one series:

To have Deity: To BE God

To have Deity from the Father: To BE the Son

To have Deity from no one: To BE the Father

And it will be evident, that among themselves they mutually correspond with each other. Thus: "to have Deity," and "to be God"; "to have Deity from the Father," and "to be the Son"; "to have Deity from no one," and "to be the Father" are in agreement. Though under the word "Father," as an affirmative, it is not signified which has its essence from no one. For this is signified by the word "ingenitus," inwardly born, which is attributed to the Father, though not with strictness, but only to signify that the Father does not have his essence by mode of generation. But the word "Father" by its own force and meaning is conclusive on this point. For where order is established, it is necessary that a beginning be made from some first person or thing, otherwise there will be confusion proceeding onwards ad infinitum.

But, with respect to origin, he who is the first in this order has his origin from no one. He who is the second, has his origin from the first, He who is the third has his origin from the first and the second, or from the first through the second. Were not this the real state of the matter; there would be a collaterality, which would make as many Gods as there were collateral persons laid down; since the unity of the deity in the Trinity is defended against the anti-trinitarians solely by the relation of origin and of order according to origin.

But that it we may view the sentiments of antiquity about this matter, I will here adduce from the ancient fathers of the Greek and Latin churches, some passages applicable to this subject.

BASIL THE GREAT

According to the habit of causes to those things which are from them, we say that the Father has precedence before the Son.[1]

Because the Son has his [principium] source from the Father, according to this, the Father is the greater, as the cause and the source. Wherefore our Lord also has said, "My Father is greater than I," that is, because He is the Father. But what other signification can the word "Father" have, than the cause and the beginning of Him who is begotten from Him?[2]

The Father is the root and the fountain of the Son and of the Holy Spirit.[3]

When I have said "one essence," I do not understand two [persons] distinguished from one, but the Son subsisting from the source of the Father, not the Father and Son from one superior essence. For we do not call them "brothers," but we confess them to be "the Father and the Son." But essence is identity, because the Son is from the Father, not made by command, but begotten from nature; not divided from the Father, but while he remains perfect, reflecting perfectly back again the light. But that you may not be able to charge these our assertions against us as a crime, and lest you should say, "He preaches two gods; he announces a multitude of deities;" there are not two gods, neither are there two fathers. He who produces two original sources, preaches two gods.[4]

The way of the knowledge of God is, by one Spirit, through one Son, to one Father. And, on the contrary, natural goodness, natural sanctification, and royal dignity are transmitted from the Father, through the only begotten Son, to the Spirit. Thus we confess the persons [in the Godhead] and at the same time the pious doctrine of the unity is not undermined.[5]

1. Basil, *Ever.* Lib. 1.
2. Ibid.
3. Basil, *Discourse Against the Sabellians and Arius.*
4. Ibid.
5. Basil, *On the Holy Spirit*, Cap. 18.

GREGORY NAZIANZEN

The essence is common and equal to the Son with the Father, though the Son has it from the Father.[6]

How is it possible for the same thing to be greater than itself and yet equal to itself? Is it not, therefore, plain, that the word "greater," which is attributed to the Father in reference to the Son, must be referred to *cause*; but the word "equal," attributed to the Son, as to his equality with the Father, must be referred to *nature*?[7]

It may indeed be truly said, but not therefore so honorably, that, "with regard to the humanity, the Father is greater than the Son:" For what is there wonderful in God being greater than man?[8]

AMBROSE

Though Christ has redeemed us, yet "all things are of God," because from him is all the paternity. It is, therefore, of necessity that the person of the Father has the precedence.[9]

AUGUSTINE

If that which begets is the original source of that which is begotten, the Father is the source of the Son, because he begets him.[10] He did not say "whom the Father will send from me," as He said, "whom I will send from the Father," that is, plainly showing the Father to be the source of the entire Deity.[11] Therefore this was said concerning the Father: "He doeth the works;" because from Him also is the origin of the works, from whom the cooperating persons [in the Deity] have their existence: For both the Son is born of Him, and the Holy Spirit principally proceeds from Him, from whom the Son is born, and with whom the same Spirit is common with the Son.[12]

6. Gregory Nazianzen, *Fourth Discourse on Theology*.
7. Ibid.
8. Ibid.
9. St. Ambrose, *On 1 Corinthians* 15.
10. St. Augustine, *On the Trinity*, Lib. 5, Cap. 14.
11. Ibid. Lib. 4, Cap. 10.
12. St. Augustine, Idem., Tom. 10, Fol. 11, Col. 1.

Indeed, God the Father is not God from another God; but God the Son is God from God the Father. But the Son is as much from the Father, as the Father is from no one.[13]

HILARY

There is no God who is eternal and without beginning, and who is God to that God from whom are all things. But the Father is God to the Son; for from Him He was born God.[14]

The confession of the true faith is, God is so born of God, as light is from light, which, without detriment to itself, offers its own nature from itself, that it may bestow that which it has, and that it may have what it bestows, etc.[15]

It is apparent from these passages, according to the sentiments of the ancient church, that the Son, even as he is God, is from the Father because he has received his Deity, according to which he is called "God," by being born of the Father. This is true, although the name of God does not indicate this mode of being or existence. From these quotations, it is also evident that because the Father is the source of the Son and of the Holy Spirit, he is called the source of the whole Deity. This is not because God has any beginning or source, but because the Deity is communicated by the Father to the Son and the Holy Spirit. So far, therefore, is this from being a correct expression: "The Son of God as he is God is from no one; and, with respect to his essence, is from himself or from no one." For he who has received his essence by being born of the Father, is from the Father with respect to his essence.

I consider therefore, that those who desire to think and to speak with orthodox antiquity, ought to abstain from these methods of expression; because, by adopting them, they seem to become the patrons of the opposing heresies of the Tritheists, and the Sabellians. Beza excuses Calvin by saying, that he did not so solicitously observe the difference between the two phrases—"He is the Son per se, through himself," and "He is the Son a se, from himself."[16]

13. St. Augustine, *Against Maximinus*, Lib. 3, Cap. 23, Col. 2.
14. Hilary, Lib. 4, Fol. 60.
15. Hilary, Lib. 6, Fol. 87.
16. Theodore Beza, preface of *Dialogues of St. Athanasius on the Trinity.*

If any of us is desirous of know more on this point, I will not refuse to hold a placid conference with him either in writing or by conversation. I now proceed to the other topics, in the discussion of which I will consult brevity.

2. THE PROVIDENCE OF GOD

My sentiments respecting the providence of God are these: It is present with, and presides over, all things. And all things, according to their essences, quantities, qualities, relations, actions, passions, places, times, stations and habits, are subject to its governance, conservation, and direction. I except neither particular, sublunary, vile, nor contingent things, not even the free wills of men or of angels, either good or evil: And, what is still more, I do not take away from the government of the divine providence even sins themselves, whether we take into our consideration their commencement, their progress, or their termination.

1. With respect to the beginning of Sin, I attribute the following acts to the providence of God:

First: Permission, and that not idle, but which has united in it four positive acts: (a.) The preservation of the creature according to essence, life and capability. (b.) Care, lest a greater or an equal power be placed in opposition. (c.) The offering of an object against which sin will be committed. (d.) The destined concession of its concurrence, which, on account of the dependence of a second on the *first cause*, is a necessary concurrence.

Second: The administration of arguments and occasions, soliciting to the perpetration of sin.

Third: The determination of place, time, manner, and of similar circumstances.

Fourth: The immediate concurrence itself of God with the act of sin.

2. With respect to the progress of sin, I attribute also the following four acts to the divine government:

The *First* act is the direction of sin that is already begun, to a certain object, at which the offending creature either has not aimed, or has not absolutely aimed.

Second, is the act in the direction of sin to the end which God himself wills, whether the creature intends or does not intend that end, nay, though he intended another and quite opposite end.

The *Third* act is the prescribing and determination of the time during which he wills or permits sin to endure.

The *Fourth* act is the defining of its magnitude, by which limits are placed on sin, that it may not increase and assume greater strength.

The whole of these acts, both concerning the commencement and the progress of sin, I consider distinctly in reference to the act itself and to the anomy or transgression of the law, a course which, according to my judgment is necessary and useful.

3. Lastly, with respect to the end and completion of sin, I attribute to Divine Providence either punishment through severity, or remission through grace. These are occupied about sin, in reference to its being sin and to its being a transgression of the law.

But I most solicitously avoid two causes of offense: that God be not proposed as the author of sin, and that its liberty be not taken away from the human will. These are two points which, if anyone knows how to avoid, he will think upon no act which I will not in that case most gladly allow to be ascribed to the providence of God, provided a just regard be had to the divine preeminence.

But I have given a most ample explanation of these my sentiments, in the theses twice publicly disputed on the same subject in the university. On this account, therefore, I declare that I am much surprised and not without good reason, at my being attacked with this calumny—that l hold corrupt opinions respecting the providence of God.

If it be allowable to indulge in conjecture, I think this slander had its origin in the fact of my denying that with respect to the decree of God, Adam necessarily sinned: an assertion which I yet constantly deny, and think it one that ought not to be tolerated, unless the word "necessarily" is received in the acceptation of "infallibly," as it is by some persons. Though this change does not agree with the etymology of the two words; for, necessity is an affection of being, but infallibility is an affection of the mind. Yet I easily endure the use of the first of these words, provided those two inconveniences to which I have recently alluded be faithfully avoided.

3. DIVINE PREDESTINATION

With respect to the article of Predestination, my sentiments upon it are the following: It is an eternal and gracious decree of God in Christ, by which he determines to justify and adopt believers, and to endow them with life eternal, but to condemn unbelievers, and impenitent persons. This is as I have explained in the theses on the same subject, which were publicly disputed, and in which no one found anything to be reprehended as false or unsound.

It was the opinion of some persons that those theses did not contain all the things which belong to this decree; nay, that the Predestination about which there is the greatest controversy at this time, is not the subject of investigation in those theses. This indeed I confess. For I considered it the best course to discuss that decree of Predestination which is the foundation of Christianity, of our salvation, and of the assurance of salvation, and upon which the Apostle Paul treats in the eighth and ninth chapters of Romans, and in the first chapter of Ephesians.

But such a decree as I have there described is not that by which God resolves to save some particular persons, and, that he may do this, resolves to endow them with faith, but to condemn others and not to endow them with faith. Yet many people declare that this is the kind of Predestination on which the apostle treats in the passages just cited. But I deny what they assert.

I grant that there is a certain eternal decree of God, according to which he administers the means necessary to faith and salvation, and this he does in such a manner as he knows to be suited to righteousness, that is, to his mercy and his severity. But about this decree, I think nothing more is necessary to be known than that faith is the mere gift of the gracious mercy of God; and that unbelief is partly to be attributed to the fault and wickedness of men, and partly to the just vengeance of God, which deserts, blinds and hardens sinners.

But concerning that Predestination by which God has decreed to save and to endow with faith some particular persons, but to damn others and not endow them with faith, so various are the sentiments, entertained even by the divines of our profession, that this very diversity of opinion easily declares the difficulty with which it is possible to determine anything respecting it.

Some of them propose, as the object of Predestination generally considered, that is, of election and reprobation, man as a sinner and fallen in Adam. Others lay it down, man considered as created and placed "in puris naturalibus." Some of them consider this object to be man to be created. Or, as some of them express it, man as salvable and damnable, as capable of being created and of falling. Others of them lay down the object of election and reprobation, which they denominate *non-election* and *preterition*: man considered in common and absolutely. But they lay down the object of reprobation, on which they bestow the appellation of *predamnation* and *affirmative reprobation*: man a sinner and guilty in Adam. Lastly, some of them suppose that the object must be considered entirely in common: man as yet to be created, as created, and as fallen.

I am aware that when this diversity of opinion is offered as an objection, it is usual to reply that, in the substance of the matter there is complete agreement, although some difference exists in the circumstances. But it would be in my power to prove that the preceding opinions differ greatly in many of the things which conduce to the very matter and substance of this kind of Predestination. But that of consent or agreement there is nothing except in the minds of those who hold such sentiments, and who are prepared to bear with those who dissent from them as far as these points extend.

Such a mode of consent as this [of which they are themselves the patrons], is of the highest necessity in the Christian church as, without it, peace can by no means be preserved. I wish that I also was able to experience from them any such benevolent feelings towards me and my sentiments. In that species of Predestination upon which I have treated, I define nothing that is not equally approved by all. On this point, alone, I differ. I dare not with a safe conscience maintain in the affirmative any of the preceding opinions. I am also prepared to give a reason for this conscientious scruple when it shall be demanded by necessity, and can be done in a suitable man

4. GRACE AND FREE WILL

Concerning grace and free will, this is what I teach according to the Scriptures and orthodox consent: Free will is unable to begin or to perfect any true and spiritual good, without grace. That I may not be said, like Pelagius, to practice delusion with regard to the word "grace," I mean by it that which is the grace of Christ and which belongs to regeneration. I affirm, therefore, that this grace is simply and absolutely necessary for the illumination of the mind, the due ordering of the affections, and the inclination of the will to that which is good.

It is this grace which operates on the mind, the affections, and the will; which infuses good thoughts into the mind, inspires good desires into the actions, and bends the will to carry into execution good thoughts and good desires. This grace goes before, accompanies, and follows. It excites, assists, operates that we will, and cooperates lest we will in vain. It averts temptations, assists and grants succor in the midst of temptations, sustains man against the flesh, the world and Satan, and in this great contest grants to man the enjoyment of the victory. It raises up again those who are conquered and have fallen, establishes and supplies them with new strength, and renders them more cautious.

This grace commences salvation, promotes it, and perfects and consummates it.

I confess that the mind of a natural and carnal man is obscure and dark, that his affections are corrupt and inordinate, that his will is stubborn and disobedient, and that the man himself is dead in sins. And I add to this—that teacher obtains my highest approbation who ascribes as much as possible to divine grace, provided he so pleads the cause of grace as not to inflict an injury on the justice of God, and not to take away the free will to that which is evil.

I do not perceive what can be further required from me. Let it only be pointed out, and I will consent to give it, or I will show that I ought not to give such an assent. Therefore, neither do I perceive with what justice I can be calumniated on this point, since I have explained these my sentiments, with sufficient plainness, in the theses on free will which were publicly disputed in the university.

5. JUSTIFICATION

The last article is on justification, about which these are my sentiments: Faith, and faith only (though there is no faith alone without works), is imputed for righteousness. By this alone are we justified before God, absolved from our sins, and are accounted, pronounced and declared righteous by God, who delivers his judgment from the throne of grace.

I do not enter into the question of the active and the passive righteousness of Christ, or that of his death and of his life. On this subject, I walk at liberty: I say "Christ has been made of God to me righteousness." "He has been made sin for me, that through faith, I may be the righteousness of God in him."

Nor yet do I refuse to confer with my brethren on this question, provided such conference be conducted without bitterness, and without an opinion of necessity [that the partial view of anyone should be generally received], from which scarcely any other result can ensue than the existence of distraction, and of increased effervescence in the minds of men, especially if this discussion should occur between those who are hot controversialists, and too vehement in their zeal.

But some persons charge me with this as a crime: that I say the act itself of faith, that is, believing itself, is imputed for righteousness, and that in a proper sense, and not by a metonymy. I acknowledge this charge, as I have the Apostle Paul, in Rom 4, and in other passages, as my precursor in the use of this phrase. But the conclusion which they draw from this affirmation, namely, "that Christ and his righteousness are excluded from our justification, and that our justification is thus attributed to the worthiness of our faith," I by no means concede it to be possible for them to deduce from my sentiments.

For the word "to impute," signifies that faith is not righteousness itself, but is graciously accounted for righteousness. By which circumstance all worthiness is taken away from faith, except that which is through the gracious condescending estimation of God. But this gracious condescension and estimation is not without Christ, but in reference to Christ, in Christ, and on account of Christ, whom God hath appointed as the propitiation through faith in his blood.

I affirm, therefore, that faith is imputed to us for righteousness, on account of Christ and his righteousness. In this enunciation, faith is the object of imputation; but Christ and his obedience are the procuring or meritorious cause of justification. Christ and his obedience are the object of our faith, but not the object of justification or divine imputation, as if God imputes Christ and his righteousness to us for righteousness. This cannot possibly be, since the obedience of Christ is righteousness itself, taken according to the most severe rigor of the law. But I do not deny that the obedience of Christ is imputed to us; that is, that it is accounted or reckoned for us and for our benefit. This very thing—that God reckons the righteousness of Christ to have been performed for us and for our benefit—is the cause why God imputes to us for righteousness our faith, which has Christ and his righteousness for its object and foundation, and why he justifies us by faith, from faith, or through faith. If anyone will point out an error in this my opinion, I will gladly own it, because it is possible for me to err, but I am not willing to be a heretic.

The preceding, then, as far as I remember, are the Articles your Excellency mentioned to me, with my explanations of them produced from sincerity of mind; and as thus sincere, I wish them to be accounted by all who see them. This one favor I wish I could obtain from my brethren who are associated with me in the Lord by the profession of the same religion, that they would at least believe me to have some feeling of conscience towards God. And this favor ought to be easily granted by them, through the charity of Christ, if they be desirous to study his disposition and nature.

Of what service to me can a dissension be that is undertaken merely through a reckless humor of mind, or a schism created in the church of Christ, of which by the grace of God and Christ, I profess myself to be a member? If my brethren suppose that I am incited to such an enterprise through ambition or avarice, I sincerely declare in the Lord, that they know me not. But I can confess that I am so free from the latter of these vices, as never to have been tickled, on any occasion, with even the most enticing of its snares, though it might be in my power to excuse or palliate it under some pretext or other.

With regard to ambition, I possess it not, except to that honorable kind that impels me to this service to inquire with all earnestness in the Holy Scriptures for divine truth, and mildly and without contradiction to declare it when found. I do so without prescribing it to anyone, or laboring to extort consent, much less through a desire to "have dominion over the faith of others," but rather for the purpose of my winning some souls for Christ, that I may be a sweet savor to him, and may obtain an approved reputation in the church of the saints. This good name I hope to obtain by the grace of Christ after a long period of patient endurance; though I be now a reproach to my brethren, and "made as the filth of the world and the off scouring of all things" to those who with me worship and invoke one God the Father, and one Lord Jesus Christ, in one spirit and with the same faith, and who have the same hope with me of obtaining the heavenly inheritance through the grace of our Lord Jesus Christ.

I hope the Lord will grant unto me, that they and I may meekly meet together in his great name, and institute a Christian conference about those things which appertain to religion. O may the light of that sacred and happy day speedily shine upon me. In that assembly, I engage, through the grace of God, to manifest such moderation of mind, and such love for truth and peace, as ought deservedly to be required and expected from a servant of Christ Jesus.

In the meantime [till this assembly can be convened], let my brethren themselves remain quiescent and suffer me to be quiet, that I may be at peace and neither annoy them nor create any uneasiness. If they entertain other thoughts concerning me, let them institute an [ecclesiastical] action against me; I will not shun or evade the authority of a competent judge, neither will I forfeit my recognizances by failing to appear.

Those Who Hear Me

If the minds of those who hear me are preoccupied in my favor at a distance by some political subtlety that I display, and may believe the matter is so managed through cunning, as makes my brethren neither to consider it advisable to arraign me before the judges, nor to account it sufficiently safe to commit to my care the useful students. Thus, they may believe, therefore, that the black stain I have deserved ought to be affixed to my reputation that my pupils and hearers may be frightened away; therefore, lest the result of this should be that the deferring of such a conference be productive of certain danger, behold I now offer myself.

This would be so that I may in company with them address, solicit, and entreat those high personages invested with the power of issuing a summons for a convention of this kind, or of granting it, not to suffer us any longer to continue in this anguish and disquietude of mind. But it is for either themselves to apply a speedy remedy, or allow it to be applied by others, but still by their order and under their direction.

I consent to place myself before any assembly whatsoever, whether it be composed of all the ministers in our United Netherlands, or of some to be convoked from each of the seven provinces, or even of all the ministers of Holland and West Friesland, to which province our university at Leyden belongs, or of some ministers to be selected out of these, provided the whole affair be transacted under the cognizance of our lawful magistrates. Nor do I avoid or dread the presence of learned men, who may be invited from other countries, provided they be present at the conference on equitable conditions, and subject to the same laws as those under which I must be placed.

To express the whole matter at once—let a convention be summoned, consisting of many members or of few, provided some bright hope of success be afforded [to them], a hope, I repeat it, which I shall be able by sound arguments to prove destitute of good foundation. This day, nay, this very hour, I am prepared and ready to enter into it. For I am wary of being daily aspersed with the filthy scum of fresh calumnies and grieved at being burdened with the necessity of clearing myself from them. In this part of my conduct, I am assuredly dissimilar from heretics who have either avoided ecclesiastical assemblies or have managed matters so as to be able to confide in the number of their retainers, and to expect a certain victory.

But I have finished. For I have occupied your attention, most honorable sir, a sufficient length of time; and I have made a serious encroachment on those valuable moments which you would have devoted to matters of greater importance. Your Excellency will have the condescension to forgive the liberty I have taken to address this letter to you, as it has been extorted from me by a degree of necessity. This is not to disdain to afford me your patronage and protection, just so far as divine truth and the peace and concord of the Christian church will allow you to vouchsafe.

I pray and beseech Almighty God long to preserve your Excellency in safety, to endue you yet more with the spirit of wisdom and prudence, by which you may be enabled to discharge the duties of the embassy which has been imposed upon you, and thus meet the wishes of the most illustrious prince, the Elector Palatine. And, after you have happily discharged those duties, may he benignantly and graciously grant to you a prosperous return to your own country and kindred.

Thus prays your Excellency's most devoted servant,

James Arminius,

Professor of Theology, University of Leyden.

Leyden, April 5, 1608

Recommended Books

THE FOLLOWING ARE RECOMMENDED books for those seeking more information about James Arminius and Arminian doctrine:

Arminius, James. *The Works of James Arminius*, 3 vols. Reprint. Whitefish, Mont.:Kessinger Publishing LLC, 2010.

Bangs, Carl. *Arminius:A Study in the Dutch Reformation*. Nashville:Abingdon Press, 1971.

Clarke, F. Stuart. *The Ground of Election:Jacobus Arminius' Doctrine of the Work and Person of Christ*. Eugene, Ore.:Wipf & Stock Publishers, 2006.

Ellis, Mark, ed. *The Arminian Confession of 1621*. Eugene, Ore.:Pickwick Publications, 2005.

Forlines, F. Leroy. *The Quest for Truth:Answering Life's Inescapable Questions*. Nashville:Randall House Publications, 2001.

Forlines, F. Leroy, and J. Matthew Pinson. *Classical Arminianism*. Nashville:Randall House Publications, 2010.

Goodwin, John. *Redemption Redeemed:A Puritan Defense of Unlimited Atonement:Expanded Edition*. Eugene, Ore.:Wipf & Stock Publishers, 2004.

McCulloh, Gerald O. *Man's Faith and Freedom:The Theological Influence of Jacobus Arminus*. Eugene, Ore.:Wipf & Stock Publishers, 2007.

Olson, Roger E. *Arminian Theology:Myths and Realities*. Downers Grove, Ill.:Intervarsity Press, 2006.

Picirilli, Robert. *Grace Faith Free Will, Contrasting Views of Salvation:Calvinism and Arminianism*. Nashville:Randall House Publications, 2002.

Stanglin, Keith D. *Arminius on the Assurance of Salvation:The Context, Roots and Shape of the Leiden Debate*, 1603–1609. Leiden:Brill Academic Publishers, 2007.

Tyacke, Nicholas. *The Rise of English Arminianism:c. 1590–1640*. London:Oxford University Press, 1990.

Scripture Index

385

Revelation